NEW YORK REVIEW BOOKS
CLASSICS

I USED TO BE CHARMING

EVE BABITZ was born in Hollywood to Sol Babitz, a violinist and musicologist, and Mae Babitz, an artist. She is the author of several books of fiction, including *Sex and Rage: Advice to Young Ladies Eager for a Good Time*, *L.A. Woman*, and *Black Swans: Stories*. Her nonfiction works include *Fiorucci, the Book* and *Two by Two: Tango, Two-Step, and the L.A. Night*. She has written for publications including *Ms.* and *Esquire* and in the late 1960s designed album covers for the Byrds, Buffalo Springfield, and Linda Ronstadt. She lives in Los Angeles.

MOLLY LAMBERT is also a writer from Los Angeles who was born in Hollywood. She has written for publications including *The New York Times Magazine*, and co-hosts the podcast *Night Call*.

I USED TO BE CHARMING

The Rest of Eve Babitz

EVE BABITZ

Edited by

SARA J. KRAMER

Introduction by

MOLLY LAMBERT

NEW YORK REVIEW BOOKS

New York

The publishers wish to thank the following people for their help in tracking down some of the more difficult-to-find essays collected here: Joie Davidow, Boris Dralyuk, Ellie Duke, Zac Frank, Elisabeth Garber-Paul, Courtney Garcia, Leonard Koren, Susan LaTempa, Sylvia Lonergan, Manjula Martin, Carolyn Vega, and Morgan P. Yates. Special thanks is extended to Mirandi Babitz and Erica Spellman Silverman for their assistance throughout.

THIS IS A NEW YORK REVIEW BOOK
PUBLISHED BY THE NEW YORK REVIEW OF BOOKS
435 Hudson Street, New York, NY 10014
www.nyrb.com

Library of Congress Cataloging-in-Publication Data
Names: Babitz, Eve, author. | Lambert, Molly, author of introduction.
Title: I used to be charming : the rest of Eve Babitz / by Eve Babitz ;
    introduction by Molly Lambert.
Description: New York : New York Review Books, 2019. | Series: New York
    Review Books classics
Identifiers: LCCN 2019021978 (print) | LCCN 2019022407 (ebook) | ISBN
    9781681373799 (alk. paper)
Classification: LCC PS3552.A244 A6 2019 (print) | LCC PS3552.A244
    (ebook) | DDC 814/.54—dc23
LC record available at https://lccn.loc.gov/2019021978
LC ebook record available at https://lccn.loc.gov/2019022407

ISBN 978-1-68137-379-9
Available as an electronic book; ISBN 978-1-68137-380-5

Printed in the United States of America on acid-free paper.
10 9 8 7 6 5 4 3

CONTENTS

INTRODUCTION

> And because we were in Southern California—in Hollywood
> even—there was no history for us. There were no books or
> traditions telling us how we could turn out or what anything
> meant.
>
> —*Eve Babitz*

MY GOD, isn't it fun to read Eve Babitz? Just holding this collection
in your hand is like being in on a good secret. Babitz knows all the
good secrets—about Los Angeles, charismatic men, and supposedly
glamorous industries like film, music, and magazines. Cool beyond
belief but friendly and unintimidating, Babitz hung out with all the
best rock stars, directors, and artists of several decades. And she wrote
just as lovingly about the rest of L.A.—the broad world that exists
outside the bubble of "the Industry." Thanks to New York Review
Books putting together a collection of this work, we are lucky enough
to have more of Babitz's writing to read.

Alongside the Thelemic occultist Marjorie Cameron (whose husband, Jack Parsons, cofounded the Jet Propulsion Laboratory) and
the Bay Area Beat painter Jay DeFeo (Babitz's romantic rival), Babitz
was one of a handful of female artists associated with L.A.'s landmark
Ferus Gallery, which showed local contemporary artists and launched
the careers of people like Ed Ruscha and Ed Kienholz. Babitz knew
(and dated) many of the Ferus personalities; she was a mainstay at
their hangout, Barney's Beanery. As she details in "I Was a Naked
Pawn for Art," the famous photo of a nude Eve playing chess with

Marcel Duchamp was the result of her trying to make her married boyfriend, the Ferus Gallery founder, Walter Hopps, jealous.

A bridge between the Beat movement and burgeoning sixties psychedelic culture, the Ferus group rejected all prescribed rules of art to follow a strict internal code of its own, dictated only by individual interests. What her boyfriend Paul Ruscha's brother Ed did with paintings, Babitz did with essays. Reading her is like looking at Ed Ruscha's gas station paintings. She makes you reconsider things you might have dismissed as ugly, strange, or even boring, and look at them as if for the first time to find that they are in fact the most beautiful things you've ever seen in your life. Everything Babitz writes is both pop and intellectual, shiny but deep, like an artificial-snow-flocked Christmas tree, every bit as real and sentimental for a Tinseltowner as a Douglas fir. She makes sure you are stimulated, and when she occasionally does say something portentous, you're never far from a punch line. She always writes with an eye toward entertaining the reader because, well, Hollywood. Women are automatically dealt low culture; Babitz doubles down, writing about Archie comics, ballroom dancing, what it's like to have big tits. She doesn't care about being high art because high art is humorless.

"The ideas you have about cities that you've always known don't work in L.A., and once you toss those aside you'll be much better off," she writes in "My God, Eve, How Can You Live Here?," explaining the whole city in one elegant swoop. (People still ask how we can stand to live in L.A., although they tend to do it months before they themselves move here and decide they invented it.) Los Angeles does not have one center because it has many centers. It does not have a monoculture because it has so many cultures that coexist, and none of them require validation from East Coast Yankees. This baffles the Yankees, who are used to thinking worlds have centers and they are somehow in them. It's freeing to give up on the delusion that you matter and can control anything at all.

To navigate L.A. the Eve Babitz way is to give yourself over to the unpredictability and slow tempo of your environment. Sure, you could complain about the heat and the freeways, or you could eat this perfect sandwich and listen to the birds sing. She tells you where to go to see what's off the beaten path, and where to go if you want exactly the cliché Beverly Hills luxe surrealist experience you imagined L.A. would be. The garish architecture and people are there if you want them, just don't go mistaking one part for the whole. The real tourist attraction in L.A. is not the shitty, pay-for-play Walk of Fame, or any museum or arena, it's the chance to immerse yourself in the human carnival. Around the time you make peace with being in a city that makes you feel anonymous, you come to realize that Los Angeles is a small town, just spread out, and if you stay here long enough you will eventually keep running into the same twelve people over and over again (and that's when you move to the desert).

The loping Western pace that those transplanted from faster-paced, European-style cities so often bemoan is likewise celebrated by locals like Babitz. It allows for constant detours and longer looks. L.A. doesn't dictate an agenda, and like all of the American West it celebrates restless individualism. Babitz is at home anywhere, and everywhere she goes she finds the most interesting person, the weirdest place, the funniest throwaway detail. She makes writing seem effortless and fun, which any writer can tell you is the hardest trick of all.

The flightiness of Babitz's narrator persona, in pieces like "All This and *The Godfather* Too," may have been slightly exaggerated to catch people off guard while she took a good long look, making careful mental notes throughout. In slow-paced Los Angeles it's easy to get distracted by a good sunset or a flock of butterflies and forget to produce any work at all, but this collection shows Babitz to have been insanely prolific while also attending every good party in the L.A. hills and many long nights at the Chateau Marmont. The parties are part of her process, just like those long drives to the beach she recommends.

Babitz is the ultimate Hollywood local, and like any true Angeleno she is laid-back and open-minded about seemingly everything—from high-priced stationery to female gym rats. Like Babitz, I am from L.A. and am fond of it in all its weird extremities. I was born in Hollywood but grew up in the San Fernando Valley, and have had plenty of "How can you live there?" questions directed my way—which compelled me to go searching for all the reasons I could. Anyone who thinks Los Angeles is only gorgeous would-be starlets dangling over the maw of destruction has never had jury duty here. It's just a regular city that is also bizarre in ways that even a local will admit are beyond full human comprehension. The smog makes for gorgeous sunsets.

California is known for its erasure of visual history—whether through quake, fire, or purposeful human intervention. Like the pictures she takes with the Brownie camera she brings to the set of *The Godfather, Part II*, Babitz renders perfect snapshots of San Francisco and Los Angeles. She describes the constant California moment of bland apartments and bland people ruining the weird, spooky charm of L.A.'s beach cities, like Marina del Rey, or high-rises in San Francisco turning from funky artists' spaces into offices for investor-funded media companies. The cost of living in L.A. has gone up absurdly ever since then, even as wages have stagnated, leading to a housing crisis that has pushed thousands of people into tent villages all over the city.

Although L.A. has changed since Babitz wrote about it in the seventies and eighties, many parts of *Eve's Hollywood* remain. You can still take the Raymond Chandler driving tour she suggests through L.A.'s "amazing streets" that run across the whole city, although today there are potholes galore due to civic decay. You can still get the taquitos she raves about in *Eve's Hollywood* at Cielito Lindo, and any reader of the great food critic Jonathan Gold will know that L.A. is even now full of cheap incredible meals.

Despite the timelessness of her subject and style, there are certain things that do mark Babitz as a working writer from another era. The piece about *The Godfather, Part II*, for instance, would be impossible to pull off today. It's remarkable for a freedom of access and a forth-rightness about difficulties on set that are unimaginable in today's PR-directed magazine climate. Babitz isn't afraid to dramatize the ways the powerful are built up by people around them. And gossip is part of her reporting style, because so much of gossip is news that powerful men don't want made public; it reveals them as silly, or petty, or cruel. Babitz can't help but make important men look as silly as they really are. But she isn't gratuitously cruel. Just as she doesn't shy away from recording men at their most ridiculous, she doesn't shy away from objectifying beautiful men (and she does it so much better than anyone else). She's nobody's sycophant, and that commands a certain kind of respect from her subjects, who've grown used to being sucked up to.

I was nervous to read the title essay to this collection, Babitz's first sustained writing about the 1997 accident that largely put an end to her writing career, because I worried about what it would do to the intertwined mythoi of Babitz and L.A. Time and again in her work Babitz had crushed the notion that women were objects rather than subjects; she simply effortlessly embodied both roles. Despite being a writer myself and knowing full well that writing is an act of pro-longed seduction that involves portraying oneself as maybe a little funnier, sexier, more self-aware than the reality, I was afraid to discover that there was a sadder, more vulnerable soul inside the confident public Babitz. Could she, just like me, have been projecting a fearless-ness in her writing that isn't fully representative of who she really is? The answer of course is yes, of course she is vulnerable and human and cognizant of her own brashness (and so am I), and it's not only fine, it's wonderful.

"My friends would kill me if I died" is what Babitz says about her accident, joking—but telling the truth. To be a female artist is to put your own stubborn obsessions above all else in a world that still expects you to take care of other people while setting your own obsessive interests aside. Throughout her life Babitz moved among stubborn, creative men who did only exactly as they pleased, and she did the same in her own way to more radical effect. To be impulsive is to be accident-prone, to follow your passions is to risk letting them consume you, and women with great appetites for life are often demonized for their desires, just as men are lionized for theirs.

Eve Babitz was of the first generation of women who really had it in their power to decide to not get married and have children. She didn't form a nuclear family of her own but she has an artist's family—composed of her sister and friends and ex-lovers and creative admirers. And after the accident they all took care of her together, in an inspiring way. (In Lili Anolik's biography, *Hollywood's Eve*, when asked why famous and now wealthy exes like Harrison Ford and Steve Martin donated money to help her, she sits up in bed and croaks, "Blow jobs.")

Having gotten sober after a youth spent trying every hyped-up high, Babitz comes to see just living as the ultimate high. She is not a death-driven fatalist like her old friend Jim Morrison or some of the sad, beautiful female friends she writes about whose worth is so wrapped up in their looks that they failed to develop any other skills. She's a writer, who happens to be so charming and good at her job that decades later Han Solo still thinks of her fondly.

After the accident and throughout her recovery process, Babitz is humorously deflective about the seriousness of it all. She stubbornly refuses to get bogged down in the tragedy and gore of lighting herself on fire, even as she exposes that gore and tragedy for all to see. Babitz is a proud exhibitionist, in her writing as in the Duchamp photo that first brought her notoriety. Confronted with the transformation of her body by the fire, she does not let us look away. She describes the scene in the operating room, as she is put through multi-hour surgeries, as an "abattoir" then immediately quips, "All my life I had wanted to have a reason to use the word."

"I used to be charming," Babitz jokes with one of the medical aides. The real joke being, she still is! Even with third-degree burns on half of her body and in unimaginable pain, she is recording the details for the story she knows she will inevitably write. The accident is one misadventure among the many misadventures she has turned into art. Yet it feels like a different type of Eve Babitz essay from the reminiscences she's written before. Here she self-consciously addresses the lapses in her own memory and takes stock of her mortality in a way that seems simultaneously inevitable and contrary to her core beliefs. Babitz's willingness to go her own way throughout life is inspiring, even as she admits it's not on purpose exactly. The haphazardness of her own choices comes back to her throughout the essay about the fire, but Babitz does not ascribe any kind of grand apocalyptic or spiritual meaning to it. That's what outsiders do. To her it is just a fire, and fires happen all the time in Los Angeles. They're a thing that might happen to you if you live here, a known risk worth taking.

Babitz writes about the "perseverance of vision" in the work of auteurs like Francis Ford Coppola, and it's her perseverance of vision that comes through in her own work. Like any artist or auteur, she came to earth with a strong point of view she had no choice but to share with the world. Reading her now, it seems she achieved the ultimate goal of any Hollywood girl—leaving behind a beautiful everlasting afterimage where you are always a little sexier, a little funnier, a little more charismatic than maybe you really were, or anyone could ever be. But Eve Babitz, like her beloved fellow L.A. native and icon Marilyn Monroe, *really is* that sexy, that funny, that charismatic. And as Marilyn's films freeze her image, Eve's writing preserves her voice.

In writing all these beautiful interesting things, initially meant for ephemeral mediums like alternative weeklies printed on rapidly yellowing newsprint and produced in a "transitory spirit"—not unlike the wildflowers that pop up on the sides of L.A. freeways in spring—Babitz paradoxically created a long-lasting canon of work. Impermanence should be freeing, not frightening, and Babitz writes like someone who lives life to its limits. There are no experiences in moderation for her, because what use is life if you're not going to try everything on the table? Los Angeles has always been the bleeding edge of the country, a place onto which people project everything bad about culture—much like women, as it happens. Babitz notes that L.A. is the only harbor city in history to start inland and grow west to the sea. To read Eve Babitz is to feel like her passenger, cruising down long Hollywood streets through a painted-backdrop sunset toward eternal waves.

—MOLLY LAMBERT

I USED TO BE CHARMING

Dedication
To Mae and Sol Babitz, always

Acknowledgments
To Mirandi Babitz, for my reappearance and for
this book and for everything.

To Lili Anolik for her love, her *Vanity Fair* piece,
and for *Hollywood's Eve*.

To Erica Spellman Silverman for coming back into
my life as my agent, and to the whole team at
Trident Media Group who worked so hard on all
my books, I can't thank you enough.

To Sara Kramer at NYRB Classics because this
book is really her book; and to all the editors and
publishers throughout the years, who believed in
my work, especially Joie Davidow and Susan
LaTempa.

To all my fans, new and old. I am so glad to have
found an audience to dance with.

ALL THIS AND *THE GODFATHER* TOO
Francis Ford Coppola and His World

I. THE BALMY SUMMER EVENING DANCE

"They're shooting the party scene outside at night," I was told. "Bring mittens and wool socks, and wear a fur coat if you have one."

Fred Roos took over the phone and said, "You'll love it here. It's a chance to get away from Tana's."

I bought some socks and flew to Reno.

"Thirty degrees and that wind, coming off the lake like a mother! And them working till four in the morning! Boy, I don't know how they do it!" The cab driver who picked me up at the airport had his own thoughts about the movie. He asked, "What'll you be doing up here?"

"Watching," I said, and made him pull over so I could buy a fifth of tequila to be on the safe side because Fred Roos and other working movie people often forget to drink.

"Washing?" the guy asked, puzzled, as he drove through groves of shimmering aspens turned golden for the fall.

"No, *watching*... I'm sort of a writer," I replied.

The sun was setting by the time we'd driven through Reno; soon we were almost to Tahoe City, where a large and carefully assembled cast and crew were making their first attempts to shoot a movie called *The Godfather, Part II.* Al Pacino was now a star. Francis Ford Coppola had 6 percent of the first *Godfather*, which seemed in danger of becoming the biggest movie success the world has ever known. Fred Roos, who had once been a casting director, was now the coproducer (with Gray Frederickson).

Suddenly, the lake appeared. It was a mirror of the sky, pinkish from the sunset; reflections of pine trees rippled in the breeze.

The location was a cluster of little wooden houses, a retired motel with strange English countryside pretensions. Trees grew all around and a guard waited by the narrow road with orders not to let in *any*body who wasn't supposed to be there.

It was beginning to get chilly.

Fred Roos, from his office in one of the bigger little houses of the compound, offered to try to find me some long underwear. I was apparently about to face a frozen evening—when I could have been at Tana's, The Bar Where We All Go to Pick Each Other Up, the Italian restaurant where I once saw Al Pacino and the very place I'd caught Fred's eye across a crowded room one night a few months before and we'd been introduced. Tana's was always warm and electric.

The electricity at Lake Tahoe was provided by a loud generator that chugged away through the night, scaring animals. It provided power not only for the filming, but for the real focal point of the evening—the Mets/Oakland game.

By nightfall the first shots were being readied.

The extras were dressed in clothes suitable for a balmy summer evening; between takes they rushed into giant khaki army coats and boots. Long underwear was stuffed under delicate gowns and there were people about whose only function was to tear the coat from a star's back the instant the cameras went on and to put the coat back on the instant the camera stopped.

"Feel this," said Francis Ford Coppola, clad in a thick bunch of clothing and wearing a ridiculous-looking woolen hat that sloped over to one side at the top. "Feel in here."

He indicated his pocket. I felt, and out came a red velvet box that looked like something that diamonds from Tiffany's might come from.

"For me!" I said. It was so soon!

"Just feel it," he said. And I did and it was hot. The gold lettering on the top, I noticed then, did not say "Tiffany." It said "Hand Warmer." Inside was a burning coal.

"People's mothers used to send those things to guys in Korea so they wouldn't freeze," Fred Roos said.

"Why, Fred, I didn't know you were in Korea," someone said. Fred Roos looks like he's about twelve, but for his slightly graying sideburns.

"There were guys stationed in Korea *after* the war, you know," Fred said.

And then Francis Ford Coppola, with gargantuan patience, began to apply himself to the shooting of the film.

I don't suppose I will ever really understand Francis. My main feeling about him, which gets stronger and stronger as time goes by, is simply abject belief in his greatness. I want to be on his side.

If you read pieces about Francis, you will notice that anyone who writes about him, from *Time* and *Newsweek* to *The New Yorker* or even to *The Esoteric Film Quarterly for the Finest Minds*, all writers (except Joyce Haber), are spellbound by him.

He talks about schemes to create the greatest shows on earth, simultaneously superimposing upon them the subtlest artistic inspirations. And who, after all, is going to refuse that offer?

On Francis's side are Righteousness and Truth, Pure Untainted Visions of Ancient Glory and Modern Goodness. On the other side are the Capitalist George Grosz Money Masturbators, amassing Power in secret vaults.

You refuse this offer, you say, and you're sure Francis isn't all that great and he's just like the rest of them and besides you can't be bothered with adolescent crushes? I challenge you to talk to Francis for fifteen minutes (or for four days) and find a gap.

Mistakes he makes, flaws he's got. But he's only thirty-six and he's still just a beginner.

2. THE ONE-HOUR MISUNDERSTANDING

Pacino and Coppola fought in Las Vegas and people quaked in their boots.

"He..." Pacino began. "Look, why the hell does it take so long to shoot a scene? Lumet shot *Serpico* in eighteen *days*! And I go up to Francis, I've got a problem I want to talk to him about... So what does he *do*? He tells me *his* problems. What do I want to hear *his* problems for? He's the *director*!"

Francis is strange about actors. He believes in them. He takes a lot of trouble to cast them, and then he lets go. He doesn't try to improve them. He hardly even says "Good" after a shot that's a take; he just goes on to the next shot.

He once told me that he was terrified when he learned that Brando would actually be in the original *Godfather* movie. Imagine trying to tell someone like that how to act. Things became stranger still when Brando came up to him and said, "Now, look. I'll tell you how I like to be directed. You just tell me 'Louder, softer, madder, kindlier'... You just tell me. You want me to look a certain way? You tell me. You want me to look up? Down? I'll do anything you say."

"And he *did*," Coppola added with a lingering sense of amazement. "He *did* anything."

If there is anything an actor hates more than a director who won't let him alone, it's a director who trusts him to such an extent that he forgets about him entirely. The actor's art is the art of physical presence. His body, his voice, his eyes, and his inner spirit are leased to a film for the time it takes to shoot.

Of course, films are a lot more than actors. There is the camera, for example, which can express things the actor is thereby absolved from—distance, light, a certain kind of drama. There are sets, with their minute detail. There is the Studio, which wonders why everything has to cost so much and why one of the actors was seen out with a certain person who will tarnish everyone's image.

Everybody knows that Francis Ford Coppola is brilliant. And it is not just the brilliance of casting, script, or camerawork. It is the brilliance of stamina.

And because everyone knows how brilliant he is, the actors hold on, trusting that his trust in them is part of his brilliance. But for a person whose art is his body it's frightening to be trusted so much.

What if you're a New York actor like Al Pacino, who's used to having friends and lovers right around the corner, used to having little playhouses where he can watch colleagues working. All of a sudden, out you step onto the lot at Paramount where huge empty soundstages testify to the glory that once was Hollywood—probably the glory that made you become an actor in the first place.

You live in a hotel and they've given you a chauffeured car and out you step into the middle of an empty day. Should you read? But you can't concentrate on books. You're supposed to be thinking about your body and soul. Maybe you should go back and watch the shooting, but it's so hemmed in by the director's fastidious perfectionism that the thread gets lost and you, along with the extras, are overwhelmed by boredom.

You could go drink, but... And you *would* go eat except that working on a full stomach, as you know from past experience, is wrong. You decide you hate Hollywood and if you ever get out of this picture alive, you'll only do plays on the East Coast, even if they're performed in hovels, or in Maine. You'll never come back here to this damned fucking wasteland, even for brilliant fucking Francis Ford Coppola.

Or you could talk to girls. But the girls out here are different. They're not people, they don't know...They're too pretty. Too crazy. They don't do anything except be tall and drive fast cars. You, yourself, don't drive. You've learned from past experience that you are not to be trusted at the wheel.

You met a girl the other day who is a health-food freak. She wore no makeup or underclothes and she was gorgeous. She gave you some ginseng root and told you if you chewed on it, you'd feel better.

The camera pans away from you as you stand in the middle of the crisp, clear, empty afternoon, chewing on a distasteful, tough root, waiting to feel better. It's something to do until 3 p.m.

You are one of the chosen. Francis has chosen you and Francis is brilliant. You remember that, bear that in mind, because sometime, somehow, Francis will come forth with a dark golden thing of beauty. Just like in the movies. And everyone will say, What wonderful actors! Just like in the movies.

"Listen, babes," he growls, alternating between a glass of ginger ale and a glass of Olympia beer. "If there's anything I know, it's never try to tell anyone how much pain you're in . . . And never expect anyone to answer any question."

Or at least never expect Michael Gazzo to answer any question. Because he starts in the middle of any given topic of conversation, and it's like you've missed the first act. But he *will* tell you about the pain, very elaborately and very well. He is not unable, like most actors are, to find the words to exquisitely describe the exact quality of the pain, because Gazzo is also a dealer in words. He wrote *A Hatful of Rain*, they told me, and *he* told me that he only acts to support his writing, his three children, his dog, and his wife.

His wife watches carefully to see that he doesn't run out of beer, that his ashtray is empty, that there are matches . . . They eloped twenty-nine years ago to Point Pleasure, New Jersey, when she was working in an insurance office and he was a machinist. It is impossible to imagine what Michael Gazzo looked like twenty-nine years ago, he looks so himself now—so baleful. They live in a brownstone on Forty-Fourth Street, which they own—a whole house in the middle of the theater district. He has an acting workshop there and it is there that he writes. He's thinking of moving to Los Angeles, he says, because "the theater is sociologically dead." All that's left are movies, and movies treat actors like shit, he repeats, over and over. "The studios have everything ass backwards. Listen, babes, all you have is the script, the director, and the actor, and anyone else is full of shit . . ."

"I don't give a shit if Francis hears this or not," Gazzo says occasionally. "Francis is a . . . a *brilliant* man. But Francis is *not* an actor."

("Gazzo's probably going to get an Academy Award for this," they say on the soundstage, and slowly shake their heads.)

The Lost Hour occurred on Friday, November 30, 1973, at Paramount Studios on stage #27 during the Senate Investigating Committee scene.

Extras dressed in painful clothes comprised the audience, the press, and the FBI men, and, between takes, they all spoke mostly about the shoes that the women had to wear. "How can you walk in those things?" The shoes had narrow high heels and pointy toes, and were killers. I was one of the extras, hired by Fred Roos on a "waiver" to impersonate a member of the press. Waivers are for people who are not professional extras.

The professional extras are used to being bored beyond words. They are used to hardship, temperamental stars and directors, interminable waiting, and waking up at 5 a.m. The rest of us, and about one-third of the courtroom was "us," were on waivers. We weren't used to it at all.

The first day, Thursday, I had to get there at 7 a.m. and the sky was black outside at six when I heard the alarm. By eight I was wearing the ghastly clothes that they wore in 1958, had on the hideous red lipstick and the stupid black line on the top of my eyelids, and was shifting my feet. But at least I got to sit down the whole time, not lean against the back wall like some of the poor women.

Over in one corner, I saw one nondescript extra who looked like Al Pacino's brother's friend. Someone told me later that he was Robert De Niro.

It was not until 10:30 that we moved into the courtroom. Why had I had to wake up at six if they weren't going to do anything until 10:30? I tried not to think about it. I tried to be cheerful and optimistic.

My second day as an extra was Friday, and that was the day of the Lost Hour.

Michael Gazzo plays a character called Pentangeli in *The Godfather, Part II*. He is the star witness, an ex-mobster turning state's evidence. He's going to tell all about the Corleone family and hopefully send Michael (Al Pacino) to jail.

But most of the extras didn't know this. We were just told to act excited when the man was shown into the courtroom.

The cameras rolled. Suddenly, a presence entered—a flamboyant, smiling, huge presence. Gazzo was led to his seat and he ran through the scene with so much fire that even the girls pinched into their shoes against the back wall, sixty feet away, took notice. It was like an injection of pure show business.

Then he ran through the scene again. It was a complicated dance, hard to block, with photographers flashing, Gazzo smiling, cigars lit, questions asked . . .

Then we broke for lunch, and the extras grumbled because we only got forty-five minutes, which meant that we couldn't dash out to Nickodell's for anything decent, but had to eat off the truck—cottage cheese and V8 juice and dumb sandwiches.

I had seen the rushes of one of Gazzo's earlier scenes, a dinner party that had to be relit and shot from six different angles so that the reactions of each of the diners could be recorded. Throughout the shooting, Gazzo was drinking wine. Finally, in the last take, Diane Keaton (who was playing Pacino's wife) looked into the camera and said, "I hope everyone's having a good time. I know I certainly am." Gazzo's chin was nearly on the table.

So when lunch came, I had it in the back of my mind that even though they weren't letting the extras get anything decent to eat, they would, in the interest of the scene, watch Gazzo closely. If he could get drunk in front of the cameras, just think what he could do alone in forty-five minutes.

When we regrouped, all was well. Everyone found his place and we waited for the scene to begin. Gazzo, this time, was equally a presence. But he slurred his words, and there were these . . . pauses.

Francis called to his henchman, Newt. (Newt has a black eye patch and an invisible whip, and he told us to be quiet 127 times in my two

days as an extra.) "All right," he said to him. "Have everyone break
for an hour."

And that was the Lost Hour.

The professional extras regarded this as a splendid opportunity to
get on with their needlepoint and to worry about whether they'd be
back on Monday.

Everyone, somehow, knew that it was because of Gazzo.

But how, I wondered, do you fix these things in one hour? How
do they do that in the movie business? They send for an ambulance,
a nurse with an alligator bag, and plenty of oxygen, food, and Coca-
Cola. That's how. He was all better in an hour and they shot from
there until 9:30 p.m. But he wasn't the same as when he'd first come
in. He was fine, but he wasn't the same.

And now I had come to see Michael Gazzo in his rented apartment
in the middle of downtown Hollywood.

The apartment was barren of personal effects. Gazzo rented it
when he discovered that he couldn't abide the Holiday Inn. A couple
of blocks away, three days before, an eighteen-year-old kid had shot
a policeman in the head and a dragnet had been thrown out over the
area so thick that Gazzo couldn't even get out to go to Paramount
and pick up his check. The kid had been captured the next night
after holing up in a motel for four hours. He finally gave up saying,
"I didn't do it."

"*I* didn't do it," Gazzo said, about the Lost Hour. "It was their
fault. You see, the whole thing was their fault, babes, and I'm gonna
tell you why."

The story, which started somewhere in the middle, of course, came
out like this: the dressing room didn't have a bathroom.

The chauffeur was late and didn't know what stage they were on.
The dressing room had to be shared with two other guys who were
supposed to be FBI agents. There was *no* men's toilet on the soundstage. The man who was supposed to play Gazzo's long-lost brother
wasn't introduced to him until ten minutes before they started, and
then, it turned out, the guy spoke no English at all. And last but not
least, nobody told him where to go for lunch.

"So I went out the front gate to this bar where it was dark and had four Scotch and sodas. And, babes, I don't get drunk on no Scotch and soda. It was just that since I was working, I hadn't eaten all day. Who can work on a full stomach? And I don't care if you play this tape for Francis. *I* was the reason for the scene! It was Pentangeli's testimony that was the reason those four hundred people were all standing around. And the driver didn't even know where the fuck the stage was!

"A lot of people forget that actors are people," Gazzo said, "and they aren't paying us to be people. They're paying us to get it up twenty times a day. They pay us a lot to get it up twenty times a day. And probably there are some guys who can do *that* too, but this is... Listen, babes, Francis comes over to me and says 'Look scared' and I'm thinking to myself, I'm not afraid of anything. The only thing that scares me is insanity. So in two minutes I transform all the senators, all the audience, my lawyer, the FBI guys, everyone, into lunatics. That's my craft. I'm prepared. That's what they're paying me for. But my God, they should have shown me my brother earlier, 'cause I never even saw the guy..."

Then he changes without a missed step. "Whoever's casting that thing is brilliant! Did you see that guy? My brother? Jesus Christ! What a brilliant piece of casting!"

And so goes the movie. It's all like that. They hired the most qualified people on earth and when Francis could control the environment the way he did at Lake Tahoe, where the actors were isolated in a village which was the set in which they acted, things held together. Everyone knew where dinner was. Gazzo ran an actors' workshop in the afternoons so that the actors felt like people and that acting was a dignified profession, an art.

But once things came to Hollywood, they fell apart for the mostly New York actors. In Hollywood, actors are left to their own devices. The huge old soundstages, the detailed sets, *everything* had to stop for one $10,000 hour because nobody thought to show Michael Gazzo where the commissary was, or to tell him how good he is.

And when your own body is what the finished product of your art is, there really ought to be a bathroom nearby. And two double Scotches seems like a good idea, babes, it really fucking does.

And I don't care if Francis sees this or not.

3. THE CONVERSATION

Francis Ford Coppola, one hundred years ago, would have been writing grandiose operas about impossible topics (like bullfighters and cigar-rolling girls) because Coppola finds stories where everyone else is blind.

So Francis decided on a terrific idea about this guy who is the best eavesdropper in the country, is a Catholic, and likes to play the sax, alone, in his apartment. And this guy, see, does an ultra-impossible job recording an impossible conversation between a young woman and a young man in Union Square in San Francisco. Cindy Williams plays the girl and except for about three seconds at the end of the movie, the few minutes of conversation she has with the young man is the only footage of her. But that's OK because it is repeated over and over, the same words, the same groan, "God," when she sees a wino, collapsed on a park bench, the same mundane remark about "He must have had a mother..."

Her voice fades and grows louder, a repeated coda, as various meanings become possible and the conscience of her unlapsed Catholic recorder slowly turns on him like Chinese water torture each time she groans "...God."

The film is called *The Conversation*, and in it, San Francisco, for once in its life, is presented as it must seem to conventioneers. There's not one single little glimpse of Victoriana anywhere and the bridges are overlooked completely, as are nice shots of the bay, the hilltops... The Jack Tar Hotel, however, will never be the same—no matter how terrible it is when you're actually there, what Francis turned it into is worse.

There's a convention for buggers at the hotel—booths displaying new kinds of secret recording tricks ornamented with ladies past the age when they could make more money with their looks doing something else. Here, Mr. Caul, Gene Hackman, is obviously the hero. Once, it turns out, he recorded a conversation between the president of a Teamsters local and his chief associate which took place in the middle of the ocean on a boat twenty miles from anywhere else. That Mr. Caul's recording seemed to have resulted in the death of the chief associate, his wife, and his child has churned up an inner conflict between the American Way of "Just Doing My Job" and what Caul Catholically knows to be a sin, murder. But it's almost impossible to think of sin or murder at the convention, where everyone thinks you're the craftiest mother alive in the world today.

Francis blithely presumed that this was a terrific idea for a movie. But they only finally let him try out his idea after *The Godfather* turned out the way it did.

4. THE GODFATHER, PART FIVE

They were in Reno first, then Las Vegas, then Hollywood; then it was "Do you wanna go to Santo Domingo?" (I heard that they had to keep the stars locked in safes at night so they wouldn't be stolen as hostages and that the natives were unfriendly and that one twenty-two-year-old female crew member who'd been remarkably pure of heart when shooting began was now, under the influence of Santo Domingo, drinking with the grips, that Al Pacino was sick there, that people were coming down with a local bug which only a doctor examining one's stools could detect . . .) Well, no, I didn't want to go to Santo Domingo. But then they said, "You wanna go to New York and go to the *Gatsby* party?" Santo Domingo—*no, Gatsby—sí!*

New York was Part Five.

*

It was about a week before the end of March. My mother had been in New York two weeks before and described it as "balmy"—a description which I bore in mind as I packed. As it turned out, it was my mother who was balmy; New York was troublesome and horrendous, as crazy as it was overwhelming, and as *cold* as it had been eight years ago when I had left vowing never to return unless I had a suite at the Plaza and my own personal limousine.

My relationship with Fred Roos, struck up in the usual way that any of Fred's alliances for progress are struck up, was decided when he realized that he could stand me and thought I'd come in handy and, besides, I went to Hollywood High. The Hollywood High Mafia. He's the one who showed me a photograph of the time Hollywood beat Hamilton High at baseball. "It's been all downhill since then," he explained.

It's difficult to make Fred Roos laugh, but once you're on his A-list, you're allowed to once, sometimes twice, a day. We are also allowed to make him furious—cold empty long pauses on the telephone. His A-list, besides me, includes Cindy Williams, Harry Dean Stanton, Monte Hellman, a guy named Brooks he was in Korea with, and the newest member—whom Cindy and I insisted on for two hours one night at Tana's—Ed Begley Jr. Jack Nicholson, too, is one, and so is Marianna Hill. I'm the only one besides this guy named Lloyd (Fred's truest friend, the one who goes to basketball games with him), who is not really in the movie business. And his mother.

"When are you coming to New York?" he asked. Like grand Guy Grand, Fred likes nothing better than to make it "hot" for people. So it's twelve midnight and he's calling to find out when I am coming to New York and if I get a taxi in twenty minutes, I can be there by dawn and we can have breakfast. "They're shooting the 1918 street scenes," he added. "Robert De Niro is in it and your friend Bruce

Kirby. And Francis wants to talk to you about that magazine . . . And we're all going to the *Gatsby* party, lots of good eats."

"Party?" I said. "A party?"

"Yeah, we're all going. After the *Gatsby* premiere?"

"Are we going to the premiere?"

"No. A private screening."

"What if I come tomorrow?"

"Just say what time," he said, "and things'll get rolling."

My book had just come out a week before and a friend of mine had written a review of it in the *Los Angeles Times* that was so violently opposed to me in general and to my book in particular that I'd run immediately to the Las Palmas newsstand to get a Tucson paper to look for a job as a waitress.

Suddenly, cooling it in New York seemed like a sensible thing to do.

I hate planes.

I hate airports.

I hate packing.

I never know what to pack.

I hate being afraid.

I am always afraid when I travel.

"How do I get from the airport to you?" I asked.

"I'll send a limo for you."

Well, that did it. I started thinking about going to the laundromat and how long it would take to touch up my roots.

"Where'll I stay?" I asked finally. (He was staying at the Sherry-Netherland.)

"Here," he said.

How was I to know that when Fred said "here" he meant New York? He'd booked me into a place on Times Square called the Edison. I'd never heard of it but after I was all packed and humming the next day, I made one final call to my best agent in Hollywood, who was delighted to hear I was going to have such fun, delighted about the party, delighted about everything up until the very moment when I said the word "Edison," and then she stated simply: "Don't go."

"What?"

"Don't go. I refuse to let you stay at the Edison. It's unsafe. Call them back this minute and say you won't go."

"I just got an ugly message from you," Fred Roos said after I had tried to call him back.

"Fred, you're sticking me into the middle of Hell's Kitchen."

"Ed Begley is right down the hall from you. And your friend Bruce Kirby. All your friends are there. I thought you'd have fun."

"...Oh..." I said.

"You've hurt my feelings." He doesn't mince words. For a producer.

"I'm sorry. I'll see you tomorrow for breakfast. And if I can't stand the Edison—there's this other place I think I can stay."

"Why do you always do this?" he persisted. "Why are you so obnoxious?"

"Because it's the only way you'll listen to me," I admitted. "I'm jealous."

"What's 'jealous' got to do with this?"

"I don't know," I said.

Another cold pause. "Well...OK...see you tomorrow. The guy'll pick you up at the airport and take you here."

Meanwhile, my girlfriend, upon learning that I was going to New York, called an old friend of hers who had a penthouse with a guest room and a private entrance, private keys. A penthouse in the upper fifties on the East Side. The only safe place in New York. The penthouse friend didn't like women as anything more than friends, she explained, but he was a peach and I'd love him. ("You'll love him," they always say. "When you get to New York give him a call." And you never do, do you? Because you know you'll hate him and besides there isn't time.) Members of the Gay Community have never liked me much the way they like my girlfriend, who's "got great bones and ages well," and it was only the sheerest and most utter desperation which would finally throw me into the penthouse of someone who was to become one of my most cherished friends.

*

The Red-Eye Special was hellish. I felt murderous rage at those who slept through it. We landed at 6:30 a.m.

My chauffeur looked like Al Pacino, only he was Jewish. He was an ex-cop wounded in the line of duty in Bedford-Stuyvesant; he knew supercops "Batman and Robin." All the women in Los Angeles are in love with dark, fast-talking New Yorkers, and my chauffeur was a dear. (All the women in New York have posters of Redford on their walls. If they came to Los Angeles, they'd find Redford parking their cars and saving their lives on the beaches of Santa Monica. Redfords are a dime a dozen in L.A. Pacinos are de rigueur in New York.)

"Don't take your purse with you when you go outside the Edison," my ex-cop chauffeur advised me when he dropped me off at the Sherry-Netherland.

Fred was wearing pajamas and the same bathrobe he wears to pad around reading scripts in in L.A. Darling, darling Fred, all sleepy and darling Hollywood High.

"Two more hours," he said, and went back to bed. He keeps his room so hot it's embryonic, and I paced, took a bath, washed my hair, and wondered about the Edison.

At nine we went down to breakfast. He made three phone calls first. He always makes three phone calls right after he says, "We're going right now."

After breakfast, the chauffeur dropped Fred off at the Gulf and Western Building and then took me to the Edison. I wondered if I could stand the Edison. All the men in the elevator looked as though they were just waiting to open their overcoats and reveal the worst.

The bellboy opened the door to my room, looked in, and said, "Oh, good, the bed's made up." I gave him a dollar and sat down. I asked for Ed Begley on the phone and the operator said she'd never heard of him. I couldn't remember Bruce Kirby's last name.

I called Jay Rank, the penthouse friend-of-a-friend. I called him at work where he supervised a Seventh Avenue high-style clothing manufacturing house with four hundred people working under him.

"I was expecting you at 7:30," he said. "Just go to my apartment, tell the elevator man, Scott, who you are and he'll take you to my apartment."

"What about the key?"

"Don't worry about the key," he said. "The door's open."

"You just leave the door open in New York?"

"In my building it's all right. It's owned by the Mafia."

(They are not allowed to say the word "Mafia" in *The Godfather* because the Mafia doesn't exist except in buildings where you don't need to lock your doors in New York.)

By 12 o'clock I was opening the door of Jay Rank's penthouse.

Safe.

Huge ceilings, large white couches and chairs, space, a terrace, clean.

Three cats looked at me; one ran, one didn't bother, and one, a Persian princess, came on purring. Ohhhhhh . . . home.

Thank God for the Mafia. Because of them I was safe and because of them Francis Ford Coppola was making another gigantic work of *art*.

"*Gris, gris, gra, ca-ca pistasche*," I sighed, my Cajun great-grandmother's voodoo chant for safety. And I put in a good word for the Mafia, the New York one and the Hollywood High one.

My bedroom at Jay's was a shambles; boxes of photographs were stacked up three feet high on top of the bed. But it was a safe bed and I got the boxes off. The Persian came in to see how I was doing and when I put a beautiful patchwork quilt over the bed, she jumped on it to see how she'd look. Divine as usual.

"*The Great Gatsby* was boring pudding—$6.8 million, brought-in-right-on-schedule, boring pudding."

*

The Persian came to the door looking worried. Jay Rank was still not home and it was almost six o'clock. I wished Jay Rank would get home so I could find out who he was. He had no rock-and-roll records, just Broadway shows and European singers. I knew that much. He had lots of flowers.

For a man who'd been up since 7:30 working in a giant factory designing clothes all day, Jay Rank looked hysterically immaculate and kind when he arrived.

"What would you like to drink?" he asked, removing his gloves and hat.

"My God," I said. "How can you look like this? You're so neat, you're perfect, and I'm . . . I'm just from L.A."

"Scotch?"

I followed him into the kitchen, where he filled up a silver ice bucket and I followed him back into the living room, where he filled two gorgeous Swedish glasses full of ice, Scotch, and soda. He smoked fine Shermans and had a Dunhill black lighter with gold trim.

From the time he came home, at about 6:30, until 1 a.m., we drank dinner and talked. He did not loosen his tie. He remained perfect and only I got drunk.

The plan was to meet on the twenty-ninth floor of the Gulf and Western Building, see *The Great Gatsby*, for which Francis had written the script, and try not to die. Then we were to get into the limousine, go to the Sherry-Netherland to change, and go to The Party at the Waldorf Astoria for "eats." The party was supposed to be "black tie" so Fred had ordered up a tuxedo from wardrobe. Francis was so disgusted by the movie that he refused to change out of his corduroy.

Gatsby was boring pudding—$6.8 million, brought-in-right-on-schedule, boring pudding. But no use crying over spilt pudding. And besides, *The Conversation* was coming in for the home stretch, ten lengths ahead of everything else, smelling like a rose.

Everyone had forgotten about the roses.

Everyone had forgotten what they liked.

Except Francis.

"It's a perseverance of vision," he mentioned *en passant* one after-noon to a reporter. "That's all."

Francis perseveres. He remembers what we like.

And we like movies. We like movies with plots, with people we care about, with scary parts, with mystery…We like to go to the movies, sit down, and let someone take over the controls. And all the promotional campaigns in the world cannot make pudding into roses. *Gatsby* is the proof of that.

The party was just great.

They gave you enough caviar. The waiters wore white gloves. The plates from which we supped hadn't been brought out since Queen Elizabeth had been there in 1966. They gave us pheasant and some-thing so good that none of us could figure out what it was. It was halfway between asparagus and potatoes. Or maybe it was gnocchi.

Dessert was flaming! (Once someone derided me by saying, "Eve likes champagne cocktails and everything flaming." But it's true.)

Cindy Williams, the star of *American Graffiti* and *The Conversation*, my friend Cindy, sat at our table nearer to Fred than I (she's much more manageable).

After a tirade of untold brilliance in the limo about what was the matter with *Gatsby*, Francis didn't mention it again, and the caviar seemed to cheer him up. It certainly cheered *me* up.

5. THE STREET

They took over Sixth Street between A and B and turned it into New York, 1918.

The attention to detail was marvelous. The pushcarts, the dogs, the goats, the chickens, the horses, the ancient cars, the newspaper racks with all 1918 newspapers on them, some in Italian…

(On a day when I wasn't there, seven hundred extras had filled the re-created street dressed in immigrant clothes and the three most important items on that extra call were:

1. No tweezed eyebrows.
2. No dyed hair.
3. No nose jobs.)

Since the most difficult way to shoot the particular scene they were doing would have required a two-hundred-foot-long dolly shot, they decided to do it that way.

Robert De Niro, playing Marlon Brando as a young man, looked less peevish than most actors who have to wait and wait and wait and wait. Debbie (Fred's assistant) and I huddled together and watched and I brought my camera so I wouldn't be too bored.

Francis strolled around throwing chocolate-covered almonds into everyone's mouth.

"It's just a crime, anyway," I said to Francis. "Just when *The Conversation* comes out, Pauline Kael has to stop writing for *The New Yorker*."

"Who is that other one, anyway?" someone asked. A New York sharpy interviewer who knew everything said, "It's that Penelope Gilliatt woman. She and Canby from the *Times* go and sit and neck during screenings."

"Really," I said. "Aren't they a little old?"

"Eve," Francis said, "Take me away from all this. Take me to some little apartment where I can write all day and dawdle around in the kitchen and when you come home from work I'd make you a nice dinner."

"Yeah, but would you wash the dishes?"

"You wanna know something?" Francis replied. "More men wash dishes in America than women. That's a fact. It's true."

I believed him. I don't know where he got that information but I believed him. So, I said, "So, I'd go work all day and you'd get to stay home and write?"

"Yeah. In fact, that was the best time of my life one time when I had a setup like that."

"So why'd you blow it?" I asked.

A production assistant poked his head in. "Newt wants to talk to you about tomorrow."

"Why?" Francis asked.

"Because if it's raining we shoot inside and if not we shoot outside."

"Good," Francis said. "Tell him 'good.' Why does he have to ask me these questions?...Why can't I just have a little apartment somewhere and do nothing?..."

The phone rang. Francis picked it up himself. There are no buttons on these phones in Francis's and Fred's offices. There is one phone for Fred in the Moviola room and one phone for Francis. There are no secretaries. When a phone rings, whoever's nearest picks it up.

"...Yeah, this is him," Francis said over the phone. "...You just saw it, huh?...Well, it's a funny thing about *The Conversation*, because a lot of different people saw it and I think that each person should decide their own ending...In fact I rather like it when people see it a whole different way from the way I thought it was..."

The conversation went on, a conversation about *The Conversation*; someone who'd obviously just been to see the movie was calling up to find out what it was all about. It went on for twenty minutes. Francis wouldn't budge. He would not tell whoever it was what the movie they had just seen was about.

"Golly," Fred said when the phone was finally put down. "Who was that?"

"Some chick says she's from *The New Yorker*..." Francis replied. "Gilliato or something like that."

"Oh, no," the New York sharpy said. "And you mean she's calling you to..."

(A half hour later, I heard someone say, she phoned again for the shooting script. I wonder if she'll ever find out.)

Francis sat back. The phones had stopped ringing.

"What'd you do yesterday?" Fred asked.

"Oh, nothing," Francis replied. "I just sort of hung around in the morning and then, oh, yeah, I watched five hours of dailies. The whole picture that we've got so far. It was really interesting, watching it.

There are just a couple of scenes that need to be reshot. And then there's the scene with the lullaby that I'm going to make a lot stronger. I thought it was too corny, you know, at first, to have Vito Corleone go straight from killing that guy in the white suit into singing a lullaby for Michael and holding him in his arms—the kids are the wrong ages on that by the way but we're going to fudge.... But it has to be strong because we go straight from there into Michael Corleone holding his own baby in arms, and we're going to segue that by thematic music so we give Michael some character because he's such an executive in this one you don't know who he is ... De Niro is stealing the picture because his character is so much more defined ..."

The street on the Lower East Side which *The Godfather, Part II* has taken over is almost completely movie-ized—almost, but not completely. Two dark little bars are still open, in which real people sit drinking real drinks. One is Ukrainian and the other is Puerto Rican and they are always open, Hollywood or not.

The locals are madly eclectic. There are the real faces, the real children of Ellis Island, the faces that you see in those Museum of Modern Art photographs from 1911. Then there are the sharp young black men, young guys with high, high platform shoes. There are the transvestites from David Bowieland. There are the beautiful leftover hippie mothers with sons who look like daughters. There are the omnipresent limousine drivers who grow familiar and important for they are the means of escape.

All the people who were not "principals" or in the extra business had to scoot away into the bars or hallways whenever Newt said, "Now anyone who's not in this scene back away, please ..." or "Anyone wearing modern glasses, take them off, please ..." or "Would you mind getting that dog off the dolly tracks, he's going to get killed standing there ..."

My hair, which I had only recently bleached a kind of shocking fox color (I went to the *Godfather* Christmas party and no one paid the slightest bit of attention to anyone but blonds so I decided to go

orange and finish them off once and for all), my hair and my fox collar and my green shoes and my Brownie had become notorious within
an hour of my arrival and I was known as: "Did you see that girl with
the red hair and the green shoes and the Brownie?"

"Let me try that Brownie," Francis said, stretching for another
interminable stretch of waiting. "How do you do it?"

Everyone I let try that camera that day did better than Francis.
He took a picture of me, only it was mostly sky and, well…

"What's the matter with you, anyway?" I asked. "Don't you know
a *thing* about cameras?"

"No, I don't," he said, and handed me back my Brownie.

6. CANNES

The Conversation was the last film to slip in under the wire at the
Cannes Film Festival and so Francis and his entourage went, while
I returned to Hollywood. I learned that Paramount was so mad that
the rain had made everything take longer on *The Godfather, Part II*
that they canceled their original offer to provide room and board for
some of the actors in France, but Fred Roos had already notified a
bunch of people that their future in Cannes was secure (if only they
got there themselves—Paramount wasn't going to pay for no flights,
mind you). So Fred, I heard, had to pay for everything. It couldn't
have sat well with him, having to pay for actors' room and board
himself. (The one time he ever took me out for a legitimate dinner
in Los Angeles, where we went all by ourselves without the rest of
the A-list, he took me to his favorite restaurant, which turned out to
be a Mexican one without dash or fervor and the bill came to $4.06.)

One day, I went over to the Paramount offices in Beverly Hills
and mailed out Xerox copies of my chapter about the filming in New
York to them all. I noticed that page 29 was missing and I realized
that I'd gone from page 28 to 30 and neglected 29 altogether. It occurred to me to mention that there was no page 29, but I forgot. I
was hungry and it was lunchtime.

The phone rang one night, a few days later, and the connection was scratchy and far away. A man's voice said, "You don't know me exactly...Are you Eve Babitz?"

"Yeah?" I said suspiciously.

"Well, my name is Victor Ramos and I..."

"Oh, yeah," I said, "you're doing something on the *Godfather* movie aren't you?"

"Yes," he said, "and I'm in Cannes and I don't know how to tell you this...But...Well, I was reading your New York piece and I..."

My immediate reaction was, This guy's calling to tell me they're suing me and that if I should so much as allow another soul to see anything I've written about Francis, they'd clap me into jail.

"What's the matter with it?" I asked.

"Well, Fred wanted me to call you even though I don't know you because..."

"What!? Come on. Tell me!"

"Page twenty-nine is missing and Fred wants to kill me."

"There is no page twenty-nine," I said.

"There is no page twenty-nine?"

"No...There isn't one. I forgot about page twenty-nine. There isn't one."

"You mean I just spent $34 to find out there *isn't* one?"

"Yeah," I said.

"Ah...Fred wants to talk to you. Hold on a second," Victor Ramos said. "The piece by the way is really very funny."

I had to wait for Fred Roos, as usual. I could hear his voice in the background all the way from Cannes making me wait.

"What happened to page twenty-nine?" he said when he finally came on the line.

"I forgot it. There is no page twenty-nine."

"What have you got against the number twenty-nine? You don't like that number or what?"

"When are you coming back?"

"Well, tomorrow I go to London for three days and then..."

"When are you coming back to L.A.?"

"Do you miss me?"

"Yeah, when are you coming back?"

"The first two weeks in June, sometime."

"Terrific. How is it there?"

"I'll tell you about it when I see you."

"And can I come up to San Francisco and watch you edit?"

It seemed like the pause had come in again but it was only the poor telephone line. Fred said, "Why don't you come to Cannes?"

"I've got an ulcer," I explained, "I'm sick."

"From New York?"

"Yeah, it's like one of those Evelyn Waugh things where you hear about this little boy getting shot in the foot on game day and casually throughout the book you find out he's had his leg amputated and then finally he dies…"

"What?"

"Nothing. I'm sick." I wanted to hang up and go back to bed. "I'll see you then in two or three weeks if it doesn't rain. And we all miss you."

"Good."

7. ANYTHING ELSE IS PREFERABLE

The shooting was finally finished. Everyone who could scattered as far away from the editing as possible.

In San Francisco, Francis has bought a building which is eight stories high, called the Columbus Tower, which used to be a nifty place to rent an office for small, exquisitely hip enterprises but is now, floor by floor, giving way to Moviolas and their more up-to-date counterparts.

In the basement, there is a tiny screening room where they had showed, the day before I got there, the five-hour version of *The Godfather, Part II*. They had to edit it down to three-and-a-half hours, or maybe just three…

An atmosphere of lethargy prevailed.

It may just have been because I arrived there on a Monday and Monday is when Francis doesn't eat anything all day. It makes him anxious and bored.

(In L.A. a week before at a party, Francis had run into John Milius, who'd just lost thirty-five pounds and was gloating impossibly at his newly trim condition.)

I knew that things had slowed down to a summer-vacation pace because when I got off the plane, expecting to be picked up by some dispensable member of the crew, it was Fred Roos himself who came for me. When the producer comes and gets you at the airport, it's an empty time.

Three things were supposed to happen while I was there. I was supposed to "watch Francis edit," and I actually did see him sitting in front of a Moviola at one point. I was supposed to "talk about *City*"— *City* being a magazine Francis fell upon and took over to give himself something to worry about in his spare time. And I was supposed to convince everyone that a piece I'd written for *City* was much better than they'd thought it would be when they asked me to write for them.

Mainly, though, I was just looking forward to the old *Godfather* razzle-dazzle once again.

Usually, I dread going to San Francisco, because it's always raining there and it's always raining anywhere *The Godfather, Part II* movie is, anyway, and that seemed like fabulous odds that it would be raining when I got there. However, in Los Angeles that week the weather was humid and desperate from a Mexican storm we were experiencing by osmosis. It was ninety-five and wet. I'd rather it were just *wet* I decided, so I went to San Francisco gratefully.

And somehow San Francisco was bright, gorgeous, not too windy, not foggy, clear, blue, and luxuriously just right.

Of course, this would happen just when everyone had to go into dark little rooms all day and squint at footage on little flickering screens . . .

Fred Roos picked me up in his rented Mustang II and drove it like a dagger through the freeway traffic, asking me gossipy questions and telling me about the five hours of film they'd watched the day before, and I noticed the same uneasy look in his eye he'd had when he'd been worrying about *The Conversation*. They'd worked on editing *that* for months and months . . . And I'd read an interview with Francis where he'd confessed that the ending could have been different and that perhaps, if the movie did well in Cannes, more people would go see it.

(The movie did well in Cannes. It won. I don't know if more people went to see it, though. Fred didn't either, when I asked him.)

"What am I supposed to do," I asked. "About watching?"

"Oh, you can just watch," Fred said, trying to not sound too vague.

My friend Lynzee Klingman is an editor and I'd once watched her for fifteen minutes, which was as much as I could stand. Another time, when I'd worked for a month on *Woodstock* on the same floor as the editors, it never even occurred to me to watch. It would have been too much like watching a file clerk or . . . well . . . Watching someone make Xerox copies is more exciting and adventurous than watching someone edit.

But I believe that in the middle of all things like movies and wars there comes a point, a time, when everything suddenly falls completely out of control and there is a moment, a day, when chaos is so nearby that anything else is preferable.

Chaos, the eternal human madness-fear (when you have all the power and still it doesn't work), is usually fixed in Moviolas.

To the editors go the spoils.

England lost World War II. The fact that they *won* was too obvious. No one liked it much that they won. What happened to Germany was much more interesting.

To the editors go the spoils.

Nobody likes the editing room.

It's the worst part of art.

Mozart wasn't being too funny when he said the most important, *important*, part of music was "the rest," the silence. What they cut out.

I was just waiting for a place to inject the above. It was written right after I returned from San Francisco and was trying to figure out why suddenly there was no glamour and what would I write about when there was no glamour.

My father once remarked that the reason Francis might have moved to San Francisco was because they both had the same name, but I read in an interview that Francis says he moved to San Francisco because it wasn't too far from Hollywood but wasn't *in* Hollywood. It takes about fifty minutes to fly to Los Angeles from San Francisco and Francis has his own plane so he doesn't even have to wait in line.

Walking around in North Beach with Francis I could see why he moved there and what he likes about it. There is a strange twist to his personality: that although he likes things grandiose and massive, he likes them grandiose and massive in a personal, Italian kind of way, a way in which the details of the thing stay manageable. There is something very theatrically Italianate about everything he does, a kind of quality I learned to appreciate when I lived in Rome—where even on the most medieval cobblestone street the girl who walks past you wears shoes like a Dior lady.

"I kinda like this place," Francis said painfully, because it was Monday. He looked around and the scale was right for him. I have never felt about San Francisco the way I felt when I was with Francis. I didn't feel like it was a city I'd never quite understand (the way all native Los Angelenos truly feel). I got the impression that the whole place was one big soundstage. Walking around San Francisco with Francis felt like it must feel to walk around Rome with Fellini.

About two blocks away from the Columbus Tower, Fred called out to a Chinese gentleman who was passing on the street. The Chinese gentleman waved back and went on his way across the street. "That's Francis's business manager," Fred laughed, embarking on a story which sounded like pure Francis. "He got a Chinese business manager and it really terrifies everyone. See, everyone knows that the Chinese are the best businesspeople in the world, right? So Francis got this guy, he's had him for years, and whenever he has to have business meetings he says, 'Wait a minute, I have to fly my business manager in' and then they all just don't know what to do when this guy comes in."

Amateur theatricals, I thought to myself, even in business.

The Columbus Tower is eight stories high but each story is no bigger than three thumbs and they are all narrow and triangular-shaped and awkward, but on the top is a cupola, in blue. (Was my father right about why Francis moved to San Francisco?) When I was in the building years ago, the music business and other chic pastimes had all painted each office whatever color they thought best but now Francis had had all the paint taken off all the woodwork and all the walls painted white and the place, with its caramel-colored wood and white walls, looked like an old Breck Girl ad, pure and simple and daintily sensual. All the windows had pinewood venetian blinds on them and at sunset a color that I had thought only came from Siena shot through the rooms casting such a romantic glow that one could hardly talk.

The elevator was slow and ordinary and had room for about four people. It stopped sometimes at every floor just for the hell of it.

Fred and I dropped by the seventh floor where Francis has his office; it's totally monkish except for the color of the caramel wood and the pinkish hues cast in through the venetian blinds. (Francis is a fool for Bertolucci and has his very own print of *The Conformist*, in which the venetian blinds played a big role.) Francis was not there but "would be back," so Fred and I went to eat lunch.

When we came back, we found Francis in front of an editing machine with his hands folded across his stomach looking out the window.

They were rerunning the five-hour cut in the basement and Fred suggested that I should be allowed to go down and watch but Francis didn't think "anyone should see it until it's done," then changed his mind and decided I could go watch until he was "finished" and could come take me over to *City* magazine.

The room in the basement was so small that it was hard not to trip over things, but I finally sat down and saw the "Havana" scene (shot in Santo Domingo), but I couldn't help thinking things like "I wonder how they got all those extras to jump around like that?" and "God, Al Pacino looks tired." Meanwhile, a man in back of me, named Walter, kept telling someone in the projection booth that this or that section should be relooped. The feeling of glamour just wasn't in the air.

The only thing I noticed about the film, in fact, was that the color was gorgeous and the sets were heavenly.

A man I know who wants to be a producer is always quoting someone who said, "The worst dailies make the best movies." But these weren't the dailies. These were part of a five-hour monster that had to be edited down to three hours, and I couldn't help wondering how they were ever going to do it.

Francis came in at last and offered to take me over to the magazine office.

Magazines are the most superior pastime of civilized man, I've always thought, and Francis, it seems, is not immune to such feelings himself. There is something about starting a magazine which is even better than setting out to discover America. All my life I've been starting magazines or been the sidekick of people who've just started them. There is no creative endeavor more fun than magazines.

Francis came to buy *City* because he liked the idea of a "service magazine" which told you what you could do and see in a particular city. The first time he showed it to me was up in Reno when they'd just begun shooting the movie. We were standing in his living room and he tossed the magazine across the room onto the couch and said, dramatically, "What's the matter with this magazine?"

I picked it up. It felt awful. It was printed on newsprint and the cover was hideous. Inside were more articles about the Jefferson Airplane than anyone could bear to think about.

"The matter with this magazine," I said, "is the artwork and the writing."

That was in October of 1973, and now it was July of 1974, and those two things were *still* what were the matter with the magazine, although the artwork on the cover had improved and the quality of the paper was less untouchable. Francis had been interviewing potential editors and had found one guy who he'd thought for sure would be good because he'd worked for years at *Newsweek*, *Rolling Stone*, and other publications of that ilk. I did not envy the editor who had to try to turn *City* into something other than what it was. It wasn't like starting your own magazine. It was like trying to save the Titanic.

The building which houses *City* is three stories high and Francis bought it. It's only a block away from the Columbus Tower and it's right next door to a little theater with a hugely baroque lobby and a small seating capacity, which Francis also bought.

"We went to the Chinese tea cake restaurant for lunch," I told Francis, as we were on our way back passing the coffee shop which is the bottom floor of the Columbus Tower. "Why don't you buy *it*?"

"I don't just buy everything," Francis said. "I just buy what I need. Like this coffee shop ought to be a cute little restaurant that sells cappuccino. But they own the lease."

You're thinking of starting a restaurant too? I thought. My second favorite thing to do is to start restaurants.

On the second day, Fred took me to lunch with Walter Murch, who had worked on the editing of *The Conversation* with Francis and was now doing *The Godfather, Part II*. "He's not just an editor," Francis told me, "He's working on this *with* me."

I'd just seen a piece of film of what I knew to be the end of the movie, since I'd read the script. I saw it in a room that had light coming into it on a screen as big as a TV screen and it wasn't what I had expected at all. It seemed slower than the way I remembered thinking it would have been from the script and it seemed disjointed and flawed by unnecessary people.

"How'd you like the alternate ending?" Walter said.

"Alternate!?" I said, "I thought that *was* the ending."

"No, we changed the ending...That's the alternate ending."

"Well, what's the new ending like?" I asked.

He told me that it was very smart, a solution to one of the major problems they were having with the movie which is one of those way-back-there art questions about motivation. "It's the same problem," Walter Murch said, "that we had with *The Conversation*. Remember?"

Walter explained that in the first *Godfather* movie the problems hadn't been the same, since when Al Pacino is first seen he's entirely different from how he comes to be and yet we all remember what he was like at the beginning. "It's like he's this guy who is told that he has to swim underwater twenty miles to an island," Walter went on, "and we see him before he goes under and then how he is submerged... But in this one, he's still swimming underwater and we never know who he is, we forget, and it even seems that he never was anything else. We can't tell if he's telling the truth because he's been lying so long, he's turned so completely into another person, we never know who he is... So maybe with this new ending...If we..."

The thing about movies like *The Godfather, Part II* is that they absolutely *must* appear to flow gracefully from beginning to inevitable end. None of those washed-out artsy endings for this movie. It isn't that kind of a movie. What is inessential must be cut away and what remains must convince us it's essential, not like England after it won/lost the war.

My editing friend, Lynzee Klingman, said when I came back to L.A. and tried to describe the confusion, "Oh, has it gotten like that? Yeah, it gets like that... I knew this girl who worked editing the first *Godfather* movie... She quit. She told me that Marlon Brando was awful in it and nobody knew what it was about or what they were doing. It was just a giant mess. She couldn't stand it anymore so she just quit."

It happens, then, with magazines and restaurants and wars... It's so much fun at the beginning and you can envision how wonderfully it will turn out. And without warning the moment appears when what you've begun is no longer yours. The glamour flees and no one can remember it except perhaps Francis with that remark about "perseverance of vision" as he sits with his hands folded across his stomach, his eyes fixed on some point out the window with an idle editing machine in front of him agonizing with Mozart's "rest," the part that's not there, cut out by the artist to make the remainder flow easily from beginning to end so people will have a nice movie to go to where they won't be bored, and Francis can start on a new one.

8. THE GREAT AMERICAN NOVEL

We used to hang out at Barney's Beanery for years before Barney died and say, "I wonder who's going to write the Barney's novel?"

Suddenly Ed Kienholz made his huge construction of Barney's and that was the end of it. The Barney's novel was executed.

In New York, people used to say, "I wonder who's going to write the Great American Novel?" When I came out of the screening of the final, three-and-a-half-hour *Godfather, Part II*, I knew that Francis had finished off the idea. The Great American Novel is two movies based on a book that Mario Puzo once told me he wrote "with one hand tied behind my back." It's funny no one thought of it before.

"How do you feel?" I asked Francis, once the film had come out and the lines were circling the blocks.

"I'm glad people like it," he said. "Now I want to get *City* on its feet so that it will break even..."

"And then?"

"What I really want to do, Eve, is to start a radio station. That's what I *really* want to do." There was a pause on the phone.

"You know, Francis," I said. "Your movie is really a masterpiece... You know how I can tell?"

"How?"

"It's flawed."

"Thanks."

"A radio station, eh?"

"A *little* radio station," he stressed.

Just like *The Godfather* was a little gangster picture.

9. THE PERSEVERANCE OF VISION

I used to watch them, those guys with their maroon and white sweaters at Hollywood High, their handsome faces and their invincibility and the way they smiled and said Hi. They were the casual popular young men who were taller and smarter than the rest of them and if you weren't one of the fifty or so girls who were their rightful mates, they rarely tossed one of their Hi's your way. The most you could hope to be if you were on the outside was an observer, a receiver of secondhand gossip, a chronicler of The Way He Looked at Her in Physiology 1 and the Way She Looked Away.

Whatever we were all going to be when we grew up, I used to think, will never be anywhere near as vivid and bloody as this. And because we were in Southern California—in Hollywood, even—there was no history for us. There were no books or traditions telling us how we could turn out or what anything meant.

The years passed. The successes turned out to be: the most beautiful blond with the green eyes who married an insurance salesman and moved to the Valley, where she's living happily ever after with three children, not even divorced; the tall strong young football player who teaches art in a high school in downtown Los Angeles; the nervous, brilliant guy who is being nervously brilliant over at Warner Brothers directing his first movie; and the girl with the flaming red hair who is the director of a stewardess school and lives in Marina del Rey.

And whenever I run into one of them, no matter what has become of him or her, I feel a kind of curious affinity with them, because we have managed to live so long after graduating from Hollywood High, because we have managed to live at *all* once we got out of there. For Hollywood High never pretended to be a microcosm of real life. Everything that we knew about real life, *everything* we gleaned from books and movies and history classes and comic books, had snow in it.

On the day before Thanksgiving, when they began putting up the giant tin Christmas trees along Hollywood Boulevard, we had to bow to the realities of real life as determined by the rest of the country, the world.

Perhaps it is this shared empty confusion about reality that draws me to the alumni of a Hollywood childhood, those tin Christmas trees tipped white for snow. Those Christmas cards where everything is peaceful and white.

Very few of those guys in their maroon and white sweaters and their easy walks have survived real life. The casual nonchalance which we prized them for has been dashed to pieces by the real world which, even in Los Angeles, exists. The fierce battle on the baseball field has been plowed under by the fierce battle some of them have just getting up in the morning.

Out of all of them, I know only one who remains practically identical with that image I have of the boys as they walked across the quad and said Hi. And he once told me, showing me a picture of himself as he was the day that he hit the home run that won the game between Hamilton and Hollywood, even *he* told me that it's been all downhill since then. And he's probably going to spend the next twenty or so years of his life winning Academy Awards and mixing with a lot of dazzling people like he did at Cannes the year the movie he coproduced won "Best."

He was the sports editor of the Hollywood High newspaper when Carol Eastman (who wrote *Five Easy Pieces*) was editor. "But it was so hard to write," he told me, his casual grin flashing the past into the present. "I decided that I didn't have to write. I've been happier ever since."

"You're a bastard, Fred Roos," I told him. "You make all the rest of us write and you get to go around being the producer and the casting director and meeting all those people and people like me have to try and think up good ideas to tickle your fancy."

He laughed. "You don't have to do that. You don't have to do anything. I'm not making you write."

But even as I wrote the above and even as I sat there, I was so pleased to be at last in the company of one of those tall, sweet young men who once wore maroon and white sweaters, that I was faintly delirious. It's not as vivid and bloody as it would have been. But then we're in real life now, not Hollywood High, and it's about art and money and Francis Ford Coppola and Paramount. It's about power and glory and casting Al Pacino's wife. It's not Hollywood High, but nothing ever will be again.

And when I come into a room, Fred smiles, kisses me lightly, and always says Hi.

And once he said, "Hey, I've got a great idea. Why don't you come up to Reno? You can write something…"

"What?"

"Anything… I don't know. You're the writer."

Francis once told me that when he went to Le Conte Junior High School (where one-third of everyone at Hollywood High came from) he couldn't think of anything but the girls. "They were so fantastically beautiful," he told me, "and they walked around every day at lunch in a circle, around and around and around. I never forgot it.

"I used to wonder what they were like and why they kept walking around and around and around and why they were so fantastically beautiful," Francis said. Francis, who went to twenty-six different schools when he was growing up in all parts of the country, must have seen those Christmas trees before Thanksgiving too. He, too, had a patch of time with no history and he must have decided to invent his own because he has, through a "perseverance of vision," invented a way to be an artist through movies—and historically that's next to impossible. The movies, like the girls, went around and around and around, and some were beautiful and Francis wondered what they were like, only this being real life, of course, by the time he found out, Hollywood was on the verge of collapse. The beautiful girls have become pale in remembrance.

Time recently reported that *The Godfather* has made $145 million so far. *The Conversation* won the Cannes Film Festival, but hardly anyone went to see it. Francis and Fred became members of the board of directors of something called Cinema 5, a distribution company. Francis held a laminated copy of a check he got for $1,700,000 (for being the executive producer on *American Graffiti*), which he inspected thoughtfully one afternoon and said, "I wonder what I'd do if I were broke tomorrow..."

He added, "I wouldn't *mind* being broke."

Before that he'd said, "I'd like to start this place up in the North Pole... A sort of toy factory where all the toys were made by little people, children..."

Which is more or less the whole thing. Having the children make the toys is like having Francis make the movies.

Historically, of course, there is no precedent. But, then, Hollywood has always been unprecedented, ever since I can remember, when the girls walked around and around and around, their arms linked through the arms of boys in maroon and white sweaters in a past so vivid and bloody.

And even Fred, even *Fred*, who is still one of them, says it's been "all downhill" ever since.

Coast
April 1975

MY GOD, EVE, HOW CAN YOU LIVE HERE?

WHEN MY sister and I were still rather short (before I turned thirteen and refused to go on any more vacations) my parents used to insist on wild adventures during which two weeks out of an otherwise perfect summer would be devoted to mountainous roads, flat deserts, or even the *crise de folie* when my father decided it would be a good idea to drive to Mexico City and back in our '48 Pontiac in fourteen days. San Francisco, however, was a different story. My sister and I loved San Francisco and we couldn't see the point of going anywhere else.

We loved Golden Gate Park, the Cliff House, Fisherman's Wharf and Nob Hill. We *loved* it. We'd save up our money to spend on ravioli and Grant Street. It never occurred to either of us to wonder what kids who were raised in San Francisco would think if they had to go to L.A. But now it occurs to me all the time because half my friends live in San Francisco, and flying back and forth all the time as I do, I am under constant fire with such questions as, "But how can you live in L.A.?"

My poor friends from San Francisco mostly get booked into hotels other than the Chateau Marmont or the Sunset Marquis. The Chateau Marmont and the Sunset Marquis are the only two places people from San Francisco are ever even marginally content (unless whoever's paying for the trip can afford suites at the Beverly Hills Hotel or the Beverly Wilshire).

The Chateau Marmont, with its slow elevators, high ceilings, and amazing views, is a bastion of grace holding on by its fingernails against time.

Sunset Marquis is pure L.A. but, like the Chateau, it doesn't have room service and this seems to be what makes the difference—you cannot pick up the phone and get that deadly hotel food. But the Sunset Marquis has more than that; it has a kind of jolly ambience like a summer camp for people involved in the Industry. (There are only three business constants in L.A.: aerospace, real estate, and the Industry.)

Since most of my friends from San Francisco come down to L.A. to do business with the Industry, they should tell whomever it is who's making their reservations to forget about the Holiday Inns or any other of those Inns, and that they'll take *anything* in the Chateau, even an eight-by-ten cell. Or that they want to stay at the Sunset Marquis.

I realized what happens to people from San Francisco when they get off in the Burbank Airport and suddenly it's hot, the buildings lie low, and it's "My *God*, Eve, how can you live here?" the first time I returned to L.A. after having "moved" to San Francisco. These "moves" are periodic notations in my life for the times I've decided to grow up and leave Hollywood. They last, at most, three months and then I am drawn back to L.A., irresistibly. "Just for a day or so," I say to myself, and then suddenly I'm back. My "moves" to San Francisco seem to occur about once every seven years.

People from San Francisco never come to L.A. for a vacation the way I'd fly up north just because it's so nice. People from San Francisco think L.A. is horrible enough just standing there like that without having to actually go, voluntarily.

It's funny, too, you know, because it's a snap to convert New Yorkers into giving up and loving Los Angeles. Italians take to Hollywood without a backward glance. Englishmen come practically armed with more knowledge about L.A. than even I know and plunk themselves right into the mainstream with awed remarks about the engineering miracles of the freeways (of all things). And the French . . . well, they can live anywhere. But my friends from San Francisco won't budge.

Like an evil sister who's gone on the stage and enchanted the world, L.A. may be all right for everyone else, but San Francisco knows all about her and is *not* impressed. "She simply won't *do*!" ladylike San Francisco says, "She won't do at all." And when it's unavoidable, for business reasons, that the northern sister make a trip to the grisly south, she holds her breath until she once more flies over the narrow escape of water that is the San Francisco Airport. Meanwhile, people from L.A. think, "Wouldn't it be nice to go up and visit darling San Francisco. I know she won't mind."

It's like that, I think, from what I've been able to see. And I wouldn't have noticed how little they can stand us up there if I hadn't become aware of the adverbial clause "too L.A." Looking at a horrible gold chain that you're supposed to wear around your waist, a person from San Francisco will say: "Too L.A." A person from L.A. will say, "My God, how horrible, it's so Las Vegas."

RENT A CAR: THAT'S RULE ONE

Let's say that you were from San Francisco and you had to come down to L.A. for a whole week on business although you've tried everything to avoid it, but it turns out you *have* to and that's all there is to it. The first thing to do, if you haven't done it already, is learn to drive. You will be abjectly miserable in L.A. if you're at the mercy of other people's cars. You must have your own unit. After you've learned to drive, all you have to do when you get to L.A. is rent a car and drive to your hotel which hopefully is not the Continental Hyatt House or a Ramada Inn. (Unless you really *want* to immerse yourself in orange plastic.)

Once you have the keys to your rented car and are in the airport parking lot ready to go, check your attitude. After all, it's your life. The ideas you have about cities that you've always known don't work in L.A., and once you toss those aside you'll be much better off. (Also, don't break any traffic laws in L.A. The LAPD is incorruptible and humorless.) Forget about downtown museums, parks, and all the other things pointed to with pride in every town worth its salt, except L.A.

The fact that L.A. *does* have a "downtown," museums, and parks has nothing to do with it and everyone here knows it. I was downtown once four years ago to pay a ticket; it was awful. The museum, designed to look like a riverboat floating down the Nile with water and bridges all around, is no fun at all now that the water's been drained and it never was much fun anyway unless you've seen this gorgeous Vuillard they've got upstairs with the French Impressionists—or the L.A. artists' exhibit that's always there. Or if you like Varèse's music and you go to a Monday Evening Concert where pieces that are too far-out for anyone else to touch with a stick are performed regularly by L.A. musicians who are so adept at sight-reading from all the studio work they've done that they can pick up Alban Berg and just play it.

L.A. doesn't have anything as much fun as Golden Gate Park, but it does have Griffith Park which is nice to wander in, especially by car, especially up by the observatory where James Dean tried to save Sal Mineo's life in *Rebel Without a Cause*. There are two babbling brooks up there, one in Ferndell which is a primeval heart's desire, just smothered in huge ferns, mossy stones, and wild strawberries. The other brook is in the Bird Sanctuary (where the Byrds' first album cover picture was taken) which is across the street from the Greek Theatre.

If you went to Vermont and Hollywood Boulevard and loaded yourself up on Italian cheese, artichoke hearts, and salami from Del Monico's and went next door to Samo's pastry shop and bought fresh Italian strawberry tarts, you could then drive straight up Vermont north and go sit down on the luscious green grass by the Greek Theatre and look at the trees. Or you could take the same stuff over to Barnsdall Park which is just two blocks away, south of Hollywood Boulevard and about half a block west of Vermont. There, you could look at more trees and grass and see some rather crumbling Frank Lloyd Wright buildings which sometimes house sweet little exhibits of Maxfield Parrish paintings or photography shows.

NOT FOR PEOPLE WHO LIKE THE TRIDENT

However, if you're like most people, you won't probably drive farther east than La Brea and so won't know. *Nobody* knows about anything in L.A. except the people who already live here, and most of us never think of taking our out-of-town friends anywhere but those daffy fake places in the Marina.

Don't go to the Marina.

Whatever you do, don't even let your business associates take you there for Sunday brunch. You'll fall into a slough of despair which will be almost impossible to shake. Don't go the Marina even if you *like* stewardesses; they're all out of work now and aren't smiling.

The Marina is of doubtful interest. These fantastic and troubled new apartment buildings keep incessantly going up and the stewardesses who move out of one and into another, newer one (when it gets dirty which usually takes six months) share the unbelievable rent so that they can get tan and ride their bicycles along the bicycle paths in the hopes of meeting their male equivalent or someone "interesting." If you really wanted to see a bunch of stewardesses, you'd already be living in L.A. or you'd live in Sausalito and think the Trident is just wonderful. I'm not writing this piece for people who like the Trident.

But suppose you'd really like to see something grandiose and flashy, something that lives up to every expectation of Hollywood and Southern California that you've ever, in your weaker moments, owned up to? Then you should take your car out of the parking lot of the Chateau Marmont or the Sunset Marquis and point it west on Sunset and drive to the Beverly Hills Hotel. Like all truly great hotels on earth, the Beverly Hills is an unflinching masterpiece better than any museum, shopping center, or the Paris Opera House. There is nothing going on at the Beverly Hills other than a constant battle to maintain perfection.

It's better than Chartres because there are no groups of tourists moving from place to place under the supervision of a knowledgeable guide. You can wander around, instead, at your own pace and no one has to tell you what to look for. Everyone knows that the Beverly Hills Hotel is the best hotel in the world and not just because it's so beautiful on the outside but also because they have the best beds and the most flamboyantly efficient telephone system left in civilization. When you pick up your phone in the Beverly Hills Hotel having just arrived eight seconds before, the woman says, "Hello Miss Babitz." She knows! They also take down your phone messages in triplicate, leaving one in the lobby, one under your door, and one for their records in case the other two get lost.

The best thing to do is to park your car along Crescent just north of Sunset Boulevard and then walk over to the back of the hotel where an insanely luscious garden is always abloom around what they call "bungalows" which are little pink houses you can rent for about a thousand dollars a second. Orange trees and jasmine, bougainvillea and palms—everything along the pathways is tended perpetually by three gardeners per square yard. There are never any dead leaves. Nothing ever dies at the Beverly Hills Hotel. It's not allowed to.

After strolling around the winding maze, in which you can easily become lost and even lose sight of the main hotel although it is four stories high, you could gild the lily by going to the Polo Lounge either for a light lunch (they don't believe anyone should eat more than three shrimp despite what they charge you) or a drink, and you could watch movie people. Watching movie people is child's play in the Polo Lounge because they are the only people in there besides you. In the lobby you might run into James Baldwin or Dr. Joyce Brothers (or both at once like I did long ago), but they don't usually go into the Polo Lounge unless it's with a producer.

A good thing to do is to ask someone to meet you in the lobby of the Beverly Hills Hotel (so you can go to the Polo Lounge for a drink). Then you should arrive about twenty minutes early so you can just sit and watch. You will see people you never thought existed pad softly across the carpeted floor, silent testimony to the fact that Los Angeles is, after all, the center of the universe as far as the Industry is concerned. (If you're a woman and want to go to the Polo Lounge for a drink alone at the bar, they won't let you. Vestigial amenities, I suppose. There is no women's lib at the Beverly Hills Hotel. Even if you're going to be a hooker, you have to sit at a table.)

Los Angeles is a city of amazing streets, streets that go on for miles and miles through slums (which in New York would be unattainable delights), fancy business sections, car lots, and palatial mansions. Wilshire Boulevard (an oxen cart road up until about fifty years ago) is a great street to drive to the beach on if one has the time although Sunset Boulevard is even prettier.

Los Angeles is a strange city as far as the ocean is concerned, because no other city so close to the sea has ever started inland and branched out later to the beach. San Francisco—like Genoa, Venice, Boston, New York, Tangiers, Palermo, Athens, Honolulu, Amsterdam, and New Orleans—is based on the premise of harbors for ships. Los Angeles is the only giant-sized city by an ocean that got around to harbors after the place was already established.

GO WEST

Santa Monica used to be a day's jaunt from downtown L.A. There was nothing in Santa Monica except the beach and there was nothing between the city and the beach except huge ranches and trigger-happy bandits. When the railroads came, people could move about more easily than by ox and they scattered all over the countryside growing oranges to send east. Los Angeles is a railroad town and sometimes, right in the middle of Santa Monica Boulevard at night, strange trains make their way across La Cienega causing drunk people to shake their heads. They tell me that the train is run once or twice a week for tax purposes. Early diagrams of the railroad tracks in the city are strange and wonderful to look at; they show a city pushing west to the Pacific Ocean rather than a city pushing in from the sea.

Perhaps it is because of the railroads that the beaches in Los Angeles are the most fun in the world. Before anyone knew what was happening, Santa Monica just kind of emerged as the most beautiful beach in the world open to anyone and not restricted to either the rich or the shippers.

Although the rich are now doing their best to ruin the Marina and have crept north into Venice Beach with their stewardess constructions, I feel that Venice will always survive man-made determination to turn it into a place for rich people. In the early 1900s a crazy scheme was devised to turn Venice into that other Venice by building canals, "casinos," and archway boardwalks, but the whole thing had to be abandoned because oil was discovered underfoot. Oil wells ruined the layout but made it possible for just ordinary people to live by the Pacific Ocean in peace without it costing an arm and a leg.

A drive at twilight down Sunset or Wilshire or Olympic Boulevards toward the sun setting into the ocean is a very romantic Raymond Chandler thing to do and ought to be appreciated as such. Raymond Chandler things are easily come by in Los Angeles and not to be sneezed at, for they bring sweet romance, danger, and memories of things past (even if they aren't your own past) into focus. And there is no smog at night.

One of the best, most secret Raymond-Chandler-things-to-do in Los Angeles is something I discovered quite by accident when I went through a period of being unable to "go on the freeway." If the given is that you can't go on the freeway, then suddenly you are stuck to the streets, the streets with Raymond Chandler names like Chevy Chase, Oletha, or Cheremoya. Just at the time I could no longer stand going on the freeway, one of my dearest friends became tractioned in a hospital in Pasadena where he waited for anyone to come visit him. The Pasadena Freeway is more gentle, slower, and vastly superior to the whipping L.A. freeways, but I couldn't even go on that. I was suffering from the Freeway Sorrows, and even the Pasadena one terrified me.

To go to Pasadena by surface streets is just about like driving the Raymond Chandler Memorial Parkway. Almost nothing new has been built along those interior and forgotten roads since the forties;

it's intact, perfect. It involves going east of La Brea once again, but then an adventurous San Franciscan can be relied upon to brave the almost unknown hinterland for a true look at the Los Angeles he scorns.

THE RAYMOND CHANDLER MEMORIAL PARKWAY

To take this trip, however, requires about three hours and should be started at about 9 a.m. If you have meetings in the afternoon, it's perfect.

You get to Vermont (find a map; they sell them at Schwab's) and again go north to Los Feliz, the street below Griffith Park. On Los Feliz you turn right and all at once you'll be right there at around the time Humphrey Bogart drove a '38 Plymouth (poetic license; I don't know what he drove). On Los Feliz are the well-to-do houses of the upper bourgeoisie with lawns, rubber trees, and magnolias. In my experience, most of these houses are owned by men who at one time were members of the Communist Party but who later went into law, real estate, or cars. Members of the Industry rarely move there, too square.

Heading east on Los Feliz you suddenly come to its end, but it isn't really. Here it twists leftish and on your right you will find a wondrous shop called the Horse Laundry with a plaster-of-paris palomino on the roof of one of those 1930s buildings styled after the idea of a yacht. Across the street from the Horse Laundry (which sells saddles, saddle soap, and stuff like that) is a place to rent horses.

Continuing along Los Feliz for about a mile brings you unexpectedly to a street called Glendale Boulevard and here, turning left, is where the Raymond Chandler Memorial Parkway begins, becoming even more so as you turn right again onto Colorado Boulevard. Once you're on Colorado Boulevard, you've done everything and you can relax and look out the windows; there are no more directions.

Colorado Boulevard goes on for miles, all the way to Pasadena. What Los Angeles was thirty years ago is now on Colorado Boulevard.

The little bungalow houses with their front yards and porches and unbelievable motels, buildings, and peace. The dreariness of it; the fact that mountains and hills come so close down to the main streets. I always find it heartbreakingly unselfconscious. It never tried to be anything. All it wanted to do was scratch out a small square of tranquility in a city where the only weather was earthquakes—no snow, no hurricanes, no famine. Just little houses, nasturtiums, and the San Gabriel Mountains in the background when there was no smog.

Pasadena is my favorite phenomenon, which is why I got you out there with stories about Raymond Chandler. Once you're in Pasadena and Colorado Boulevard turns abruptly from almost a country road into a sort of a city and the freeway exits and traffic lights begin again, you have probably come to Orange Grove Drive. Turn left.

A WHOLE HOUSE BUILT AROUND CLOUD DESIGN

Once you're on Orange Grove, you're on your own and you should forget the map, time, and how you're going to get back. Just find a street to wander over. If you're a good sport, you'll stop about two blocks north of the Colorado Boulevard–Orange Grove intersection, and go to look at the Gamble House and see if it's open.

The Gamble House was built in 1908 for a rich Cincinnati family (part of Procter and Gamble) as a winter house. It was designed by the Greene Brothers who were the architects of a number of unsurpassed Southern California residences. The Gamble House is open to the public on Tuesdays and Thursdays from 10 a.m. to 3 p.m. The inside of the house is mostly made of polished teak, carved by one of the Greene Brothers in a pattern called the "cloud design." Seemingly the whole house is given to the cloud design, even the rugs, lamps, and banisters. The feeling that you've come into a splendid, spacious creation is true. The windows, lamps, and even the rug designs are by Tiffany and everything in the house is as it was when the Gambles returned from their trip to the Orient to see their house for the first time.

Resident architecture professors at USC get to live in that house. I once went and visited one, and we had cheese, crackers, coffee, and ham out on the porch on a wicker table, much to my disbelief. The gardens of the house, which used to stretch out for Versailles miles beginning with the back Japanese lotus pool, have now been built over with other, lesser houses. But it's still the same, somehow; it must be.

If the Gamble house isn't open, it's all right to just park and walk around it anyway and to try and see in; but it's much more fun to be taken around by one of the ladies who'll show you the secret window in the upstairs master bedroom from which you can see who has just come in downstairs.

Then you should get back into your car, go north a few blocks, and turn left down any one of the streets that looks the most glorious, or strikes your fancy, and just wander.

LOOK CAREFULLY AS YOU DRIVE BY SO QUICKLY

"How can you live in L.A., Eve, my God, the *architecture*," my friends from San Francisco *always* say. "I love the architecture," I answer, without thinking. I love the architecture, but you have to know how to look, you cannot stay on the main drags or go on the freeway and see anything. You have to be willing to wander off, up in the hills (even the hills in back of the Sunset Strip are pretty cute).

The whole lay of the land, the history, and the weather have divided San Francisco and Los Angeles for so many years, maybe it's impossible. Maybe it's impossible for you San Franciscans with your history all around you—the downtown, the proximity of the harbor, the rain and fog, the narrow houses, streets, and driveways—it might be impossible for you to travel the short distance of only an hour and find yourself in wide-open placid spaces, in a rented car, driving down streets which seem unrelieved in their garishness, the tacky obviousness of a railroad town, spaces flat and seemingly without purpose with freeways going off in all directions, and then have your business associates point with pride at the Marina.

But there is another town here that you could find if you wanted to, a more subtle city beyond the translucent hamburger chains and gigantic billboards...

You could find it in back of the Beverly Hills Hotel, or up a winding road into the hills, or down a side street lined with little houses which are covered with flowers. You can find the transitory spirit of Los Angeles if you look carefully as you drive by so quickly, beyond the false fronts, the pancake makeup, and the sequins of your regrettable sister who's gone on the stage and captured everyone but you by a simple determination to sprawl indifferently out into the sunset after her long train trip across the country.

City
April 30–May 13, 1975

NEEDLES IN THE LAND OF FRUITS AND NUTS

THOSE stories about Southern California's comprising a population of fruits and nuts used to land around my feet like kites that wouldn't fly when I was growing up there. People who lived on carrot juice were all around, and they *did* have rosy cheeks and they *were* cheerful, but I, even as a child, was too sophisticated for regional nonsense. Penicillin, after all, had been discovered and Hollywood was not the center of the medical firmament.

But later when I went to New York, I discovered that the L.A. health mystique had overtaken me. Why else would I find myself appalled, as only someone from the coast can be appalled, by the vast quantities of white sugar New Yorkers put into everything they eat. And the donuts! Watching them eat donuts as though they were fit for human consumption made me realize what a schism had developed between me and the rest of the country. I was a full-fledged crank—penicillin or no.

It might have been the time I read that oranges lose vitamin C ten minutes after squeezing and so I gave up juice. Or maybe it was the combination of sleazy stories girlfriends told me about sex-crazed gynecologists and how women's-lib centers were now teaching women to do their own Pap smears. Maybe it was that the AMA toppled out of my circle of respect when some years ago my fourteen-year-old friend Suzie, too young to get a diaphragm legally, ended up having to go to Tijuana for an abortion. Even closer to home, it might have been the time I consulted an MD about my feet, which were killing me, and almost bit off the hand of the nurse who was helping the doctor inject my arches with cortisone.

My own mother, who had all her life scoffed at alfalfa sprouts, had gone and got her consciousness raised, so when my sister brought over a young man who was a doctor, he found himself backed into a corner with no answers, by my mother, who outdistanced him by fifty yards on the subject of the AMA and nutrition.

"Jesus," he said, "how do you know all that stuff?"

"How come you don't?" she softly, but menacingly, replied.

At any rate, one day when I was about to bite into a hot dog and suddenly the newspaper exposé of what was really in them flashed before me, I knew that I had become at least a semi fruit-and-nut freak. And when my feet finally gave out, I discovered I was ready to take the next step over the line—I was ready for acupuncture.

And in Southern California, we do have acupuncture. Two kinds, in fact. The first kind is the AMA kind, where you have a doctor—a legit MD who'll feed you white toast as soon as look at you—who decides that what you've got he can't fix, so he puts you into a room with his Oriental; the Oriental tells him where to put the needles and for a mere $50 to $100, he follows instructions. The second, the illegal kind, is the kind I go to—a guy who knows what he's doing and does it at home with no smelly hospital, and only takes friends.

Ever since I'd heard about acupuncture, I was anxious to see if it worked. And I kept my eyes open for an authentic practitioner. My feet were beginning to kill me, and I didn't think I'd be able to survive another day or sleep through another night—and believe me, I had gone to doctor after doctor about it. Anyway, just as I was about to give up, I found Sandy.

Sandy was not my idea of what an acupuncturist ought to look like. I imagined an ageless inscrutable who'd just *know* at once what was wrong with me and cure it in two visits. Sandy, however, is someone I'd seen around in L.A. society for years and had always thought was a photographer or something. Sandy is a peer, too, which made it hard to have faith in him. How can you trust someone your own age? But anyway, I went. Maybe it was his blue eyes and dark eyelashes. My feet were killing me, so I went.

When confronting a doctor, I figure that I should be able to describe my woes in lyric phrases like "My whole left side feels like it's going to fall off," and he should take it from there. So I told Sandy, "Look, my feet are killing me and it goes all the way up my leg and my ass falls asleep when I'm writing and I wish I were dead."

Sandy, who'd seemed a friendly sort at first, began to turn into something much different. As I babbled randomly, he fell deeper into concentration, and out of it—the way a karate black belt looks before he severs a redwood plank.

He took my wrist, and I shut up and wondered if they took pulses in China too, but it felt good to have my wrist taken with such authority, men being what they are nowadays and never even holding your hand in the movies. Styles of love have changed abysmally for the worse. I sat happily and he held my wrist for a nice long time. When he finished he looked at me, at my good skin, which usually fools most doctors into thinking I'm a hypochondriac.

"Tell me," he said, "how much are you drinking?"

"*Drinking*? This is supposed to be about my feet."

He looked over my shoulder at the green branches of his crank organic garden outside the window of a room that was like a tree house and he felt my wrist again. He turned his gaze back to me finally and began describing symptoms which I had neglected to mention because they didn't hurt like my feet.

And so my doubts about the mystic capabilities of a blue-eyed member of my own peer group vanished and gave way to the realization that *this* is how it ought to be.

"And," Sandy continued, "your system is so imbalanced and your stomach is so messed up that you're going to have to take some time off and consider yourself as 'healing' because you're really in bad shape, and I won't answer for the consequences unless you decide you're going to spend the next few months healing."

"*Then* what happens?" I asked warily.

"Then you can do whatever you want except take heroin or cocaine." (The kind of people he dealt with were prone to risky extravagances.)

"Well, I don't take heroin and cocaine's passé," I told him, "but I drink like crazy."

His eyes turned toward the garden again, and I could see he was trying to figure out the best way to tell me, without scaring me out of my wits, that I'd better stop drinking. He seemed totally concerned with my well-being. And in this day and age to have anyone even vaguely interested in whether you live or die is refreshing. I knew I wouldn't touch another drop!

The best thing that happened to me when I quit drinking (I'd been on the Drinking Man's Diet since time immemorial) was that I could eat everything and not gain a smidgen. I could eat dandy linguini, for example. I could eat rice, bread, apricots, peaches, and most of all, potatoes! I even found someone to eat them with, a new lover whose eyes were even bluer than Sandy's and who liked to do things like kiss my back and hold my hand and bring me flowers on the rare occasions that we managed to get out of bed. This acupuncture stuff, I thought, as I reviewed the fortunate effects of my sole visit, is not to be sneezed at. And only $15.

But did my feet get better? Yes, I suppose—whenever I look down to remember them, which isn't often when one is in a romantic entanglement of Herculean proportions.

On my fifth visit, I asked Sandy how he'd come to interest himself in the act of sticking needles into people. He told me that eight years before, he'd suffered from bloodshot eyes, eyes so dry they were painful, and that no doctors seemed to be able to fix it.

"I was at this party one night and someone told me about this guy who could do acupuncture and that I ought to try it. I figured why not? I went down there the next day, downtown to this old guy, and he told me to lie down. Then he put two needles in the points of my ear, took a drop of blood from my forehead, and handed me a mirror. My eyes were perfect, all cleared up!"

"And?"

"And I told him I wasn't leaving until he promised to teach me how to do it. I'm not at all pushy, but I was determined to make him teach me, and he was giving me answers like 'We don't teach whitey ancient Chinese secrets,' but I just sat there and wouldn't budge. So finally he told me to be there the next day at 5 a.m., and when I got there he gave me a list of things to do like take his clothes to the laundry and dumb stuff like that. And then he let me sit there and watch while he treated people. After two years of this my big day came. He gave me my own set of needles, and for the next two years, he let me serve my apprenticeship working on his patients."

But how had he been able to tell that I had a bad stomach from taking my pulse? No one else ever had the slightest idea I had been going around with cramps nearly all the time.

In front of him was a giant chart of acupuncture points on the body of a man who Sandy called Karl because that was the name of the person who designed the chart. ("All right, now face Karl," Sandy said when he finished with the needles and fire and was ready to give me a massage that was so organized that "bad blood" rushed from deep inside you and rose to the surface of your skin—and your neck and shoulders didn't hurt anymore.) "See," he nodded toward the chart, "all the meridians..."

"What's meridians?" (I'd been hearing about meridians and who knew? I thought they were like latitudes by which sailors could tell where they were.)

"They're the nerve cycles where the points are, the acupuncture points that affect parts of you... like what's the matter with your feet is on the same meridian as your stomach."

When I had gone to the podiatrist he had referred to something called, bleakly, the Circle of Pain. I figured it had something to do with meridians because it seemed to make sense especially when a needle that was stuck into my elbow sent an electrical pulse straight to my feet. Anyway, I believed in meridians.

"All those meridians," he continued, "pass through your wrist, and each one has a different pulse; there are six different pulses in your wrist."

"So that's how you can just take someone's pulse and tell what's the matter with them without their saying anything?" I asked.

"Your pulse is like a symphony. If everything's in balance, I can feel it. But when your stomach's off, then everything goes; it throws everything else out."

All my sessions had begun with him holding my wrist and informing me of what was getting better or not doing anything.

What I wanted to know was how he remembered after perhaps thirty patients a week or more, what my particular pulse had felt like that last time I was there.

He smiled his bright smile, closed his eyes, and said, "I don't know. I just don't know why, but when I take your wrist and concentrate, I remember exactly who you are and what you were a week ago."

If anyone is wondering whether it hurts to have needles stuck into you, the answer, no matter what some brave US diplomatic visitor to China says, is yes. It hurts. But only for a second usually. It's like saying it doesn't hurt to have your ears pierced; it hurts.

Lesser known, but a legitimate practice in acupuncture is burning incense on the body. Apparently this is to draw up to the surface whatever's wrong so it can be heated out. First they put something on your skin to make sure you don't go up in flames, and then they apply the tiny burning pieces of incense and wait until the heat becomes unendurable. When Sandy did this to me the first time on my feet, side, and back, I went into a hypnotic trance, and felt like an angel coming down from mescaline. It's my favorite part.

"In Japan they call it scaring," Sandy said brightly, then added good-humoredly, "Those Japanese!"

"They're nicer in China," I had to admit. "Owww. But not that much nicer."

I have this feeling that in any therapy, three-fourths of what's beneficial about it is that someone's paying attention to you for a whole hour—just to you. Any pain endured during this time is worth it. In psychiatry they make you remember horrible things you've seen fit to shove out of the way. In gym classes they kill you health-club style. With acupuncture, it's exotic and it seems to work.

And my newest friend with golden eyes, who rubs my back with geranium-scented apricot oil says, "Maybe it's me or something... but you seem to be so much better than when I first met you. More relaxed or something. Happier."

"Mmmmm," I agree and think of Sandy's thoughtful trance that first day when he was trying to figure out how to tell me to straighten up and fly right. And I could almost hear him say, "I'll relax you," as I turn languidly to gather rosebuds while I may.

Playgirl
November 1975

MY LIFE IN A 36DD BRA
Or, the All-American Obsession

WHEN I was fifteen years old, I bought and filled my first 36DD bra. Since then, no man has ever made a serious pass at me without assuring me in the first hour that he was a leg man. Tits! Why, he hadn't even noticed!

The tacit understanding was that if I did indeed have those giant knockers one hears so much about in locker rooms and sees flopping across magazine covers, why he simply hadn't seen what all the fuss was about! Instead he had been quietly pursuing his bird-watching of ankles, knees, and nicely turned calves.

For years I believed these men, which goes to show how dumb one can be when one puts one's mind to it. And for years I felt sorry for the men who, by some sad twist of fate had gotten stuck with me when they'd have preferred legs. On the other hand, I always knew that if I ever really wanted anything, all I'd have to do was lean forward slightly. Suddenly the world was waiting to hear what it was I wanted, how fast I wanted it, and whether they could get a better one for me wholesale.

Now, my legs aren't that great. They're OK—with feet on the end of them and toenails at the ends of the feet. They're not the long legs that you see in *Vogue* magazine, those grasshopper stems glistening out in Vaseline bronze for "this summer it's white linen, briefly" copy. (And as for my ass, well it's so nondescript that no one's ever presumed to tell me that was what they were after.)

In fact, I inherited my legs from my mother, and her apple-dumplingly adorable (but short) legs used to cause my father to laugh for what my mother described as "no reason." Then my mother would blush all the way down to her amazingly taut and gorgeous breasts. Perhaps that was the real reason my father laughed at her legs.

I inherited my breasts from the women in our family, judging from old photographs taken in Russia in 1905 and old photographs taken in Louisiana in 1907. Only I was what is euphemistically described as a "Late Bloomer," but which might better be called The-Heartbreak-Hotel-Death-Row-No-Love-Low-Down-End-of-the-World-Blues. There I was fourteen years old in Hollywood with all these incredible girls around me bulging out of these powder-blue sweaters, these salmon-colored sweaters, these pink and charcoal-gray sweaters, these full-fashioned cashmere navy-blue sweaters. And I'm in huge white blouses coming out of my skirts because I'd rather have people think me a pig or a slob than flat-chested. My best friend, who'd spent hours with me in the seventh grade laughing and talking (she was really a smart funny girl and we had splendid times), suddenly turned up after one summer in Lake Arrowhead with beautiful 34C tits in pink sweaters—and she never spoke to a girl again. (Yes, she did—to the only girl in school with tits bigger than hers. But that girl wasn't beautiful the way she was, or smart.)

Then, it happened to me.

It was in the summertime, I was fourteen. I started my period and then I started "blossoming" in the most phenomenal display of glorious last-minute cavalry rescue. It was, as the English say, gratifying. Now, at least, I didn't have *that* to worry about any more.

Later I noticed that men would view my tits and become aflame with desire for them, and they would fantasize about having a pair of their own: "God, if I had tits like those I could fuck my way into a million bucks..." I also started getting plenty of, "Shit, she must really be horny." (They get horny so I'm supposed to.)

Recently, in Ralph's, my local supermarket where anything often goes, there I am, trying to decide on some lettuce—lost in thought, idylls of watercress—when I feel a man behind me and quickly, before I can turn around, he says in a low, authoritative purposeful salute: "Big tits." And he's gone.

That's like seeing a movie star. You run up—with all kinds of fantasies beaming through your regular thought process—you run up to Cary Grant and say "Cary Grant!"

What's he supposed to do? You've just said his name to him—a tradition, a heritage, a massive plethora of dreams and meanings. It's the same with men and my tits. They cannot imagine my doing anything that isn't somehow connected with how big my tits are. And my tits aren't even *that* big. I mean . . . they're not Cary Grant. They're more . . . John Garfield or Dean Martin. You know, there's that shock of recognition but not the fainting spell Cary Grant would inspire.

The other night I went out on the Last-Blind-Date-I-Shall-Ever-Go-Out-On-Ever-Again. The other night this friend, who keeps saying how smart and funny and wonderful she thinks I am, calls me and says she's going to fix me up with this smart, funny, wonderful ex-lover of hers. I'll just love him, she says. So I get dressed in these clothes that I wear when I don't know what I'm about to encounter—clothes vaguely reminiscent of those awful white blouses I wore in junior high to hide whatever was there. This tall, unfunny, unwonderful, stupid man picks me up (I could tell at once he was stupid because he was stupid), and on our way into this restaurant he brushes against my breasts and says, "Why, shit, Jeannie was right! You do have gigantic tits!" Home, James.

He'd have done much better if he'd insisted he was a leg man and you can see why, all these years, those other guys did.

When a man who I don't love and am not sexually engrossed in talks about my tits, there's something that makes me want to pour cold water into his lap and leave a loose carton of ice cream on his car seat overnight. Legs are much less tiresome to listen to under those circumstances. However, if I'm beginning to be madly whipped into a frenzy of lust, a polite mention that I have beautiful breasts is a nice touch. And of course, after I've known the guy awhile and he's proved himself funny, smart, an ace lover, and a man of distinction, then he can say any fucking thing he pleases. And only then have I found out what men were really thinking the first time when they poured me a glass of cool white wine and nonchalantly admitted their preference for legs.

"I remember one time," my gorgeous friend David told me after I told him I was going to write this piece, "I met this girl, Lucy Sanders" (I knew her—we'd shared a dressing room in Hollywood High together once and even then I thought it was hilarious because I was a 36DD and she was a 36DD and we'd get our bras mixed up—a truly uncommon coincidence) "and I was like nineteen and she was sixteen and there they just *were*, you know!..." and his voice softened in memories of things lust, "and I *ran* home, I mean *ran*, I pushed people off the sidewalk so I could get home in time to jerk off thinking about her tits..." He started laughing, "And then I asked her out and I was going to kiss her for the first time and she said something about being careful because she was swollen because of her period and I said, 'Swollen? Where?' And then I went into a whole thing about how now that she mentioned it I did notice she was perhaps larger than other girls but since I was a leg man myself..."

I love revelations.

So for all those years when I was having to make do with men who were a trifle *triste* because they were leg men and they had to accustom themselves to all this extra baggage... And then how they pounced when the coast became clear, and those revelations afterward that from the moment I'd come into some party they couldn't take their eyes off my... But of course they *had* to. Because if they *hadn't*, I would have thought they were pigs and brutes and you know how women are about pigs and brutes. We like them to clean up their routine in polite society at least. We like to at least *know* they could maintain an air of respectability if they had to.

There are other little tricky situations that arise from big tits. Sometimes other women, a lot of the time when they're drunk, can't keep their eyes off them. They think you're doing it on purpose. It's like big guys in bars getting picked on for fights. But that's OK, I don't really mind about women. Deep down they know I know they can't help it and eventually they turn their venom on their escorts for liking women with big tits and leave me out of it.

There's also all this having to bundle up. Whenever I go into the street, I have to cover myself with clothes that flow and drape. I cannot wear a tight anything on the street if I hope to have a moment's peace. Suppose, for example, you wanted to go for a nice walk and look at the sunset and breathe in the air at eventide, nice idea, right? No, no, no. Not if you've got big tits and you're not bundled up (Cary Grant can't do it either).

Putting on disguises is one of my daily tasks. "Now what shall I wear today that'll billow around?" I say to myself, squinting into my closet. If I'm going to see friends and I have to go on the street first, I usually have to wear a coat ("Eve, a coat? It's eighty degrees out there!") and then take it off (sweating) upon arrival. If they're really true friends who won't make remarks about my tits when they get drunk enough, and if I can really be sure they aren't going to turn on me for being Cary Grant, then I sometimes really get luscious and I try to dress like Claudia Cardinale in *Cartouche* or try in some other way to otherwise become a visual social asset to the proceedings.

If I'm with a man I want to entice, then I have a special bunch of immoral things I wear for in-house functions, but only if the guy is six foot seven do I presume to wear them at large.

There is one other problem—not a *problem* but a little matter of concern—about having big tits, and that is that a lot of sensitive, smart men are terrified because they're consumed by lust and they haven't learned the old "leg man" line. Also they have this nervous feeling that anyone with tits like that must be vulgar. Or insensitive. There I sit, reading my Proust and minding my p's and q's and keeping up with current oddities—no slouch more or less—and I see them shrink from my gaze as though I were a tramp.

Having spent the day defending myself from the slings and arrows of outrageous truck drivers and busboys, I am sometimes ill-equipped to suddenly assume an air of sensitive melancholy—and a couple of years ago I gave it up for a bad show. I mean, to be given the feeling that one is inelegant after one has just found the strategy for getting from point A to point B without having to walk past a little group of fourteen-year-old boys . . . It's too hard and life is too short, and I want to be happy and laugh . . .

Occasionally, I sit in a restaurant and I watch as a lithe, long-limbed creature with daisies embroidered on a sheer organdy blouse (beneath which she does not now, nor has she ever had to, wear a bra) enters. I see the face of the man who awaits her; it has a particularly familiar look and until lately, I couldn't place it. He kisses her, she sits down, and he reaches over to pour her some cool white wine. And then, I'll bet you anything, he says, "You know, even though we've just met, I think I must tell you right off... I'm a tit man."

Ms.
April 1976

NO ONIONS

They seemed to understand that the consequence of Archie saying "no onions" would result in an "out-of-gas" car with hearts coming up from the roof—they all knew and I caught on, but not really. I was perpetually ill at ease with how kids blandly sat through Crimes Against Nature like the first grade and I didn't want to understand too much about Archie either because I was afraid I might become one of those kids.

I grew up on a steady diet of comic books and movie magazines. Archie comics are the only ones I read out of a sense of duty, in the same way other kids had classic comics shoved in front of them or read them for "knowledge." I felt obliged to learn *some*thing about America, I was living here after all, and Archie was as American and not-what-I-wanted as Mom's apple pie. It seemed that Americans about to run out of gas were very particular not to have onions beforehand. I knew it by the time I was eight. But Veronica never knew it; she'd just sip her strawberry soda and step blithely into Archie's car, completely unaware that hearts were about to come out of the roof in the next frame. I would never be such a fool, I thought—jaded and worldly at nine—as to let a man take *me* to a soda fountain and not have onions. Not an American man.

The deal was that Veronica was ready to give Archie one kiss, period. Archie had to have more. Veronica could be persuaded to overcome her natural girlish abhorrence of kissing if Archie made sure not to have onions and ran out of gas. These Americans, I thought . . . How could she stand Archie? How could he stand her? Why didn't he like Betty who was a regular person? How could anyone stand Reggie? Where did Jughead spring from? How could they all just casually drink Coca-Cola when one sip, and it tasted like musty trunks? How on earth could anyone eat a hamburger unless they were starving? Where was the America that had soda fountains? Did kids actually eat large slabs of raw onions on strange meat, dubious lettuce, awful mustard, and untouchable "buns"? How did Archie Comics know that the kids reading them would understand that when Archie leered "no onions," it meant hearts?

BAD BREATH

From toothpaste commercials, I discovered that onions gave you "bad breath." Why Veronica, who didn't like kissing that much anyway, had to be seduced by "no onions," I finally figured out. Americans went crazy about "bad breath" and sweat and in fact, from TV commercials, I learned that the only things they liked were Camay, pies, and toothpaste. They loved toothpaste.

When I was kissing someone, like my mother or father, I loved kissing *them* so whatever they smelled like was fine with me. I loved kissing beautiful women with perfume on unless it was horrible like Old Lady Hard Candy perfume. My favorite smell to kiss was Harry, a friend of the family who wrote TV and radio music. Harry smelled like Scotch. I still love kissing Harry. Men who smell like Scotch remind me of him, but they're not him. Stravinsky must have smelled like Scotch but I never kissed him much. I kissed Mme Stravinsky and she smelled like the French Riviera in May covered with flowers, growing roses, happiness in spring, and Salems. (Now she smells like Carltons, she must have smoked Camels or Luckys when I was little, before filters and menthol.)

ARCHIE AND ERROL FLYNN

The first boy I ever kissed smelled like his V-neck sweater and birthdays. (It was at a birthday and we played spin the bottle and seven minutes in heaven.)

The first illegal boy I ever kissed (no adult supervision) was ice-skating in the ancient high-up bleachers of the Polar Palace. He ate hot dogs with onions. I was enraptured; he was CUTE and one of the most popular boys at Le Conte and there he was at the Polar Palace every Friday night skating couples-only with me and necking. If only the popular kids at school could know that every Friday night for a year he kissed me. But they never knew because he never spoke to me at school, he only spoke to popular kids.

A pirate expelled from a Birmingham, Alabama, school system came to Le Conte when "his mother couldn't handle him." He had burned the principal's office down and threw a chair at the vice principal so they sent him to Hollywood to his father—a "Man's Influence." He took one look at his father and moved to the Hollywood Stables in Beachwood Canyon where he shoveled manure and slept in the hay. He, this pirate, devastated the Archie comic social system of Le Conte because he was Impossible. He alighted upon our American Way of Life like Errol Flynn's Robin Hood. He had tattoos and I think the basic trouble was that he was Irish. The Concrete Block of cute girls and cute boys, the Ping-Pong blandness, the toothpaste popularity and Spray Net gruesome crap of the Darling just stood, with wide-open blue-eyed confusion at his "How do you do?" smile that didn't notice them. He was polite. The guys turned into boys. All the "Oh, hi's" in the world and best smiles from the three most cutest; blond, brunette, redhead darling adorable earth angels got nowhere. The day he got kicked out of algebra, he walked me to the middle of High Society's segregated inviolate stair-steps, sat me down, and together, before the school, we read *Mad*. He laughed like Errol Flynn. I was in uncute, undarling, unadorable tears of laughter. He smelled of Brylcreem, alcohol and tobacco when we kissed in a stolen car a week later.

Predictably, after the *Mad* lunch, on my way to class, the guy from the Polar Palace struck up a conversation. I looked at him, his cute popular casual face, and I decided he was a coward. I never kissed him again. Unlike the American Veronica, I had not noticed the onions on his hot dogs during the year he kissed me on Friday nights. I did notice he was a fraidy cat and hoped he'd burn in hell. I hoped they all would. (When Robin Hood got out of jail a couple of years later and came to visit me we still fell on the floor laughing with each other, but I was still a virgin—my major flaw—so after many Irish evaluations on the "Silliness of Virginity" not working on me, he shrugged and left me to my own devices like I deserved. I was left back with the toothpaste crowd.)

GARLIC AND DORIS DAY

After junior high, everyone smelled like beer and pizza, especially me. "You'll have to marry an Italian, dear," my mother told me one day, "the way you eat garlic." Garlic was not in Archie comics because they were too American to have garlic. Veronica needn't smell *onions*—though she'd probably heard of them—but she certainly was not to be subjected to the dreadful vulgarity of *garlic*. I loathed Veronica and starting when I was eight I wanted her to take her pearl necklace and strawberry soda and shove it; she was rich, they lived in a mansion, poor Betty didn't stand a chance. Betty was the only one I felt deserved mercy, but Betty wanted Archie. And surely it would be more merciful for some pirate to clear things up for her. There were no pirates in America.

As I grew older, Doris Day and Rock Hudson carried on the onion tradition. You can easily imagine her not-quite-thereness as Rock, in a soft aside to the waiter, says, "No onions," after she's just said, "Two hamburgers please." After he doesn't order onions, we know he'll stop at nothing to get into her pants. And she, like Veronica about kisses, simply won't have pants gotten into; she may perhaps not mind being kissed once or twice, but he's going to have to marry her for pants. She smelled like lipstick and Camay and he smelled like clean money. No onions anywhere.

Then everything fell completely to pieces, thank heavens.

Dennis Hopper got rich, Doris Day collected dogs, and her son employed a full-time bodyguard and never ever went out again into America. *Life* folded, Edie Sedgwick stuck her head into a toilet for Art, the Beatles came on Ed Sullivan and tore girls from the path of pearls and virginity, heroin and alcohol became outré among intellectuals, and ladies and gentlemen... the Rolling Stones. Ozzie and Harriet, toothpaste, and running-out-of-gas just couldn't hold a candle to a fifteen-year-old meth girl asking for "spare change," if you kissed her you'd get hepatitis or suicidally depressed. If you ate hamburgers you'd get poisoned. If you ate anything, it turned out, you'd get poisoned. Everything in the whole world had been quietly poisoned while Archie was worrying about onions.

ELIZABETH TAYLOR

I'd forgotten all about onions, myself, once everything fell completely to pieces until a few months ago. It was an article about Elizabeth Taylor in *Cosmopolitan*. She was in Russia making *The Blue Bird* and of course she'd brought her dogs along as well as the poor used car salesman who'd figured who was he to wonder at God's mysterious intentions when Elizabeth Taylor picked him. Elizabeth held the interview in her Russian hotel suite and was in a good mood. She ordered caviar for the interview and acted human which was a change from the last time the interviewer had seen her when she'd acted like Elizabeth Taylor. Elizabeth told the interviewer that she had recently come across the simple pleasures of being human, shopping, etc., and much to her amazement, she liked them. She liked being "just a woman" (or something) and going for drives in the country. Meanwhile, the interviewer had been forewarned not to talk about RICHARD and the used car salesman sort of lurked in the shadows as Elizabeth rambled on about her New Life. Elizabeth is not stupid.

The impression a clever reporter would receive from having Elizabeth Taylor be nice to them and be human is that Elizabeth Taylor is enjoying life without RICHARD and has discovered a girl can have fun without RICHARD, simple pleasures like drives in the country take precedence over RICHARD and besides, there's the used car salesman.

Everything was going splendidly. The clever reporter was totally engrossed and believing it. The caviar arrived. Elizabeth made a graceful gesture of "go ahead," the lurk from the shadows stepped forward for a cracker, and Elizabeth—being human to perfection—spread caviar on a piece of cracker, continued about how nice Russia was, and... But it couldn't be... But it *was*! Elizabeth Taylor who was "so happy living a normal life with the used car salesman," sprinkled *onions* on her caviar!

The used car salesman who had been watching her carefully, buttered his cracker with caviar, *and* AFTER *she* sprinkled onions on her caviar, *he* sprinkled them on his.

Now... The clever reporter was baffled. How could this be? How could a woman just sprinkle onions on a cracker without first making some kind of eye contact with her lover.

One lover simply doesn't go ahead with onions. Especially if, as it turned out, he had to watch to see what she would do before he could feel free to have onions. A woman who eats raw onions, in Western civilization, doesn't care what she smells like. A woman who doesn't care what she smells like is not in love with anyone present. And that meant, as far as the reporter was concerned, that something was wrong.

What was up, it turned out, was that Elizabeth Taylor, at the time of the interview, was having secret negotiating long-distance phone conversations with RICHARD. The used car salesman was sent out to walk the dogs. RICHARD was in Switzerland and Elizabeth was in Russia, eating onions.

By the time the piece was written, the reporter was, happily, no longer baffled. RICHARD and Elizabeth were remarried. (The used car salesman was banished, the Lord giveth and the Lord taketh away

Elizabeth Taylor.) And everything fell into place; it resolved itself. No longer did the clever reporter feel a sense of thwarted strangeness— Elizabeth's human act, brilliant as it was, had instantly collapsed when—without looking at her lover—she brought to her perfect lips, onion.

LIFE WITHOUT ONIONS

And so, it seems, that even now, with the world in pieces around our ears, the air, water, and food poisoned, the American Way of Life out on the street—dirty, no toothpaste— Elizabeth was totally transparent in the midst of her human routine. All that's left of the soda fountain America is that if you eat onions in Moscow, your lover is in Switzerland.

My lover now is supremely clean. He told me I'm not the only one to complain about his unearthly odorlessness. It's fairly creepy but I adore him so I try not to smell like anything either and wouldn't touch an onion with a stick. Except if he's going to be out of town for a few days, I bring them out of the closet—them and garlic—and . . . well, you'd be surprised. When he comes back I act like nothing's happened and so far, I've been able to be Archie to this ridiculous Veronica in my heart. He must never learn of onions . . . not from me, not *my* onions. I'm not the only one, either, who thinks he looks like a pirate—one friend thinks all he needs is a patch. I myself wonder about Brylcreem. But I wouldn't press my luck, even though I've seen them do it since childhood when I imposed a steady diet of comic books and movie magazines upon myself to deal with Americans. I live here, after all, and I know all about "no onions."

Wet: The Magazine of Gourmet Bathing
December 1976–January 1977

ON NOT BEING A TOMBOY

THE VERY idea of the word "tomboy" enraged me when I found out about it. It was such a stupid trap. Either you were a "girl"—sugar and spice—or you were a "tomboy"—puppy-dog tails. The idea that they only had two categories and those were they turned me white-hot. With silent, guerrilla impatience, I sat alone in a school in Hollywood feeling like Che in a business suit, walking through the city of Havana before he got rid of Batista. I couldn't wait to be out.

It was insulting enough that they expected you to be a cute little girl. It was an outrage that the ones who wanted to play baseball until dark were "tomboys" and would "grow out of it." I hid. I was neither a cute little girl nor someone who'd grow out of my present indifference and *become* a cute little girl. I could understand the pride of the ones who were cute little girls, though. They were behaving well and able to stand it. Who wouldn't be proud? But I didn't trust the stoic, grim dignity that I sensed from the girls who allowed themselves to be called tomboys—who basked in the word and proudly wore a sort of distant, "loner" mantle. They were buying a crummier product, yet they seemed to feel they'd outsmarted us. They were traitors. They hated girls. They became boys and hated girls the same as boys. They were just as good as boys. This made them proud.

One, Delia Rogers, sat next to me for a semester. She skimmed through school like a dry leaf over a windy pavement. She drew horses. I could draw anything, but it was probably because of my horses that she invited me home for dinner. After dinner, Mr. Rogers began shooting BBs at a bronze liberty bell in the living room, and into this my mother entered to pick me up. She turned ashen, she was so furious, and told me, "You're never to go back there again. If you want, you can play with Delia at school. That—*tomboy*."

Mother didn't believe in guns after dinner in the living room.

Mostly, our tomboys concentrated on hitting home runs after school in games where they were the only girl. They hated girls' games. Girls played smaller games, in smaller courts, with softer balls. The lines around the space were different for girls.

I wanted to go home. At home there were books, and I could sit outside under the tree on our savage crabgrass and read, and pet my cats, Liliocalani and Nefertiti, and yearn for European capitals. I didn't want to be inside anyone's lines.

I was nineteen, and I'd been in Rome for six months. I stood at the bottom of five flights of steps, looking for an apartment. Someone told me one was for rent at the top. I was determined to have my own address.

At the top I was dying, but I knocked anyway, and a young American opened the door. It was Delia Rogers. All dressed up, looking at me and my jeans doubtfully. Delia wore stockings and gloves, among other things. Her hair had never been blonder and was back-combed within an inch of its life.

Over coffee she told me that she was dating a married man. He was a movie star. He'd taken her to Moscow and Madrid. "If there's one thing living in Rome has taught me," she remarked, about to leave, "it's to be a lady." "Oh," I said, closing my mouth from when it had fallen open after she told me, "his wife doesn't understand him."

I watched her make her dainty way down the street. She still walked with stoic dignity. Her now fragile shoulders straightened under her grim "loner" mantle. But I could see how, when she was being especially flirtatious, she might confide that in her youth she'd "really been a tomboy."

The glamour of being an expatriate, of having my own address, of actually living in Rome, faded that afternoon, and Hollywood began taking on a cosmopolitan, even worldly aspect.

In French, tomboy is *garçon manqué*—a missed boy; a boy lost. Maybe, I decided, as Delia got into a cab, I'll go home. Besides, I didn't really want to be in Rome that night after dinner in the living room when Delia got nostalgic for her lost girlhood.

womenSports
August 1977

LOSING WEIGHT MADE ME A NEW PERSON—A NOVELIST

FOR YEARS—years—because it started when I was thirteen, I was made gravely aware of my being the wrong thing to be: plump. The first remark was my father's precise assessment that what I had wasn't "baby fat." He said, "It's candy fat."

It was. It was M&M's, Milky Ways, this special See's candy they sell mainly in L.A. that was so fancy I actually had to save up for it, and Three Musketeerses. It was also the crumb rolls they baked at our junior high. It wasn't that I actually was fat or anything, it was just that I wasn't supposed to be eating all that candy—it showed. It showed at the beach. It showed in "tight" skirts. It showed in gym. But I was never dumb enough to think I was Fat; because I wasn't, I just wasn't perfect. And I have never liked perfect things, they give me the creeps. So, altogether, I didn't feel that awful, because you couldn't tell in a loose skirt; and, besides, in those days, people were so preoccupied with breasts that they could hardly take their eyes off mine long enough to notice my waist wasn't a slinky willow branch. I was gravely aware, by the time I was thirteen, that my waist *should* be a slinky willow branch, to give me an hourglass figure; but being gravely aware and being seriously disturbed enough to stop eating candy are two different things.

Everything went OK until the Beatles' amphetamine skinniness. Then I stopped eating candy. But by that time it was too late because, to be Beatley enough, you had to have been raised on English boiled cabbage and milky tea. Anyway, by the time the Beatles trotted out onto Ed Sullivan's stage with those heartrendingly sexy toothpick legs—THWAP—*every*one had toothpick legs. Except mine weren't

81

right. The heart of the problem wasn't really my legs; for, actually, alone, my legs could stand by themselves. The heart of the problem was my ass. It was no good. It was there, for one thing; and no serious Beatle person's ass was there. But mine was worse, I'd never seen one like it even in a Rubens painting. It's low. Someone once told me that it's got a name: "saddle-ass." It seemed about right.

I discovered that, if I took a lot of uppers and didn't eat anything, I could get myself down to 132 and people would begin to make approving remarks like "That's more like it . . . ." Usually, I weighed ten pounds more. I'm 5'7".

Finally, when I was in my late twenties, I discovered the "Drinking Man's Diet." Because I drank like crazy, this seemed exactly the right premise for me. With the diet, amphetamines, and the gentle augmentation of cocaine, I, for a month, weighed 128. It was a triumph. Photos document the occasion.

Of course, this couldn't last. Amphetamines make you lose all your friends, and my life fell apart. I even resumed smoking cigarettes after having quit for four years. Only I didn't lose weight when I smoked—so I was back to 142 *and* smoking and then, when one day about six months ago it said on the scales that I weighed 154, I decided that something would have to be done—so I gave up scales. And I was drinking like crazy every minute.

One day, having given up scales, I decided to stop drinking. It seemed to me that my perceptions were always coming in as they would to a drunk person and that drunken perceptions had been fully covered by brilliant minds like F. Scott Fitzgerald, Malcolm Lowry, Hemingway, and, well . . . just *everyone*, more or less. Most writers, it seemed from what they wrote, drank all day and all night. And they were really good. They had Being Drunk, Hangovers, Bitter Martini Quarrels, and Guilt totally monopolized as far as writing about those things was concerned. Especially that guy who wrote *The Lost Weekend*. That guy, I thought, was as drunk as anyone was going to get and live to tell. So, it seemed to me that perhaps I should stop drinking and that way maybe some opportunities for different points of view would happen by, ones that so far had not been Mailered.

It turned out strangely I'd been such an alcoholic that the first six weeks, the amount of time allotted for your liver to rise from the dead, were like being on this ocean liner traveling through fog that cleared. Giant liftings drifted away with each moment. I didn't feel I had to move, hardly; I was on the edge of my chair, bolted wide-eyed with amazement at the procession of clearer and clearer marvels.

It didn't even matter that my nerve endings were sticking out of my skin an inch and a half. Or that the softest breeze ruffled against my skin like fire. It didn't matter that the first four weeks found me crying due to lost numbness. It didn't matter that the clearness made me weak; because the next clearness made me wildly joyous, and the one after that made me tenderly peaceful. All of these were very different from Numb-Brittle-Coarse-I-Love-You type evenings that came from fashionable alcohol.

So I sat on the edge of my chair in the middle of this giant marvelous incredible movie. Now and then I'd feel hungry and eat whatever was around, until I'd feel really hungry and have to go to the store, which was not too bad because the movie went to the store, too; it just wasn't as intense to me in the supermarket as lying on my couch looking at the ceiling, or talking on the phone to my friends who turned into different people as each day brought more and more vivid clarity.

Some friends, unfortunately, became blurrier. They were patches of fog that burnt off my ever-changing adventure to find the source of the Nile. Some friends, it turned out, could only be tolerated if I were numb. It wasn't their fault, it was just that when they drifted grayly by my exhibition, everything had to stop while they were dull. When they weren't looking, I'd steal off to my barge; and, when they called, I told them I was "busy," although what I actually was doing was lying on my couch looking at the ceiling.

Now, after about four weeks, I stopped crying my usual two hours a day and virtually could count on being able to go into public without being triggered accidentally into water-water-everywhere. Not that I minded water-water-everywhere; and, I discovered, other people didn't really mind either. I could just say, "Look, I'm afraid

I'm going to cry, but it's not about you or anything, it's just crying..."
They'd pause, about to raise their soup spoons to their lips, and—seeing it was *serious*, they'd take my word for it and finish their soup.

I walked very carefully at that time, like an invalid, which is why, probably, I didn't really hurt myself the first time my elastic-waist trousers tripped me. They went under my shoes and tripped me. "What is the matter with these pants," I wondered, "they're falling down!" Maybe the elastic is old, I thought, and safety-pinned them more securely.

Only it wasn't just those trousers, it was all my pants. Every one of them was falling down. I had to keep holding everything together so I wouldn't trip or blow away, in spite of my invalid pace that kept me edging along, holding onto the railing.

"You've changed," the few people who saw me said.

"Please..." I'd say, shyly, "...just go on with what you are doing. I've been sick."

Somewhere in the fifth week, a sort of unearthly stamina took hold of me. Things I'd never even turned to grapple with because they were too complicated and demanded a concentration beyond my known range became simple as pie. All my writing people—my agent and my editor and those who knew what to do—had been harping at me that if I were going to write, I had to write a "novel." A NOVEL!? Have you ever thought about what it takes to write a *novel*? It takes a concentrated intensity, an idea that you can hang things on for one city block at least. It takes a strong rope that knows what it's doing with a major tree at either end. It takes something that could keep me in front of a typewriter for more than three hours. Three hours was all I could do before my concentration broke and nothing could hold me longer except amphetamine.

Writing on amphetamine is tricky because *Mein Kampf* has been done already, better. A long time ago, I saw photographs of three spiderwebs in *Scientific American*: One was done by a regular spider to catch flies, and it was OK—not great, but it'd catch flies; the second was done by a spider on LSD, and it was a perfect mandala—perfectly centered and equally radiating from the middle so that, even though it was creepily perfect, it looked as though it'd catch flies all right; the third one was done by a spider on amphetamine, and it was a fantastic undertaking, convoluted stratagems, nineteen possibilities-taken-care-of; however, they all took place over in the bottom right-hand corner—at least nine-tenths of the space was empty; flies could swoop through and never notice the wonderful trap in the corner. So amphetamines weren't what you'd want for writing a novel. A novel has to be its own world, to fill its loom. If you know what I mean.

On the fifth week, a rope-end fell into my hand and it appeared to be knotted at the opposite end of the city block to a tree. All I had to do was tie it to a second tree where I was and anything would hang on it. It was an Idea, a novel, a simple tale of outrage, lust, and drawing-room faux pas—a sure thing. The chapters were so simple, a nice seven. It seemed hardly necessary to write them down; but, on the other hand, why not—so I did. In fact, since I was "why not" about the chapters, I figured "why not" about the entire deal; and, in the next eighteen days, to sparkle up the time, I took notes, so that when I recovered from the voyage certain aspects would be recalled. Four hundred and thirty-two pages of openhanded observations. If you slanted them in a certain way, some people might call those notes a novel. I sent the manuscript off to my agent, who dropped dead.

"This," she telephoned to say, "may be a novel."

"This," my editor at the publishers said, "*is* a novel. Do it over; and, for God's sakes, don't get bored. I can't wait to operate on it."

I thought it was a little greedy of her. After all, I was the one who'd gotten the corpse from the guy in the alley at midnight; and now she wanted to dissect it all by herself, and I hadn't even finished drinking the blood.

My book had a title that didn't bore me, a title you could wake up to on mockingbird hill and not yawn and clean the oven. I decided to call it—simply—SEX AND RAGE. It was not the kind of title that those accustomed to my breezy landscapes were, at first, about to say "yes" to. They thought it sounded like *Bondage & Desire. I* insisted it was more in the category of *War and Peace, Crime and Punishment,* or *Dombey and Son*. I could hear them frowning at me over the phone all the way from New York. They were bartering with a difference in my soul.

For, from my cocoon of sobriety and obsession, had emerged this 119-pound blinking fawn, caught, for a moment, in a shaft of misty sunlight.

"WHAT HAPPENED TO YOU?"

"WHAT DID YOU *DO*?

"*YOU* LOST WEIGHT!"

"Is that *you?*"

Accusations barked from the mouths of friends: I'd lost weight! And, I was shy enough already—naked like that, my skin un-numbed and fresh to the air. I backed away hastily from diabolically turning civilization inside out, turning out the way I had. *I* was supposed to be this numb white-wine-drinking robust woman who wrote short pieces. *Now* I was this slinky willow—a shy, vulnerable, Perrier-with-a-twist fawn who looked like a dewdrop starlet. An irresistible impulse made me wear black mascara and peachy rouge and lighten and wave my hair like some fifties picture of innocence they used to "groom" over at Fox. No one had seen me in such a long time, they thought I'd pulled out to do this to them on purpose.

One night, my lover and I went to a party; it was Halloween, so my wavy hair, stockings, black mascara, and adorable nose were OK. This particular set of friends hadn't seen me in six months. Most of them were writers, but Jewish writers of comedy who didn't drink like crazy. Most of them were "plump" and forever up or down on the weigh scales.

The way those people treated me was as if I'd won the Nobel Prize for Literature—or is it the Pulitzer? They approached me as though I were, from some dramatic collision of circumstances, now the Queen—whereas before I'd been this droll woman they could pal around with who was often better with one-liners than they.

"How did you *do* it?" they demanded, "you really look great!"

They were not spouting accusations. Each one had a romantic notion that by losing all that weight, he or she too would turn into a fifties starlet. The transformation was so utterly a stumbling block that they sidled; they could hardly look at me, because they didn't *know* me.

"My dear," my mother said at lunch, "it's so lovely since you stopped drinking. You look your age. Sixteen."

I weigh less than I did when I was sixteen. I can eat candy these days and stay this weight. I can eat potatoes, rice, bread, meat, ice cream, chocolate mousse, it *all*! My drinking metabolism had been so out of kilter that it had been turning celery into fat, because I drank on my "Drinking Man's Diet" a trifle too enormously. My lover, who is skinny, calls the way I now consume dinner "pigging out."

When people come to me to say that I am how I am because of "weight," I am at a loss as to what to tell them. It's not weight. It's *me*. It isn't because I lost those pounds and my pants tripped me, it's because I am a new person and they are right not to recognize me. *I* don't know me.

People, bearing grudges from the olden days when I used to get drunk and insult people, approach me at parties—drunk—and insult me. They say hard things, things you have to be numb to laugh about and to return with wittier insults. Then, something happens to them; they sort of begin to explain that I had once said such-and-such and that's why they said what they said. A case of mistaken identity, they suddenly see. I am not the same person. They go away in strange shame for what they've said to a person they didn't know.

The hardest part of all is being "beautiful." I stopped drinking because I hoped to find some place that hadn't been done—wasn't being done—better. A place where I wouldn't be automatically on a low rung. It's hard to know what to say to people who ask how I did this; so, when they accuse, "You look so wonderful!" I answer, "Well, so do you." My lover thinks I'm rude, that I should say, "Thank you." But I cannot bring myself to act as though how I look is something I set about to do, when it was an accident, this perfection. I told you I never liked perfection. I, myself, would never set about to become a slinky willow. . . . All I started out knowing was that the most fashionable hotels were full, their bars were jammed. I didn't know Versailles was empty. The ceilings all have cherubs, blue skies, and white clouds—the beds are enormous—and I'm Queen.

Vogue
September 1977

SHOPPING

ABSOLUTE luxury always has been champagne and caviar, or was until all-night supermarkets stole the show and you could shop in the still of the night, hushed in empty splendor. No one but you and three other people who came there to stay out of your way. Empty aisles, all yours.

At last, not only can you stand there long enough to make up your mind whether to buy three-pound cans of coffee—anyway coffee, like everything, comes in so many sizes—or whether next time it has got to come down; but you also can take forever musing over how sophisticated Americans are these days when imported cheeses from far and wide sit where once Swiss was exotic. Products that have become stars on TV are finally where you can change your mind three times about buying them, and you can sink into a reverie smelling the Brylcreem because it'll always smell like teenage romance unless some mean expert improves it.

I had the beginner's luck, when I first moved to West Hollywood, to be a couple of blocks from Ralph's which not only was sort of an orchestra seat distance from the Sunset Strip but also was open twenty-four hours a day unless something like Christmas brought it to a halt.

Until about 11 p.m., this Ralph's was so fraught with live action that cashiers used to shake their heads sometimes; but one nevertheless proclaimed, "Work anyplace else? How could I after all this?" But at night, even Ralph's—or *the* Ralph's as I impatiently call it— would finally unwind. The hordes would scatter leaving *the* Ralph's to 3 a.m. drifters like me catching up on the twentieth century, our

carts rolling on silent wheels of rubber through the enchanted tab-
leaux.

In Los Angeles, the supermarkets all have kosher sections, health
food sections, Mexican and Thai shelves. These packages of foreign
hungers mirror the city with their bilingual instructions. The "Gourmet" section bespeaks with marmalade and Bird's Custard, imported
from England; teakettles and coziness uprooted, too. All those people.... In the daytime, remembering who *you*'re supposed to be is a
full-time job in supermarkets; but, at night, there's leisure to think
alone in those empty aisles, a new luxury. Once, champagne and
caviar were all there was. And they only came in one size.

Vogue
November 1977

SUNDAY, BLUE POOL, SUNDAY
A Story

IT WAS HOT, of course, since it's July. It was rich, which is not "of course" at all, since it's hardly ever rich; it's usually so-so. It wasn't *really* rich, but it was rich enough for the house to overlook L.A. and for the pool to be so covered in bougainvillea blossoms that I could swim entirely naked when I swam—that's how rich it was.

The man whose house I swam in had always been my friend, since I was sixteen—half my life ago. He was now, maybe, fifty. His newest girlfriend had just gone off on some excursion; his wives had divorced and divorced him. But I'd always liked him—you could let your head fall backward and laugh loudly at the way he tricked language into his poetry, his fast-street, immensely brilliant Manhattan-bred poetry. I had always liked him, but it was his son I had once slept with, not him—he'd always been too married or too in the throes of one thing or another.

Behold me now just as I am, Colette once said in a beautiful piece about how she was in her early thirties (my age) and alone, living in a one-room apartment on the first floor, a Parisian room near the Bois de Boulogne. Beholding herself in the mirror, just as she was.

The man beholding me just as I was did so through the blue swimming-pool water where I swam naked and would get no tan marks; he let me swim suitless. That afternoon, I dried myself off and went to lie on his white bed that a manservant (it was that rich) came and made every morning. He beheld me in the dim room, sprawled across his bed where I waited for him to come out of the sun and be surprised. He said, "Oh, Jesus, how beautiful you are!"

Now lookee here, kids, I have to tell you that the last time a man came into a room, saw me naked, and said, "Oh, Jesus, how beautiful you are!" was . . . I can't remember. I think about maybe five years ago a very strange Middle Eastern Oriental yanked me in front of a mirror when I complained of being too fat, and said, "You are not fat. You are beautiful."

Now this man, the blue pool man, was no slouch. His smile has charmed the pants off many a charming girl. His words had charmed the diamond earrings off many a mature woman wise to the world (not so he could steal the earrings, so he could take her to bed without losing them). He is rich; his friends are smart, powerful men. And he's got a pool you can swim in naked overlooking the city.

Behold me, then, just as I am. I have brown eyes that can be vastly improved by mascara and eyeliner; my face is large; my forehead is high; I am not the nervous little fox with the dark circles under her eyes that Colette beheld in about 1910. I am taller than she, five feet seven, and two weeks ago I weighed 152; now I weigh 140. I didn't look fat weighing 152 no matter what *Vogue* would have you believe; I looked voluptuous because I am; but, on the other hand, it's a whole lot better weighing 140. When I weigh 130, my friends think I'm dying and use words like *gaunt*. When I weigh 125, which is almost but not quite what *Vogue* might be able to deal with, I look as old as Jeanne Moreau when she's just murdered someone.

My last/current boyfriend was/is beautiful. He is tall and slender; he is grace itself and has the manners of someone whose mother hoped he'd marry better than she had. But he *never*—in the whole three years we have known each other or in the last six months, when things got hot—he *never* came into a room and gasped, "Oh, Jesus, how beautiful you are!" His manners were not *that* good. That was because he was not in love with me. I was/am in love with him. That was/is the trouble. The two weeks that I lost the twelve pounds ended on the Sunday I swam naked and got called beautiful. They were triggered by the realization that he didn't love me. I loved him and he didn't love me (he wasn't "in love" with me was how he put it—a semantic problem if there ever was one).

When I beheld myself at the end of the two weeks without the twelve pounds, my waist was a lot better, I had to admit. My ex/non-lover told my therapist that he "didn't mind the contrast of being so slender and she so plump" (the swine!). He'd never said that to *me*; he'd always told me he *liked* flesh! Now it turns out in front of my mental cleaning lady he is not unaware that perhaps we're clown-like together. I once told my lover who didn't love me, when we were calm and civilized, that when I was suffering from periods of depression or actually acted crazy, he didn't *have* to evaporate. He *could*, I even suggested, stick around and offer solace and maybe I'd get better faster. But a person who doesn't love you doesn't stick around when you're not at your best. That's part of not loving you.

Some people stick around when you're crazy even though they don't love you, just out of Christian charity and all, but my lover, who wasn't in love with me, had some notion that abandonment would, for some reason, "help." Do you understand that? Are there others who think that leaving someone who pleads for you to stay is "help"?

I realized he didn't love me when he decided to go home for two weeks to his midwestern hometown in the middle of a 110-degree summer to see someone he used to know—I realized that no one in his right mind would go where it's drop-dead heat unless he was in love. And if he were in love with this other person, then he was not in love with me. I realize this is cliché reasoning and all, but beholding me then, just as I am, that's my way of reasoning.

Sam, as we shall call the one whose pool is so beflowered that you can let bougainvillea petals float into your mouth swimming naked, used to lust after me so much that it gave him headaches and he'd always be asking for water to take his Fiorinals. So when we finally got to his manservant-made bed, I wasn't surprised when he said, "I cannot make love to you and look at your face. Your face has always been too beautiful." Which was more like it. When we finished making love that Sunday, we lay in each other's surprised arms looking out the open wall of glass windows at the pink sunset sky and the lavender-tinted garden. All I could say was "I'm hungry."

Oh, I was *so* hungry, for the first time I could remember. I could eat shrimps and roast beef, and I did because he happened to have them in his organized manservant kitchen. We sat wrapped in towels, gobbling shrimps. I'd come to have him look over the uncopyedited version of my new book, to have a real mind look it over and tell me the truth; his real mind. I hoped he still could tell me the truth and think I was beautiful at the same time. I can always find someone *else* to tell me *all* the truths—the ones about not minding us looking peculiar walking down the street together or not being "in love" with me.

Now, the day after the shrimp/roast-beef dinner, behold me again. In my mind last night (when I came home from Sam's), I created this Colette scene for me and my soon-to-be ex-lover whom we shall call—let's see—Scott, since F. Scott Fitzgerald was so weak and gentlemanly. I imagined a whole gorgeous Colette scene where Scott and I would meet, prearranged, in a restaurant's private room. He would be looking forward to seeing me because, what with his escapades in the last couple of weeks (which began after I had crazily dragged him to my mental-health lady where he said he was not "in love" with me), it had been some time since he'd been able to talk comfortably to me and gossip and laugh and receive all the other slender gifts, all I had to give him, that he'd have missed. Although he didn't know they mattered.

In my scheme, we'd meet in a beautiful room, this imagined private restaurant dining room that perhaps would overlook a garden with a fountain. It would be in the afternoon, because I wasn't about to have it wind up at night, when the possibility that I might be overcome by his beauty would make me want to be in bed with him again. I would arrive, twelve pounds less, my hair a few shades lighter, tan, and fresh from the bed of Sam, who cannot look at my face when he makes love to me because I am too beautiful.

"Darling..." I would say, outstretching my hand and sliding down into one of the nice seats while a waiter handed us two elegant menus. (I'd be starving, of course, having just been with Sam.)

We would have white wine from a silver cooler and he would find his beautiful self reflected in the polish. He also is thirty-three, but he is graceful and well-mannered. He'd be easy and proud of me, perhaps, because I would be so in control of myself and not like I'd been two weeks before when I realized he didn't love me and had begun to cry and had run out into traffic. He might wonder where I got tan, but he'd never ask. He never asked anything. The same as he never was the first to call when we fought. Just as he never stayed with me when I fell into despair. He wouldn't ask where I'd gotten tan.

"What have you been doing?" he'd ask, all charming curiosity.

"Oh...you know," I would say to the menu, "the usual carryings on."

"You look *wonderful*!" he would say (not "Jesus! How beautiful you are!").

"So do you," I would answer, "but you always look marvelous. So tan."

The waiter would pour the wine (which Scott doesn't really like), and we'd clink and sip.

"I have something to tell you, Scott," I would then say. And he would know, then, that things weren't going to be too funny. "But don't worry," I could add, "I'm not mad. I'm not anything. I'm all right. Don't worry. No scenes."

"Well...What is it?" he would ask, realizing belatedly that he'd been holding my hand in a sympathetic grasp, and now disengaging it wasn't the simplest thing on earth. I would make it easy for him by reaching for my wine.

"Well, the thing is, Scott," I would begin. (Oh, Colette, Colette, how did you do it? How did you manage these scenes so well? If it were really happening to me, things would have spilled all over the table by this time, and the waiter would have been an old friend wanting to know how my father was. Scott would have come into the lunch with a face totally shaken, knowing something horrible was going to happen from the tone of my voice over where we'd meet; he'd be so drawn and pale, I wouldn't have the heart to do my beautiful speech.) "The thing is, Scott," I would begin, "that since I've realized that you don't love me, that you are not in love with me, I

have had to think about a few things. One of them is that I realize
that nowadays getting any kind of relationship with any kind of man
is very nearly impossible, everything's so scattered and me not being
eighteen and all… I mean, if I had any sense at all, I'd be satisfied
with your half-measure affection and not rock the boat. But you see,
Scott…" (the waiter would come in and whoosh down some butter
lettuce with freshly sliced mushrooms and divine dressing, and there'd
be a pause) "…you see, I don't mind being alone. Most of the women
I know just hate being alone; it drives them crazy; they search for
men; they do anything to keep them. I have many women friends
who live with men like you who don't love them and who just use
them to cook and listen so they won't be alone. The fact that I am
sometimes amusing, in our affair, must be a bonus to you and for a
long time I thought I could make you love me. But I realize that I
cannot make you do anything; you don't love me and you never have.
You use the word *love*; you say you're not 'in love,' and then you take
my hand warmly and say that, however, you do *love* me."

"But I *do* love you," he would say, worried, trying to capture me
in his titanic gray eyes.

"Well, good," I would answer. "The thing is, Scott, that it's very
nice that you love me, believe me, I realize it is just dandy and all. But
I'd rather be alone. Or with a companion who truly loves me. I realize, of course, that these days no one truly *loves* anyone, but in that
case I'd rather be alone. Because if you look at it from my point of
view, Scott" (and at this point, I'd dip a shrimp into some pale green
sauce, brought by the waiter during the first part of my speech, and
take a ladylike nibble), "it's actually humiliating to be in love with
someone who doesn't love you."

"But I never meant to humiliate you," he would say. "I never meant
to hurt you."

"I know that, darling," I'd say; the shrimps in this restaurant
weren't as good as Sam's; but then, Sam's a better chef than the guy
they've got in the kitchen of this restaurant. "I know you've never
meant to hurt me and I know that you always told me you were not
'in love' with me, but I was so stuffed with illusions, I thought I could

change you...Could I have some more wine? Thanks..." I would watch as he poured carefully. He never dropped things from nerves the way I did. "So the real reason I invited you to lunch today was not just to explain the reasons I don't think we should see each other anymore..."

"Reasons?" he'd say. He doesn't drop things, but his mind goes on the blink.

"The humiliation and so forth...you remember?"

"Yes, but I never meant... "

"The reason, actually, that I invited you out to lunch was to help you."

"Help me?" he'd ask. By this time his mind would have come to a halt.

"Yes, help you, Scott..." I'd continue, frowning slightly at the half-eaten shrimp and deciding for once against it. (Around Scott, I always ate everything, perhaps because I knew he didn't love me.) "Scott," I would begin, "I've been thinking about you. Thinking if there were any way I could *help* you, you know? The thing is, Scott, that while we were together, going to parties and all that, a lot of people began to think that there was a lot more to you than they'd thought at first. Because at first a lot of people thought you were all manners and no content, you know? At least, the ones who knew about your manners, because your manners are so wonderful." (I was not about to tell him that people actually thought he was empty-headed because what good's that going to do when you're trying to help someone?) "But now that I'm no longer going to go places with you, now that we're no longer going to be an item—I've been worry-ing about you. I mean, I understand my position pretty well. I'm a thirty-three-year-old woman, but I'm a writer and people think writ-ing is glamorous, so I can go places alone or not go places and people still sort of think I'm doing what I want and not that I am alone because I'm no fun. Now, of course, no one's going to think that you're alone because no one loves you, but Scott, you need someone—someone with a certain weight—to give you presence. What was so nice about us together was that people...Well, Trina was telling me the other day that when she first met you, she just hardly noticed you, but that when she saw you with me, her whole attitude changed . . ." (No way could I finish this without telling him that people actually thought he was stupid and that when I suddenly turned up beside him, they thought he was charming and marvelous—they saw him through my eyes; it's the truth. How could I tell him this, this poor sweetness whose only crime was that he didn't love me and I loved him? I couldn't!) "Look, Scott, I'll just say this once and you can think about it at your leisure, but here it is. What you should do, if you decide to get another woman friend, is get one who's older, even older than me . . . so she's more frightened and willing to give up a lot more rather than lose you. Get one whom you don't even have to make love to, who's just so happy to have you with her. For you are, Scott, a charming companion and a gorgeous escort . . ."

"But, darling, I don't want another woman," he would now say. "I've . . . never loved another woman as much as I love you."

(The tag end of that joke is "I've never loved another woman as much as you in L.A. with brown hair who's five feet seven.")

The trouble with him never having loved another woman as much as he loves me is that the person he really loves is a man. That was the person he went to visit in the hot midwestern city. To this man, Scott tells me, he says, "I've never loved another man the way I love you." That man, says Scott, doesn't like that sentence any better than I do; that man knows about me. I have to tell you—I'm not happy about this—I've known about this guy for a good while. Scott, being Scott, assumed I'd be sympathetic. Jesus! Sometimes he would wipe his brow forlornly and say, "You know, sometimes, between the two of you, I feel like *Sunday, Bloody Sunday*." Until finally I snapped, "So what's going to happen in the end, Scott? Are you going to leave us both and run off to America?" That put a lid on the *Sunday, Bloody Sunday* grousing.

So behold me now, as I am. I am alone at the typewriter. I've made an appointment to see the cleaning lady in charge of my head whom

I've seen before with Scott. She's under the mistaken impression that what I need is a "real man." Robert Mitchum wouldn't fit in my apartment; how could I make coffee with him in the kitchen? What I need is to be alone, to write, and to lie in beds where the man thinks I'm beautiful and will let me swim naked in his pool till his mistress comes home.

The truth is, I will never be able to maneuver Scott into that little scene I devised so gorgeously if we could only be Colette. But, too, he will never ask me where I became tan without marks. Sam would. He notices things like that—it's why he's always divorced and divorced and his mistresses don't trust him, as well they shouldn't. He was always "in love"; he'd been "in love" with me since I was sixteen—his being in love with me would have given him the right to demand to know how I'd become tan this way. He's a real man.

Anyway, now Scott has called. He's back and he's brought me a present, he says. He brings everyone presents—he can't go out the door anywhere without nine complicated gift-switching arrangements (he always knows who goes with what—it's just he's always going back for more because he remembers how much they liked it last time). He's missed me, he says; it was dreadful in his hometown; his mother is maniacally lonely. Hot, he says, thank God he's back in L.A. where there's a breeze.

We are going out to dinner. Why not?

I've been through my closet and found the slight, bluey dress with a square low neckline that, until now, I've been too big to wear. It slips over me and fits perfectly—I wore it a night, six months ago, at the party where Scott, whom I'd known for years, suddenly saw me. His eyes lit up, he dragged me into the bathroom and pinned me to the green cool tile wall, insisting that we leave at once. He will love me in this dress; I can just see his eyes the way they narrow when he sees me looking beautiful, but he will be too well-mannered to say, "Oh, Jesus, how beautiful you are"; he will only say, "Well . . ."

My hair has just been washed and now comes curly to my shoulders and I have gone outside and picked a gardenia; they grow here—everything in California grows. I stand back then, from the mirror in this bluey dress and the flower in my fresh hair and behold myself, just as I am. The last two weeks of tragedy without Scott have turned out to seem like a comic to-do at some rich Marienbad spa where ladies pay fortunes to perfect themselves, rest, and sunbathe naked beside blue pools.

Sometimes, as the sun slants against the twilight a certain way, Scott looks like a pillar of strength. It cannot be easy to love me. Maybe if he were "in love" with me, as Sam says he is, he couldn't be trusted to tell me the truth, and I could not love him so. Which I do. I love him so. Yes, behold this blue pool/bluey-dressed ambivalence that I choose to call love, whose footsteps I hear coming up the path. Whatever scenes I imagine, whomever Scott goes to visit, it doesn't matter, or at least not enough. Behold me, then, smiling. Waiting for my lover, just as I am.

Cosmopolitan
August 1978

VENICE, CALIFORNIA

I HAVE moved to Santa Monica, into the rafters of this handmade 1906 house that is on a rambling flowery hill overlooking what could be Fairbanks, Alaska, and Maui, and Tierra del Fuego—but *not* Boulder. I have two bedrooms—and two cats, one for each of me.

Santa Monica and Venice, I'm convinced, are now the center of the universe and nothing happens anywhere that doesn't happen out here on the boardwalk first. The boardwalk in Venice, three blocks south of me, is screaming with violet fur shorts while Frank Sinatra sings "Violets for Your Furs" from the jukebox in Robert's. Robert's is a white gallery-looking restaurant with lots of those obscene red lilies with yellow stalks sticking out the middle, waiting leeringly. Robert's is so hip, it's practically *in* the ocean. People roller-skate there; and, at night, you'll see Mick Jagger and Lena Horne gorging themselves on strawberries dipped in chocolate topped by amaretto-spiked *crème fraîche*.

In Venice, looking like Linda Ronstadt—cute satin shorts and cute brown hair and pigeon toes—is all the rage. It's a little hard doing punk out in broad daylight, though, because all that cerise neon hair loses something when it's ninety-six degrees and glaring. The men are all doing *L'Uomo Vogue* with a vengeance—and "primaries" are screeching across your eyeballs like a chalk on a blackboard every Sunday brunch in Robert's (where everything starts first, even firster than the rest of the boardwalk). Primary taxi yellow, primary blue, primary red, primary all-in-satin.

In Robert's, you sit watching people come in, and you say to yourself, "Yes, yes, no, *non*, no, yes—oh YES!" People's bodies, what with all these roller-skating, cutie-pie outfits, have gotten so primary themselves that I've overheard lines such as "I saw a body yesterday, I mean, it was gorgeous—but then it spoke."

Where I'm living—two blocks from Main Street—is getting worse than Rodeo Drive. They've got these horribly outrageous stores selling neon-purple spiral extension cords and little magpies made of straw from Red—rather the People's Republic of—China. Across the street is this evil den of iniquity called the Buttery that makes croissants fresh every morning starting at 7:30 a.m. They also bake cinnamon rolls that taste exactly like the ones I used to lust after in Le Conte Junior High in Hollywood. Everything is hot there and people wait in this ravenous line starting so early that the sign still says CLOSED outside.

Also down here on Main Street is the Café California, an exquisite place so L.A. and so French that they practically pick the asparagus out of the garden (California, unsprayed) one minute before they bring it to you cooked perfectly (French). They put capers on anything you ask them to, and I love capers more than life itself. In case you're wanting things a little richer, they also have those New York desserts that they bring in crystal punch bowls filled with whipped cream.

Fortunately, also on Main Street, there's a little restaurant called Le Central that hardly anyone knows about. It will never be mobbed, because the food just isn't anywhere near the Café California's, which is why everyone who lives down here goes there. The wine cellar of Le Central is upstairs, and the place reminds me of something out of *Babar the Elephant* because it's all white-white with smidgens of color from Babar-looking French watercolors that are on *zee walls*.

My photographer friend Annie Leibovitz is on one of her upswings into health and has been here shooting a magazine cover as well as jogging on the beach in front of my house while I sit home eating milk and honey. We went roller-skating together, maniacally, on a weekday morning when no one was around and it was bliss. I have my own skates which Paul Ruscha (my adorable boyfriend, the only one in captivity, it seems) found for $2 in the Goodwill. Brand-new! And my size!

Michael Franks has a new record (Warner Bros.) called *Tiger in the Rain*. The title song—about his cat—has *purring* from a stand-up bass in it. Michael Franks also has another song that goes: "When I saw you there in your Danskin / Then the wolf jumped out of the lambskin." I just love him. I mean who else has purring on his record?

Vogue
August 1979

HONKY-TONK NIGHTS
The Good Old Days at L.A.'s Troubadour

NOW I WANT it known right off that I was fourteen years old the day I first walked into the Troubadour. That was in 1957 and I was a virgin. The Troubadour was over on La Cienega, a little more east of Doheny but still sort of West Hollywood-ish. It had just opened; Horace Silver was playing "Señor Blues" on the piano, while a friend of mine, Barry Salvin, was washing dishes in the kitchen, claiming that life was worth living because the owner, Doug Weston, had given him a job next to the music. But the original jazz Troubadour closed and my friend Barry Salvin died before the Beatles ever became famous.

In 1961 or so, Weston opened what he called the Troubadour II on Santa Monica and Doheny. It was a kind of beatnik place, a folk club seating about three hundred people, where Odetta or Peter, Paul and Mary would play acoustic sets.

In those days, the only place you could hear live rock and roll in L.A. was up at the Whisky a Go Go on the Sunset Strip. Johnny Rivers used to rip it up there until the Beatles changed the world; then suddenly the entire Strip was one long problem for the West Hollywood Sheriff's Department, what with the Whisky, the London Fog next door (where Jim Morrison and the Doors used to play in 1966), the Trip, Ciro's (where the Byrds first started), and even off-the-Strip places like Brave New World and little clubs around Hollywood. The cops were just awful. In those days, they used to just bust kids wholesale as they came out of the Whisky and the Trip and handcuff them and throw them into police buses out of what seemed like sheer exuberance.

It wasn't until 1967 that Doug Weston allowed rock and roll to darken his doorstep, and that was, according to my friend Dickie Davis, one night when the Buffalo Springfield came and played a set with amps. It was odd that they were the first to play rock and roll in the Troubadour. Stephen Stills's lyric in "For What It's Worth"— "a man with a gun over there"—was *about* the very West Hollywood Sheriff's Department in question. But after the Buffalo Springfield played, rock and roll took a turn off the Strip and came to the Troubadour, where for some reason the West Hollywood Sheriff's Department didn't bother anyone. The Byrds, the Dillards, Joni Mitchell, the Nitty Gritty Dirt Band, Neil Young, Poco, Linda Ronstadt, Jackson Browne, and all sorts of L.A. surfer-cowboy types played the Troubadour after that.

But as far as I'm concerned, it was in the Troubadour's bar that L.A. rock and roll really happened, and by the time I walked into Weston's Troubadour in 1968, I was neither fourteen nor a virgin at all.

From the outside during the day, the Troubadour looks like a mild-mannered Swiss restaurant among the shabby commercial realities of West Hollywood; Beverly Hills, only half a block west, is so flat, green, and safe that it seems immune to any reality at all (a disguise that fools no one). At the intersection of Santa Monica and Doheny is an indigenous jumble of Porsches, Rolls-Royces, '55 Chevys, London taxis, and ramshackle Jeeps driven by movie stars. Half a mile back is the Tropicana Motel, where at least three rock and roll bands are always waiting, ready for anything (though these days they're punk, whereas in the late sixties when the Troubadour was in flower, they were cowboy Beatles). Half a mile ahead in Beverly Hills, God knows.

From the inside at night, the Troubadour looks surprisingly large and homey. The bleeding-heart folksiness of the club's original atmosphere still warms the hardest rock and roll. Until a few months ago, people thought the Troubadour's day was over and that it couldn't possibly stay open another season; it had been petering out for so long that by the fall of 1977, when Doug Weston got Jackson Browne to do a benefit for the club, most people felt it was more like a farewell performance. But now the lines have begun to form once more, and when I went there for a couple of nights, the place was as mobbed as if the years of emptiness had never happened. Even the bar, a shadow of its former self, seemed prepared for any occasion, though God knows the future would have to be awfully checkered to live up to this bar's past. Not that I doubt it will be.

Like more than one carefully educated young woman watching TV the night the Beatles were on Ed Sullivan, I was a groupie. I posed as an album-cover designer and photographer, while others disguised themselves as tailors, record-company secretaries, or journalists. For women like us, hanging out in the Troubadour bar every night was, you know, business. I mean, I told people—even myself—that I had to do it. But when I dyed my hair the color of a pumpkin, even my sociology professor uncle, who only knows what he sees on *The Merv Griffin Show*, wondered if I hadn't become "one of those groupies."

That I today have some album covers and photographs to show for myself is a monument to the attention-to-detail of my disguise; for by the age of twenty-four, when most young ladies were married, having babies, and immersed in the "business of living," the Troubadour had traded folk for rock and roll, and I was there in its bar every single night for just about five years, a slave to skinny boys with long hair who sang and played guitar.

Of course, people who *had* to come to the Troubadour bar—publicists and rock and roll record promoters and reviewers—*hated* the place. And others who only came to watch the acts didn't even notice the bar. And there were some who knew about the bar and wouldn't touch it with a ten-foot pole.

"How *can* you, Eve, every single night!?" they'd ask, frowning.

"I love it!" I'd exclaim.

"Love?" they'd ask. "That place? In God's name, *why*?"

"Why?" I'd reply. "The *people*!"

They'd stare at me a moment longer, sigh and finally leave, sure that if only I applied myself, I could be somebody, but I obviously wouldn't, so what could they do: I just wouldn't listen. "The *people*," indeed.

To those of us who spent all that time in the Troubadour bar, it didn't matter what was going on in the rest of the club, though hundreds of people paid to get in night after night. It seemed like performers who'd begun their careers there would have to play the Troubadour even after they could fill the Forum, because they had signed contracts with Doug Weston, exchanging his club as a showcase for them when they were obscure newcomers in return for an agreement to get them later on when they were Elton John. People would line up around the block, drooling to get tickets, not knowing that the stars they'd come to see loathed playing the Troubadour and were only there because they couldn't get out of Weston's contract, which they'd signed back in the days when they thought a week at the Troubadour was an honor—before they began to think of Weston as a snaggletoothed, greedy son of a bitch who didn't understand artists. Weston rarely came downstairs into the bar because, people said, he was upstairs cackling over his good fortune. I myself thought that any nightclub owner who let a bunch of rock and roll types like us hang around in his bar for 365 nights a year doing nothing couldn't be *that* good a businessman.

Monday nights, "Hoot Nights" leftover from the folk-club hootenanny days, were the most insane evenings, because the Troubadour's stage was flung open to any kid or band determined to wait in line Monday morning and pass the audition, and the audience only had to pay a dollar to get in. The bar was just jammed with record-company people, friends of the bands, the bands themselves, and groupies. Passion licked through the room, burning with wild desires.

"You had to wear a diaphragm just to walk thought," Susan Smith, one of the waitresses, told me. "The semen potential was so intense it was enough to get you pregnant just standing there."

It seemed like anyone who went home alone Monday nights had to be supernaturally unlucky.

Tuesday night was almost as insane as Mondays because new acts opened Tuesdays and the record companies were paying. Every journalist and friend and rock and roller got a tab for free drinks and ended up in the bar trying to get laid, get high, or get a deal together.

The rest of the week was just a usual mixture of youth, beauty, fame, and unknowns, aflame with lust—just like Mondays and Tuesdays—only less touristy.

People immersed in the business of living could tell at a glance that the Troubadour bar was "too L.A." for anything more serious than trying to look like a cowboy surfer—if you were a guy—and young-but-dangerous, if you were a woman. Looking back on it, the whole time seems like the longest one-night stand in history. Anyway, I bet the people having lunch every day at the Algonquin back in the years when they were all so witty and brilliant looked back eventually and thought of it as all one lunch.

Perhaps when a certain group of people enters a certain place for a while, the time is so electric and crackling that later it all looks the same—washed in a blur of amazing grace. And I don't think it was just the tequila, either, at least not entirely, though I'm not saying all those double margaritas poured over ice cubes in large tumblers with no salt didn't have something to do with the rosy glow in which it all still basks. Coming into the bar early some Thursday night, slipping through the crowd in line outside, it was almost a relief to see that hardly anyone was there yet except Jim Dixon, a yachtsman who was one of the earliest people to hang out with the Byrds. He'd be talking to the bartender, John Barrack, about sailing to Maui.

Sullenly, leaning against the bar, was the waitress Reina, the queen who ruled that room all those years, in sickness and in health, with exactly the same attitude: not amused. (Indifference and scorn were the only variations.) She was gorgeous, with long brown hair down past her waist and a face like a pinup girl. But then, all the waitresses at the Troubadour were too much. It seemed like the place had a laissez-faire arrangement with them, allowing them to do anything they wanted as long as they didn't mix up the orders or let anyone escape the two drink minimum. The waitresses at the Troubadour, therefore, were infamously hot.

"Hey, Babitz, you still here?" A smug voice in the corner would demand.

I knew it was Glenn Frey, because though I was there early, Glenn always got there earlier. In those days, Glenn was not in the Eagles amassing a portfolio of stocks so he can retire and play softball like Bob Hope plays golf. In those days, he was just another cowboy in patched-up jeans at the Troubadour every night with no other ambition, seemingly, but to misspend his youth.

Of the two members who went on to make up Longbranch Pennywhistle, Glenn Frey and J. D. Souther, it was difficult to say which was skinnier, since both of them together weighed about 208 and combined to look like one toothpick. I met them on a Monday night and thought they were much too cute and way too young, which made me feel old, but not old enough to go home and get married. By 1971, it seemed like Glenn and I had been hanging out drinking tequila in the corner of the bar forever, and that we never went home, that one or the other was "still here."

"What do you mean, you were here first," I'd say. "You're always here. You're worse than Jackson."

I'd bring my drink over to Glenn's table, and just as I'd be sitting down, Jackson Browne would appear from the kitchen, where he'd apparently moved from Orange County when he was seventeen, or else had such a casual arrangement with the place that they let him come in the back, through the kitchen, like he lived there and didn't have to go around to the front like everybody else. He'd get a beer and go back into the kitchen, having nodded to Glenn and me like the host's teenage son being polite.

If you're going to drink the way Glenn and I did, you should do it when youthful exuberance and an iron constitution let you wake up the next day ready for more trouble and not wait till you're so old that you wish you were dead the morning after and are unable to appreciate plummeting headlong into oblivion the way God intended.

Anyway, that's how it seemed to me then.

Maybe everyone saw it like that.

Everyone but Steve Martin of course. Steve, sitting at the bar drinking a single glass of white wine in the midst of all that cigarette smoke, could never bring himself to look on the bright side of total debauchery or "overboogie," as it came to be known. It was almost as though he didn't realize that if it weren't for the Beatles, we'd all be stuck pursuing reasonable lives. In fact, sometimes I'd look at Steve sitting there and say to myself, "Oh, poor Steve, he just has no sense of humor."

By about 9:30, the bar would begin to fill out and get that padded look I liked so much, and which melted into my second margarita and blended with everybody there. Low-powered, hyphenated groupies (photographer-groupies, Topanga-groupies, etc.)—beautiful girls with tans and Marlboros and soft hair and clear eyes and without that look of contemptuous impatience that one sees nowadays in this age of cocaine (this was B.C., Before Cocaine)—would settle down to tables and laugh at things. Young musicians from places like Tucson and Boulder and Lubbock would watch and be funny, having smoked dope behind the Troubadour before they came in.

Glenn Frey, by this time, was making diabolical observations about some poor tourist who soon realized that white folks in suits and ties weren't supposed to be there (unless they were presidents of record companies).

Outside by now the traffic had thinned. At the light would be a chartreuse Lotus, a '52 Lincoln Continental painted cream, dentless and virginal, and a beat-up hearse full of kids from West L.A. who were on their way back from cruising Hollywood Boulevard and who were listening to Jim Morrison's apocalyptic lullabies on AM, while out back, Jim Morrison, drunk, would be flung into a Red & White cab, having hung by his knees from the balcony, among other things. A girl would be trying to bribe the cabdriver into taking him to the

Alta Cienega Motel and not worry, and finally the cab would be just about to pull away when Jim, totally sober and out of nowhere, would tell her: "You know, I've always loved you."

Anyone could see he'd die young.

Inside at one time or another during this one-night stand, strange combinations came together at the bar—like Gram Parsons and Mike Clarke drinking champagne and Wild Turkey, or Arlo Guthrie falling in love with one of the waitresses. Hoyt Axton and Jack Elliott and David Blue made things seem legit even on nights when Gatsby, Steels and Nosh (what someone dubbed Crosby, Stills and Nash during a particularly horrendous time when they were in the middle of recording that first album and everyone was thinking it should be called *Music From Big Ego*) came in and made things seem too Hollywood for words. Janis Joplin would sit in her nightgown with a pink boa, all by herself, drinking. Paul Butterfield would hit the Troubadour the minute he came to L.A. and didn't wait till he opened to order adult drinks like gin and tonic. Van Morrison glowered in corners, and Randy Newman was all innocence and myopia. Nothing was impossible. Unknowns became stars.

Steve Martin used to say, "You're like Linda. You've got opinions about things."

I used to worry about that, since having opinions about things— if you were a woman in those days—didn't seem to inspire mink coats or foaming lust or even songs written about you, but it was true that Linda and I were somewhat alike, because we both read (Linda's house was piled high with thick novels, history books, and amps), and we both were always on diets. In our opinion, the best way to lose weight fast was to go on a fruit fast, and we did this once together—telephoning the other when we ate so much as a single orange—until at the end of one week, we'd each lost twelve pounds. At this transcendent moment, I took a bunch of pictures of Linda to document her perfection: she looked like a French convent girl on her way to seduce a lecherous old count.

"Look innocent," I told her.

Like most people, I was in love with Linda's voice, and when she sang "Long, Long Time" (her biggest hit around then), I turned into one large, aching teardrop.

John David Souther used to come to the Troubadour and scorch the bar with his eyes, ignoring all the girls in case they thought their souls their own. He hardly had to be there at all to make you worry, and he was only twenty-three. "Everybody knows boys from Texas are conceited," Linda once told me. He burned with an amber light so that his green eyes seemed on fire with it. He'd drink San Miguel beer (he's probably still the most elegant gourmet from Texas the world has ever known), his long fingers curling around the glass. It made you think that the amber from the beer bubbled down his throat and ignited him further, he was so intense.

Jackson Browne was always the Kid. You couldn't help but love him (nobody even tried), for when he stood there with his too-large shirt on and his determined stab at becoming Robert Mitchum by not shaving for three days (which made him look like a Botticelli that needed dusting and not like Robert Mitchum at all), the world came to a complete stop.

"And those cheekbones," one of the waitresses used to sigh. "Those eyelashes and those cheekbones. God."

Now of course, if J. D. and Jackson weren't bad enough already, all of a sudden Ned Doheny would come in from outside, wearing his gray serape jacket and his eight-by-ten glossy smile, looking like one of those kids who went to Beverly Hills High and who got a convertible for his sixteenth birthday (only Ned would drive Jeeps).

And of course there was always Glenn Frey. Glenn and Jackson wrote the Eagles' first song, "Take It Easy." But I was so used to seeing Glenn all the time that I took him for granted and didn't have any idea he could even tune a guitar, much less go out onstage and make girls scream.

*

Sometimes it all got to be too much for me—all that beauty showing all that promise—and I'd grow morbidly paranoid and filled with grave doubts, comparing us there—that all-one-night at the Troubadour—with the hero in Henry James's story "The Beast in the Jungle," who starts his life knowing that something so great and special is going to happen to him that he never attaches himself to anything real, and finally, just before he is about to become old, he realizes that the special thing—that beast in the jungle waiting to jump out at him—is indeed unique, because it's nothing—nothing will ever happen to him. Sometimes I'd think that nothing would ever happen to us either, or at least that it would be all downhill from then on. The latter isn't far from wrong, I think sometimes.

But then other times I knew everything would be all right and that no matter how terrible we were or how great our futures were, it was inevitable that some beast was lurking, if only Doug Dillard. He laughed at everything and smiled this regrettable smile that had a way of convincing you to let the devil take the hindmost and fling caution to the winds. Standing there six feet two or so, Missouri wiry, wielding a violin case or—worse—playing the violin, his eyeballs would spiral out in opposite directions. And then a look of saintly seriousness would fall over his face, like Prince Mishkin in *The Idiot*—practically religious. And wiping his lips free of beer foam, he'd open his mouth and a note of sheer angelic beauty would ring through the bar.

"Amazing grace ..."

And he'd raise one eyebrow, waiting, mock holy.

Minding her own business, Linda Ronstadt would just be coming into the bar, talking a mile a minute about where can she find a bass player, but at the sound of his voice, she'd be flattened.

"How sweet the sound ..."

Linda, challenged, couldn't resist and her voice would lift in perfect a cappella harmony. Since she lived upstairs from Doug Dillard, they might have planned this, but I rather doubt it. Her voice was always the same: perfect, like an angel.

"That saved a wretch like me ..."

Gene Clark and Jackson and David Crosby would all be in it by this time, suddenly Baptists. It was Sunday morning.

"I once was lost

But now am found . . .

Was blind but now I see."

By 1972 nearly everyone had signed recording contracts and went straight. By 1975 the Troubadour bar was a shell of its former self.

Outside a few nights ago at only 8 p.m., two twenty-year-old kids sat on the cement sidewalk by the Troubadour box office like they'd been there for a while. The box office was closed.

"What are you doing?" I asked.

"We're waiting for it to open," the girl said.

"To buy tickets?"

"To see the Pages," she said. "And we're first in line."

I've never heard of the Pages, but by 8:45 the line was halfway to Doheny, four deep. From outside, the Troubadour, as usual, looked like its mild-mannered self located on the wrong side of Doheny Drive. Lots of silver Porsches, pastel Cadillacs, limos, and beat-up vans from West L.A. wait as—even now—you can hear Jim Morrison's lullabies of fire in the AM air. Inside in the bar, anything might happen—a beast in the jungle. Back at the Tropicana it's mostly punk now. Ahead, God knows, the future—checkered with amazing grace —will always belong to unknowns.

". . . Was blind but now I see."

Rolling Stone
August 23, 1979

A CALIFORNIAN LOOKS AT NEW YORK

"LADY, with that hat," he said, "you gotta be from California."

The hat wasn't that different from lots of hats on the streets of New York. It was one of those little crocheted coffee-with-cream-colored hats; only on the part next to the brim, I'd pinned these silk flowers from the dime store which looked exactly like bougainvillaea. Anyway, he must have meant that only a Californian would go around in a city already ablaze with color with flowers pinned to her hat against the mere terror of trying to get a cab.

"Oh, please come," my friend Sarah had said, "The leaves..."

Everyone said that the six weeks I'd be in New York—from the end of October to the first week in December—were the best ones to be on the East Coast.

"You'll be able to see the fall," they all said.

"But still," I said, "New York."

"But don't you *like* New York. It's so exciting!"

And I'd be able to see all my friends and finish the grisly last details on my book and meet all these people in New York who run everything and find out how to write for television.

Writers have been hired to go out to the coast and work on unlikely projects since before anyone was born but it was always the *West* Coast they went out to, not the *East* Coast as I was. I'd been asked to come to New York to work on a TV play about New York models. The reason this was unlikely was that I knew nothing about New York models and had only gone along with the project in the first place because it sounded like so much fun who could resist.

Plus I'd be able to see Sarah, my best friend, and she had invited me to stay with her for a few days up in Connecticut before New York.

And so there we were, Sarah and I, driving through blurry blazes of leaves of crimson, marigold, and blood rust, past stately Henry James mansions with low stone fences. We sat together on a boat pier jutting into a bay where sailboats in the distance looked so crisp in the fall air that the perspective seemed out of one of those Renaissance architectural drawings where a few stray people linger in the foreground. It hardly took us any time, in this illumination of leaves and horizons, to get back into our old ways of spending hours together without speech.

On our way back to Sarah's house in the car, we drove past heaps of raked-up leaves.

"Would you like to jump in the leaves?" she asked.

"Jump in the leaves?" I asked.

"Oh, I forgot," she said, "you didn't grow up here. Whenever I fall in the leaves now, it brings back *everything*—my whole childhood."

In the sky were those Kennedy clouds—little white wispy ones which they surely must have had at Hyannis Port and which there never will be in California.

Sarah and I took the train into the city together from Greenwich and passed miles and miles of more gorgeous leaves until at last the train was flying above Harlem and I knew we weren't in Kansas (which is a lot like L.A., people complain) anymore. It was New York full blast from then on and the last I remember of peace and quiet.

The park, Central Park, was not quite as ablaze with color as Connecticut had been. It must take something out of the leaves to have to contend with being stared at every daylight hour by the hungry eyes of people determined to get their money's worth out of fall. In New York, they make a great issue out of something they call the Exhilaration of the Seasons and here one was. So the leaves had better be good. The leaves in Central Park looked drained and numb with overwork; however, they performed valiantly and did not simply drop off all at once into a swooned faint as I would have.

For a long time, I felt that the "energy" of New York was not for me because it was all I could do to buck death crossing the street going to and from the office. I didn't even work at an office, really; because it seems that when you write TV plays, in the beginning you never actually do anything until you've gotten "the feel" of things. This meant I slept.

The "energy" of New York along with the "excitement" boils down to "terror" if you ask me. If I went around with my purse unsnapped the way I always did in L.A., older women accosted me saying, "Dear, your purse is open. Anyone could just grab your wallet." They made me feel my purse's being open was an affront. How dare I go around with an open purse when the city was so dangerous. I had to be some jerk from out of town. I'd tell them, "I don't care."

But you have to care in New York or you'll die. It's not like L.A., where you can go around with your purse unsnapped or lost in thought even on the freeway. In New York, the gossip will get you if crossing the street doesn't; for the gossip is so dense and thick that it hovers over the entire city like an enraged bear, ready to snap its teeth on anyone who isn't fast enough to cover herself with alibis, low profiles, or return red herrings aimed strategically somewhere else. The gossip is like a lightning game of backgammon with rolls of dice leaving behind broken hearts, the dissolution of entrenched power, and awkward guest lists. Everyone (who's left) waits for the next roll, eyes glued to the die. You cannot *not* care in New York. Even I know that. You'll die just crossing the street. It's exciting.

It was always exciting.

It's changed, though, from when I used to live on the Lower East Side in 1966 and acid was in flower; and it's changed from a few years ago when my first book was published. It's even changed since last year when I stayed at Sarah's in Connecticut and took the train into the city every day, braving the streets, going to magazine appointments.

The people were all different somehow, I decided, but the ones I tried to explain this to insisted that New Yorkers were just glad because it was fall and because the winter rains and horrors which were predicted on TV every night at dinner hadn't come.

"No . . ." I would say, trying to think, "it was something else."

Then I knew.

"It's the dogs!" I exclaimed. "The sidewalks, you can walk on them! Those signs everywhere saying 'Curb and clean up after your dog' are *working*!"

"Well . . ." some said, "you could be right." Their usual New York contempt for hick opinions grew dull regarding my theory. Perhaps this was because they could walk beside me as we talked without having to guard every step they took, and we could look up into the sky at flocks of birds swooping low, flying south for the winter.

Having been in New York before, I knew that buying clothes for, or in any way trying to figure out something suitable to wear in, New York would get me nowhere. They already have all the clothes in New York, there is no way one can hope to attain the look the women there have unless you become one of them, twenty-four hours a day, year in and year out.

The best thing to do, I decided, was not anything. I would wear just what I wore in L.A. (only with a coat over it) and that would be that. What I wear in L.A. is old jeans and this grey sweatshirt with a hood that my boyfriend found at a garage sale for $2 and is my favorite shade of gray. And I like these old thirteen-button navy uniform pants which aren't too bad and are intensely nondescript and can be rolled up into a foolproof sausage if you turn them inside out like sailors do and they'll have no wrinkles. Then I have these sort of wretched muddy-looking khaki pants that everyone's wearing. And these snaggletooth old sweaters along with one silver sweater (in case I got invited to a party). These were what I took with me for six weeks in New York. I could carry all of this—plus shoes—aboard the plane.

Besides, I thought, when I was packing, if I need any clothes, New York is sure to have some. One must shop in New York, I remembered from experience, in order to know one is alive, practically.

Bloomingdale's has changed. This time, I can't go into it. Last time and the times before, I could endure the break between life as we know it and Bloomingdale's and enjoy the sensation just about; but, this time when I went to Bloomingdale's, the information blitz was too overwhelming. All those people and all those promises. If I bought only $15.69 worth of carnation bath talc, I'd receive $79.95 worth of gift samples, and on and on. After only three minutes of Bloomingdale's I was out onto the feckless sidewalks, back on earth.

In the beginning, for the most part, the shops in New York this time paralyzed me into an inability to speak; though, by the fifth week, I was buying $130 cashmere cable-knit sweaters from André Oliver on Fifty-Seventh Street as if a person could just go into a store and do such a thing. I mean, four. Two for me, one for my boyfriend, and one for my sister. The sea-blue one was for my boyfriend, the gray for my sister, and the forest-green was for me—though the reason I got started buying these things to begin with was that they had one in a kind of neon violet. This color miraculously cured my paralysis from inside the store window; and before I knew it, I was barging up to this delicate young salesman in this luxury men's sports clothes place saying, "Can girls wear these purple sweaters or just guys?"

"You're from out of town aren't you," I was told.

And once André Oliver kicked through the door to my heart, it was no time at all before I was in Henri Bendel's hovering over little wooden boxes with cats painted on them from the People's Republic of China; they were filled with little black licorice mice that looked like they were carved out of onyx. Each box cost $7.50.

"I mean, $7.50 for *mice*," I said to myself.

"But they're so cute," I replied, "and besides, they're useful—you can eat them."

So I bought six boxes.

I suppose I was lucky that the shopping lust didn't overtake me completely until it was almost my sixth week and I flew away from such seductions. At least now I know what it's like to be consumed by fashionable desires. But I can see how, if I lived in New York in real life, I'd plunge joyfully into enormous debt swathing all my friends in cashmere; and as they carried me off to the psychopathic ward at Bellevue, I'd be fashionably pleading, "Let them eat mice!"

"Oh, please come," Sarah had said, "the leaves . . ."

By the first week in December, the first snow had fallen and I'd been able to walk invincibly down Madison Avenue in my new New York fleece-lined galoshes and my secondhand sealskin coat. I was so sentimental that I bought violets for my furs (for $12.50—silk violets) because New York always reminds me of Frank Sinatra singing. I had finished the television play, finished the grisly details on my book, met all the people who ran everything at an opulent East Side party where I wore my silver sweater and sailor pants and everyone said I hardly looked "too L.A." at all. I'd seen the leaves alone with Sarah and seen them in Central Park in the crowds, faintly shopworn. I'd felt the "energy" and "excitement" for six whole weeks and not gotten run over.

And there I sat watching the rectangular skyscape recede as the cab driver took me to the airport, when he turned and gave me this look, saying, "Lady, with that hat—you gotta be from California."

New York City lay sleeping curled up like a bear hibernating across the river, ready to wake up again the instant I come back next time.

Vogue
October 1979

ANNA'S BRANDO

IF BY PAGE five he's a bad lay, then you have nothing to look forward to and who cares? In Anna Kashfi Brando's *Brando for Breakfast*, we learn that Marlon Brando is "not well appointed," is "selfish," and was hardly ever home for dinner (much less breakfast, since he rarely woke up till after lunch); we get movie reviews, frank opinions on what a gauche genius poor Marlon is, and a flashily exposed solution to this man's innermost mystery—that he's really nothing but a poly-sexual and that he'll stick it into any port in the storm, up to and including a duck. Anna wouldn't mind, she explains, except that she feels his behavior is bound to taint their now twenty-one-year-old son, whom she always called Devi and Marlon always called Christian (after the boy's godfather, Christian Marquand, the French director and very close friend of Marlon's). Anna and Marlon were married for about a year and a half back in the fifties, but it has taken her all this time to give us The Book. She probably would have kept silent forever except that she took an overdose of drugs recently and was in the hospital for a month or so and when she was all better, she knew the world need no longer go on in ignorance. She decided to tell all.

Anna and her coauthor, E. P. Stein, elaborately go into the story of Brando's entire life and how his father thing and mother thing were the reason he turned out to be such a rat. The book includes details of how no screenplay, movie director, studio, or fellow actor involved with Brando was safe once he came into the room. It tells of all the naive young girls, all the illegitimate children, all the suicide attempts, wigs, sleeping pills, tearings up and down Mulholland Drive at midnight, and on and on unto the night of legal papers quoted at length. The last third of the book is almost entirely about judges and lawyers and what a liar Brando was but how everyone believed him because he was Brando and she was only this little starlet trying to raise her son and not take too many pills.

Describing his appearance on their first date, she and Stein write: "He balanced a steatopygous form on squat, sturdy legs and moved with a lissome stride that conveyed a forceful yet feminine grace." (Roughly defined, *steatopygia* means fat ass.) Nevertheless, she lets him take her out to dinner, and when more than two months later she goes to bed with him out of "curiosity" and he is a dud, you'd think she'd call it a day and date someone better appointed.

But if she had, where would we be today? All her thoughtful insights would have been lost. Such as:

"In short, Marlon Brando is modern gothic: grotesque, contradictory, impossible."

"Marlon's sexual tutti-frutti comprise several shadier flavors."

"Marlon reserves his favors for Orientals, Latins, blacks, Polynesians, and Indians, both east and west. When I accused him of choosing 'inferior' women as partners to satisfy his need for superiority feelings, he was incensed."

"Marlon flaunted his dominance of women by humiliating them whenever they dared display an independent mien."

And last but not least:

"A naive young girl probing her way through the world meets the suave seducer."

Well, not naive exactly—more like a B-movie adventuress.

Anna Kashfi was born in Calcutta in 1934 of "an unregistered alliance" between her mother and father. When she was eighteen, she went to London to study, and though she was supposedly a naive young girl probing her way through the London School of Economics, she ran off to Paris with an Italian jet pilot. Unfortunately, in Paris she ran into her father, who was supposed to be home in India with Mom. Dad cut her off without a penny. Anna was forced into "modeling," a pursuit she explains by saying she couldn't type. Luckily, Spencer Tracy agreed to cast her in a movie with him. When the cast and crew moved from their location in Chamonix to the Paramount soundstage, she was whisked off to Hollywood. A week later, she was sitting in the Paramount commissary in her red sari and minding her own business when from across the room (where he was nuzzling Eva Marie Saint), the sly seducer clapped eyes on her. She did not, she says, even know who he was the first time he called and they went out, but it wasn't long before someone told her, and perhaps who he was outweighed her objections to how awful he was, all squat and steatopygous.

When I was sixteen, I took up with a band of vicious Hollywood starlets who were all older than I (real old, like twenty-two or -three). They spent their days working on tans at the Beverly Hills Health Club and devising diabolic revenge for schmucks who crossed them in any way at all. They spent their nights drinking martinis and wearing Jax dresses with necklines so low that their bulging breasts were all anyone could think about. They drove Thunderbirds, dated celebrities, and always knew beyond a shadow of a doubt that there was a prince for them, a handsome, rich, clever, hip prince who was famous, had famous friends, and drove a Cadillac convertible down the Sunset Strip in the afternoons listening to jazz on the radio. A man with a large appointment who was never selfishly premature.

And a man who came home to dinner and stayed home, not like the man who was always running around with Rita Moreno—who left her wig in the bedroom, as Anna tells us. Marlon would have been perfect except that he had other ideas. But from afar—among those vicious starlets—Marlon was the ultimate score.

Not a single one of those girls found a prince—including Anna Kashfi. In her mixture of rectal conjecture and quotes from Pauline Kael cut in half so that they say the opposite of what was meant, Anna seems to speak for all of them—one long wail of howling outrage. A tirade against the audacity of the way things turned out compared with how they should have been. Marlon Brando has "toes (at least) of common clay," she screams, and he did it to this duck in Paris besides! The world is no longer to be kept in ignorance of all Anna has suffered.

Perhaps there's something marvelous and brave about Anna and my vicious starlet friends, out for blood and evening up the score so long after everyone has gone home. But we do worry when we realize that Anna, though she's out of the frying pan Brando-wise, might be someplace hotter with this E. P. Stein person cowriting her book. Anna seems to have a fatal fascination for sticking with the hopeless. But this time, instead of winding up in divorce, it ends up, after pages and pages and pages (I mean, who wants to hear Anna and E. P. Stein's critical essay on *Bedtime Story*?), a book.

I was almost gasping with relief upon coming across one small holdout during a time when Anna and Marlon were recently estranged: "Newspapers played up the theme of 'Brando's two loves'—France Nuyen and Barbara Luna. Miss Nuyen displayed her usual tantrums for the press, while Barbara Luna withdrew with grace. Asked her feeling for Marlon, she replied, 'I'm not in love with him.'"

Oh, Barbara Luna, tell us everything. What was he really like?

Esquire
October 1979

THE GIRL FROM GOLD'S GYM

THE GIRL in Gold's Gym was standing with her face to the mirror and lifting weights. She was small, only about five feet three inches tall, but her arm muscles were perfectly defined, each muscle clearly showing, almost statue-like. Her calves were perhaps just a little too well developed to win a beauty contest. She wore a green workout leotard and a cutoff T-shirt stamped with a rose on the front; her torso was girdled by a wide leather belt, apparently the same kind of belt worn by most of the men there (who greatly outnumbered the women) to prevent their spines from collapsing under the strain.

"Listen," Lisa Lyon said when I came in, "just sit somewhere and watch; I'll be with you in half an hour or so. I can't really talk till I'm through."

So I sat down on the floor, on a green rug. Gold's Gym is near the northwest corner of Second and Broadway in Santa Monica, California. Windows opened to Second Street and were lined outside by an audience of passersby who could not tear themselves from the sight of all those men with all those muscles trying to lift more and more and more. The atmosphere of seriousness inside Gold's Gym came through in spite of continuous rock and roll FM radio blasting away. Everyone was suffering to a rhythm—maybe the wrong one. You couldn't help thinking that Gold's Gym should pipe in some Wagner, which, with its lofty aspirations and blond passions and force, would be so much more suitable.

Lisa Lyon looked adorable.

Her perfect little Bardot-Ronstadt face was framed in curls of chestnut brown caught up in a ponytail. Her brown eyes, edged by unmade-up eyelashes, sparkled, and her white teeth were perfect. Like all the truly serious people working out in Gold's Gym, she wore Nike running shoes.

In the center of the workout room at Gold's Gym were machines for pushing and lifting weights backward and on your knees and in other superhuman positions. All around the walls of the gym were signs saying REPLACE ALL WEIGHTS and low racks lined with weights and mirrors.

At the end of Lisa's workout, she and her training partner, Jay Silva—who has a transcendently angelic smile above a body packed with wedges of iron muscles and covered with ebony skin—stood in front of a full-length mirror and reviewed what needed work. "Come in here," she said to me when they finished.

I figured we'd go into a dressing room where she'd change into something else so that we could go out for lunch, and indeed she did unbuckle that wide leather belt and take it off, but that was all she took off. She makes a point of wearing her workout clothes wherever she goes; it is her idea of spreading the good word. (To my surprise, I noticed she wasn't sweating even underneath the belt around her waist, and I asked her why. She showed me another pad that encircled her waist underneath her T-shirt. It was designed to stimulate sweat—and it does—but Lisa just doesn't look like she sweats.)

"I started this bodybuilding two years ago," she told me while we were still in the gym. "Before that, I studied dancing and kendo—that's Japanese fencing. I wanted to be strong, and when I met Arnold Schwarzenegger, I saw there was potential to do something dramatic with myself." (It seems that everybody who meets Arnold gets their life changed.)

"I'd been an art student, I'd wanted to do medical illustrations, and I loved the suppleness and grace and understanding of power, plus"—she looked around as we were walking out of Gold's Gym—"I fell in love with the scene." And with that, she laughed this bad-girl laugh and her curls curled more roundly around her face, making her look even more adorable.

Lisa went to University High in L.A. Her father was an oral

surgeon; her mother, an interior designer. At UCLA, she was very political and studied criticism in its graduate film school, which, as everyone knows, is where in L.A. Karl Marx resides, at least in spirit. Today, at age twenty-six, she has a job reading and synopsizing books and scripts for American International Pictures, a job she can do mostly at home between Gold's Gym workouts.

"I could have gotten a job as story editor, but it's worth four hundred dollars a week to me to have my freedom," she told me. "I could never sit down inside all day like that."

Somehow, out in Santa Monica and even at the elegant Café California, where we went to lunch, Lisa Lyon in her workout clothes, with her sweatshirt tied around her shoulders, looked OK enough not to rock the boat. Except for her sculptured biceps, she might have been simply a tennis single from the marina or a runner from the beach. The Café California is not where I thought I'd wind up one day with some lady bodybuilder—I had thought she'd probably want to go to a health food place and drink carrot juice. But now, here she was eating an omelet and drinking café au lait just like a normal person.

"I *am* a normal person," she told me. (By this time, I was feeling that she might indeed actually be a normal person, at least the kind of normal person I usually know—the kind that every so often goes off the deep end into something.) "I mean," she went on, "everybody thinks that to be a bodybuilder you have to be a freak, but I don't think bodybuilding is very different from basketball. Except that in bodybuilding, the end you're striving for is aesthetic. That's why I think it should be taken seriously.

"Plus, even the most freaked-out, untogether person from the street who goes into Gold's, you know, just to see what's happening, well . . . the discipline transforms anybody who tries it. The energy and desire inside that place are so high, and the people are so nice and understanding. I think," she said, "you should feel free to pursue whatever you feel will benefit you. I think women should be able to have a choice in ideals of physical beauty. I mean, we're going into the eighties, and we're headed into androgyny anyway, so why not? Besides, how many women do you know who can do this, man?" she asked, and suddenly, when no one in the Café California was looking, she flexed her arm, and it turned into a burning-alive map in bas-relief of incredible muscles. Then she flashed me one of those hooky-girl smiles again and said, "It's art. It's living sculpture. Plus I can deadlift two hundred and sixty-five pounds."

"What's 'deadlift'?" I asked.

"That's from the ground."

Lisa and I know all the same people in the movie business and the art world and even in jazz (she knows the piano player who's playing with Art Pepper, who's married to my cousin). But she can deadlift 265 pounds. And she spends as much time as she can in Gold's Gym getting stronger and stronger and stronger.

This year she won the first World Women's Bodybuilding Championship. She wants to be on the President's Council on Physical Fitness. And she means to define the New Beauty for Women. "Since I started doing this," she told me, "I'm happy all the time. You just can't help it."

But she looked out the window impatiently from the Café California into the blue skies over Ocean Park, and I remembered that as she had left Jay Silva, her training partner, she made plans to meet him later at the gym. And I thought she'd be far happier once she was working again at her machine . . . on one knee bending forward as she pulled heavy lead plates . . . with rock and roll blasting overhead . . . back in Gold's Gym.

Esquire
October 1979

THE TYRANNY OF FASHION

QUENTIN Crisp once wrote something like this: "When you say things are better than they are, they call you a romanticist. When you say things are worse than they are, they call you a cynicist. But when you say things are exactly as they are, they call you a satirist." George W. S. Trow's wonderful volume of stories is a victory for things exactly as they are.

Terrible images conjured up in these stories seem bound to linger for a lifetime in one's brain. Images of restaurants "that had to close because of the small green snails appearing suddenly everywhere." Or this: "Like my ex-wife, my rug wants to exist in a nonjudgmental atmosphere."

Part of the time, Mr. Trow writes in a terminal travel-brochure style, as when his prose attempts to transcend by cheeriness an intractable resort hotel called the Hotel Reine-American, which is located on a strip of lost-cause oceanfront property called Alani Beach. Of course, every so often, the hopelessness of Alani Beach leaks out, and we are given a slap in the face of what caused the hotel to fall apart in the first place: the "killing damp," for example, or the "red stinging plants that have recently been afloat, clinging together in red clumps like coagulated blood." But all the while, we're brightly assured that "Alani Beach and the whole Alani area are more nearly alive than they've been for years."

Other times, George W. S. Trow writes in an innocent style you usually see in the Talk of the Town section of *The New Yorker*. Only this time the bright and genial prose is out to make bearable not reptile exhibits or a certain special cheese importer—this time Mr.

Trow's friendly words are out to describe Mrs. Armand Reef (who "Likes to Entertain"). Mrs. Armand Reef, a divorcée who lives on the Upper East Side and endorses products like "Body Dew" and "Ultra Vodka," discusses who is asked to her "little dinner parties": "To be asked to one of my little dinner parties you must have great intelligence. And wit. I value wit. I love the clever thing—the thing that just *glances off* the truth and circles back to something topical." She then goes on to say, "I find that high-powered dynamic men like to humiliate easy women and that makes a party go..."

There is a story called "At Lunch With the Rock Critic Establishment," which to me—having spent my youth in the jaws of rock and roll, designing album covers and spending so much time with people like those he describes that I *know* he's saying things are exactly as they are—is worth the price of the whole book. The sort of rock critics Mr. Trow describes are the ones who write three-page essays on the first four notes of the Eagles' "Take It Easy," showing these notes as proof that the Eagles are corrupt and Too L.A. and that nobody could possibly take them seriously but teenagers. One of the members of the Rock Critic Establishment, Lester Rax, has "always stood for complete integrity," and when a publicist tries to fool him with a band called "Traitor," he knows the band is only hype. "This kid Calvin," Lester says, "wasn't he...didn't he...do backup for Donovan?"

"He was a *child*," the publicist protests and says: "My God, you can't hold that against him. And he was very disillusioned. He practically had a breakdown. It was *very painful*."

To have to apologize to a member of the Rock Critic Establishment for a band member because he once played backup for Donovan is *exactly* how things are.

What happens when you read Trow's stories is that you begin to see everything quite clearly. Suddenly, a fabulous place that boasts of "hotels with perfect security" becomes transparent.

And Trow, who is himself a master of style when he writes, seems to be using it to show that style, taste, those little refinements used in everyday life to separate the elegant and delightful from the rest of us, are nothing more than "specifics." So that having the specifically right shoes, the right shirts, the right old furniture and new friends is nothing but a collection of specific details imposed by those in fashion. And those in fashion are nothing more than bullies. Yet those who are bullied seem so eager to soak up the specifics and details of what is in style and what isn't, that unless they read Mr. Trow's book, they may go on and on without ever stopping to think what fashion really means.

But once you've read these stories, it will seem that in fashion, bullies are all there are. Or ever will be.

The New York Times Book Review
April 20, 1980

TIFFANY'S BEFORE BREAKFAST

I'M FORCED to pause, whenever I'm going to have a nervous breakdown, and consider the single most obvious objection: I can't afford one. I mean, if I am going to collapse, I'm certainly not going to do so unless there is so much money nearby that I needn't worry for a moment about how much it's going to cost to be whisked off to Switzerland for a two-week sleep cure; nor—in *my* nervous breakdown—would I want to mind the expense of a three-month convalescence somewhere in Italy—probably Lake Como—where, on my hotel balcony chaise, I could gaze upon peaceful scenery as I penned letters to concerned friends assuring them that I was OK. Unless I can afford a Henry James one, I'd prefer to postpone my nervous breakdown till next summer.

In the meantime, I call my sister. Only my sister, these days, has been blooming with peace of mind, occupying herself totally with fund-raising for Cesar Chavez (*La Causa*); funds for retired farm workers' pension homes and health clinics and education. She's always in places like La Paz in the Tehachapis, just when I have scrambled brains and other conditions which I'm sure could be cured if I were out picking grapes for even one day rather than sighing over Lake Como.

Oh, I nearly forgot—before I telephone my sister, if my lover happens to be nearby, I simply fly into a rage at him and then have a hot-fudge sundae and am all better. Only my lover is in South America shooting pictures and my sister is unavailable because she is ironing "There's Blood on Those Grapes" decals onto white T-shirts for future rallies. So I am forced to rely on two other women.

Ginny, the oldest of my friends, is helpful because she's a list maker. Instead of letting everything all over fall apart in your brain, Ginny lists the words and eliminates some, and, as though by magic, the world stops trembling, quiets down, life can go on. Only Ginny is in Japan with her handsome sexy boss eating sushi, and when I find out how much it costs to call Japan and the length of the list.... Besides, I probably wouldn't be able to hear her.

That leaves Tina. Now Tina and I always—well—get together for my nervous breakdowns. The great thing about Tina is that she has suggestions. I *hate* it when you call someone and say "My God, what am I going to *do*?" and they say, "Gee, uh...have you looked in the *TV Guide*?" Tina is never dreary.

Once, for example, after I'd not eaten for three days and was seeing everything twice, like Joseph Heller's soldier in white, Tina said, "I'll come right this minute, honey, what you need is red meat."

Now everyone knows that you don't need red meat ever, especially after you haven't eaten for three days, but Tina came in her white car (forever, in my mind, an ambulance) and whisked me to a place which whisked this red meat before me and Tina would not let me so much as go to the ladies' room until I finished every last bite. Despite her unlikely remedy, I recovered so fast that I began seeing everything just once by the time we were back at my place. I was so enormously impressed by how fast she'd gotten her remedy in front of me, how seriously she'd taken my declaration of collapse. But then Tina has always been a Real Friend.

"Tina, Tina..." I called last night, "...oh, I'm so glad you're home! I've gotten in too deep, I can't do anything. I've...got ants and no money! I am having a nervous breakdown just *thinking* of these things. I've got ants, Tina. *Ants!* But I can't..."

"Oh, honey, what you need is something to eat," Tina said.

So we met at Nickodell's, a thirties Hollywood restaurant which has stuff like "turkey croquettes" on the menu, it's so Mildred Pierce. Nickodell's—it's sort of the only place in L.A. you can go without accidentally bumping into an alfalfa sprout. It makes you feel grounded. It's a good place to discuss your nervous breakdown.

"Shall I pick you up?" Tina had asked.

"No..." I'd said. I shall never again be that shaky, I hope, as to have to be driven in her ambulance.

It wasn't just the ants, you see. It was that in a burst of some inner will to let go of the railing and drop into the snake pit, I said, "yes," I'd just love doing all these projects. I'd allowed my lover to talk me into going on a five-day publicity junket near the Cook Islands—to a place called Rarotonga—a place I'd subsequently write about for two magazines that I'd breezily telephoned and convinced it was a wonderful idea. Since I hate traveling, why did I do that? One of the magazines would want an In-Depth, encyclopedic inventory of this place or else I'd be rejected, which is just about worse than ants. I'd also known all along that any moment now a gigantic reedited six-hundred-page manuscript of my new book was going to land on my head from my editor who'd expect me to be thinking of the book, the whole book, and nothing but the book so help me God, until it was finished or I died, whichever came first. In the meantime, I was to write a piece for a local magazine about an old haunt of mine, a place the magazine wanted me to sort of sneer at but which practically made me burst into tears of past desire just remembering all those nights.... And then there were these ants!

"Well," Tina said, "you pay for the dinner on your card and I'll give you cash and you stop off at Ralph's supermarket and get ant poison if all that's between you and the ants is no cash. Why didn't you get cash from the bank on Friday?"

"Because on Friday, I couldn't..." I moaned. On Friday, I couldn't speak. I couldn't put my shoes on on Friday. How could I get to the bank?

"Now," she said, ordering another carton of milk, "about Rarotonga."

At one time, Tina had been the secretary of a very responsible, very respected American author whose reputation was flawless and whose literary career was unstained by mad Rarotonga-like insanities.

"Whenever he'd got himself on overload..."

"*He* got *himself* on overload? *Him*?" I mean, my image of him was a majestic master of evenly spaced considerations, calm voices, clarity and peace of mind.

"Oh, he'd always do that," she said. "I mean, he'd wind up throwing all the dishes at the kitchen door, he'd be so furious at the holes he'd walked into himself, eyes wide open.... Anyway, what he'd do was, he'd write these notes—on Tiffany notepaper with the engraved monogram—about how he'd simply gotten some 'unexpected unavoidable thing,' how he'd be 'so happy in the future to work with the editors' or whoever and how 'if there were *anything* he could do to help....' It was the Tiffany's, of course, it just killed 'em."

"The Tiffany's?" I asked.

"Sure," she said, "you go to Tiffany's and you go to their stationery department and you order yourself this engraved notepaper with your name and address and all on the envelope ... I'm telling you, it'll have you out of Rarotonga in two seconds. *And* they'll think you're responsible."

On my way home from Nickodell's, I bought the ant poison and brought their march to an abrupt halt. I then lay down upon my bed and thought about Tiffany's and stationery and life, and how much calmer it would be having my own stationery than causing all that commotion collapsing in front of editors. Besmirching my reputation.

Not pausing for breakfast, I was at Tiffany & Co. at 9:45 the next morning. Before the place opened, it looked as though only stone could be behind those doors—the doors to Tiffany's in Beverly Hills are every bit as enormous and twelve times as forbidding as the Gates of Paradise in Florence. But at ten, you hardly saw these gigantic gates as you floated into several large and well-lit rooms of silver, porcelain, and diamonds.

"May I . . . ?" asked a man in charge—who was used to seeing people in jeans and shirts with paint on them—this being California—entering Tiffany's and knowing what they wanted.

"Stationery," I said. And I was led to the special stationery lady who was also absolutely blind to how L.A. I was and how Fifth Avenue she and the store were.

For about an hour, we went over just exactly what it was I had in mind. *I* didn't know. I mean, I knew I wanted this paper to write notes to editors which would make them think I was a fine upstanding bastion of the community, but on the other hand, the papers were so beautiful, I wanted them all. Only all I needed was one simple card and one simple envelope. And the stationery lady eventually extracted this information from my reluctant lips. Just exactly what it was I had in mind was too tangled; she would, instead, give me just what I needed.

"So you need one hundred cards and one hundred envelopes," she decided, "to begin. Afterwards, if you decide that you want more, we will have your information, the die, and you will be able to reorder whenever you feel it necessary."

So she got me with sanity on the amount and the size. But on color, she lost. Of course, what I ought to have gotten was "Ecru-White Kid" with black engraving or, at worst, dark green or brown script. What I ended up extracting from this valiant woman was a sort of buff-peach, a shade only lately introduced into the line. In the line only two months, in fact. (The other new color was ribald Shocking Pink, a jet-set color.)

And if it weren't bad enough that my first venture into Tiffany stationery was cards of buff-peach, it turned out that the color of the engraved script I wanted was turquoise.

Her frozen downcast eyes immediately told me I was never going to get by with anything so demented as turquoise.

"Well…" I sighed, scanning the chart—*I* didn't want proper brown, proper forest green, proper dark gray, "how about red?"

"A deep red," she reluctantly agreed, ready for me, "here…this might look very nice with that color paper."

The red she pointed to was this sort of proper maroon. *I* didn't want proper maroon. I wanted bloodcurdling scarlet. I submitted to proper maroon for a whole five minutes, until I realized that I wasn't even getting turquoise, this was costing $100, and I *wanted* bloodcurdling scarlet! So scarlet it was. She had to bow to my demand—after all, I was a customer and this was Tiffany's—and after advising the customer three times upon the simple goodness of maroon and getting a cool insistence upon bloodcurdling scarlet...what could she do?

"Maybe next time," I told her, "I'll get the darker red."

"Well, if you like the color you have chosen..." she said. "Perhaps—who knows—at any rate, it will certainly be original."

"Next time, I'm getting the turquoise," I was thinking as I flew down the street of Beverly Hills, dressed in my jeans and sandals and shirt with the paint on it, composing demure but conscientious little scrawls about why I'd never be able to write about Rarotonga, although "perhaps in the future...."

I had breakfast at lunchtime.

It'll take five weeks for my first Tiffany cards to arrive from wherever Tiffany feels is best insofar as engraving is concerned, and in the meantime, I've had to write short little notes on ordinary stationery—notes which nevertheless appear to any beholder to have been charmingly composed by the firm hand of one of our country's less neurotic writers, one of our nation's leading women who understands tradition and good manners.

And my lover should be back within the week, thank heaven, because it's his fault I had to spend $100 on stationery, and I shall fly into a rage, have a hot-fudge sundae, and feel slightly sorry for poor Henry James who had to go all the way to England and change his citizenship when a simple trip to Tiffany's might have saved him the trouble.

Vogue
September 1980

SKIN DEEP
A Story

MY FIRST irrevocable loss with a man was the afternoon in a Mexican jungle when it was raining so greenly it seemed made of lime juice, and my own father absolutely refused to buy me this leopard skin with the bullet hole in its head. I was twelve.

"But Daddy," I pointed out in disbelief, "we'll never see one again."

"It's $24," he snapped, handsomer than men in those days used to be, "and you spent all your allowance. This is what happens when you don't save! And besides, you can't have everything."

"But Daddy...." I wept all the way to the end of the green jungle and up onto dry land into New Mexico, where blue corn enchiladas made us all wish for peanut butter even more desperately than we had in Mexico City, where everything made us wish for peanut butter.

"I'll never be happy again," I said, pushing the black tortilla (blue corn looks black on a plate) under a napkin.

"What would you do with it anyway?" my nine-year-old sister wondered later that night, when we lay in the same motel bed with the horrible highway outside with horrible trucks and I longed for my bedroom in Hollywood—Hollywood where everyone knew you *could* have everything.

"*Do* with it," I cried. "Lie on it naked when men were in love with me. What do you *think*?"

"Oh," she said.

"Now no one will ever love me," I moaned.

"Ever?"

"Well, they might love me," I sighed, "but it won't be right. Nothing will ever be right for me again."

And of course it was true, because nobody ever did love me right—or if they did, well, take Buddy for example.

Buddy Fiore (which everyone pronounced Fury) was the legend by which girls who went to Hollywood High judged cuteness. They'd say, "This guy's eyelashes were a lot like Buddy's—his eyes were plain old brown like anyone's—but his *eyelashes*...." Or: "We were at Bob's having hamburgers last night when Buddy drove up in that ice-blue Impala convertible, and Roz thought for sure this time he was going to ask for her number, but he didn't. When he smiled, I thought I was going to faint." Or: "From behind I thought it was Buddy, but then I saw he was much shorter. Plus he didn't have the shoulders."

The trouble was I arrived at Hollywood High a year after Buddy had graduated, and because I wasn't "in" with the sorority girls, I never got invited to parties where guys like Buddy might devastate me in person. And all I wanted—if I couldn't lie naked on the leopard skin—was for someone like Buddy to buy me a Coke at Bob's.

As the hot skies of Hollywood High flashed above in May, and summer drew closer, my best friend, Dulcie, and I grew more and more restless. Here we were, sixteen years old, and *still* nothing had happened.

"I know what let's do today," Dulcie blurted one morning. We were on our way to school in her moth-eaten Hudson, and it was so smoggy that smoking cigarettes seemed redundant, though we did it anyway.

"What?" I said.

"Let's go to the beach," she said.

"You mean ditch school?" I was scandalized.

"It's so hot," she moaned. "We could get tan, go swimming."

"Ditch school?" I was still scandalized.

"Everyone else does it," she pointed out.

"Where are our bathing suits?" I wondered.

"In my trunk. From last summer," she said.

"Oh," I said.

"So let's," she said.

"Well...." I said, "OK."

Fun seemed the easiest thing in the world, and if we couldn't have The Prince, we could at least be sophisticated and jaded and world-weary and ditch school.

Dulcie began to sing torch songs, and the skies over school were behind us.

But as we got nearer the beach, the day grew overcast and cold, and by the time we arrived at the poor ocean, it was ridiculous. We were the only two human beings in the Western world in a car in the parking lot in Santa Monica, and even the lifeguards were home watching TV.

"Well...." Dulcie said, looking around in the icy silence.

"Maybe it'll clear up," I said.

"I hear you can get tan even when...." Dulcie said doubtfully, because how a ray of sunshine would reach our bodies was beyond us both.

We doggedly changed into our bathing suits—Dulcie into her adorable pink bikini and me into my Cole of California leopard-skin one-piece that made me look exactly like Sheena, Queen of the Jungle. To see me in this suit, in fact, with my long blond hair almost to my waist and breasts so spectacular that to this day I've never gotten a traffic ticket, you'd realize that I was cute enough to get in with the popular girls, and it must have been something really demented in my attitude that kept those sororities from having a thing to do with me.

We threw our towels down on the damp sands of Sorrento Beach and threw our freezing bodies gamely on top, trusting we could get tan even in Iceland.

"Uh...," Dulcie said, "let's not go in, don't you think?"

"Go in? Where? The ocean!" I squeaked, "No, let's *not*!"

And with that we both burst into such hysterical laughter that maybe the gods decided to give us a break out of largesse.

Not that the skies cleared or anything remotely like that. What happened was that suddenly....

Suddenly a third body was lying next to ours. To mine. A man's. Beauty.

"Hi," he sweetly—like mangos, sweet with exotic impulses—said.

"Oh, hi," I said, as nonchalantly as I could, considering I felt like I'd been hit in the solar plexus with a bag of cement. Even his hands were gorgeous.

"I'm Bud," he said.

"Buddy?" I asked.

"You know me?" he sounded surprised.

The funny things was, Buddy looked a lot like that leopard—or at least a panther. His cheekbones were so pronounced, and the skin covered his face so tightly, but aglow somehow, that he not only seemed to burn from within but to be constructed of deep pile, like sleek fur. He was a panther. And it was no wonder that girls sometimes called him a tiger—not because of fierceness but because of the way he moved, the way his eyes were set aslant in their sockets, eyes the color of golden lagoons. He was slender as a reed, and his shoulders made a triangle to his narrow waist. And if that wasn't enough, his legs settled things once and for all. Even his feet were tan, tensile paws. And his hands were the hands of Prince Charming.

And to think I almost didn't come.

"Huh?" I said.

"You know my name," he said. By this time, I was so lost in his eyes I wanted to cry from joy. They were why art was invented, to convey just his particular beauty. It never needed to be sunny again as far as I was concerned. Just so long as he smiled.

I felt my insides had marbleized.

"I really think you're cute," he said. (By this time I was laying on my side so he wasn't stuck just flirting with my back.) "What's your phone number?"

"I don't have a pen," I said. There he was in cutoffs; how could he get my phone number? But Dulcie had a ballpoint in her purse, and he wrote my number on his hand.

"Is it all right if I call you?" he asked.

(THAT SMILE—THOSE TEETH—THAT OOOOOH
VOICE—NOT FAIR.)

"Call me? Yes. Tonight!"

"I can't tonight," he said. "Tomorrow night."

"OK," I said.

"Is it OK if I call you late?" he asked.

"Yes," I said, deciding to sleep with the phone in my room.

So he rose to his heartbreak-hotel height and vanished into the fog, and I felt like my life had begun.

"He looks like Elizabeth Taylor," Dulcie screamed. (For her, guys who looked like Elizabeth Taylor were the only reason to go on.)

"No he doesn't," I said. "James Dean."

"James Dean. His hair's black. He's got those Elizabeth Taylor eyelashes. James Dean?" (But what did she know.) Let's just say he looked so much like a leopard skin that all you wanted to do was lie on him naked.

And that night I slept with the phone in my room, even though he said he wouldn't call. But he did. He called at 5 a.m. I had slept in my leopard bathing suit for luck.

"Hi," he said.

"Buddy?" I said.

"What are you doing? he asked.

"Nothing," I said.

"Can I come over?" he asked.

"Uh...." I said. I slept downstairs, my parents and sister were upstairs, danger was rampant. "You could climb in my window. But you can't make any noise." So I told him where I lived, and he was there in fifteen minutes.

Now, I want you to know that I wasn't even the kind of girl who ditched school, much less the kind who invited a boy to her room at dawn—I was simply too square. And yet there was Buddy in my virgin bed, enfolding me in his firebird arms.

Nevertheless, I wouldn't even let him pull my bathing suit top down. All we did was neck with a vengeance. That's how square I was. Besides which, I was afraid if I did what he wanted, who would know? No one at Hollywood High would have the least suspicion. And what was the point of Buddy Fury if nobody knew?

He may have loved me, but it wasn't right. If it were right, he'd take me to Bob's in his ice-blue Impala and buy me a chocolate Coke in front of everybody and then, well, who cared if you got pregnant? At least everyone would know it was a holy cause.

Of course, I never asked him where he was until five in the morning, and for the next three weeks when he kept calling and leaving before my parents woke up, all we did was tangle. For some reason, he let me get away with this—maybe because he loved me.

What I did in class was pass notes to Dulcie telling her each and every heartbeat, and what happened was I left a note lying on my bedroom floor, where my mother found it and nailed my window shut. Plus I couldn't sleep with the phone in my room ever again.

But the very next morning after my window got nailed shut, Dulcie and I were on our way to Snow White's Café, where we always had our nine cigarettes and hash-brown potatoes before school, when I noticed the headlines on the *Los Angeles Herald Examiner*, which said: SALOME NILES SUED FOR ADULTERY. And not only had they printed a picture of this gorgeous redheaded movie star, Salome Niles, who did a lot of B movies, but they also printed one of her handsome agent husband, Monte Butler, *and* what looked like Buddy's high school yearbook picture. And under these pictures it said that Salome was being sued for being caught one weekend with William Fiore, a nineteen-year-old Hollywood High graduate whom she'd met doing stunts on this movie she was shooting at Universal.

"Jeez, Evie," Dulcie said. "Can you believe it?"

And that day in school all the popular girls looked very huffy and said things like, "How could he like her, she's so *old*." (She was twenty-eight.)

For months afterwards, I woke up at 5 a.m. armed with a hammer to help him undo the window in case he came back, but he never did.

Of course, I thought about him, especially once I wasn't a virgin and men did love me but never quite right (which I attributed to my leopard-skin bathing suit having worn out). But it was hard talking to people about him, because if I ran into some girl from Hollywood High and said, "Remember Buddy Fury," they'd say, "God, what a dreamboat! You didn't date him, did you?" And I couldn't say about him coming in the window because it made me sound—well, it sort of went with how bad my attitude was that I let him climb in the window like I was some backstreet wife.

Anyway, last week I was standing in line at Ralph's when I saw this strange-looking Hun in jodhpurs from some WWI movie, with a riding crop. Of course, this particular Ralph's on Sunset is in the heart of the most peculiar part of Hollywood, where punkers and weirdos and people with bad attitudes like me feel right at home. This was the same Ralph's that Joan Didion meant when she wrote about standing in line in her bikini and this lady making some remark about indecent exposure. How anyone could be indecently exposed there was up for grabs. The cashiers got so jaded ringing up checkouts that they wouldn't know what to do in someplace normal. Anyway, I was enjoying the way the Hun stood when I noticed he had hands so beautiful they tore your heart out.

Then I noticed he was 6'3", and when I saw his profile, I knew he'd have eyes like gold lagoons.

At that moment he saw me.

"Eve," he said, twenty years later.

"Buddy," I said.

"I . . . uh . . . missed you," he said.

"You never came back," I said.

"I called," he said, "but no one answered."

"Oh," I said. (It never occurred to either of us that he could call at any time but 5 a.m.)

"Where do you live?" he asked.

I had walked to Ralph's, so we got into his silver Ferrari and drove the two blocks back to the little bungalow court where I live in the back of all this wisteria and night-blooming jasmine.

He was still unbelievably beautiful, only now his hair was neon silver, and as he draped himself across my couch, I sensed the smell of Sea & Ski—which was how he always smelled—fill the air, and my insides marbleized.

He was Grace itself.

"The thing was," he said, pouring us both some wine which we forgot about, "I would go see her [Salome] and then leave and come see you. I really liked you, you know. After I met you, you were all I thought about. But things were really crazy with the divorce, and she wanted me to drive her Rolls from Rome to L.A...."

"Drive it?"

"Well, you know, go pick it up...." he said offhandedly. "And we wound up there in Rome, but I really couldn't stand being so far from L.A. But by then, two years had gone by. I stopped by your house, but you weren't there."

"Oh," I said.

"I never stopped thinking about you."

"Me either," I said.

And with that, he swooped on me like a firebird and wrapped me in his silken arms. Our clothes were off in two seconds, and for the next few hours, we mangled the past and intensified the moment in such heat that I wondered if life were really like this—love done right.

Maybe he was just a stud.

Or maybe it was just me he burst into such flames over.

Now I was older and wiser. But not much wiser.

If I had done it then, would he have stayed? Knowing men, I don't think so. On the other hand, maybe a virgin was worth more than a movie star. Even in Hollywood, where movie stars have such an edge. They say that L.A. is a shallow place. That people fall in love for stupid reasons like looks, and that beauty doesn't count, it's only skin deep.

And I suppose finding Buddy again was no reason to just go straight home to bed with him. But somehow, it was the right thing to do. It made up, somehow, for the lime juice jungle and the irrevocable loss of leopard skin of things past.

He says when he's done with this movie (he's got his own stunt company now—what he's doing for this movie is jumping out of planes), he'll take me to Bob's and buy me anything I want.

But the really great thing is yesterday morning he stopped by at 5 a.m. on his way to the studio with this illegal leopard skin he found somewhere for me. It doesn't have a bullet hole in its head, but even in Hollywood you can't have everything, so I guess my father was right.

L.A. Style
September 1985

OUT OF THE WOODS

WHENEVER I think about James Woods, it is either as the affront he was in *Split Image*, where he plays the cure almost worse than the disease for a family who wants to have their kid deprogrammed from some Moonie-type cult, or else—and this is worse, especially since I was about to go to the Beverly Hills Hotel for one of those "interview breakfasts" in broad daylight—or *else* I see him hovering over Deborah Harry in *Videodrome*, helping her indulge her decadent, perverted taste for pain, sticking long needles through her earlobes, licking drops of blood as she slinks orgasmically beneath his hot breath, his hot eyes, his hotness—his coldness. Even Pauline Kael calls him James "the Snake" Woods.

"He's such a sleaze, Eve," says the only woman I know who's immune to him. "He's like the only guy in the eighth grade who knew about sex."

"But someone had to," I reply, thinking of the moment in *Videodrome* when James Woods spots this TV show of torture that at first he flinches from, but from which he cannot turn away.

Which is exactly how I feel about him.

The Polo Lounge (or the room right next to it where they serve their gardeny breakfast) is graced by ladies in pink outfits to match the pink tablecloths and pinkness of the Beverly Hills Hotel since time began. However, most of the patrons are *in the movie business* with a vengeance not to be denied. If you like this kind of thing, then the Polo Lounge is *it*.

He arrives looking like something fresh, aslant in the sunlight and breakfast shadows of an L.A. morning. His clothes are light, his feet are light, and his expression is blank. He seems as capable of being blown out the door as a tumbleweed.

An agent clasps him on the shoulder and says in his ear: "How would you like to do Dracula for Ken Russell?" Woods tells me about it as we move into the Polo Lounge, and I feel suddenly that he is as at home here as a hustler is in a pool hall. All that energy he usually uses to punch weasels into High Art is whirling through his bloodstream.

"Dracula," I mutter, thinking it's redundant: James Woods *as* Dracula—he already *is* Dracula.

"Hi Olivia, do you have some cream, sweetheart?" he greets our waitress as we settle into one of the ivy green booths. "Did you cut your hair? You look adorable," he adds as he takes a menu from Olivia, whose hair is short, permed, and gray.

"Thank you," she says, laughing. "It looks nice for about a month, then it gets too long."

"Then you look like, uh." He pauses. "Angela Davis."

Olivia brings us breakfast, which for the forty-year-old Woods consists of a large orange juice, bacon ("real artery jammers, babe"), and a toasted bran muffin. No cigarettes—he gave them up several months before. Not long ago, he confesses, "I actually had one in my mouth and a match lit. And I thought: If God wants me to smoke this cigarette, he's going to put this match right to the end of it and I'm going to inhale. And that very moment, God, believe it or not, masquerading as a second AD, came to the trailer and said, 'You're needed on the set.' And I thought: Well, it may not be Jesus in a crèche, but it's good enough for me."

I am anxious to know how he feels to be nominated for Best Actor in *Salvador*. "It was the single happiest day of my life," he says, looking very sincere and very unsnakelike. "It's hard to explain, because people sort of expect me to be outrageous and cynical—and I am, about things that deserve cynicism. But I'm not cynical about things like having all your colleagues toast you with something like an Oscar nomination."

"How did you find out about it?"

"I unplugged my phone in the bedroom and didn't set the alarm clock, hoping to sleep through the nominations because they were at five thirty in the morning, and I couldn't imagine getting up to be disappointed one more time in my life. And I kept hearing the phone ringing in the other room. And I looked at the alarm clock and it was, like, five thirty-one. So I picked up the phone and it happened to be a friend of mine who had told me that I wasn't nominated for the Golden Globes, when I was, because he got the information wrong. So I thought he was teasing. He said, 'You got nominated.' And I said, 'This is not funny.' And I hung up on him. And then the phone started ringing some more. He said, 'I swear to God. Turn on CNN.' And I turned it on and I was stunned.

"Actors pretend to be so blasé about this stuff: 'Ah, the Oscars. They don't mean anything.' And yet I've never met an actor who hasn't been rehearsing a speech every day of his life on his way to an audition."

The agent bobs back, smiling loudly at Woods. "We just want to know, are you prepared to shoot *Dracula* in four days in between two pictures?"

"If I don't have to do any overtime," Woods replies.

The agent proceeds: "Listen, when we first tried to put this picture together four years ago, we got a call from this rock star and we flew to Washington, DC, where he was doing a concert, and the guy actually told Ken that he would be prepared to drain his blood before shooting so he could really look the part—and he said he would actually sleep in a coffin to get into the role."

Olivia serves us coffee, and the agent, at long last, leaves.

"This guy wants to drain his blood and sleep in a coffin? It's like Laurence Olivier's great line to Dustin Hoffman, who stayed up four days to look tired. He said, 'Can't you try acting?'"

I am wondering whether he felt *Platoon* had anything to do with the renewed attention being lavished on *Salvador*.

"Luckily, *Salvador* was on videocassette at the time, and people started saying, 'Gee, *Platoon* was good. I wonder what *Salvador* is like.' The problem is that you try to put a film like *Salvador* in a theater when there's fifteen hundred theaters with *Pretty in Pink* playing for the fifteenth week. Even though the theaters might be empty by the fifteenth week. But a lot of times, when you go to these sixplexes in some shopping mall somewhere in Costa Mesa, it's the same six studio pictures."

"So now that *Platoon* and *Salvador* have made it, are we going to see a slew of movies about Vietnam and Nicaragua and Beirut?"

"You know, for eighteen years of my career, I'd always hear that I wasn't a leading man. I would say, 'Well, how about Humphrey Bogart? How about Dustin Hoffman? Al Pacino? How about ...?' Even Bill Hurt is a good-looking guy, but he's not some classic walking surfboard. Each time, they sort of get it, but they only get it that one time. It seems like they go out of their way to avoid quality, to find an excuse to hire every football player and model they can. It's almost uncanny how difficult it is to convince them that maybe, instead of a run of movies about kids getting laid in the back seat of the car, maybe you could have a run of movies about Vietnam or Central America. There are two kinds of movies being made: There's *Ferris Bueller's Day Off* and there's *Ferris Bueller's Day Off*, you know, John Hughes's imbecilic movies. Will I get invited to the prom or not? Who gives a rat's ass.

"Now *Platoon* has finally done it. But if Oliver had the script of *Salvador* right now, and he brought it to a studio, they probably would say, 'God, you're great. And *Platoon* was sensational and we really want to be in business with you, but do you have anything else, maybe? Instead of this thing about Central America?'"

Before I met Woods for the first time, his press agent had told me, "The great thing about Jimmy is that you don't really have to interview him. Once he gets going, he's off." It's true.

"I hate the guy I played in *Salvador*—I think he's a total asshole. I don't hate him; I'm indifferent to him—the kind of guy who is a drunken, boring, disgusting fool who's always gypping people with money and lying and bullshitting and all the other wonderful things that compulsive obsessives do—but I loved the story. And I found a way of turning that character into a fictional amalgam of what he is and what I hoped he could be in his life, which caused untold amounts of violence between me and Oliver Stone, but the final synthesis was worthwhile."

"I hear Oliver Stone is pretty intense."

"Well, he met his match the day he walked on the *Salvador* set in Mexico with me. But our arguments were over the right stuff. They were about interpretation, balancing the picture, not making it a polemic. Not making the character too heroic, which Oliver didn't want. And not making him such a loathsome scumbag that the audience would be so turned off that they wouldn't get any of it, which was my point of view. And so we had two very antithetical points of view that resulted, I thought, in a very constructive synthesis. And I like to work that way. If it's all peaches and cream, you're in trouble, believe me. It's a cardinal rule of filmmaking that if everybody's happy at the dailies every night, you've probably got a piece of junk on your hands. We struggled through that thing like a war. We're great friends now."

"Give me an example of a fight."

"One day Oliver and I were having a terrible argument. And he said, 'You know, you're a rat and a goddamn weasel and I hate you and I hope you die!' I said, 'This is great—ten minutes before a scene.' The next day, we're doing the scene where I'm trying to convince Elpedia Carrillo to marry me. I was supposed to say to her, 'OK, so I've done some bad things in my life.' Instead, I said, 'OK, I'm a rat and a goddamn weasel!' And I threw it right in. And he said, 'Oh, you had to embarrass me, right? You have to throw it into the take.' And that came out of an argument that Oliver and I had. And he was gracious about leaving it in."

"What did Richard Boyle think of your Richard Boyle?"

"Richard was pretty content to sort of try screwing the extras and having free lunches and free drinks—which I say affectionately. He was always on the set and, in all seriousness, was concerned to make sure the Salvadoran uniforms looked right, and that the peasants looked right, and so on.

"At one point, one of Boyle's friends there said, 'Richard would never wear a Hawaiian shirt.' I said, 'No, but on the other hand, what Richard really wears is so frigging ugly that if you put it on the screen, people would walk out of the theater.' I mean, he has the worst taste in clothes imaginable. My shirts weren't what he would wear in actual fact, but they did poetically capture the spirit of Boyle more than what Boyle himself would actually wear."

"So I guess you'd work with Oliver again?" I break in, spearing a strawberry.

"He wanted me to do *Platoon*, but I didn't want to go get any more tropical diseases this year," he replies. "I'll stick by Oliver, even if his next one isn't courted and wooed by the critics. I know the vagaries of this business. I know that they can turn on him like a lightning bolt. They may; I won't. You know, John Daly, chairman of Hemdale, is doing Oliver's film after the next one. When the bigwigs who all turned down *Salvador* and *Platoon* wanted it, he said, 'Hey, John Daly was my friend. John Daly's got it.' I had a studio exec say to me, 'Well, Oliver Stone doesn't want to talk to me.' I said, 'Well, he knows that you hate him. You may work on the premise of "Hey, if it's big bucks, screw it!" But there's a moral consideration. You spit in a guy's face, he doesn't wipe it off with a hundred-dollar bill. You think I'm a piece of crap? Then I'll just stay a piece of crap and now you can't have me, even though I've been dipped in gold. Oliver believes in something. You don't. That's the difference.'"

I first met Woods in a nunnery—that's right, a *nunnery*—in downtown L.A., built on a giant estate overlooking the entire smog-laden city baking in eighty-five-degreeish desperation. The bougainvillea are staggered on the terraced garden walls; the walls are stained an Italian sepia, like a Leonardo line drawing. The mixture of downtown L.A. and this thrust of pastoral, idyllic Italy is unnerving.

But then, what about Jimmy Woods isn't.

The movie is called *Best Seller* and it's about a Joseph Wambaugh–type cop-writer (Brian Dennehy) who is contacted by a white-collar hit man (Woods) who wants Dennehy to expose the corporation he works for.

When filming stops for resetting the cameras, Woods comes to me in his Armani suit and we begin to walk down to his trailer.

Me: "Let's get serious. Where do you get your technique?"

Him: "What kind of technique?"

Me: "Do you have any technique other than plowing forward?"

Him: "I don't even know what you're talking about—technique for what?"

Me: "Acting, acting, what you do."

Him: "Yeah, I put batteries in my alarm clock and try and get here on time."

Me: "Do you have a philosophy of acting?"

Him: "I admire the James Cagney 'plant your feet on the ground, look the other guy in the eye, and tell the truth' school of acting. I'm not into the 'four hours before you go to work pretend you're a radish' school of acting."

By now we've reached this kind of luxurious trailer and spend the next few hours facing each other in claustrophobic air-conditioning across a table in a breakfast nook meant for old retired couples to play gin rummy.

Me: "They said you quit the Tavianis' new film because you were afraid of being kidnapped and wanted a twenty-four-hour-a-day bodyguard."

Him: "Actually, it was a stronger reaction. It was when I read that France and Italy provided safe havens for terrorists—and had a tacit agreement with them. And I thought: You bastards weren't objecting when we left half a million American bodies here to protect your grandmas from being raped by Russians drinking gasoline in 1945. You know what, why don't you rely on Libyan tourism?"

Me: "Are there any kinds of roles that you don't want to do, or that you wouldn't accept?"

Him: "I have made a conscious effort in the past year or two to avoid villains, only because I did a couple that were rather well received, even though they were extremely different characters. But the press can tend to typecast you. *Best Seller* is my farewell to villainy, but it was such a delicious character, I couldn't resist it."

An AD comes to summon Woods to the set. He stands in line with the rest of the people, assembling his lunch—pork chops, applesauce, peas, mashed potatoes with *lots* of gravy, and chocolate milk. Director John Flynn comes over and says, "He acts with a pin stuck through his muscle. It gives him that edge. Otherwise he falls asleep."

"Yeah, with you directing, I'm surprised I don't have narcolepsy."

"Yeah, when you sit through the rushes—"

"We could bottle those babies and sell them for Valium."

Fade to pink and the slanting sunlight of a Beverly Hills morning. We're back at the Polo Lounge. These days, Woods is busy on a new project for Atlantic Releasing Company, except that this time he's behind the camera, as well as in front of it. He's coproducing a film based on the novel *Blood on the Moon*, a murder-suspense thriller in which he stars as a Los Angeles police detective. I wonder whether, in his role as a producer, he is "nice"?

"I'm never going to be nice. Nice is what studio executives are when they're offering your part to somebody else behind your back after they've already made a deal with you."

"So what's it like to be a producer?" I ask.

"It's great, because I treat people the way I would like to have been treated when I was only an actor," he says, pushing his plate aside. "It's easy, if you're honest—if you're straightforward. If I'm asking somebody to work for less than the usual salary, what I do is bring out the budget and show it to them. I don't bullshit around with them."

"There's been a big stir about David Puttnam coming out against inflated stars' salaries," I say, glancing at the movers and shakers at nearby tables. I can talk Industry with the best of them.

"But it's not just the stars' salaries, it's the executive producers' salaries. I know that people do not go to see a movie because Jon Peters produced it. They go to see a movie because Robert Redford is starring in it. Or Oliver Stone directed it. I mean, the people who make movies should get paid for making movies, and the people who make phone calls should get paid for making phone calls—by the hour. Unfortunately, they've got it all backward in this business."

Suddenly he looks almost remorseful. "Don't get me wrong," he says. "There are studio heads who are friends of mine, whom I like very much. I always dump on these guys and I don't mean to, because I do not envy them the task they have before them. If I had to answer to the people they have to answer to, I'd probably hang myself. Their job is to make money. *The Killing Fields* was a studio movie. *Terms of Endearment*, finally, was a studio movie. And they were great movies."

This is almost too nice, so I change the subject. "You once told me that it's usually a bad sign if everything's going peaches and cream. Do you know when it's working and when it's not working?"

"Almost invariably. Not only the performance, but the feeling on the set. I mean, if I see, like, an unbelievably stupid costume on somebody, chances are that there's five other unbelievably stupid costumes on other actors, because people are either good at what they do or bad at what they do. And usually they're bad, not for lack of talent, but for lack of dedication. And that drives me crazy. The one thing that makes me want people to disappear from a set is that they're too busy doing something else and don't have time to do the job that they're getting paid for. You know, buying a string of condos in Marina del Rey or whatever else they have on their mind. My attitude is that when you make a film, you eat, drink, and sleep it. And be thankful that you can go twenty-two hours a day, because if you're spending any time less than that, you're probably not giving it your best shot."

"Are you interested in directing?" I ask.

"The T-shirt at Creative Artists Agency—have you ever seen it? It's an agent sitting behind his desk, holding his head in his hands, and there's a chair with a dog sitting in it, smoking a cigarette, and the suitcase he has says, 'Ralph, the Talking Dog.' And the caption is, 'Of course, what I really want to do is direct.' So, you know. If I ever direct, you'll know when you go to see the movie, and you can tell me."

"Is there anything else you've always wanted to—"

"—tell the world? No. I'm fine. See, I wasn't terrible after all. It's all a myth."

I actually had hoped not. But maybe so.

American Film
May 1987

THE PATH TO RADIANT PAIN

WHEN YOU live in L.A. you occasionally run into people who have lost lots of weight, started exercising and suddenly look as though they've been run backward through a time machine—which was what must have happened to my old friend Karen. I barely recognized her when I ran into her at an art opening a few years back. But then, Karen had gone too far, for not only was she slender and willowy, she also seemed to possess something else—an alarming grace. Whereas I didn't even have a flat stomach.

"What happened to you?" I asked.

"I'm doing yoga now," she said.

"Oh," I sighed. "You poor thing."

I had once gone through two months of taking yoga seriously, and I knew that yoga was too hard—and it hurts.

"Come to the Yoga Center with me," Karen kept saying. But I kept thinking of the place as the Ivan the Terrible school of yoga, because when I had gone there, an instructor named Ivan used to make us stand in the warrior pose until we got it right—which meant that I couldn't walk down the stairs afterward.

I had heard that yoga was supposed to be relaxing, but Ivan had been a devout student of B. K. S. Iyengar, who didn't think yoga should be relaxing at all. He thought it should be perfect. Iyengar's idea was that unless I held poses until my nose fell off, I was a straggler.

"Is Ivan still there?" I asked Karen one day.

"Ivan who?" she replied.

"You're sure there's no one there named Ivan?" I insisted.

"That must have been a long time ago," she said. "Now they've just got Eric and Patricia and Chad."

So I found my old brown leotard, some tights, and a barrette, and I agreed to meet Karen for one class.

There was a guy in the center of the room who was bending over to touch his toes, only instead of touching his toes and getting up, he kept his hands flat on the floor and his legs went up in a handstand. I gasped because nobody had ever done handstands when I was there before, and I'd never seen one done like this. This man removed one of his hands from the floor, folded his legs in the lotus position and just held it.

And that was Eric.

Anyway, as I recall, he only made us hold the warrior pose until our arms fell off, and not forever, which I felt was a nice change. But I did notice that we didn't do the sun salutation right at all—for instead of the liquid series of moves that I remembered, this thing involved the amazement of push-ups and these tiny jumps that seemed to me very undignified and unyoga-like. Suddenly, I had the feeling that Eric had made this routine up that minute out of a perverse impulse to throw yoga to the wind and just go crazy.

I had never seen anything like it. I made a mental note to ask Eric to please never make us do this again, but by the end of the class, I forgot and decided to sign up for a month.

At the Yoga Center you can pay for one month and take as many classes as you like, and I decided to take maybe three a week—except with me, I can't do anything in moderation, and before I knew it I was there the next day. When I realized another teacher was making us do the same weird variation of the sun salutation, spiked with push-ups and stupid little jumps again, I was extremely incensed.

The name of this exercise, I found out later, is Ashtanga yoga. Two things I noticed right away: One, nothing that happened to me the rest of the day, no matter how terrible, even remotely struck me as painful. Nothing, not emotional things like getting rejected, nor spiritual crises, nor dragging three bags of groceries straight uphill, which left everyone else panting, came close to just a few minutes of burning with shame, unable to do push-ups. All my pain was in that room and the rest of my life was simple. No wonder Karen had looked so noble and serene.

And two, I had a flat stomach. In a month.

In fact, I began to look great, and after just a few months of all this, I was up to my ears in an affair with a man I thought of as the Last Rock Star. The thing is, I never really liked rock stars. Only now I was living with one.

The only good thing about it was that the way he behaved, which had in the past driven other women up and over walls, was—compared to yoga—a distant disturbance.

The Ashtanga routine I was doing—ten minutes of perhaps an hour-and-a-half class—was nowhere near what a true Ashtanga class did: solid movement, push-ups, jumps, and sweat for an entire class. After my friend Lois took the class, she told me, "It's two hours, Eve. I thought my wrists were going to snap—and the thing is, I loved it. But when I came home afterward, my husband. . . . Well, I was just too much for him. I decided, for the sake of my marriage, to stop. Because unless you're both doing it, it's too weird. You become too advanced, in this metaphysical and physical and spiritual way—and the other person, they know."

"What do you mean," I said, "'they know'?"

"They can see it," she said, "you're sort of—I don't know—too radiant."

"Too radiant?"

"You sort of get, I don't know, drained of impurities," she explained, "and it makes you look radiant. Like you were having an affair. Or at least in love."

"No kidding," I said, feeling tempted.

But the next time I was there when the class was going on, I looked in the room and all I could see was push-ups.

By this time, I knew that the point was not to do a pose perfectly, but rather to become so warmed up that your body could do things you never thought possible.

Of course, there are those teaching yoga in Los Angeles who think doing Ashtanga is courting disaster, that people's wrists can't stand the constant push-ups, and one man told my sister, "No one over twenty-five should even think of stuff like that."

But the thing about Ashtanga is that everyone, once he or she starts doing it, comes face-to-face so quickly with the brick wall of their own physical resistance that the challenge is—or was for me, anyway—too much to ignore.

It struck me as odd that in this day and age of instant trends and people with glints in their eyes looking for the ultimate in physical insanity, Ashtanga had kept such a low profile—except that it's so hard. Too hard, in fact.

It's not just brute determination, it's something else—something more. I had no idea what I was going to do, but I knew the Rock Star had to go.

The day I came back from yoga and found the woman in red in our living room, I moved out, and a friend of mine, a woman from New York, asked me to come with her to the Hollywood YMCA and do Nautilus machines. The Y was noisy and filled with old people and kids, and I felt so at home there, it was as though I'd just returned from the moon.

At first I joined the Y, thinking I'd go to yoga at the same time. But the truth is that the Nautilus machines made my stomach so effort-lessly flat, my arms so apparently toned and my legs so willowy, I didn't really care if it was all fake—I'm so shallow, cuteness is its own reward.

So when people now hear that I walk five miles a day with weights, swim, skate, do Nautilus, and I've even signed up for ballroom danc-ing at the Y, a lot of them think I've gone crazy.

But physical insanity is in the eye of the beholder.

And now that I am no longer locked in my balancing act with the Last Rock Star, I no longer need any physical insanity to make my emotional life pale by comparison.

If I learned anything about push-ups, it's that.

Los Angeles Times
March 6, 1988

SUNSET TANGO

I USED to think that Le Dôme was a ridiculous bastion of iniquity. I mean, from the moment the restaurant opened, it was infamous for things rock stars did there at night, reflected in mirrors opulently framed in gold rococo, and the things movie stars did there at lunch against the walls of forest green. It reminded me of some Northern Italian palazzo that had been commandeered by the Nazis.

But then we are, after all, in Hollywood.

And Le Dôme is where you go for lunch when you are involved in a Hollywood scheme so preposterous you need to remind yourself that just because something's impossible, doesn't mean it can't be done.

Today, in fact, I am on my way to Le Dôme to meet two friends, both agents, both women, both victims of the cocaine wars that raged inside my head back in the days when I fired my original agent, Janet Wilton, because Megan Stanton, who wasn't an agent but a lawyer, had—I am ashamed to admit it—such great hair.

I recently went back to the first agent, having just fired the second (who didn't care), and now all I want is for Janet to meet Megan and see for herself what great hair she has, which is, I'll admit, probably impossible and definitely unbusinesslike.

But then, business has always escaped me.

After all, I grew up in Hollywood and graduated from Hollywood High School with a very strong sense that nothing on earth mattered except looks and romance.

What has been happening in my life lately though, is that looks, which I used to consider my inalienable birthright, have suddenly stopped mattering so much—because everyone is waiting for the other shoe to drop in the AIDS mess, and no matter how irresistibly gorgeous anyone is, everyone else has begun to resist. Even me.

And without lust to inspire me to some mad obsession, my urge to describe it all on paper had dwindled to going to the gym and wandering around looking for something mature and adult to capture my imagination. It wasn't until I saw this movie, *Dirty Dancing*, that I felt myself again.

Eight years ago, my casting director/producer friend, Fred Roos, called, and said, "I'll pick you up in a few minutes, we're going to Westwood."

"Westwood?"

"A movie," he said. "I want you to see something."

Only instead of a movie, we saw this horrible kids' picture called *Skatetown U.S.A*, which is about two skate gangs—the good boys, loathsome dorks led by Scott Baio, and the bad boys, motorcycle-gang types led by this guy who could skate to music so intensely he put me under a spell. The plot was that the good guys won.

"How did you like that guy?" Fred asked, on our way to Dan Tana's afterward.

"Scott Baio?" I cringed.

"No, the other one," he said, "in black."

Fred so seldom went in for rotten teenagers that I was surprised, until he told me he was looking for kids to cast in *The Outsiders*. Anyway, he knew enough about my brand of lust to believe me when I said, if the guy who could skate could talk, he should go find him right away.

It was Patrick Swayze.

I never saw *The Outsiders*, but when *Dirty Dancing* came out and I saw him again, I fell under a spell. The spell was Patrick Swayze to music.

He does a mambo at the beginning of the film that is so good, I found myself unable to breathe, sitting on the edge of my chair. If you can't have sex, at least you can have dancing.

I told everyone I knew to go see it right away. My aunt Tiby, who'd been a dancer with Martha Graham, went so nuts she told all her friends, too. I wound up taking my mother to see it, my second time, and the thing was, I loved it even more, because I knew how great he was and what was coming next.

Then I went alone.

And then I was hooked.

I began thinking about it all the time, and because the theater where it was playing was just two blocks from my gym, I began going more and more often. My sister thought I was endangering my sanity, but what sanity? All that actually happened to me was that I began taking ballroom dancing lessons at the Hollywood YMCA and, except for the tango, I wasn't that bad. The tango is harder than it looks, danced entirely on bent knees with the woman continuously backing up.

I arrive at Le Dôme five minutes early, so I go to the ladies' room downstairs, which looks like a set from a Bertolucci movie. In the dark mirror, I check out my blond hair, cut in a long, shaggy, semi-hysterical mess, which on good days, if it's spiked right, causes truck drivers to think I have great legs. But on normal days, like today, if I shake my head upside down enough, I look like Rod Stewart's idea of a good time, which is, unfortunately, slightly passé. I'm wearing black pants, a black jacket, and a silver art nouveau pin that someone gave me back in the days when Gene Clark was still in the Byrds. I don't look like a businessperson at Le Dôme. If I look like anything, it's Talent. Talent stands out loudly against the suits, especially Music Talent.

Once my hair is as good as it's going to get, I leave the bathroom and emerge into the small forest-green oval foyer, where I stand for a moment, suddenly imagining a man dressed in black, holding a shadowy woman in his arms, bursting into a wicked tango.

When Rudolph Valentino arrived in New York at the age of

eighteen in 1913, Irene and Vernon Castle were so hot, people were doing Castle imitations down the aisle to get married, and tango dancers were so sought after that women who danced married society millionaires, and men, like Valentino, who worked at Maxim's, were paid fortunes to dance with rich matrons in special ballrooms set aside just for the tango. Valentino hated rich matrons so much (except a cute one named Bianca from South America), he became too good to be a gigolo and danced professionally on the stage for hundreds of dollars a night.

Unfortunately, Bianca, who was married to a complete lout named Jack de Saulles, shot her husband dead one day, and her lawyers suggested that the farther Valentino got from New York, the better her case in court would be. So he wound up in Hollywood, where nothing was impossible even then, and left behind that lavish life in New York, where the girls wore chiffon frocks and satin shoes and were newly brazen and free. And it all must have seemed like madness, even to Americans, much less to boys from small towns in Italy just learning to speak English, tangoing the nights away.

The idea of a whole city wild over tangos, all that money, Bianca with her gun—

But I'm at Le Dôme, where nobody cares about Valentino except crazy old ladies and me.

The hostess leads me to a table in the back of the restaurant where Janet Wilton is sitting with the sun in her hair, because we are at the Wrong Table, the fault of whoever made reservations without explaining to the maître d' Who She Is. The Right Table would be in front, where we could be interrupted by everyone who comes in. But this room is almost empty enough to be cleared out for the tango. This room, in fact, could be Argentina with a little more Joseph Cornell ruin around the edges.

"Hi," Janet says. "You're still thin."

"Eternal vigilance," I reply. "I'm so glad to see you." I'm still unable to believe my luck that she agreed to take me back, after everything. Gratitude is the only emotion I seem to enjoy these days. To me,

Janet is the ultimate New Yorker, and those people don't suffer fools gladly, whereas I always am one.

"You still seeing that movie?" she wonders (she knows).

Janet is all in green, which makes her resemble some edible cloisonné object, especially with her glistening lips of purple opal. Her hair is titian and curly, and the sun frosts it like halos from behind.

"What are you doing now?" she asks, hoping it will be about sex.

"The last guy I was with," I sigh, "was such a dork, I haven't touched anyone else with a stick in maybe decades. What I do now is date tall men with good manners whose names I can't remember. If I can even remember to kiss them goodnight."

"French kiss or what?"

"Shy, sisterly, dry things," I reply. "You wouldn't be interested."

"So what *are* you doing?"

"I'm learning to tango, sort of."

"And seeing that movie," she remarks.

"Well, at least he wears shoes in this one," I explain, and proceed to tell her how much better life would be if they made a movie of Valentino in New York starring someone who could really dance, smolder, and look embarrassed and young.

"He's not going to make another dance movie," she says abruptly. "They won't let him. They'll want him to play real people."

That's all we need, more real people.

"Look," I say, "everything about him, the interviews, says he's a dancer. He grew up studying ballet in Houston—his mother taught dance. He's not going to stop just because nobody else can dance."

Janet lives in New York, where flamboyant careers like Swayze's can be overlooked, and she's surely never seen *Skatetown U.S.A.* In New York, as soon as the fake-o dancers like Jennifer Beals or John Travolta can be yanked into normalcy, everyone's relieved.

"Maybe. . . ." she shrugs, although New York wisdom is against dancers who aren't Russian.

I can see that this is one of those green occasions, when anything I want to convey has to get through a forest of New York prejudice.

This has happened before with me and Janet, but the great thing is that if you can convince *her*, you can convince *any*one.

At which point, Megan arrives looking like an Irish Valentine— her lacy collar, her bulky sweater, her low-heeled shoes, her pale skin, her hair swirling out the way I've always wished mine would.

I thought, wrongly of course, that if she represented me, I might become her. Fortunately, we are in Hollywood where being a fool for beauty doesn't always end unhappily.

"Hello," Megan laughs. "I'm late."

She sits down, and I can feel Janet Wilton beside me, all alert. Megan's sweater is perfect for Wuthering Heights.

"What are you doing in that sweater?" Janet blurts out. "People in California don't dress like that."

"Oh, I know, I know," Megan shakes her head. I have nothing to wear. I . . . never know where to go."

She sits down.

I suddenly realize that this is my dream come true, having two people I love not hate each other. Of course, I realize that rival agents aren't that likely to fall madly into eternal friendship just because I think they're both gorgeous, but I still hope that two such powerful women can rise above the fact that this is the eighties and business is business and just trade lipsticks.

Seeing the three of us, sitting at our Wrong Table at Le Dôme, people might think—because we laugh so much—that we're the Wives, instead of the Biz. But the Biz takes over the conversation as Megan and Janet swing into primary gear, feeling around for subjects that they can safely discuss without betraying themselves. Whether, for example, some guy who reads Proust is really an asshole, or if the fact that he reads at all is an extenuating circumstance.

"When you consider," Megan says, "how many of the people out here come up through the mailroom and have never even heard of F. Scott Fitzgerald—"

Megan comes from a family of Irish readers. She's read every Irish writer who ever went into print and read Joyce's *Ulysses* while she was preparing for the bar exams, graduating from Harvard number one in her class with one hand tied behind her back—so she has a soft spot for people who read anything. Janet, however, comes from a family of Jewish writers, editors, agents, and general New York literati so, to her, Proust is no excuse.

Their conversation lets me slide out from under and back into the past and into possibilities of how much better the large room would look, slightly empty of tables, chairs, dessert carts, bald men—with the light casting itself from the south, slashing smokily through the dark green and gold windows, with my friends speaking, to and fro, of F. Scott and Michelangelo—while Carlos Gardel spills out in heartbroken tango of exile and a slender-waisted young man clasps his partner against his midriff, she all shimmering in beads, sagging slinkily through layers of light, layers of time, layers of romance and lust and memory.

In the tango, the woman always looks like a bird fluttering out of a tree, caught just in time.

There is a scene in *Dirty Dancing* when the Innocent Virgin sneaks into Johnny Castle's tent (Patrick Swayze's bungalow), where he's standing naked from the waist up with stomach muscles worth all of Dante. And when the Innocent Virgin asks him to dance, he does a slow ballet—which, danced by any other man of our generation, would cause kids at Saturday matinees to squeal with derision. But Swayze dances with such hot momentum and vulnerable sweetness that the whole theater comes to a full silence.

At which point lunch arrives, a salad with no feta—but I don't feel deprived with Janet and Megan at the table and what's going on in the rest of the room. I feel sated.

"…and the dancing wasn't dirty *enough*," Megan is saying as I return to audio, "*that* was the trouble."

"Not dirty enough!" I protest. "Any dirtier and—" Well, to me it was already a porno movie. God knows to what level of degradation Megan aspires.

I wonder if people looking at us can see what a maniac I've become. The waiter, apparently, doesn't notice, because when he comes to take my salad plate, he asks if I'll have dessert.

By this time, Janet and Megan can hardly wait for him to clear the plates away so they can dump their purses on the table, and they're trading blushers—which to me signals victory.

"... and so when I come to New York, after the Tea Room," Megan is saying, "you'll take me to the sweater lady. You'll go with me."

I've won. I've turned enemies into shoppers.

And it only took one lunch.

Janet and I leave Megan at the parking attendant to wait for her car and walk down in back to the lot where I've parked for free (I'm just too L.A. to hand my car over for money). Janet says, "Her hair *is* great, it really is."

But then, once Janet gets to know Megan, she's going to find out a lot of things about her that don't meet the eye—like how miserable she was in Boston about parting with all her clothes, until finally her sister came over with a Polaroid, took all her clothes out on the front lawn and recorded for posterity every miniskirt, saddle shoe, and jacket Megan ever owned, so Megan could come to California without feeling bereft. I'm sure Janet will understand, since she can't give old clothes away, either.

And Megan and Janet will have other things in common, too, including the belief that brains are everything, and if you're not smart you're in the way.

It was like that in my family. When I was growing up, my father and all his intellectually intense friends could flatten you with just a whisper of contempt.

My aunt Tiby, the one who danced with Martha Graham, was always ridiculed by my father and his friends because, in their opinion, if dancing was an art, it was the lowest one. Doing anything that involves physical exercise puts you in a good mood, and they thought the proper condition of mankind was torment and despair.

They were so pissed off, these men, that they all married dancers and kept them home so they couldn't move at all anymore. But most of these women grew much smarter as time went by and got depressed, too.

My aunt Tiby, in fact, was so wrapped up in this union organizer she married that she decided never to dance again. And it was only when he moved to Seattle and divorced her that she somehow began practicing, and I actually got to see who she was.

It was at a fund-raising benefit for Israel—and there I sat beside my father, eleven years old, all his prejudices firmly ensconced in my head, when suddenly the lights dimmed, and Tiby leaped out of the wings on wings herself—creating a giant space between her feet and the floor, a smile on her face, her arms hooked to the sky, all in black—and all at once, I knew that there was more to art than brains.

She kept exploding like firecrackers every time she moved. So when she was the one who said, "That Patrick Swayze can *really* dance," it was the ultimate recognition. I am a complete fool for dancers and have been ever since I realized there was such a thing as *physical* genius, too—people who cast spells of balance, grace, strength, and instinct. Geniuses of tempo. People who can move.

I mean, I loved my father, but eyes are eyes.

And ever since then, I've never been one of those people who think critical thought is better than beauty. It's one of the things about me Janet Wilton thinks I'll outgrow when I come to my senses and realize New York is right and Hollywood is just Hollywood.

"So you really think they're going to let that Swayze guy play Valentino?" Janet says, getting into my car. Her green slinky outfit and purple opal lips, now in broad daylight, look like a Fabergé object.

I start the car and pull out of the lot, onto the glorious Sunset Strip, which today, because it's so clear and windy, is like a painting of Monte Carlo by the sea.

The whole of Sunset Strip, in fact, looks like it's dancing, swirling, and blowing, the way people who came here before I was born say it used to look. It occurs to me that maybe my aunt Tiby thought she could fly.

"God, it's great today," I sigh, the sky so blue.

"You really think they're going to let him dance in another one," she persists, though I can feel her relaxing. She misses trying to dissuade me from my harebrained schemes.

"Look," I say, "he's a great dancer. And he's great."

She's glad to see that I'm just the same as always, but she wishes I'd just go home and write a short story about the way things are now and forget about wanting to see Patrick Swayze do the tango.

But for me, ghostly lovers from the past have always been the way things are now. I can't escape them. They slink out of the walls in layers of light, layers of memory, layers of lust, through layers of time. They burst into full-blown layers of dance.

And you don't become a dancer unless you think you have wings.

L.A. Style
May 1988

SOBER VIRGINS OF THE EIGHTIES

NOT THAT I like the eighties, but the sixties, if you ask me, weren't that great, either. I mean, in the fifties, for men to get girls into bed, they had to be good lovers, to persist, to be sensual and seductive and inevitable and spontaneous and say things like "Stay away from me, I can only mean trouble."

When I finally managed to get myself deflowered at the age of eighteen, the man was from that earlier milieu where being a good lover was the least men could do if they weren't going to marry you. It really wasn't until the "sixties" began, in about 1965, when the Beatles made being cute the be-all and end-all of the man's part of the bargain. I think it was at the party for Donovan when Jim Morrison stuck his fist through a plate-glass window that I began to realize that love and sex in the sixties was really more like a bunch of people tasting appetizers, wondering who might be good for them if they ever, in fact, decided to stay in one bedroom longer than overnight.

To me, the sixties were . . .

Well, I remember this guy named John who was so beautiful he looked like Henry Fonda in *The Grapes of Wrath*, and it was impossible to deny him anything except what he wanted, which was usually, "Let's go to Mardi Gras; I've got thirty-three cents."

"Mardi Gras?" I gasped, realizing I was about to deny him yet another thing.

"Oh, come on," he said. "We'll have fun. I've got LSD."

"But what if it rains?" I complained.

"It won't rain," he explained.

"But how will we go?"

"Hitch, sell drugs," he explained.

I also remember going to this house in Malibu that the Buffalo Springfield were renting. I dropped by one afternoon when no one was there except this girl so gorgeous in a peach satin chemise and high heels it took me a moment to realize that what she was doing, standing there in the living room, was ironing towels.

"Why are you ironing towels?" I wondered.

"Oh," she sighed, "because these guys are so beautiful, and I just love them so much. They deserve the best!"

The trick in the sixties was to grab the most sought-after member of the opposite sex and see how long you could keep him from leaving, from trying to get more than just you into bed.

It seemed that there was no hope.

Of course, now that it's the eighties, most desirable members of the opposite sex give rise to dark wonderings like "If they're so cute, why aren't they dead?"—which for me really put a damper on sex and made me actually take up chastity for almost two years. I watched everyone I knew who used to be hot stuff either drop out from what J. D. Souther called "overboogie-related" conditions like Epstein-Barr or join "programs" like AA or Cocaine Abusers Anonymous, where they seemed to come to their senses. This created clusters of what my friend Julia calls "sober virgins," for although none of these people were by any stretch of the imagination virgins, once they were sober, getting undressed in front of total strangers became a whole new ball game.

And everyone in the world went to the gym. Suddenly, men I always thought of as wispy poets had shoulders as if there were no tomorrow. And flat stomachs, Bruce Springsteen arms, and cute rear ends. And women I knew who had regarded having to park a block away as a hardship were suddenly talking about people called "trainers" coming to their homes three times a week and Palotti machines in their guest bedrooms. I myself got leg weights and went hiking around the Hollywood Hills, wondering if this was better for me than closing down the Troubadour every night.

In the meantime, I had taken up ballroom dancing, thinking that it was a good way to spend time with the opposite sex up close without having bodily fluids change hands. But the trouble with doing the tango, I discovered, was that it makes you sort of *more* sexy and languorous and in the mood than something old-fashioned should do.

Doing the tango made guys who had been "just friends" suddenly look like hot stuff. I rethought my position with one man in particular whom I had always considered too short, and I took him to bed. The truly weird thing about it was that after all those years of men who were my type being all wrong, the one I thought was all wrong was the best. Here was this man who'd been waiting and waiting and waiting, and he actually was this brilliant, fabulous lover.

In some sad way, I realize that I have AIDS to thank for my current amazing grace—since without the dread fear of death I would never in ten thousand years have slowed down enough to notice someone who I thought didn't go well with high heels. But then I remember this photograph of Igor Stravinsky and his beautiful wife, Vera—he so tiny and intense, she so overblown like a rose in summer. She always wore high heels, but then women in those days, I sometimes think, were *born* with character, whereas some of us have character thrust upon us.

But now that I have it myself, I can actually see how love and sex might have something to do with each other, rather than what I learned in the sixties: that sex was something two people did until one of them thought he'd fallen in love with someone else.

Now all I want to do is iron his towels. In a chemise and high heels.

The great thing about the eighties is that if you're still alive, there's hope. That, anyway, has changed.

Smart
Fall 1988

ATTITUDE DANCING

It used to be that if a place were the hippest and innest and most likely to attract major beauties and stars of our generation, like Helena's when it opened three or four years ago, you couldn't keep me out. I mean, I'd move there. Nothing makes me feel worse than knowing I'm missing the right party.

And yet I've never felt that way about Helena's. In fact, I have never even been to Helena's. I mean, I don't even know where, downtown, it is.

All I know about it is that it was a huge triumph the minute it opened and that everybody who's anybody living in Los Angeles or anybody from, say, New York who's attempting to see what's really going on in "this town" wants in. But even the few times when that great Christian Ed Begley Jr. offered to take me to Helena's, I never lashed myself to his side securely enough to wind up there. It's as if I have an aversion to seeing Helena if all she's going to do is run a nightclub. I mean, why would anyone, in my opinion, go see Helena if she's just going to stand there?

You see, I have already spent my passion for traipsing after her. There were days when I would show up anywhere I knew she might be just to watch her move. I was in love with her body, her eyes, the rose tattoo on her shoulder. . . .

The first time I saw Helena I was just sixteen. My mother and some of her friends dragged me to this peculiar event in Laurel Canyon— an event that entailed paying $2 to go to a party to enable some girl to get her car fixed. Or a new car. Or something to do with a broken car, a girl, and money.

"There's going to be music," my mother said, "and dancing. You'll be able to see Satya dance." Satya was this Hindu Brahman from Delhi who ran a restaurant half a block from Paramount, and he was famous in India for his dancing. And since all you ever had to say to me was that someone great was going to dance and I'd be there, I overcame my terror at being seen with my mother and went.

There were maybe a hundred people in this abandoned house in Laurel Canyon on Kirkwood. It was not a Hollywood crowd—but then in those days there was this sort of beatnik/cultural mixture of people who cared about something other than the movie business (while waiting to get into the movie business, if you see what I mean). There were old cars parked up and down Kirkwood, and from outside I could hear a Greek band.

"She's going to dance," someone told my mother.

"Who?" I asked.

"The girl whose car it is."

Satya danced first (to a record); there was a red dot on his partner's forehead, a black one on his, and greasy black eyeliner on both. They were really very silky and yet all corners—Indian dancing is all knees, elbows, and heels—but the crowd was really buzzing and humming in anticipation of the girl whose car it was. Then a wild note from the oud pierced the air, a feeling of "at last" hit the crowd, and from the kitchen, through wretched torn curtains, a blinding flash of red began tornadoing out into us. People leaped backward.

The girl had this black hair that came down to her waist like a cartoon cloud; she had this white skin on a body so taut and undulating that the red chiffon skirt had trouble keeping up; she had little cymbals on her fingers, clashing against the dreariness of the day, clashing away. Her face was covered by the red veil, but her eyes were mad with remembered violations, unmet complaints. The oud was going wild with inspired lust. Slowly, the veil fell away, and I just about stopped all bodily functions. The girl was looking at us with such naked contempt it was an art form. She was a reason to give up paradise.

Then she stood on the balls of her little white feet, lowering herself backward until her hair spread out behind her on the floor like Ophelia floating downstream—only this was an Ophelia who would have spit at Hamlet. She was a snake, a fire snake—the snake that's gonna get that eagle in the flag of Mexico, just when it thinks the snake is dead. She was like that line from the old Coasters song "Down in Mexico," where suddenly the lead vocalist's voice breaks in half and he moans, ". . . and then she did a dance like I never saw befo'."

And suddenly that moment in Laurel Canyon was filled with money. Money cut through the air like soft gray-green leaves—mixing with the dry leaves of fall. Helena stuffed bills into her costume, but she didn't stop. I, who had $3, gave her $3. The air was hot and filled with money, oud music, retsina fumes, people hypnotically chanting, and Helena's contempt—Helena, the violated Medea ready to kill her children on a matter of principle. The Medea who gave her husband's fiancée a cloth that turned into flames when the girl put it on. The Medea who killed her own brothers to help Jason escape with the Golden Fleece. The Medea who, after killing her children and making Jason pay, was sent a deus ex machina to get her away from Corinth. The Medea who escaped to Athens, where she married a king named Aegeus and caused a lot *more* trouble.

Helena was everything every tragedy of Medea has ever been—but she was alive, a girl in Laurel Canyon, getting her car fixed. And if this took mesmerizing us into cosmic shock, then so be it.

Helena's dancing so overwhelmed me with awe and happiness that when I heard later that she was at a place on Hollywood Boulevard called the Greek Village, I dragged every date there and made him pay clip-joint prices so I could see the girl move. The same oud player and band were there, and as far as I was concerned, this was it—even though people in the clip joint on Hollywood Boulevard didn't get it the same way they did in Laurel Canyon.

I heard later that Helena was married to the oud player, and once, when I was doing my sheets at a laundromat on Bronson, I saw her there—with the oud player—doing laundry.

"Oh," I said, "you are the greatest dancer."

She acted as if this compliment were ruining her day; what was she supposed to do—thank me? She just shrugged and threw stuff into the dryer. It was perfect.

Then, suddenly, Helena was in the movies. She scared people to death in *Five Easy Pieces*, talking nonstop in the back seat. And when she played that mean bitch in *Kansas City Bomber*, trying to do in Raquel Welch, I hated seeing it because people who saw her might have taken this for the real Helena, rather than the one in the red costume. But when she decided to take the roller-skating thing into society, renting the Reseda Roller Rink and inviting enough of the right people to make all the wrong people sick with envy (I got invited, thank God), her skating was so gorgeous that I felt relieved. No one who saw her skate—her discipline and passion and beauty—could mistake her for anything but what she was: an artist. The art of motion. Medea on skates.

When roller skating became so big that she couldn't keep the riffraff out, she decided her own club would be best. And after some wear and tear on those around her, from what I've heard, she had her way. And so Helena's came to pass. And she became queen of all she surveyed and even scarier than before.

About a year ago, this friend of mine—a man—was invited to Ed Ruscha's fiftieth-birthday party. This event was the hippest, innest type of occasion, held in Ed Janss's house, which is the size, I've heard, of an airplane hangar but filled with art instead of DC-3s. *Le tout* L.A. was there—Michelle Phillips, Timothy Leary (can you imagine?—just when you think you've seen everything, Timothy Leary becomes a hip insider). It was a grand meeting of the glamorous survivors up to and including Francis Ford Coppola's producer, Fred Roos, who arrived with a date. And his date was Helena.

According to my friend, Helena was dressed in a white dress so well fitted a girl of nineteen might feel it showed her flaws. But Helena's body is taut and dancer-perfect, her black hair is a cloud like Ophelia's, her shoulder has the rose tattoo, her eyes are filled with smoldering contempt. She was, as always, herself. No flaws.

"How's it going, Helena?" my friend asked, not wanting in any way to arouse in her more indignation than is normal in just plain, everyday Helena-at-a-party.

"Oh, God, I don't know. I need to find a new location."

"You don't like where the club is located now?"

"No, no," she said, "it's too far away. I need something more in West Hollywood, where you don't have to drive so far. Someplace big."

"Oh," he said. Obviously, being queen of all she surveys in the place she has now is no longer enough, and if it were she'd be mad anyway because people would think she couldn't complain—and God knows she doesn't want anyone to get off that easily. I mean we might just think we could relax and go on a picnic, just when something came up demanding our obedience.

So, now it's that Helena's isn't big enough.

I mean, if anyone told me—when she opened her club downtown, where no one in L.A. had ever been except to go to court or renew a passport—that suddenly that entire body of the population whose every move is the envy and focal point of most others, who think being in the right place at the right time with Harry Dean Stanton is what life's about, if she could drag them all the way downtown, well, anyone else would rest on his laurels.

She got them down there without moving so much as a shoulder blade. Just the you-better-do-this-for-me-right-now-or-else about her got demographics to shift. But now that she's queen of Athens, I don't know....

For me, I've gotta have more than Harry Dean.

If I'm going to follow Helena around, I want her to wrap a packed roomful of afternoon-in-gray-heat people around her torso, atop a lust-racked oud. I want the red veils, the gold coins, the oud, the money, money, money. I mean, Helena sweeping out from behind the wretched torn curtains—a blaze of Medea red—the Helena of "...and then she did a dance like I never saw befo'."

For that I would go anywhere.

Smart
January–February 1989

RONSTADT FOR PRESIDENT

I HAVE been thinking that Linda Ronstadt is more politically effective than Jane Fonda. Linda has made the world safe for Mexican music. I mean, all Jane's done is to go from being a movie star's daughter to not quite apologizing for Vietnam with that Tom Hayden, the reason, I've heard, the women's movement was instigated in the first place. The worst that Linda's ever done is to think Jerry Brown was maybe a little cuter than he actually was, and who can blame a girl for that? At least she didn't marry him.

Watching Linda sing that great mariachi song at the Grammys was what gave me the idea—because it was really the first time I'd heard her sing anything where she wasn't getting a knife in her heart over some man (unless that was what was happening in Spanish and I didn't notice). Her voice and everything about her was so opulent with happiness and excellence that it seemed to me she could take this entire country for a grand ride that would last at least eight years, if not more, if we elected her to something she deserves, like president.

She could date all the other heads of state and we'd hear a lot of great songs and meet a lot of new musicians, and there'd be a lot of great parties and the *bon temps* would definitely *rouler*. Naturally, it would be a musicological term of office, since there's really nothing that Linda does better than sing—the notes floating out of her throat into the sky like pale-pink and yellow and lavender clouds one day and hot chili-pepper reds and *anaranjados* and *negros* the next, when she's in a less pastel and more *caliente* mode.

I mean, talk about making a silk purse out of a sow's ear—Linda has gone from what in most of us would lead to heart disease, obesity, and gas (i.e., Mexican-restaurant ambience) and she's turned it into this great *Songs of My Father* album and gets to wear the dangling earrings, a rose in her hair, and those cute little boots. It's really adorable—another adorable episode in a life already strewn with adorable moments. And the great thing about Linda is that none of her adorable moments has involved Republicans even for an instant, proving that no matter how cute a guy is, there's a point beyond which she will not go.

I remember the first time I ever saw Linda Ronstadt in person. It was in the Troubadour, and she was on her way into the club part, talking a mile a minute to two gray-haired business types, complaining about not being able to get a band together. This was in the late sixties, after she'd broken up with the Stone Poneys—and all these men in the music business were dreaming of producing a hit album with her, something that would show off her incredible voice. And yet, despite her incredible voice, for a long time, well, she would do albums that weren't hits, and so another producer would be a thing of the past.

Meanwhile, men like Hugh Hefner would be propositioning her with "Let's just shoot you with no clothes on, why don't we?" and casting directors were trying to interest her in movies.

"That's not what I am, Eve," she said, laughing and laughing. "*Me* with no clothes, imagine!"

"But what about movies?" I said.

"Too boring."

That was one thing about Linda: movies were absolutely too boring for her—if she wasn't singing and on the stage, she preferred lying around reading the *Wall Street Journal* and adding to the piles of books stacked up in her living room.

She was sure that one day she'd get around to buying bookcases, but it wasn't until I saw her house in Brentwood with built-in bookcases that I ever saw one of her living rooms not perilous with volumes you had to step over or around. When she wasn't lying around reading or finding herself embroiled in some romance and isolated beyond phone calls, she was running around the Hollywood Reservoir, taking aerobics at some gym, or otherwise endlessly battling her constant impulse to make chocolate cakes, brownies, or thick stews. Or going to Lucy's El Adobe for the wrong kind of Mexican food or eating stuff like the papaya chicken at Nuclear Nuance.

Her favorite books in those days were political histories and F. Scott Fitzgerald's *Pat Hobby Stories*. I kid you not. I mean, Linda is just your normal good-time overeater type of person, whereas Jane Fonda, as she mentions in her book, was a bulimic—one of those sneaky people who eat and eat and then throw up. And bulimia is not what I want in a politician at all. I want things to stay down. And I want Linda to sing a slow, sexy double-entendre version of "You're Just Too Marvelous" to Gorbachev.

Anyway, we've missed Linda, stuck up there wherever she is with George Lucas, making brownies, and it was great to see her on the Grammys, looking so Rosarita-y and confident.

She certainly has my vote.

Smart
May–June 1989

RAPTURE OF THE SHALLOWS

L.A. ARTISTS have finally proved that good art and the good life can blissfully coexist.

Three years or so ago, a woman friend of mine from SoHo (the type who looked like Laurie Anderson, although I was so dumb and untraveled in those days I had no idea a whole slew of girls looked that way) began telling me about an art exhibit that was coming from New York to the Margo Leavin Gallery in Los Angeles and would be here in three months, then two months, then a month, a week—and suddenly we were there. I in this sort of go-to-art-opening, Matisse-looking skirt with my usual because-I've-got-a-flat-stomach tank top, which by then no one was wearing and hadn't for about five years.

And she, à la Laurie.

But even the men were dressed like her.

Anyway, the art was black-and-pink checkerboards with rococo gold ornaments, and I was just saying to myself, "My God, *this* can't be true," when there he was, Walter Hopps III, drinking Scotch, smoking as if his life depended on it, and looking—as usual—as if he were about to become invisible and slide into a two-dimensional cardboard replica of Marcel Duchamp. Just the sight of him made all the difference, for if Walter was there, then surely there was some excuse for it all.

Meanwhile, my friend Leslie dragged me back to the gallery office, where a woman friend of hers, an artist, was talking on the phone and wearing all black, looking like New York City itself. Finally, her friend hung up and Leslie introduced me, and this artist looked at my passé clothes and said, "God, it must be awful being stuck in L.A., where nothing's happening and there's no art."

The meaning of being nonplussed filled my body from the top of my too-blond L.A. hair to the bottom of my pearly-pink toenail polish, and I was about to say, "Listen, you uppity bitch, you button your navy-blue lips. Ed Moses was doing hideous pink and black before you were . . ." But then, of course, I didn't—because in L.A. you don't. It ain't cool.

Surfers don't.

Our myth is to smile and nod and say, "Golly, is that right?" and get on with things, since, after all, as my friend Peter Alexander once told me, "they don't have surfers on the East Coast."

In New York, people feel about art the way they feel about wine in France: if it's from California, it ain't wine because wine's French, and if it's from L.A., it ain't art because art's from New York. That's their mythic definition of art. Art comes from the squalor of Jackson Pollock drunkenly demanding to be famous, to be taken seriously, to be great. Art comes from New York because they've got the history, the family trees, the museums that won't let you in until it's too late or else *will* let you in because you're Willem de Kooning and your abstract-expressionist pictures of women look like Marilyn Monroe in a kind of East Coast depressing angst-filled way. (Whereas *our* Marilyn Monroe just kept it simple. But then she once lived in Van Nuys.)

Anyway, the myth—as Joseph Campbell has pointed out repeatedly—is what gives our lives power. Priests used to be the ones who devised the myths, but now artists are doing it. And myths depend on their geography—their places of origin—for their meaning. In other words, you can't have a myth about kayaks in Peru. In New York you have to have fame to rise from squalor, whereas in L.A. fame is squalor and, for their survival, even the famous look to the Pacific Rim countries for ways to Zen out. In L.A. power is a man alone on a surfboard in a blue atmosphere, walking on water with nothing to do all day but catch waves; in New York power is a limo, the right clothes, the right tables, Leo Castelli, vacations in the South of France (where no self-respecting surfer would last two days because the Mediterranean sucks. I mean, I've been to Cannes, and you can't so much as bodysurf on that ridiculous body of *el blando* water). The myth of L.A. is Maui. It's ashrams in India, Tibet, Nepal; Japan in cherry-blossom season; those Japanese woodcuts of mountains, snow, and water. Of course, water means everything if you live in L.A., whereas if you live in New York, water is the least of your problems. In fact, the thing is to *avoid* water.

I grew up in L.A. during the fifties, when the only thing in the county art museum that was the least bit alluring to me and my sister was the Egyptian mummy, half unwrapped so you could see its poor ancient teeth. As children, we both decided this would be the way to go, petrified and put in a museum, immortal.

In L.A. at that time, in other words, if you wanted to see real art, you went to the Henry E. Huntington Library and Art Gallery and saw *The Blue Boy* and *Pinkie*, those portraits by Thomas Gainsborough and Sir Thomas Lawrence. Nobody knew in those days about Joseph Campbell's theory that every geography has its own myths, that myths are necessary to give life meaning, and that today it is the artist who is the priest, the holy man bringing the local myths back into focus.

Meanwhile, growing up in Eagle Rock was an intuitive and entrepreneurial young man named Walter Hopps III, whose father was a doctor but who himself had decided to major in art history as well as in premed and to rustle up some galleries.

I remember him telling me, somewhere in my past, that while he was majoring in premed he happened accidentally to open some galleries just for diversion. But it wasn't until 1957 or so, when he opened the Ferus Gallery with John Altoon and Ed Kienholz, that the myth of the West began to solidify: "Whatever Walter says goes."

And what Walter Hopps said, subliminally but with perfect control, was, "*This* is the place."

"*This*," we all sort of wondered, "is the place?" We thought New York was the place. New York *says* it's the place, and we all know New York's right, so how could this—L.A.—be the place?

But soon Walter was crackling and sparkling, putting on shows at Ferus such as Kienholz's installation *Roxy's*, the whorehouse assemblage with a jukebox playing World War II songs and a madam, made of a cow's skull on top of a dressmaker's dummy, brandishing a long cigarette holder. And little by little, what with Wallace Berman getting busted for obscenity in *his* show, before we knew it people who went to the Ferus Gallery began seeing things. Things they would never forget.

That is why, to this very day, people who lived here then and remember that time, even if they were eighteen-year-old girls like me, get a reverent hush in their voices and say, "Ohhh, Walter, my God, he taught me how to see."

Now at that time, Walter, still in his twenties, was wearing mostly navy-blue suits, white shirts, dark ties, and Clark Kent glasses that chopped his face into rectangular squares and made him seem as square and cool as celery, while everyone else was burning candles at both ends, going to Barney's Beanery every night, and if an artist didn't dress like a surfer—relaxed and elegant and tan and cool—he dressed in black capes, exuded an Aleister Crowley aura, and otherwise gave the Powers of Darkness a run for their money. Walter scrupulously upheld his portrayal of a trustworthy businessman in those days when there were already enough businessmen and people were sick of them. Except rich matrons with money to buy art, of course.

There were lots of art galleries on La Cienega at that time—and one that even sold drawings by Matisse and paintings by Bonnard and Picasso—but there wasn't another spot besides the Ferus that claimed this town for its own and said, "We don't care if we are L.A.—this is the place, the rest is all noise, come here and wrap your eyes around these hypnotic Robert Irwins and sublime Larry Bells. Look at these Kenneth Price ceramics; nothing like them has been seen before. Here are Peter Alexander pyramids that'll sink you into a trance, and regard, if you will, the silly charm of Ed Ruscha, who not only paints but also throws words across his canvases like floating mementos of type and wonder. Think about Billy Al Bengston's chevron stripes and Billy Al Bengston thinking about these things as he surfs away his mornings on the blue seas of the Pacific, a man alone, walking on water, thinking about art."

It was the myth of the place, and the artists who made these myths were all *of* L.A. because they were nothing if not out for a good time, a few laughs, girls, wine, and roses. Or beer and cactus, at least.

Was surfing a powerful-enough myth to give New York's Jackson Pollock—suffering bloody murder, acting like an idiot, being mad because he wasn't famous—a run for its story line? In New York the myth was to be famous and to convince people that you were a genius *or else*; here the thing was that art was what you gave up surfing to do, and it better pay off or the priest would retire back to Maui, to his primary focus. Even people who didn't surf, who were from Oklahoma City and came here only to go to Chouinard (then one of three art schools), such as Ed Ruscha and Joe Goode and Jerry McMillan, were able to assimilate themselves into the L.A. myth because they had such an adept way of standing. They looked as though wherever they stood was the place—and L.A. was where they chose to stand. Suffering was not in our repertoire.

Now Walter Hopps did a lot of weird things in his life—things that came as rude shocks, in fact. The first incident I remember is the one where suddenly Irving Blum was running the Ferus and Walter had this job as a director of the Pasadena Art Museum, which was shaped like Grauman's Chinese Theatre, only it was in Pasadena.

Suddenly, Pasadena was the place, too—except it was not about surfers; it was about rich people with old money.

Anyway, what Walter did at the Pasadena Art Museum was persuade Marcel Duchamp not only to have a huge show there but also to stay in L.A. long enough to have the Party of the Century at the Green Hotel in Pasadena and to lay that Duchamp ethic on us once and for all—the Duchamp myth being that whatever an artist said was art was art, that art wasn't serious. You didn't see old Marcel groveling around in the gutter, drunk, grousing because he wasn't famous. Old Marcel was a dandy. A French elegance permeated the very smile he smiled, the way he stood, the way he washed his hands of art in 1923 or whenever it was and went on with the myth—playing chess. Of course, he didn't really retire, but he lied and said he did, making art seem like something you could retire from and lie about rather than something you were driven by Furies to do so you could get famous. And, anyway, once we saw old Marcel in the flesh and realized for ourselves that his smile was in earnest and not just something out of an art book and that he was, indeed, capable of having a good time in the company of outlander renegade surfers who refused to work in New York because either (a) they were from L.A. and thought this was the center of the universe or (b) they were from Oklahoma and just getting out of that place was enough for one lifetime, the Duchamp effect was cemented in. *This* could be the place.

That was just what we wanted to hear, because if old Marcel was right that art was art and not what New York decided was something you had to suffer in pursuit of, then Billy Al and Kenny and Bob Irwin could still surf.

In New York, of course, having to wait as long as Ed Ruscha has waited in order for New York to think maybe he wasn't just kidding might be considered suffering, but here it's just an easily endured reality that you can sigh about but not go overboard or get demented about its being unfair because it's usually too nice a day to do anything but gloat.

During that early time, I befriended as many of the Ferus Gallery boys as I could possibly fit into my totally abandoned, twenty-year-old social life. My criterion was cuteness, and of course the cutest has always been Ed Ruscha, who had the added allure of talking with a foreign accent, being from Oklahoma City as he was. Ed used to come to my mother's house on Thanksgiving and say, after he finished eating, "Boy, Ma Babitz sure is good to her boys."

He used his hick-sounding accent to say the most ridiculous things, and I remember an entire winter he worked in a mail-order house, painting names on cups for Christmas presents, so he could publish a small book, wrapped in classy paper and nestled in a small slipcover box, called *Twentysix Gasoline Stations*.

Inside were photographs of every gasoline station he had stopped at from Oklahoma City to L.A. When I realized this, I was so flabbergasted that all I could say was, "But Ed, how come you did this?"

"Why, *somebody* had to do it," he replied, sounding like John Wayne explaining some heroic feat. And with that, we both exploded with laughter in his old Citroën on our way downtown to La Esperanza, his favorite Mexican restaurant. La Esperanza is gone now, but Ed is still doing things because *somebody* has to, and he's the only one silly enough to care.

When Joe Goode (one of Ed's best friends from Oklahoma who moved here also) left L.A. about five years ago and moved to a farm outside Fresno, a lot of people thought he'd gone too far—that you couldn't be that distant from the water and expect any good to come of it.

But last winter, at the James Corcoran Gallery in Santa Monica, Joe had a show called *Ocean Blue Series* that was so beautiful and radiant that just seeing the things made you feel lit from within. The paintings were so blue you could feel your heart go out to them; it was as though light were shining through them from behind instead of on them from above. It was like being underwater and looking up toward the sky. I went back five times to feel those paintings on my eyes, and the whole crowd at the opening just wallowed in elation, as though they were suddenly children again.

"I'm going to write a piece about Joe Goode and maybe Ed Ruscha and Laddie Dill and ... " I told my friend Aaron, a New York collector who lives here but hates it.

"Those phony-baloney bullshit artists," he scowled. "They all suck. They're just for restaurant openings, tea at Trumps. They're all just for company. They're what you buy if you don't know about art or *care*. They're typical L.A. artists. The only good artist in L.A. is Ed Moses, and you never catch *him* at any of those places!"

"You think Joe Goode is phony?" I began, although I had a whole list of objections—I mean, Ed Moses will go have tea at Trumps (or 72 Market Street anyway) as soon as look at you. Well, maybe not tea exactly, but a drink anyway.

"Joe Goode used to be OK, *maybe*," he said, "but that Ed Ruscha hasn't done a thing but dine out since that Spam painting, and I'm ashamed of you for even mentioning their names!"

But then this is the deep-down typical reaction of a man from New York who doesn't think it's art unless the poor guy stays at home and doesn't have any fun or eat anywhere cool. I mean, it's *OK* for *him* to go to Spago on Saturday night, but God forbid he should run into Laddie John Dill there. To be an artist, the guy should be on medication, just barely keeping body and soul together on account of nervous breakdowns caused by not being famous.

Old Marcel would have been quite able to handle both Spago and art, but maybe for some people the two might get confused. Although no matter how much of a hick Ed Ruscha seems, I myself think he too can tell the difference. Of course, my friend Aaron would be a lot happier if Ed were still going to La Esperanza, but it's not open, and besides, Ed likes movie stars (who are a lot more fun to be around than to be).

But, jeez, I'm thinking to myself, I know Aaron knows a lot about art because the paintings in his house are too overbearing for words; they clash with your sensibilities here in L.A. They're like hearing the subway, and you don't want to hear the subway in L.A.

"Until five years ago," another L.A. artist told me recently, "I couldn't make a living without going through the New York art system. But over the last few years, I'm doing great and haven't had to go there once."

Compared with the fifties, when the county art museum was downtown and the only thing I liked was the mummy, L.A. has changed incredibly—I mean *now* at the art museum you can see Kenneth Price ceramic cups and saucers and Gila-monster gravy dishes, and you can see Peter Alexander's huge black-velvet painting, and you can see, well . . . who we are. The artist-priests have converted the locals enough so that the locals have now got a raging case of art fever. They are incredibly busy, buying art hand over fist, building new museums, collecting huge collections, pushing and shoving to get one of everything with a gold-rush mentality that is actually not very dignified but at least it has kept Laddie Dill in a nice lap pool, which he says I can use anytime I want.

The vision of Walter Hopps III has come to pass, but Walter has been gone forever.

So you can imagine my joy upon seeing him at the Margo Leavin Gallery that day. Finally, he was wearing more fashionable clothes and looking like an English country gentleman instead of a businessman from Denver. Of course, he'd been gone over twenty years, to New York and Washington, DC, and, I heard, now Houston, where he is running the new Menil Collection, but without him we'd just be curled up in our cocoons here, afraid of New York, mythless and unrealized. At least, maybe we would.

Anyway, I drew him aside and said, "Walter, tell me really—this is horrible, right? It all sucks?"

"No," he said.

"No?" I replied.

"It doesn't," he said, looking me square in the eye.

"Oh, *no*," I cried, realizing that if this were true, everything I knew was wrong. Which was OK, of course, since whatever Walter says goes.

I looked around again, this time trying to see with his eyes, to see what he saw, to overcome this rude shock, which Walter, after all, had been subjecting us to since time began. And suddenly the pink-and-black checkerboard with the gold rococo ornaments on top like an Atlantic City bedstead sank in. I looked at it for a long, long time. And you know, I've never forgotten it. And if I see it again, I'll be glad.

It is true that in New York life is horrible, just as it is true that in L.A. life is perfectly sublime and that all you need to make it interesting are a few sprinkles of cosmic bleeps to keep reins on the mythic blue horizon. Or, like Ruscha, a little wink of silly words that, from across a room, seems like an old friend smiling and saying, "Ain't life grand, aren't you great, isn't it perfect to be here, and aren't you glad you're not in New York?" We must remember, I suppose, that for others the truth that life is horrible *is* as true as rococo Atlantic City bedsteads, and it's not cool to make light of their plight no matter how certain we are that they brought it on themselves by putting up with the place for one minute. But to them the painful truth is the rapture of the deep, whereas to us the rapture of the shallows is more than enough.

Even old Marcel might agree to that.

Smart
July–August 1989

THE SEXUAL POLITICS OF FASHION

FOR ME, fashion is like sex: unless it's attached to a face I know or at least fantasize about, it's not worth the candle.

The trouble with these two books* is that one is about someone—Elizabeth Hawes—we come to know, and to dread in so doing, and the other is a collection of ideas about fashion written by people who aren't quite as bad as college professors trying to publish so they won't perish, but still . . . they're a long way from Diana Vreeland.

Vreeland can make you *see* the romance in clothes, whereas the introduction to *Men and Women: Dressing the Part* begins: "The freedom to choose and to create an image of self, whether in the tangible forms of appearance or the abstract qualities of self-concept, has been a celebrated source of self-expression and a chronic source of conflict."

I mean, *really*.

And this is after they've just run about ten pages of luscious color illustrations of the Beatles, a topless lady, women in satin, and an 1850 etching entitled "the Bloomer Waltz" showing a man and woman waltzing with her pantaloon bottoms peeping out of her knee-length dress—illustrations that would make you think maybe there's something alive inside this book.

But the luscious photographs and illustrations are given a continuous cold shower by the prose: Every time you get a romance or

Men and Women: Dressing the Part, edited by Claudia Brush Kidwell and Valerie Steele; and *Radical by Design: The Life and Style of Elizabeth Hawes* by Bettina Berch.

200 · EVE BABITZ

fantasy going in your head with, say, the Arrow Collar Man, you are smacked into rectitude by phrases like "gender-specific," or just the very word "gender" itself, which is enough to keep me from wanting to hear more, no matter how cute the people in the pictures are.

There's one chapter entitled "Clothing and Sexuality" by Valerie Steele that has a few faintly arousing things about it (arousing to your curiosity, if nothing else). She quotes a study that says "porters and soldiers preferred photos of large-breasted nudes in 'bedroom poses'... whereas the psychologists liked young, *predominantly dressed* girls who were 'unconventional' or 'provocative,' and who were 'displaying arms and legs'." Similarly, working-class women, according to this study, tended to like photos of "mostly undressed 'muscle men,'" while professional women "preferred unconventional, *mostly dressed* men."

She also notes that "recent research indicates that men and women often disagree on which clothes are most sexually attractive." While women in one study believed that "men were most attracted to clothes such as midriff tops, short skirts and revealing slits," the men said they were "most attracted by women's clothing that reveals the bust (such as see-through blouses or the absence of a brassiere)."

This is such old news, you could die.

This book attempts to trace all the different fashions and how they were affected by work, sports, Hollywood, haute couture, and what sex you are. The only thing I found gratifying in it was that shoulder pads lasted five years longer than French fashion had decided was good for us because of World War II when (a) French fashion went out of business, and (b) the United States government issued Order L-85 prohibiting fashion from changing so women wouldn't "discard their existing clothes" and cause a fabric shortage. So women got to have shoulder pads for five years longer—a fact that made their waists look smaller. And if you ask me, we shouldn't discard them *now* either—no matter what anyone says—because they *still* make everyone's waist look smaller, including men's, and God knows, as far as waistlines are concerned, we need all the shoulder pads we can get.

Bettina Berch's biography of Elizabeth Hawes, *Radical by Design*, is the tiresome story of a completely tiresome woman who claimed that "fashion is spinach" (i.e., a pain in the neck which we should eschew as utter nonsense) while running a French-as-could-be haute couture salon of her own in New York in the thirties and charging as much as she could for her clothes.

Her clothes, Berch writes, were "witty, distinctive, practical." They "didn't scream status" but were "just sort of easy and flattering and could be worn for ages without going out of style." In other words, they were cut on the bias; and although this is supposed to be big news, I've never seen a dress from the thirties that *wasn't* cut on the bias—in fact, I have some cut just that way. And they're not designed by Hawes.

As for her clothes being so "witty, distinctive and practical"—well, maybe they were, but in the illustrations all have high necklines, and as far as I'm concerned, you can't have fun in a high neckline—I don't care how witty you are.

Anyway, the point of this book is not about fun but rather politics and the fact that Elizabeth Hawes was determined to be radical. At Vassar she wrote her senior thesis on "the works of Ramsay MacDonald, a leading British socialist." Berch adds:

"Not surprisingly, even this very academic exposure to socialist thinking left Liz somewhat dubious about her fashion aspirations. Fortunately, one of her economics teachers...was reassuring: Liz's talents should be put to their best possible use. The world could also be a better place, the two agreed, if more people could be dressed in wonderful clothing."

Now I myself agree that "wonderful clothing" is a great idea. I don't see how this fits into politics, but if you're a person who's designing all her friends' clothes by the age of twelve and earns enough money to go to Paris by selling to a local dress shop, and if you've also studied economics at Vassar and everyone's a Marxist, I guess wonderful clothes have to be political.

Because having to go into a life of crime so she could *stay* in Paris and devote herself to wonderful clothes didn't deter her. Although some people might not think working as a "copyist"—i.e., someone hired to steal designs from the leading couturiers—is such a great political job.

She also got a job writing a fashion column for *The New Yorker*, in which she signed herself "Parisite" because much about "the fashion reporting game" offended her "on a moral level."

All her life, Hawes attempted to give herself a radical political slant—when she had her salon in New York in the thirties and visited Russia; when she went to work for *PM* magazine in the forties and then for the UAW in Detroit trying to organize women workers.

In the meantime, she was writing books, the first one being a 1938 best seller called *Fashion Is Spinach*, in which she attempted to explain to American women just what poppycock the Paris scene was.

In the fifties she returned to New York and, Berch writes, her "life at this point becomes quite obscure. She was a lot more isolated . . . she wasn't published much anymore . . . she was drinking a lot more— it seemed to soften some of the hard edges."

She died alone of cirrhosis of the liver in 1971 at the Chelsea Hotel. Berch writes that "though alcohol killed her in the end, she *did* survive into her late sixties, probably more productively than many who live much longer. After all, a life is measured not in length but in depth."

Now it seems to me if I were going to go to the trouble to write someone's biography and she ups and dies alone in the Chelsea of alcoholism, I would at least check up on what alcoholism is—and to me it is what Elizabeth Hawes was persistently about, not radicalism. I mean, if you want to be radical politically, you don't go into dress designing unless early on in life you can blur the edges enough so that inconsistencies don't get on your nerves.

To say her life had "depth" is surely a crock.

Dying alone of alcoholism with none of her friends "daring to bring it up" because "who could argue with her—who could tell her the world was worth viewing sober?"

I mean, *really*. If the world is not worth viewing sober, it's not worth designing clothes for either.

The Washington Post Book World
July 30, 1989

GOTTA DANCE

MY ONLY recommendation to a man who is even remotely thinking about ballroom dancing is to be careful. Unless you have a very large trust fund or a very strong character, don't begin at Arthur Murray. Once they hook you, they have you for life.

"Me?" you say. "Hooked? On ballroom dancing? Come on!"

I know. The only reason you'd take ballroom dancing at all would be as a joke. So that's why I'm telling you: Don't. Like a newborn duck, you'll get imprinted on your teacher and your classmates, and then they'll sign you up for lifetime lessons. Later, when you ask around, you'll discover that you could get the same lessons for less from someone who used to teach at Arthur Murray and now gives lessons himself.

Once you feel what it's like to dance with someone who knows how to dance, you'll understand what I'm talking about. You may even come to realize, as I have, that dancing is better than sex. I mean that, I really do. It's better because it's a flirtation that can go on forever and ever without being consummated; because you can do it with strangers and not feel guilty or ashamed; because you can do it outside your marriage and not get in any trouble; and because you can do it in public, with people watching and applauding. And when you're doing it right, you can't think about anything else, such as what you forgot at work or that the ceiling needs painting.

Which is why women love to dance.

There's a problem, of course. All wonderful things in life come with some sort of problem. For women, it's finding men to dance with. I've been taking ballroom-dance lessons for more than a year now and, in my class, as in most classes, the women seriously out-number the men. Not taking dance lessons is a common mistake among men. They fail to realize that dancing is one of the few things a man can learn when he's young that will come in handy later. Men who know how to dance—even a few basic steps—will never end up sad and alone, with nobody to play with, because women will always be looking for that rare man who can dance. They'll take him to night clubs and parties and on cruises, and they'll go all mushy after a simple waltz.

Men should know this, but they don't. They don't appreciate the fact that what happens between a man and a woman on a dance floor is so romantic and pure, so steeped in tender tradition that few women can resist it. There are other wonderful things about dancing. It's a return to a more innocent time, back to the days of courtship when young couples danced the fox-trot, the waltz, and even the tango, and then fell in love with the way they felt in each other's arms, moving to the music. After they fell in love, they got married. And then they stayed married.

On a dance floor, it's OK for men to take the initiative and not worry about being viewed as Neanderthals. The man is supposed to ask the woman to dance.

And once you begin to dance, the man leads. It doesn't work well if you both lead, and it's no better if you take turns. The man gets to show off his physical strength, lifting her up and twirling her around. It's a scientific fact that once a woman feels a man's strong arms around her, she feels a lot better about life in general and can't complain much at all.

Women don't complain about the fact that most of them dance better than men. If a man can't cut it on the floor, the next time he asks, "Do you want to dance?" he may get a reply such as, "I think you need more practice. Why don't we meet somewhere and try?" Women are perfectly willing to help someone learn. They'll even become the dance partner of a man they might not otherwise enter-tain in any way other than as a grave doubt. Any man who so much as wants to learn to dance is given much more slack by the women in ballroom dancing than the women are by the men, once the man has learned to dance and is totally impatient with the least imperfection. I know this marvelous dancer named Frank, who, the minute we start to tango (we take Tango Argentino class together, the dance of the truly driven), begins looking at me in the mirror and saying, "Can't you do your *ochos* on your own balance?"

Frank, in fact, had a perfectly gorgeous partner named Irena, with long red hair down to her waist and a back like a Victorian virgin, her profile so pale and sweet against his dark, Latin good looks. But Frank was such a barrel of critiques that finally, one day, she just upped and quit, saying, "I can't dance with you anymore. It's no fun."

As for me, one day I asked Frank, "Don't you like dancing with me?"

And he said, "No. Not all the time."

So I left him alone from then on, even in a class where people were expected to dance with anyone handy. I ignored him for a long time. Now he asks me to dance, nicely, and things are a lot better.

Since I began doing ballroom dancing, I've discovered that there are two types of men to dance with. There's the kind who, like me, learned everything they know from teachers and who wouldn't veer off the beaten track if an earthquake struck in midstep and with whom dancing is incredibly beautiful and brings moments of such happiness that they know they'll remember them until the day they die. And then there are the men who were born to dance, who took a few lessons when they were young and have been dancing ever since. These men regard dance as a simple way to express themselves, leading their partners into things they never dreamed of doing in a million years, and making me, at least, feel as though I've just been to a motel—or a small hotel in Santa Barbara—for the best weekend of my life.

"My God," I asked one partner, named Aldo, at the end of a slow Latin bolero. "What do you call that?"

"That," he said, smiling, "is dancing."

No wonder he has been married five times. I would have married him, if only for a few infatuated months of ballrooms, moonlight, and what he does to music. Fred Astaire was like that, I suppose. He learned a few steps in his youth and just took off when he felt like it in later life. Oh, to be in Fred Astaire's arms. Or even Ralph's arms.

I had a first date with Ralph last Saturday. We were having dinner in one of those elegant old downtown L.A. hotels that have a great restaurant, and after dinner, we walked past this hotel bar, where a combo was playing "But Not for Me."

"Oh," he said, "that's a fox-trot, right?"

"I think so," I said, wondering how a man who was only thirty-four and had been raised in Southern California would know.

"You want to try?" he said, smiling, and cherry bombs went off in my heart.

"To dance?" I said. "Oh, let's."

The floor was almost empty, maybe two other couples, and we stood for a moment while he listened for the slow/quick-quick beat, which is all a fox-trot is. And there we were, gliding away, my heart turning into cotton candy and my head in and out of the clouds. I stood up straight, my feet stayed on the floor and in that moment, I was prepared to forgive him for anything he would do for the next forty years.

The dance came to an end and he said, "That was fun." I was seeing stars so badly I could hardly talk, but when he said "One more?" I managed a feeble "Oh, I'd love to." Maybe it's the public formality of it all that makes the whole thing so private yet so intense. It took all my wits to keep from offering to be his slave for life.

"Ahhh," he said, "you're the queen of slow dances, aren't you? You're so easy to dance with, your body is the great escape."

"Now, now," I said, blushing like a love-struck kid. But I wasn't a teenager in love, I was something worse—I was a tango dancer in love.

If a year ago someone had asked me to dance a dance in a place like that, he'd have been sorry. I was worse than a heavy lead, I led myself. But now my body was fully clothed while my mind, heart, and soul were quite a different story.

"In heels," he said, "you're just the right size for me."

Was he planning our future?

When I get infatuated this completely, I tend to think of head-stones—what we'll have written on them and if he'd like the side-by-side look or prefer nice mausoleum plaques. A year ago, I might have asked his view, but now, due to the rigorously enforced charm that I acquired in tangoland, I'm as good at keeping my mouth shut as I am at keeping my back straight for the entire dance. If Ralph wants headstones, I'm sure he'll ask. I now leave it to the man to propose.

Of course, it's only a dance.

Nothing more.

But the great thing about ballroom dancing is where it can lead, if only a woman knows how to follow.

Playboy
October 1989

THE SOUP CAN AS BIG AS THE RITZ

IT'S ODD to think that last summer, while friends of Andy Warhol were waiting for the diaries to come out, Chuck Workman—this documentary filmmaker who is probably the only man hip enough to be a documentary filmmaker in New York who failed to meet Andy Warhol—was working on his new film, *Superstar*, out interviewing those same friends of Andy, friends who didn't yet know they might not like Andy anymore once they saw that book.

Now here I sit, interviewing Chuck Workman *about* interviewing Andy's friends, thinking to myself that this whole edifice is a house of mirrors, with Andy's image reflected on every surface. Well, that's what Andy was, wasn't he? A multitude of images. (Like any celebrity. Like anybody.) Only people are still trying to get to the bottom of the Mystery That Was Andy.

Andy was definitely about money, because when he died in 1987 his estate was valued at $15 million and now, two years later, I heard on the radio it's up to $100 million.

And he was definitely about being famous—except that since the book was published, Andy's image has become that of a common gossip, someone who routinely stabbed his friends in the back. People were shocked.

I wasn't surprised. I knew about Madame Récamier. After the French Revolution, Madame Récamier was considered the height of fashion in Parisian hip society and was deemed beautiful, brilliant, and kind by all who knew her. In fact, when I was younger I wanted to grow up and *become* Madame Récamier, reclining on a chaise in a backless dress, and felt mad that I was stuck in L.A.

Then I read her diaries.

She was a hog.

She was mean, vicious, and without mercy towards her friends.

Her dearest companions, she slit to ribbons.

"If that's 'kind,'" I said to myself, "I'll take L.A"

Of course, that's what diaries are for—to allow you to get out your hatred of people close to you without actually laying it on their heads and thus not getting invited anywhere anymore—but really, are artists supposed to be that craven about Warren Beatty?

Which brings us back to the first question: Was Andy an artist?

Someone once told me that she saw Andy and another painter trading silk screens and Andy was saying, "Well, these three are worth $60,000—that's $20,000 a piece."

"OK," the other artist said, "Well, this is worth $15,000 and this is worth $45,000, so we're equal."

"What I realized they were doing," my friend said later in tones of awe, "was minting money. They were creating money where nothing but silk screens had been before."

Is that art?

Believe it or not, people still debate that issue—whether Andy was a great artist or a complete fraud. Chuck Workman's documentary, for example, uses footage of an Art Students League class in which the young artists discuss Andy: some claim him as an inspiration, others insist he's bogus.

But the documentary doesn't stop at pondering Andy's artistic credibility. Chuck Workman interviewed at least twenty-five people about Andy, so you have at least twenty-five different versions of who Andy is.

So far he's talked to Sally Kirkland, Shelley Winters, Dennis Hopper, Holly Woodlawn, David Hockney, Viva, Henry Geldzahler,

Chris Makos, Ultra Violet, Joan Quinn, and Bob Colacello, among others. Three people died before Workman could get to them: Robert Mapplethorpe, Ondine, and Steve Rubell. Then there were the people like Lou Reed who didn't want to be interviewed, and Paul Morrissey, who said he "didn't want to be associated with Andy anymore" and refused to be in the documentary. For Paul not to be in a documentary about Andy Warhol just goes to show the truth about golden ages like the Age of Pericles in ancient Greece, which gets Pericles's name on it but in reality was about Socrates, Plato, and those comic and tragic playwrights. For those of us who were there, Paul Morrissey was Glue and everything else was Falling Apart. Paul got the ideas for the "Warhol" movies, cast the movies, wrote the scripts, woke the people up who were in the movies so they'd not be nodding out during their scenes, shot the film, took the film to the developers, edited it, got the movies distributed. And Andy? Andy said, "Yes."

Andy said, "Great, just great."

Andy said, "I just don't know, talk to Paul."

I suppose if you're the designated driver in a golden age, to be interviewed for a documentary about a time when you alone were awake and everyone else lived in dreams of tinfoil and superstardom, might be more than a straight street type like Paul could abide.

Then there are the people you'd expect to be interviewed in an Andy documentary, but aren't, like Halston and Bianca and Liza Minnelli, who apparently felt funny about saying anything nice about Andy after reading about themselves in his diaries.

Chuck Workman didn't ask me, but if I were reminiscing about Andy I'd say that he was about being hip. In 1963, when Andy first came to L.A., I was a teenage groupie waiting to happen. The Beatles had yet to arrive to give my life impetus and luster, but at that time L.A. was the scene of some feverish art activity. There was this place called the Ferus Gallery which showed artists who barely seemed willing to leave the beach but who somehow managed (on overcast days) to go inside and produce actual work. "I had to make a decision," Laddie John Dill once told me. "Art or surfing. I gave up surfing."

At nightfall the artists would get dressed and go off to Barney's Beanery, a hangout in West Hollywood which had the world's hottest chile and least cool jukebox (lots of Bing Crosby).

The Ferus Gallery was run by Walter Hopps, who never got tan and wore dark Brooks Brothers-y looking suits and ties. His straightness was a perfect cover for the anarchy going on in his gallery. If Walter Hopps decided someone was cool, the person was (in my opinion) cool for all eternity.

So when he explained to me one night over chile at Barney's that Andy Warhol was going to have a show at the Ferus, I said, "What? The soup can guy? You're kidding!"

How could that soup can guy be cool? (And his hair?)

In fact, when I first heard the name Andy Warhol, I thought it must be a joke, there couldn't be an artist named Andy. It sounded like a puppet on an after-school show for kids.

"He's seven jumps ahead of everyone else," Walter may have said (his way of explaining that a person was so cool you were lucky to have heard of him).

But later on, after I'd actually seen Andy, leaning against the wall at the Ferus, with his black turtleneck, his loose pants, his silver hair—looking like someone you glimpsed through blue water from a diving bell, living in another element from the rest of us, the element of fame, the mantle of self-enchantment, the wings of glamour, the aura of things to come—I changed my mind. Before the Beatles, there was Andy. No joke.

Andy Warhol, the serious, served tomato soup to those who were first come—I mean, it was ridiculous.

But it was true.

The soup as big as the Ritz.

The soup that is loaves and fishes. The soup that goes forth and multiplies. And the thing is, you can make it just as well yourself at home.

My friend Judy Henske, the blues singer, once told me regarding jewelry, "Never buy it in a store if you can make it just as well at home."

When Andy came to L.A. in 1963 and had a party at the Santa Monica Pier merry-go-round, it was the only place to be in L.A. that night. If you were with Andy in the sixties, you were in the right place. And in the sixties, being in the right place was of the essence.

Andy was usually—no, always—in a good mood. It wasn't cool to be in a good mood in those days. In 1966, when I next knew him in New York City, just about everyone else around him was pushing Tragedy in a big way. When, for example, I met Edie Sedgwick my first week in New York, she was crying. It was at this great big party, a fund-raiser for the *East Village Other* which I myself had organized in one week, seven bands playing at the Village Gate, one of which was the Velvet Underground—and there, in the dressing room, in an unironed silk blouse, Edie Sedgwick was crying tears like Tiffany baubles.

Suddenly unironed silk blouses seemed to me the perfect style. At the party that night, Yoko Ono and her first husband, Tony Cox (a conceptual artist), spent the entire evening twisting paper streamers from the rafters as part of a happening—creating more chaos than was already there, with the TV cameras and all these reporters documenting the event—well, Felliniesque is an understatement. There were dozens of reporters there, and they were more important to the audience than the audience was to them. The cameras were the news.

It was just like Marshall McLuhan said, even if he was Canadian. (But then of course a Canadian would want to think the world was a global village since otherwise he would be left out of practically everything.)

The next time I saw Edie she was sitting at the bar at Max's Kansas City with Bob Neuwirth, the famous hippest coolest art type guy of his generation, and again she was crying, this time into a gin and tonic.

Sitting there together, they were a movie—*The Two Hippest People in New York City Being Unhappy Together in Public.*

Suddenly, my ambition became to look gorgeous and miserable, but I was always so thrilled to be anywhere and do anything in those days, I never cried a single tear except when I heard that the bass player of the Fugs got drafted. But in the middle of my tears, walking across Washington Square, I ran into Jim Morrison, who'd only that day arrived in New York. "Light My Fire" was a hit and I immediately forgot why I was crying. By the time Jim was close enough to talk to, I had a plan to introduce him to Andy. I mean, one look at Jim in this black fur jacket and Andy Warhol came to mind as someone who would appreciate him. "Do you think this jacket goes with my image?" Jim asked.

So Jim and Andy met, and Andy invited Jim to come to a party with him. People invited Andy to these parties hoping he'd come alone, or just with Edie, but he always brought his own entourage— a bunch of leather-crazed beauties with Cheekbones and speedy asides. I remember one countess who lived in the Dakota gave a party for some English novelist to which Andy invited the entire Factory. She served special smoked geese and rare roast beef with horseradish dip laid out on an oaken table, which was demolished by these crazed speed freaks, who unexpectedly discovered that speed didn't ruin their appetites but rather made them eat faster. (If you weren't on speed, you weren't in New York City in the sixties. I was certainly on it. In fact, if you took speed out of New York in the sixties, it would have been Des Moines.)

Andy, however, during this particular era, ate only lemon drops in public.

He'd carry a wrinkled paper bag with him to those parties—even dinners given by hostesses in fancy penthouses—and only eat these little yellow candies.

Meanwhile, before the dinners, my friend John Wilcox of the *East Village Other* and I would go to Chock Full o' Nuts to meet Andy, who'd order a couple of toasted English muffins with marmalade which he ate for his actual dinner. The image of Andy, the artist who ate only lemon drops, was kept intact, while the real Andy couldn't resist marmalade.

That was when I discovered how much fun it was to sit beside

Andy and watch people go by Chock Full o' Nuts. Just his comments about girls in yellow boots were worth their weight in lemon drops.

After the dinner parties we'd go to the Dom, this Polish dance hall on the Lower East Side where the Velvets played and they ran movies on the walls—like *Kiss*, this movie Andy (and Paul Morrissey) made of two gorgeous kids kissing and kissing and kissing. The world's most fabulous people were dancing everywhere, and on stage was Nico, the girl lead singer of the Velvets, looking down at the audience with eyes that saw nothing but apocalyptic collapse and a voice that did nothing but emit a bagpipe-like drone.

This was definitely the place. And those were really the days. At least I, in my twenty-two-year-old wisdom, didn't see how things could be improved upon. In fact, it's been mostly downhill from there as far as Great Scenes are concerned. (Although, at the time, I did think the Velvets were too loud and not cute enough. Not as cute as Jim Morrison, anyway.)

Most people think that in the sixties Andy was one way, in the seventies another, and by the eighties he was purely a party-mad businessman. However, when I knew Andy in the early sixties he was already so party-mad that people who were serious about art were worried that a hustler had tricked the poor public into thinking he was an artist when all he was, was a manipulative genius able to marry fine art with popular culture. I thought all the people who thought Andy wasn't an artist were dragging their feet.

In fact, if you asked me, what had passed for art for the twenty years previous to Andy—that portentously tormented abstract expressionism, that Jackson Pollock, de Kooning, Motherwell stuff, was a lot harder to swallow than a nice can of soup where you could look at the picture and know where you stood. And if Andy chose to make a nightly career out of hanging around Max's Kansas City and going to parties and being surrounded by the most emaciated and gorgeous cheekbones of his generation—who could begrudge him that?

Well, if my experience is any indication, Chuck Workman has given a lot of people some very happy moments by giving them the opportunity to think about their lives with Andy. He had the knack for being around when you were having a great time (even if having a great time meant a two-day crying jag).

There's a line from Thomas Hardy about how most men at the end of their lives discover that rather than finding they've gone forth in glory, it's all they can do to retire without shame. Andy went forth in glory, and the great thing about being a real artist is that even your bullet-hole scar can be an Annie Leibovitz poster.

Movieline
November 1989

BLAME IT ON THE VCRs

WHEN I was a madwoman in the 1960s, everyone I knew was getting laid like crazy. Everyone was wild for sex: they heard the phrase *free love* and ran amok across the land. Married men, married women, squares, hippies—everyone was on the prowl, cruising for the Answer in the form of sex. Of course, if you found the Answer, you were stuck with it for all eternity, like being married, so the Answer would often change.

In the meantime, the gay men and the feminists were in the background, girding their loins against the Farrah Fawcett spun-gold hair of the seventies, trying to ruin everything. And they succeeded. Yes, men were pigs, women were exploited—yet gay men were, well, out of the closet and staying out and up till three in the morning, having more fun than anyone else ever did in the history of mankind. They made straight people jealous. Buck Henry once told me that he used to pass those bars and really get mad because the gays were having so much more fun than the straights. What the gay guys seemed programmed to prove was that, if we thought the sixties were far-out, they *really* knew how to have a party. Andy Warhol and Truman Capote *über alles.* The gay scene had a sense of mad adventure, high gossip, bitter wit, and a determination to make people beautiful, glamorous, marvelous, fabulous. The feminists, meanwhile, were having none of it. The most they'd do was buy frames for their glasses at L.A. Eyeworks, once the eighties occurred. (In *Cheap Chic,* Fran Lebowitz says that if the way people look calls attention to their clothes, they are badly dressed.)

Today the normal people who just wanted to get through life

having children and going camping have discovered that being married means both partners have to work full-time at hard jobs that take every ounce of strength and don't leave enough money—once the car insurance is paid—to *go* camping. And the peripheral women, women like me who were too neurotic to get married and have children and wanted only to stay young forever and fool around, have discovered that the available men are getting less and less interested in running amok with unbridled passion, even with women in their twenties. In fact, some of the twenty-year-old women I know never even have dates. And didn't have any as teenagers.

These days women are always telling me that "there are no men out there." This is not a new idea: *Cosmopolitan* is based on that premise, and the magazine is now twenty-five years old. But I myself have noticed that there aren't any men unless you go forage in the brush and drag them kicking and screaming into, say, a movie. But what's really amazed me lately is the number of women I know who actually have "relationships" (i.e., boyfriends, husbands, locked-in lovers) who say, "But we haven't had sex in, oh, three years." Or, "We had sex twice two years ago but ..."

If you ask me, videos are what have put the damper on most people's sex lives. People have all these incredible Glory of Western Civilization-type choices in the video stores, and they say to one another, "Oh, goody, I know what we'll do Saturday night. We'll watch the complete *Godfather*, parts one and two, and then we'll watch all these Preston Sturges movies." Their eyes are bigger than their stomachs—or some organ down there. It used to be that you'd go to a sexy movie on a thing called a "date" and come out totally inspired to go home to bed—your boyfriend with Kim Basinger, you with Mickey Rourke (or *me* with Mickey Rourke). But now Kim and Mickey are right there in the bedroom with you—because you've been too lazy to go see the movie and waited till it came out on video—and they're too small to inspire anyone to do anything but go to sleep. Sex has to be really twisted for it to do any good on a small screen.

For some reason I got the idea when I was growing up that the thing we should all be doing is having fun, but now it hardly surprises me when I learn that yet another of my women friends has packed up and left for Santa Fe, hitting the trail for the lure of cowboys and artists or other archetypes who are still supposedly interested in having fun. I can't help teasing these poor girls, insisting that heading for the hills in pursuit of romance is ridiculous and reminding them that Santa Fe is the color of pancake makeup, which makes it very difficult to take seriously.

Of course, after they get a load of what cowboys and artists are actually like, they come back older but wiser, which makes things even worse. Who needs more disillusioned people after all? Perhaps we are going to have to become dignified and resigned to a quieter, droopier time. Maybe we will all become like Henry James, eager to discover virtue, rather than vice, in situations and people.

That, I suppose, will be a nice change. Or a change anyway. But not yet. Not me.

Smart
June 1990

JIM MORRISON IS DEAD AND LIVING IN HOLLYWOOD

J.D. SOUTHER once told me he spent his first years in L.A. learning how to stand. Jim knew how to stand from the start. He stood pigeon-toed, filled with poetry against a mike with that honky-tonk Berlin organ in the background, and sang about "another kiss."

And there is something to be said for singing in tune. Jim not only sang in tune, he sang intimately—as Doors producer Paul Rothchild once pointed out to me, "Jim was the greatest crooner since Bing Crosby."

He was Bing Crosby from hell.

In those days, in the sixties, people in L.A. with romantic streaks who knew music went for the Byrds, Buffalo Springfield, Paul Butterfield—and for clubs like the Troubadour and the Trip and the Ash Grove. The Whisky, where the Doors flourished, was the kind of place where the headliner would be Johnny Rivers, a white boy who covered Chuck Berry's "Memphis." By the sixties, white boys weren't supposed to cover soul anymore, but at the Whisky it was still groovy. The Carpenters played the Whisky.

At the Whisky, the bouncers were bouncers, the management was from New York City, and the women wore beehive hairdos long after it was cool.

Rock groups who went to college and actually got degrees were not only uncool, they were unheard-of.

Jim went to college and he graduated. My friend Judy Raphael, who went to film school, too, remembers Jim as this pudgy guy with a marine haircut who worked in the library at UCLA and who was supposed to help her with her documentary term paper one night but ended up talking drunkenly and endlessly about Oedipus, which meant she had to take the course over that summer.

The Doors were embarrassing, like their name. I dragged Jim into bed before they'd decided on the name and tried to dissuade him; it was so corny naming yourself after something Aldous Huxley wrote. I mean, *The Doors of Perception* . . . what an Ojai-geeky-too-L.A.-pottery-glazer kind of uncool idea.

The Beatles were desperate criminals compared with them. The Beatles only had one leg to stand on—rock and roll. The Doors, though, were film majors. Being a film major in the sixties was hopelessly square. If you wanted to make a movie, even if you went to UCLA like Francis Coppola and then to the Roger Corman School of Never Lost a Dime Pictures, you *still* weren't cool. Even Jack Nicholson wasn't cool in the sixties. Being an actor wasn't cool in the sixties, because all movies did was get everything *all wrong*. At least until *Easy Rider*, being in the movie business was a horrible thing to admit.

Of course, Oliver Stone was *so* uncool he voluntarily went to Vietnam instead of prowling around the Sunset Strip with the rest of his generation. Oliver Stone was such a nerd he became a soldier, a Real Man. He didn't understand that in the sixties real men were not soldiers. A real man was Mick Jagger in *Performance*, in bed with two women, wearing eye makeup and kimonos. Or John Phillip Law, with wings, in *Barbarella*. Of course, Bob Dylan was even cooler than Mick Jagger, so cool he couldn't sing. He didn't bother, and he was so skinny, with those narrow little East Coast shoulders and that face. And he was mean.

Like everyone back then, Jim hated his parents, hated home, hated it all. If he could have gotten away with it, Jim would have been an orphan. He tried lying about having parents, creating his life anew—about what you'd expect from someone who'd lost thirty pounds in one summer (the summer of '65, from taking drugs instead of eating, and hanging out on the Venice boardwalk). I mean, he awoke one morning and was *so* cute, how *could* he have parents?

According to some health statistics I recently heard about, the fifties was the decade when the American diet contained its highest percentage of fat—over 50 percent. And these fifties children, over-fed, repressed, and indignant, waited in the wings, lurking and praying to get big enough to get the fuck out. Jim Morrison had it worse than a lot of kids. He was fat. And his father was a naval officer.

Then the ultimate dream of everyone who weighs too much and gets thin happened to Jim. He lost the weight and turned into the Prince.

Into John, Paul, George, and Ringo.

Into Mick.

I met Jim early in '66, when he'd just lost the weight and wore a suit made of gray suede, lashed together at the seams with lanyards, and no shirt. It was the best outfit he ever had, and he was so cute that no woman was safe. He was twenty-two, a few months younger than I.

He had the freshness and humility of someone who had been fat all his life and was now suddenly a morning glory.

I met Jim and propositioned him in three minutes, even *before* he so much as opened his mouth to sing. This great event took place not at the Whisky but at a now-forgotten club just down on the Strip called the London Fog, the first bar there the Doors played. And there were only about seven people in the room anyway.

"Take me home," I demurely offered when we were introduced. "You're not really going to stay here playing, are you?"

"Uh," he replied, "we don't play. We work."

I suggested the next night. And that's when it happened (finally!). Naturally, I dressed my part—black eye makeup out to there, a mini-skirt up to here—but the truth was that I did, in fact, have parents. On our first date I even confessed to Jim that my ridiculous father was on that very night playing violin in a program of music by Palestrina. To my tremendous dismay, Jim immediately expressed his desire to drive to Pasadena. I packed him into my '52 Cadillac and off we went, but by intermission I had had enough. He whined that he wanted to stay for the second half, but I put my foot down.

"You just can't be here," I said. "Listening to this. You just can't."

Being in bed with Jim was like being in bed with Michelangelo's *David*, only with blue eyes. His skin was so white, his muscles were so pure, he was so innocent. The last time I saw him with no shirt on, at a party up in Coldwater, his body was so ravaged by scars, toxins, and puffy pudginess, I wanted to kill him.

He never really stopped being a fat kid. He used to suggest, "Let's go to Ships and get blueberry pancakes with blueberry syrup."

"It's so fattening," I would point out.

I mean, really.

Jim was embarrassing because he wasn't cool, but I still loved him. It was his mouth, of course, which was so edible. Just so long as he didn't smile and reveal his too-Irish teeth, just so long as he kept his James Dean smolder, it worked. But it takes a lot of downers to achieve that on a full-time basis. And no fat.

Just so long as he stood there in the leather clothes my sister had hand-made for him, the ones lined with turquoise satin, trimmed with snakeskin and lizard. The black leather pants, the leather jackets. My sister never thought Jim was that cute, but then my sister was one of his girlfriend Pamela's friends, and it was in her best interest to ignore Jim, even though, for a month, my sister and her boyfriend lived with Jim and Pamela, and it was almost impossible. "He was always a very dark presence in a room," she said. "In fact, if you asked me today the feeling I got, I'd say it was of a person who was severely depressed. Clinically depressed." She's now a psychologist, so she knows.

"He thought he was ugly," she said. "He'd look at himself in the mirror trying on those clothes, but he hated looking at himself, because he thought he was ugly."

My sister and Pamela had to fight to persuade him to leave his hair long, because left to his own devices he'd get it cut preppy-short and break everyone's heart.

Even his voice was embarrassing, sounding so sudden and personal and uttering such hogwash in a time when, if you were going to say words, they were to be ironic and a little off-center. Jim just blurted things the fuck out. My artist friends found him excruciating, too, but my movie friends (who were, by definition, out of it and behind the times and got everything all wrong) loved him. He said what they meant. They might not have understood Dylan—they thought he couldn't sing—but in Hollywood they loved Jim.

Jim as a sex object and the Doors as a group were two entirely different stories. The whole audience would put up with long, tortured silences and humiliation and just awful schmuck stuff Jim did during performances. He could get away with it because his audience was all college kids who thought the Doors were cool because they had lyrics you could understand about stuff they learned in Psychology 101 and Art History. The kids who liked the Doors were so misguided they thought "Crystal Ship" was for intellectuals.

Jim as a sex object lasted for about two years.

In fact, once he and Pamela became entangled in their fantastic killing struggle—once he finally found someone who, when he said, "Let's drive over this cliff," actually *would*—he became more of a death object than a sex object. Which was even sexier.

When Pamela Courson met Jim, he began putting his money where his mouth was. Whereas all he had previously brought to the moment was morbid romantic excess, he now had someone looking at him and saying, "Well, are you going to drive off this cliff, or what?"

She was someone with red hair and a heart embroidered on her pants over the place her anus would be. He was a backdoor man, and Pamela was the door. Pamela was the cool one.

Everything a nerd could possibly wish to be, Pamela *was*. She had guns, took heroin, and was fearless in every situation. Socially she didn't care, emotionally she was shockproof, and as for her eating disorders—her idea of the diet to be on while Jim was in Miami going to court was ten days of heroin. Every time she awoke she did some, so she just sort of slept through her fast. Once, when she did wake up, she went with some friends to the Beverly Hills Hotel to see Ahmet Ertegun and fainted. Voilà, there she was back at UCLA, diagnosed as dying of malnutrition.

Good old Pamela, what a sport.

She would take Jim's favorite vest and write FAG in giant letters on the back in india ink. She would go through Rodeo Drive's Yves Saint Laurent Rive Gauche, piling her arms higher and higher with more stuff, muttering under her breath, "He owes it to me, he owes it to me, he owes it to me."

Pamela was mean and she was cool. She liked to scare people. Pamela had control over Jim in real life. He made his audience suffer for that.

And I mean, he was so cute, you *would*.

Pamela looked sunny and sweet and cute—she had freckles and red hair and the greenest eyes and just the country-girl glow. It was hard to believe her purse was stuffed with Thorazine (that horrible drug they used to give acid freak-outs). She wore mauve, and large, soft, expensive suede boots and large shawls, but even her laugh was mean.

She was so mean, she told Ray Manzarek (the worst nerd worldwide, known to his friends as Ray of the Desert) that Jim's last words were, "Pam, are you out there?" even though he actually left a note. And she *knew* that the note would establish forever the literature-movie myth of Jim's Lizard King image. Everyone hated Pam except Jim.

A friend of mine once said, "You can say anything about a woman a man marries, but I'll tell you one thing—it's *always* his mother."

"Mother," Jim sang, "I want to . . . *aggghh*." Pamela was more than happy to supply the lip back: "Oh, you would, would you? Well, fuck *you*!"

I couldn't be mean to him. If the phone rang at night and there was a long pause after I said hello, I knew it was Jim. He and I had a lot of ESP in some kind of laser-twisted, wish-fulfillment kind of way. I *always* wished he were there, and every so often, he zoomed in.

"The thing that really made people mad at him," my sister reminds me, "was that he drank. And it wasn't cool to drink in those days."

"Yeah," I say, "he *did* drink."

Of course, I drank, but I tried to keep my drinking within the psychedelia-prescribed boundaries of okayness. I drank Dos Equis, wine, and tequila. Jim drank Scotch.

Scotches.

Adults drank and got drunk and were uncool. I myself drank, got drunk, and was uncool. But I myself didn't drink, get drunk, and become *so* uncool I flashed an audience in the South. I myself didn't drink, get drunk, and then jump out of windows, get busted, stick my fist through plate glass, show up three days late for an interview with Joan Didion from *Life* magazine, drunk, unshaven, and throwing lit matches in her lap.

But Jim did.

Jim drank, got drunk, and woke up bloated and miserable and had to apologize and say he loved you, the alcoholic's ancient saving grace. Jim drank and got drunk and then was so uncool he had to walk home.

I never saw him drive—he was always on foot in L.A. He didn't dare drive himself anywhere. He *knew* in his worst blackouts not to drive. Just as I knew in my worst blackouts to put my diaphragm in and take my contact lenses out.

Jim drank, got drunk, and wanted to be shown the way to the Next Whiskey Bar. Whereas the Rolling Stones were ripping off Otis and Robert Johnson and Chuck Berry, and the cool and hip Buffalo Springfield were riffling through Woody Guthrie and Hank Williams with folkie touches or else trying to achieve soul, Jim was ripping off Kurt Weill, Bertolt Brecht, Jean Cocteau, and Lawrence Durrell. While the Rolling Stones were making it cool to be black and folk rockers were making it cool to be white trash, Jim was making it cool to be a poet. If Jim had lived in another era, he would have had a schoolteacher wife to support him while he sat home writing "brilliant" poetry.

One night I was in the bungalow of Ahmet Ertegun (this was when I wised up and quit aiming at rock stars and went for record-company presidents instead—but *cool* ones, not Clive Davis). It was the night of the 1971 moon landing, and when I came in wearing my divine little black velvet dress, my tan, my blond art-nouveau hair, and my one pair of high heels I used for whenever Ahmet was in town, who should be sitting in front of the TV watching the moon landing but Jim, a Scotch and Coke (no ice) in his hand.

Ahmet proceeded to tell a rather gross story about midgets in India, and when he was through, Jim rose to his feet and bellowed, "You think you're going to *win*, don't you?! Well, you're not, you're not going to win. We're going to win, *us*—the artists. Not you capitalist pigs!"

You could have heard a pin drop in this roomful of Ahmet's fashionable friends, architects from France, artists, English lords, *W*-type women. Of course, Ahmet *was* a capitalist pig, but still, he did write some Drifters lyrics and produce records and his acts sang in tune. Anyway, everybody was silent (except for the moon-landing reporter on the TV) until I stood up and heard myself say, "But Ahmet *is* an artist, Jim!"

I became so embarrassed by how uncool *I* was, I ran down the hallway and into the bathroom, where I stood looking at myself in the mirror and wondering why I didn't get married and move to Orange County and what was I doing there.

There was a knock on the door.

I opened it and Jim came in and shut the door behind him.

"You know," he said, staring straight into my eyes, "I've always loved you."

Later that night he came back and apologized to Ahmet. But it was too late; by then he was too fat to get away with it. The people who were there refused to remember that it had happened. It was one of those tricky nights when Ahmet was trying to make up his mind whether he was going to seduce Jim away from Elektra Records (whose contract was nearly up). Ahmet had lured Mick away from *his* label the year before. Ahmet bespoke elegance, Côte d'Azur loafers with no socks, Bentleys and Rolls-Royces. Ahmet knew everybody. Jac Holzman of Elektra was an awkward bumpkin compared with Ahmet. Jac was a Virgo, Ahmet the world's most sophisticated Leo. Ahmet had Magrittes in his living room in New York, his wife was on the Ten Best Dressed list, he'd been everywhere, done everything, and spoke all these languages. Jac liked camping.

Of course, today Ahmet might deny this was going on, but at that time Ahmet never saw a rock star who made money whom he didn't want. Especially if he could sing in tune. Jim might also have denied anything was going on, or maybe he did notice he was being seduced, maybe that's why he was on about the capitalist pigs not winning. But then, Jim was drunk and uncool, so maybe what he said wasn't about anything. That's the thing with alcoholics: Their resentments are a condition of their disease and not really political at all. A condition of their allergy to alcohol—and allergies mean if you're allergic to strawberries and eat them, you break out in hives. If Jim drank Scotch, he broke out in fuckups.

But as long as Jim was on foot in L.A.—as long as he was signed to Elektra and in a world where if he fell, it would be into the arms of emergency rooms or girls who knew and loved him—he was, if not OK, at least not dead. There was always somebody around who would break down the door. He could never get away with killing himself in L.A.

Someone in Paris told me that when she met Jim at a party after he had moved there, he looked into her face and said, "Would you mind scratching my back? It itches." Her arm went around him, their bodies facing as she scratched. Then Jim said, "You know what? I can't feel a thing." Which was really humiliating to her, since having your arm around someone who says he can't feel it is . . . well, it sounds like one of Pamela's tricks.

Jim burned his bridges in Paris. He got fatter and fatter, drank more and more, sampled Pamela's heroin, and piled up suicide notes on a table in their rooms. Since Jim had rheumatic fever in his youth, his heart was not in condition for what he did to it there—combining insult with fuckups until finally one day Pamela came into the bathroom and Jim wasn't kidding.

She pulled him out of the tub and there she was—stuck in Paris in early July, forced to put him into a too-small coffin wearing a too-large suit. (Since no one in those days had suits, she had to buy one for him. She didn't know his size.)

Pamela told me she fled to Morocco with an eighteen-year-old French count, a junkie who also OD'd on her and died. And then, having worn out her stay abroad, she returned to the West Coast and sued for her share of Jim's estate until she got it and then, since three years had passed and she was now the same age Jim was when he died, she, too, OD'd and died.

She left behind a VW Bug, two fur coats, and Sage, Jim's dog. A quarter of the group's estate was split between her family and his, and her father saved Jim's "poems" and put them in a safe place in Orange County. The wonderful Julia Densmore Negron, who had divorced the drummer, John, was given royalties as a settlement because, as she said, "By 1971 they were worth practically nothing. But they've gone up more than 1,500 percent in the past eleven years." Since she was only married to John during the last two years of the Doors, when their records didn't sell much anyway, sales must have really gone up, but *why?*

Because Francis Ford Coppola used the song "The End" to make Jim a star in *Apocalypse Now*, which came out in 1979. And now Vietnam's about to do it for Jim again.

If, in the sixties, you were white and political and had noblesse oblige drummed into you (Yale's big selling point), you might have gone to Vietnam as a soldier, as Oliver Stone did, so you could come home and write a book the way Kennedy did and then be elected president.

Being Kennedy was not entirely uncool, but I knew a guy who went to Yale and then officer school at Annapolis and then Guam and then a ship in the harbor at Saigon (if it has a harbor, I don't know; it was someplace with a harbor). And all he did there was drink, and when he got home and went into seclusion to write his book like Kennedy, he couldn't write it. It was one thing being a World War II hero and writing a book. In Vietnam there weren't any heroes.

In *Salvador* (one of the last Oliver Stone movies I'm ever going to see), he created two sleazeballs who can't handle women, who are so incapable of having a real life in a real place that they have to slop down to hell, where they are the richest and most powerful people around. And *still* these guys manage to make victims out of themselves. Stone's heroes always wind up as victims, no matter how sleazy they are.

It has been rumored around L.A. that Oliver Stone is asking everyone in connection with the Doors movie if Jim was impotent, and it makes you think Oliver Stone doesn't know much about Jim's main disease. You'd think he'd at least read up on the symptoms that show up in a person who takes depressants as a cure for depression. Taking Seconal and Tuinal and drinking brandy will bring your sex life to a grinding halt.

But what I want to know about Oliver Stone is not whether he can get it up or not, but why anyone in the sixties would *join* the army, would *go* to Vietnam and become part of the war and murder and atrocity, when the action for Real Men was on Sunset Strip, the Lower East Side, and in San Francisco. Why did he join them, and why is he now in love with our Jim?

The thing is, we in Los Angeles have always been willing to give a lot of slack for looks—for beauty—but Oliver Stone doesn't have any. He doesn't even like it. His movies are always about horrible men doing awful stuff, horrible men who are too far into their vileness to look beautiful. It's as though everything he's done is against the very premise of looks; he can't even show Daryl Hannah and understand what she's about. His idea of a good thing is a man bellowing about how being stupid is not that bad. (But it is.)

If being stupid is not that bad, then Jim's poetry would be OK, but it's not. Fortunately Jim had looks.

Maybe like Jim's other nerdy fans, Oliver Stone really believes that Jim was "serious" about breaking on through to the other side. But what does that *mean*—death, the way it sounds? It meant death to Jim personally, if what Pamela told her neighbor Diane Gardiner is to be believed, if he really died in Paris, his suicide note against a lamp, "Last Words, Last Words, Out."

By the time Jim left L.A., everyone thought he was a fool; he was fat, getting fatter, and even his fans were unwilling to look at his cock. He didn't have enough ideas in his head to keep people interested any longer.

Underneath his mask, he was dead.

But then, by 1971, who wasn't?

I certainly had washed ashore, without illusions. Everyone was afraid of Manson (Jim looked like him in his obit picture in the *Los Angeles Times*), acid had suffered a defeat, and cocaine was up for a long, ugly ride. Until Jim died, I had made a living doing album covers—psychedelic valentines for groups I loved, like Buffalo Springfield. I was in France in 1962 when Marilyn Monroe died, and now Jim was in France, dead, and I was nearly twenty-eight, unmarried, no future, no going forth in glory, only waking up at 3 a.m. with free-floating anxiety (which someone said was "the only thing floating around free anymore").

Someone said the sixties was drugs and the seventies was sex, but for me the seventies was staying home.

It was a time when I began to write for a living, and though I never wrote movies, they began seeming not that bad to me. Actors suddenly became OK (at least from afar). I began running into women who kept Jim alive—as did I—because something about him began seeming great compared with everything else that was going on. He may have been a film-school poet, but at least he wasn't disco.

People began trying to make a movie about Jim, and everyone I ran into who tried either died or wound up in AA. They wanted . . . John Travolta! Casting *anyone* to play Jim was just totally ridiculous to me.

My incredibly beautiful neighbor, Enid Karl, had two children by Donovan in the sixties, and their son, also Donovan, worked as an extra in the Doors movie (the daughter, Ione Skye, is an actress, too, but she was in a play in New York during the filming). The experience left Donovan thrilled, excited, and completely on Oliver Stone's side. (Everyone I talked to who worked on the movie—wardrobe women, actors—was on Oliver Stone's side. *Le tout* L.A.)

"In the first scene at the Whisky, I played my father—because I asked. There were four hundred extras, but I got to sit in front and wear a caftan like my father wore. I thought I was going to end up lost in the crowd with an AD in front of me and not in the movie, but Oliver saw me and called out from the stage, 'Donovan! Donovan!' and suddenly they put me in the front row."

Then they gave Donovan a blond wig to wear as an extra in the Ray Manzarek wedding scene, and once he added muttonchops and a mustache he looked so much like Ray's brother that they let him sit with the wedding party.

"The extras were all too young to have been around in the sixties," young Donovan reports, "but really, it felt like everyone loved the Doors, and it was a happening. You didn't feel you were on a movie set."

I heard that once shooting began, Val Kilmer sent around a memo demanding that no one speak to him except as Jim. And that no one was allowed to come within ten feet of him. Plus, he wore a sweatshirt with a hood so he could hide his face. Not at all like Jim, who was all things to all people, like Marilyn, but how else can a boy stay in character if he's not actually Jim? (When Dustin Hoffman arrived on the set of *Marathon Man* looking worn and exhausted because he had deliberately avoided sleep for two nights, Laurence Olivier remarked, "Dear boy, you look absolutely awful. Why don't you try *acting*? It's so much easier.")

According to everyone, Val Kilmer is supposed to have gotten

Jim's looks exactly right, but what can Val Kilmer know of having been fat all of his life and suddenly one summer taking so much LSD and waking up a prince? Val Kilmer has *always* been a prince, so he can't have the glow; when you've never been a mud lark it's just not the same. And people these days, they don't know what it was to suddenly possess the power to fuck every single person you even idly fancied, they don't know the physical glamour of *that*—back when rock and roll was in flower and movies were hopelessly square. And we were all so young.

Esquire
March 1991

I WAS A NAKED PAWN FOR ART

"His position was extraordinary," my wonderful friend Walter Hopps informed me. Walter was the One, when it came to all this—long ago, when hardly anyone knew—who *knew*. "One way to look at it—these things are never set in granite—is that Picasso and Matisse fulfilled the dream of the nineteenth century, and the two artists who hold the really extreme positions unique to our time are Duchamp and Mondrian. Art for the mind and not for the eye. The irony is, Duchamp did so many beautiful things. But not just stuff you decorate walls with. His great contribution to art was elsewhere."

Meaning that in the nineteenth century a urinal could only say—if it could say anything—"I'm a urinal." But after Marcel, a urinal could also say, "I look like a urinal, but Marcel says I'm art."

"In other words," Walter may or may not have ended, "Duchamp playing chess with a nude in a photograph may be art."

Of course, if *you're* the nude, being "art" seems beside the point. At least with the Naked Maja, you could be airbrushed and posterity would think of you as perfect, whereas on that day, sitting naked in the museum, having to play chess with someone who hardly spoke English and was so polite he pretended that the reason he'd come was to play chess—*well*. And afterward, when the photograph began showing up on things like posters for the Museum of Modern Art, and *Nude Descending a Staircase* became almost interchangeable with *Nude Playing Chess*, and Duchamp being so immortal, I just wasn't sure I wanted to be identified. Maybe it would be better to be "and friend."

On the other hand, if they'd asked anyone else—or if I'd chickened

out and some other woman was immortalized—then, *hmmph....*
Recently, when a woman called and said she was doing a book on
Duchamp on the West Coast and could she please use that picture,
I said, "You're not going to use it on the cover, are you?" But when I
found out the cover photo was to be of Marcel alone, I felt insulted.
Mixed emotions hound me after nearly thirty years of mixed emo-
tions. I want to be on the cover, immortal, but I don't want anyone
knowing it's me. Except my friends and people who like it.

Otherwise, I'll just be "and friend." Anyone who thinks the nude
should have been thinner, or in any way different—to them, I'll be a
floating image of "elsewhere."

Immortality or no.

In the 1913 Armory Show in New York, there was a scandal over
Duchamp's *Nude Descending a Staircase*. If you look at that picture
today, you might ask yourself—*Pourquoi*? It's not as though it's a
photograph or anything naked you could see. It was so diffracted and
cubistic, who could tell? Maybe it was a scandal because people had
to take it on faith that there was anything there at all besides olive-
green, beige, and black corners that may or may not have been a
staircase. That painting, however, made Duchamp famous and laid
the way clear for twentieth-century art to be not what it seemed.

The interesting thing about that painting is that it was bought
(for $350 or so) not by some hip New Yorker but rather by a print
dealer in San Francisco, who put it in his office as a publicity stunt.

In Hollywood, there was a genuine collector couple, Walter and
Louise Arensberg, who amassed Duchamp works as though Los
Angeles were a totally cultivated city where you'd expect people to
know what was happening artwise in the twentieth century—like
Gertrude Stein and her brother, who knew what was what practically
before anything was anything. Only the Steins were in Paris, where
art was in the air, whereas the Arensbergs were in Los Angeles, where
if you could draw, you'd be good if you were Walt Disney.

Los Angeles was a hick town with a vengeance, artwise. If you judged it by the L.A. County Museum, or by its nowheresville galleries, or by its public philanthropies like the Huntington Library, where they kept all the Gainsboroughs and Joshua Reynoldses, the place was hopeless. It was so impossible that the L.A. County Museum didn't admit any art from Los Angeles. In the fifties, my mother once picketed the place with her friend Vera Stravinsky, just to call the museum's attention to the fact that nobody from L.A. was inside. The museum relented and held a contest for local artists, promising to hang the work of the winners, and my mother won for a line drawing of old houses on Bunker Hill.

New York was ablaze with glamorous guys like Pollock, Rothko, de Kooning, and Motherwell, but in L.A., even if all you wanted to see was French Impressionists, you had to know Edward G. Robinson.

My parents were sort of a team to combat L.A.'s hickness, and in the fifties, they took it upon themselves to have poetry and jazz things in our living room. And although I liked only Kenneth Patchen and thought everyone else was long and boring (being a teenager who preferred Chuck Berry and Elvis), I could see that the adults were completely elated, and I could see the point in being a beatnik if that's what James Dean was supposed to be.

My father was a violinist with taste and determination, and he and his friend Peter Yates began something called Evenings on the Roof atop Peter's house. There, slick studio musicians who could sight-read anything performed never-before-heard works by, say, Stravinsky or Schoenberg, who both lived in L.A., where the Philharmonic rarely played anything newer than Brahms, and even that nobody went to.

In 1937, when my father was still playing in the L.A. Philharmonic, Stravinsky came to conduct. And Stravinsky so loved my beautiful and funny father that later on he became my godfather, and his wife, Vera, and my mother were great friends. My parents and Stravinsky and Vera used to go see Jelly Roll Morton or mariachi bands, or my father would jam with Stuff Smith in dives—they double-dated, you might say. Not that Vera ever got over there being no clothes in L.A. or anything else to remind her of Paris, the only city, in her opinion, where anyone sensible would want to live. But Stravinsky loved the climate, and after World War II, when everyone else who had been on the lam (like Brecht and Thomas Mann and Jean Renoir) returned to Europe, Stravinsky stayed—he wasn't going anyplace it snowed ever again.

So I grew up listening to adults complain about L.A. and its hopeless cultural condition, but not in that condition myself, being surrounded by such high magic.

Meanwhile, Walter Hopps was growing up a whiz, kid from Eagle Rock, in a program in high school for the truly brilliant, and once a month they went on strange field trips, one of which, in 1948, changed his life forever. Before that (he was only fifteen) he was supposed to become a doctor—he came from a family of doctors, his mother and father were both doctors, his grandfather and grandmother were "horse-and-buggy" doctors in Eagle Rock, his great-grandmother was a doctor! But then one day he was taken to the home of Walter and Louise Arensberg.

"And so you saw the Duchamps there?" I asked. "And did you get it? I mean, about Duchamp?"

"In a word?" He laughed. "Yes."

"So it changed your life?"

"The whole core of my thinking was shifted very particularly within a year," he said. In other words, he started hanging out with low-life types, going to jazz joints with fake ID, and mingling with Wallace Berman, who wasn't yet an artist but more just a hipster.

In 1957 or so, when Walter opened the Ferus Gallery with the artist Ed Kienholz, he finally dropped out of school. He had already opened three galleries by then, and he was only twenty-four. He still looked like a doctor, and he had such a bedside manner he made people feel better just by entering a room. And though he talked all the time, he gave the impression of utter silence.

Everyone else in the art world, or what little art world there was in those days, may have seemed far-out and beatniky, but Walter, in his neat, dark American suits with his white shirts, ties, pale skin, and blue eyes behind black eyeglass frames, seemed too businesslike for words. It was as though someone from the other side, the public side of L.A., had materialized on La Cienega, on our side, the side of weirdness, messiness, and art.

One of the first shows they had there, a Wallace Berman exhibit, got busted for obscenity, which got things off properly and sealed our faith in Walter. If someone so classic-American was willing to let a crack of light into fluorescent Los Angeles, a crack of darkness ... Plus, he had such a convincingly deadpan delivery that rich older ladies might actually *buy* this stuff.

In 1962, when I was nineteen, I was going to L.A. Community College (because you could park, unlike at UCLA). One day a girl came up to me, told me her name was Myrna Reisman, asked if Stravinsky was my godfather, and when I said yes, she said, "Great, I'll pick you up around eight."

She arrived in her boyfriend's Porsche and took me to Barney's Beanery, where Everyone was that night. Sitting at a couple of tables in the back of the bar were Irving Blum (who by then was the front man at the Ferus Gallery, having a presence and voice like Cary Grant and the greatest eyelashes on any coast) and Ed Kienholz, who was grizzly and manly and who was having a show at the gallery. Also there that night were Wallace Berman, the strange prince of darkness with long, long black hair, and Billy Al Bengston, the first surfer artist I met there, and Larry Bell, who I knew already because he was the bouncer at the Unicorn. I wouldn't meet Ed Ruscha, Joe Goode, Peter Alexander, or Laddie Dill until later, but I did meet Robert Irwin, who was so totally a surfer that in those days that's all he and Kenneth Price, who was also there, ever did. Sitting with the surfers was Walter Hopps, looking much too normal to be in Barney's, just this wreck of a West Hollywood chili joint.

"I met you," Walter said, "at a poetry reading at your house."

"You did?" I asked.

Somehow it was decided that we were all going to Kienholz's house in Laurel Canyon. It was crowded and rustic and I was beginning to feel left out when Walter sat beside me and offered to show me Ed's show, "among other things," if I came to the gallery the next day.

"What other things?" I asked, although I trusted him because he was so polite.

A couple days later I went to the gallery and Walter was there, alone except for the cow's skull on the mannequin's body with an arm holding a cigarette holder, alone except for a papier-mâché model of a woman over a sewing machine you pumped with your foot to make her pump up and down. The installation, titled *Roxy's*, was a scale-model World War II–era Nevada whorehouse with a jukebox that played Glenn Miller, and the skull lady was the madam.

"I'll show you other things," Walter said, and took me upstairs to a garage apartment where I saw a Siamese cat with eyes the same color and weirdness as his. He showed me a bunch of John Altoon works he'd just rescued from one of John's self-destructive attacks (he used to go after his paintings with an axe or something, I don't know), and I saw these great, hypnotic Kenneth Price ceramics. I was only nineteen and I said, "What's this all about anyway?"

"Is it OK if I write on this?" he asked, noticing the paperback I was carrying, a history of literary criticism. I handed it over and after a minute he wrote: "Eve, baby, this is another place—so walk, (right along) easy."

I still have this because I have everything he gave me except a signed Lichtenstein (I always lose the art). I have memories of his voice, a silver bullet, convictions about how to see, and of course, Marcel.

We walked back down into the gallery, which was now dark because it was night, and he turned on the jukebox so the revolving lights lit up the whorehouse, making the place frightening but cozy because of the Glenn Miller.

"Listen," he said, "I'm going to Brazil. When I get back, I'll call you."

"Brazil?" I cried, disappointed. "For how long?"

"Not long," he said. "A couple of months."

"Months!" I moaned. We could all be dead by then.

"I'll call you," he said.

This promise didn't stop me from going hog wild at Barney's, immersing myself in the scene, falling in love as any fool might with Ed Ruscha (the cutest) and Kenneth Price (maybe cuter) and Jim Eller (the "rat man," who did terrible, dark things to rubber rats with red blood on them, but then, I was so young, I went for cuteness, not content).

I have always loved scenes, bars where people come in and out in various degrees of flash, despair, gossip, and brilliance, and the scene at Barney's was just fabulous—better than Max's in New York, which I thought was too mean and too dark. Edie Sedgwick and Bobby Neuwirth sitting at the bar looking untouchable is not my idea of fun. But then, the Ferus was nothing if not fun. Every night I was getting into my car and going to Barney's or to art openings, since now it had been decided that every Monday night all galleries would stay open, and suddenly, everyone in L.A. was out—en masse. It was stupid but it was fun.

By that time, I was living in this little paper bungalow—one room with a typewriter—on Bronson Avenue in Hollywood. I had a hor-rible old Chevy with stalactites growing down from the interior like cobwebs. I was writing my memoirs, of course, because I'd been to Europe (like Henry James) and wanted to write a book called *Travel Broadens*, about being Daisy Miller, only from Hollywood. Poor Europe never recovered was the point of my book. I thought of myself as extremely decadent and thought that anyone who had graduated from Hollywood High had nothing to learn.

Maybe three months passed in that way before Walter finally called me, saying he was driving in from the airport. When he got to my house, car keys jangling in his pocket, he said, "So, shall we hear some music tonight, or do you want to see a play?"

"A play," I said, always happier around words.

In his red station wagon, we drove back to the airport and flew to San Francisco, where a play his friend had written was opening. "I had tickets to see the Dylan concert," he said, "but maybe it's better if we see this Michael McClure play, *The Beard*."

I couldn't believe someone was taking me to San Francisco on a date—nobody at Hollywood High had ever done *that*. I mean, artists were cute, but all they'd ever give you was a burrito. And so, even though Walter wore glasses, my reservations crumbled. And sitting there, hearing the opening lines—

> In order to pursue the secret of me
> You must first find the real me.
> Which path will you pursue?

—it seemed to me that there were things going on that I could pursue, that no matter what they thought in New York about everyone else being totally out of it and hopeless, on the West Coast things were happening and that it was art and that Walter was the One and these were the Times. Sitting in the audience, even though mostly I didn't get it, I at least had the feeling there was something to get.

From then on, I saw Walter frequently, which meant I was in the midst of much excitement and momentum going public in L.A. One night, we were leaving Musso's when he looked at his watch and said, "Good, I still have time to get to Bel Air and sell that Duchamp."

"Who's Duchamp?" I asked.

He seemed stunned.

"Is he French?" I wondered. "He sounds dead."

"He's not dead," he said, "but he is French. There's a lot you don't know."

But since Walter seemed willing to spend every waking hour turning uneducated fools into people with eyes to see, he tried to explain Duchamp to me, telling a story about meeting him once in the Arensbergs' garden when Duchamp, in a white-and-purple polka-dot satin bathrobe, said to fourteen-year-old Walter, "Perhaps we shall meet again."

"I've been to New York since to see him," Walter went on, "and the first thing he said to me was, 'And so we meet again.'"

Walter was like Proust, he had so many story lines going on in his head. He didn't restrict his story lines merely to the past and present, he sort of projected them into the future, and once, when we were in Kenny Price's studio, Kenny told me, "I don't like Walter to come here like this; when he sees what you're doing, he suddenly is seven jumps ahead of you. Like he knows what you will be doing. And then, he *leans*."

In 1963 Walter forsook the Ferus Gallery, and even though it was only to become director of the Pasadena Art Museum, someone should have noticed how fast he was moving. He was only twenty-eight and suddenly he was all the way in New York sweet-talking Duchamp into a Southern California retrospective. The thing about Walter was that he was able to persuade not only artists to go along with his ideas but people with money to back him up. He looked so Waspy they figured he was one of them. And he was, it was just that they were changing—suddenly the had eyes to see.

Suddenly they weren't just after a nice Matisse.

Suddenly they were becoming complicated.

Suddenly everything was a lot more fun.

Pasadena, whose sole claim to fame was the Rose Parade, was now anxiously awaiting the Big Private Party at the Green Hotel before the Public Opening of the Duchamp show. *Elsewhere* was going public!

It was around this time that Walter called me up and suggested I come meet this friend of his who was very nice, but short.

"How short?" I wondered.

"Well, he can drive a car," he said.

This sounded very suspicious. "You mean he's a midget?"

"Well, sort of like Toulouse-Lautrec," he said.

Suddenly I felt things had gotten *too* weird, even for Walter, and for the first time in my life, I realized I had a great reason to hang up on someone—like women do in the movies—a thing I'd never imagined myself doing until just then.

This was the wrong time, of course, for me to have pulled this move, because in a month the Duchamp show would be happening and the beautiful old Green Hotel would be filled with everyone in the L.A. art world, champagne, bands, clothes! But Walter never called me back, and I wasn't invited. Everyone I knew was going. Even my sister, who was only seventeen (I was twenty), was going, with this bold photographer, Julian Wasser, a *Time* photographer who drove around with a police radio in his car.

When he came to pick up my sister, Julian noticed that I was to be left behind and he invited me, but I felt so banished in spirit and it didn't seem to me the sort of thing you could crash. And obviously I'd disappointed Walter so much he forgot all about me.

Anyway, I knew that a couple of days later there'd be the public opening of the show and my parents had been invited, so I could go with them. My father didn't care about Duchamp but he did have this interest in chess, and since Marcel had announced that he was "retired" from art to only play chess, my father thought he might go and see just what a master this guy was.

At the entrance to the show, there was an old photograph from a long-ago opening in Paris that showed Marcel and a woman as Adam and Eve. I noticed this as I went in, and it seemed sweet to me, they both were so young and French and skinny.

The public opening was very crowded and lots of fun. I got myself some red wine and wandered over to a raised platform where Marcel and Walter were playing chess, and my father came by and watched with a cynical expression. (He told me later, "That Marcel is not very good, I could have beaten him on the fourth move. And your friend Walter can't play at all.")

Maybe it was the spectacle of Walter playing chess with Duchamp "for art" that gave Julian the idea. After all, by 1963 it had been about forty years since Marcel had retired to play chess (or so he wanted the world to think). For forty years someone could have come up with the idea of photographing the master of *Nude Descending a Staircase* playing chess with a naked woman. But nobody in Paris or New York thought it up.

"Hey, Eve," Julian said, grinning. "Why don't I take pictures of you nude, playing chess with Marcel Duchamp?"

Heretofore, the only nudes in L.A. were calendar girls—starlets trying to make the rent. Of course, me being the nude sort of made me feel like I was pretending I was way bolder than I really was. But then, anything seemed possible—for art, that night. Especially after all that red wine.

Still, this *was* Pasadena, the home of gracious ladies painting watercolors on afternoon outings, so I said, "You better ask people, Julian, and make sure it's OK."

I have known plenty of great photographers in my life, and if there's one thing they can do, it's trample over objections. Julian disappeared, and when he came back he said, "It's all set."

"Does Walter know?" I asked.

"They'll tell him," he said. "Anyway, he'll think it's a great idea. It is a great idea."

All my ideas about Pasadena—about L.A. itself—were undergoing a molecular transformation. We were going from Little League to a home run in the World Series. Even my father thought it was a great idea, driving home in the car, although my mother did say, "If you change your mind, darling, it won't matter."

The only trouble was, I had been taking birth control pills for the first and only time in my life, and not only had I puffed up like a blimp but my breasts had swollen to look like two pink footballs. Plus they hurt. On the other hand, it would be a great contrast—this large, too-L.A. surfer girl with an extremely tiny old man in a French suit. Playing chess.

(After I saw the contact sheets, I never took the Pill again.)

The next day Julian called to make sure I didn't chicken out, which seemed a sensible idea after I woke up and realized that I had never taken my clothes off in public—and certainly not in a museum at 9 a.m. to play chess for a photograph. I mean, maybe this wasn't art. Maybe this was just Julian trying to get the clothes off one more girl—which he was famous for doing, living across the street from Beverly Hills High School as he did and always making lascivious cracks.

But with Marcel there, I figured he'd cool it, and I knew enough about him to realize that when Julian took pictures, he took pictures. (His greatest photograph was the one of Madame Nhu and her daughter when they heard her husband had been shot, and they stood weeping in each other's arms—surrounded by news photographers, a sea of flashbulbs—which appeared in a two-page spread in *Life*.)

When Julian came to pick me up, I was wearing clothes of nunlike severity so nobody would have the slightest reason to believe I'd take them off: a gray pleated skirt down to my shins and an Ivy League blouse.

We arrived at the museum at 8:00, and Gretchen Glicksman, one of Walter's assistants, was waiting for us. I had never been in a museum before it opened—it was so quiet and cold. Gretchen told me I could change into a smock upstairs in a studio, so I ran up while Julian set up his lights. He was completely in photo mode, determined to get pictures the way photographers are once they know nothing can stop them.

The year before, I had lived in France, supposedly to learn French at the Alliance Française, but all I did was hang out at La Coupole picking up Americans. My sister, who did learn French, had to drag me to museums since going inside a building to see art never would have occurred to me. In Rome, where I lived alone for six months after Paris, I never once set foot inside the Sistine Chapel, but at least in Italy I learned some Italian, and as for art, you could watch it while you ate *tartufo* outside, and large nudes were everywhere, abundantly, galore. Except for Rome, I thought Europe was nowhere compared with L.A.—everywhere I went, everyone I met was in awe of California and dying to go to Hollywood. Not a single one wanted to go to New York.

It was hard to believe that only about fifty years earlier, in 1907, in *The American Scene*, Henry James had written: "I had the foretaste of what I was presently to feel in California—when the general aspect of that wondrous realm kept suggesting to me a sort of prepared but unconscious and inexperienced Italy, the primitive plate, in perfect condition, but with the impression of History all yet to be made."

Well, here I was—in the gallery with no shoes on, prepared to make history, my feet growing colder in more ways than one.

At 9:00, Marcel arrived alone, wearing a little straw hat he had picked up the day before in Las Vegas, where he and Walter had gone on some adventure. And these completely detached eyes, which seemed charmed to be alive but otherwise had no comment on the passing scene, met mine.

A feeling of gentleness pervaded him, he was like a very old Walter Hopps—a Walter Hopps with a history instead of just a future. Just when I was beginning to relax into his eyes, Julian violated our privacy by saying, "OK, I'm set up. Play chess."

I took the smock off, letting it fall beside me, but Julian kicked it far across the slippery floor, out of the way in a corner. I sat down quickly at the chess set and wondered if we could just pose or did we actually have to play, but Marcel—whose obsession with chess made him give up not only art but girls—was waiting for me to make the first move.

"*Et alors*," he said. "You go."

I, of course, had youth and beauty (and birth control pills) over him, but he had brains on his side—or at least chess brains—and though I tried my best, moving a knight so at least he knew I had some idea what a knight was, he moved his pawn and the next thing I knew, I was checkmated. "Fool's mate," they call it when you're so stupid that the game hasn't even begun and you've lost.

I became interested in playing and tried to stop thinking about holding in my stomach, but every time I thought I was so brilliant, like taking his queen on the fourth move, I'd lose.

Of all the things that have ever gone on between men and women, this was the strangest, in my experience. But it got stranger. For one thing, there were Teamsters in the next room, moving paintings, and they couldn't help but be amazed.

And suddenly I felt other—even more amazed—eyes on me. When I looked up, there was Walter, shocked. He just stood there like a rabbit caught in the headlights, unable to move or speak.

He saw me look up and he turned right around and went away. No hello, no nothing.

For a long time afterward, I thought he might have been pretending to be surprised, but he told me later, "I had no idea. I came into the museum as usual, a few minutes before it opened, blind and cold. I could feel weird vibes in the air, it was so quiet. But then I go into the gallery, and there you both were."

"I thought it was *fake* surprise," I insisted.

"No, it was real," he said, "but I thought it was inevitable."

Finally, just when I had this idea I might actually be winning, Julian said, "OK, Eve, get dressed." Which seemed more than OK with Marcel. I flew over to my smock, put it on, ran upstairs and got my clothes on, and came back down to play one more game with Marcel clothed—for posterity, Julian said.

Walter was back in the room, composed, and all he said was, "My, this was a surprise."

A month or so later, I went to Barney's and found Walter sitting at the counter alone with tacos and a beer, and I said, "So, are you going to forgive me?"

"What for?" he asked, indicating the seat next to his.

"The Toulouse-Lautrec guy," I reminded him.

"That Duchamp thing," he said, "made up all your points."

He proceeded to digress into a story about how this Lautrec guy was the one who had long ago shown him the work of a teenage artist whose last name was Ferus, but how before Walter could meet Ferus, Ferus committed suicide. Perhaps in Walter's mind, the reason he killed himself was because nobody encouraged him, nothing in L.A. existed where someone strange and weird could feel safe. And although Walter never said this out loud, I think the reason the gallery was called Ferus was so never again would someone in Los Angeles have to kill himself over art.

In the years I spent listening to Walter—from 1962 to 1966, when he left L.A. and went to Washington, DC, where he was with the Smithsonian—I lived in a sea of his digressions. And though I never saw what he saw, I at least learned to see through things and into and under and over what was in plain sight. Being with him, looking at anything, was an experience, and though when he left L.A. I felt he had forsaken us, I now feel grateful we had him for so long, since after the Duchamp show everyone on the East Coast suddenly noticed how brilliant he was and wanted him there, where art was art and people knew a genius when they saw one.

By 1966 his parents—or his mother, anyway—finally agreed to let bygones be bygones about his dropping out of medical school. "They figured if I was at the Smithsonian," he said, "I had a job."

I never met his parents, but nobody else did either, they never set foot inside the Ferus, the Pasadena Art Museum, or anyplace else they were likely to run into him. They probably were home wondering where they went wrong, why they'd ever allowed him to go into that program for gifted children, ruing the day he set off on that field trip for the Arensbergs', the only people in L.A. with a houseful of Duchamps.

Late in 1990, when the Duchamp-on-the-West-Coast book (*West Coast Duchamp*) was being prepared, the Shoshana Wayne Gallery used our picture, blown up big on silver paper, to announce its own show of his work in conjunction with a symposium to be held in the Santa Monica Public Library. Unlike the party at the Green Hotel, to this thing I was very invited.

"You can wear clothes," the girl who was in charge said, "or not, either way."

I arrived late, elevenish, though it started at nine and the experts onstage were sunk into flagrant detail about the Arensbergs, who had moved to L.A. in 1927, and the print dealer in San Francisco who bought *Nude Descending a Staircase*.

I saw George Herms sitting alone across the room—he was one of the dark-of-the-night Ferus artists. I sat beside him and he said, "You know, Chico is supposed to come to this."

"Yeah," I said. "Fat chance."

(George was one of the people who called Walter by his secret name, Chico, like a lot of the artists who knew him early on.)

Since Walter had left L.A., I'd seen him twice in Washington, but then he'd gone to organize the Menil Collection, in Houston, which is famous for having more money than the mere Smithsonian. He was probably down there, filling Mrs. de Menil's head with his digressions.

"It says right here on the brochure," George showed me, "he's supposed to speak, but I don't even know if he's in L.A."

In Pasadena, Walter was fairly well known for forgetting where he was supposed to be and being someplace else. So just because his name was printed on a brochure didn't mean he'd be there. At 12:30, when we broke for lunch, Walter still hadn't shown, but he wasn't actually scheduled to appear until the afternoon, so who could tell?

George and I walked to Fred Segal's, this fancy clothing store with a café inside. And sitting there, George told me Chico stories, the one I especially loved being about how, when Walter curated this huge California Art show in San Francisco, he wanted to go to the party thrown by the artists who'd been omitted—and George said he'd go with him as his bodyguard if Chico would give George money for his rent in exchange. Since Walter couldn't possibly go into this room full of people he'd personally excluded *without* a bodyguard, he agreed. "He promised to give me the money before he left," George explained, "but suddenly I looked up and he'd gone. Without paying me. The party lasted all night. The next morning, Chico shows up again...."

"No," I said. "Fearless!"

"Yeah," he said, "I lifted him up and carried him over to the pool and asked everyone to give me thumbs-up or thumbs-down. I got at least one thumbs-down."

I hated to think of Walter being thrown into a pool with all his clothes on, especially in San Francisco, where it's always so cold.

"Well, then he whispered the one thing he knew would get to my heart," George said.

"What?" I asked.

"He said, 'I'm holding.'"

"No," I said. "Drugs?"

"Not drugs," George said. "Art. He was holding art. Probably stuff he stole from me or some other guy's studio. If you caught him, he'd always say he was saving things from being stepped on, but I always knew he was stealing!"

"I'd be flattered," I said, thinking if Walter stole from you, you must be good. Art is filled with criminals. I once heard that to start the Ferus, Walter and a friend got a check for $20,000 from a guy who was really drunk, and they ran to the bank and cashed it before he woke up and realized what an art patron he'd become. But how else was a twenty-four-year-old medical student to open a gallery on fancy La Cienega back when things unseen didn't yet exist?

George and I left and wandered back to the symposium, deciding that if things didn't get a lot weirder soon, we'd leave. We sat near the side exits and were sure we'd have to go when suddenly, across the auditorium, I saw a tall man in a hat who looked enough like Walter to *be* Walter.

"It's Chico!" I said, poking George sort of hard.

I knew it had to be him because suddenly I felt so much better— that bedside manner of his permeates a room. It's, like, half desperado, half Lourdes.

Walter spotted George, whom he really loved, and then me with all our history, and he brushed everyone aside as he came over, looking radiant and filled with stories. He embraced George, who was still strong enough to pick him up, and then he looked at me through his reflective glasses and said: "*Well.*"

He handed me his hat and then bounded onto the stage and right away the symposium became a lot weirder and people were vastly relieved. Someone else didn't show, so George went onstage, too, and doubly intensified the proceedings. It's one thing to have someone talk about what George and Walter must have felt, it's another to have them personally there in public view.

Of course, New York was still New York, but right then, in downtown L.A., the Museum of Contemporary Art was staging a huge Ed Ruscha retrospective, and Everyone was in town that day and the next for the parties. Plus there was a big Art Expo thing of international renown in some place they usually use for car shows.

After the symposium Julian Wasser showed up looking younger than he did when he took the pictures. He's now such an adept paparazzo he hired a helicopter to crash Madonna's wedding. We all walked over to the Shoshana Wayne Gallery, where Julian had a display of his pictures, the ones he'd taken at the party, the public opening, and that day I played chess with Duchamp and surprised Walter. Looking at the pictures of Walter in those days, so pale, almost unearthly, I said, "If I'd known you were so young, I wouldn't have been so mad at you."

"For what?" he wondered.

"For not inviting me to the party. Everyone went but me."

"Why didn't you?" he asked.

But then I never would have gone to the public opening and Julian never would have asked me to take that picture, which was now hanging in the back gallery blown up (though not twenty feet wide like a painting some artist made of it). To me, I still didn't look like a nude, although I suppose history will have to decide.

"Let's go back," Walter said, putting his hat on my head, "I have to meet Corcoran."

We finally arrived at the gallery, where James Corcoran was waiting for Walter so they could leave and go watch the sunset at his house. I was invited and followed in my car. His house was filled with art but all you could look at was this large picture window with a view of the ocean. And as the light faded from the sky, Walter told me digressions of spellbinding magnitude. It felt like the Arabian Nights, his life still being as *elsewhere* as could be, and yet there in the room, in person. He had become much better-looking since leaving L.A. (usually the opposite is true)—instead of casting a cool glow of shadowless ultraviolet light, he now cast a warm, almost rosy, luster. But then he no longer had to worry that people didn't get it. Even here in L.A.

Walter's kiss goodbye was filled with history. He even asked, "Do you still have that silver bullet I gave you?"

"Of course," I said.

(I have it still. It's in a little red morocco-leather box and I hold it now in my hand for memories as I write this. The cotton inside is yellow with age.)

"Good," he said.

At least now he, too, has a past.

On San Vicente, as I drove home after saying goodbye to Walter, I ran into Ed Ruscha—or rather found myself driving parallel to him. At a light, we both opened our windows, and I said, "I can't believe it, I just spent the whole afternoon with Chico."

"I can't believe it," he said, "I just saw him for breakfast this morning. He's so great."

"He's going to your show tonight," I said.

"If he shows *up*," he said, knowing Walter well.

The light changed and we waved goodbye.

A couple of days later Walter called from Houston and told me that at Ed's show there was a line of people two blocks long waiting for Ed to sign his catalogue. "He was alone at a table," Walter told me, "and he asked me to sit down with him as he signed all those posters. He really has come a long way."

"Yeah," I said, "but not so long that he wouldn't rather have you sitting next to him."

Of course, by now even I have forgiven Walter for leaving L.A., and we are happy to give him any chance we can, and though most of those Ruscha fans probably had no idea the man sitting beside him was really the One as far as art in L.A. is concerned, we who were there realize that Ed couldn't have happened without the strange days of long ago.

But then in L.A., we have no sense of history, which is why I am always writing my memories. As Duchamp himself said, "It is the spectators who make the picture."

Esquire
September 1991

LIFE AT CHATEAU MARMONT
The Sequel

"IF YOU must get into trouble," Harry Cohn warned Glenn Ford and William Holden in 1939, when they were young Hollywood studs newly signed to contracts, "do it at the Marmont."

It was always that kind of hotel, a place that provided sufficient privacy, laxity, eccentricity, and thickness of wall to allow you to enjoy your trouble away from prying ears and eyes. Even getting to your room from the underground garage could be accomplished without ever setting foot in the lobby—though the lobby was so grandiose back then that most people loved wafting through it, touching the piano keys, pretending to be in a château on the Loire, which is where the Marmont (which opened in 1929) was designed to make you think you were.

In later years, though, some felt that the Chateau had taken its laissez-faire attitude a little too far, when the place began to lack amenities like showerheads and working telephones and hallway carpets—well, I mean, so little care had gone into maintaining it that even people who *liked* seedy hotels thought it was too much. Even people who *wanted* to feel depressed started staying away.

Then, a year or so ago, a pair of New Yorkers, André Balazs and Campion Platt, bought the Chateau and began fixing it up, and now they're done. And how dramatic is the difference?

"So little has been changed," Balazs says, "that even Wally Shawn didn't know the hotel had been sold, and he, you know, is the type to worry. People are worried we're going to wreck it, but we've been very careful thinking about how to restore it. We had three model rooms worked out, but there was always something wrong, something that didn't go with the history, something grating."

As he speaks he is heading toward the official model room, and there's a certain fear, as he reaches for the door, that somebody from New York couldn't possibly get the Chateau right. But then he opens the door and, except for not wanting to kill myself when I walk into the room, the Chateau feeling is the same as ever. Only cleaner. It's as though the Chateau had died and gone to heaven. Even some of the same all-wrong furniture is there, like the kitchen table that looks like it belongs in somebody's living room—but then the Chateau was never much for housewives, it was a place where women who didn't cook ordered up from Greenblatt's, and all that went in the little refrigerator was vodka. (Except maybe for Garbo, who used to make vegetable stew in her room.)

I had been worried that the kind of people the Chateau used to attract—the kind of people who *like* to spill things, things like wine, blood, whiskey, cocaine, ashes, and bodily fluids, people like John Belushi, who spilled *everything* here one night—might no longer feel at home. Then I look further inside the room and see the Martha Washington bedspreads still in place and that none of the lamps match, and I know that it isn't going to be too much of a shock.

In L.A., the impulse to tear down anything good but old and rebuild it crummy and different is so rampant that the only things anybody tries to restore are women's faces. Now the Chateau Marmont is getting a chance to come into the present and be charming again, and even if the romantic depressiveness of the hotel is lost, I have to rise above my nostalgic despair and be glad.

Esquire
January 1992

THEY MIGHT BE GIANTS

IT'S DANGEROUS to call anyone the new James Dean, because even the old one found being himself somewhat impossible. You don't fly around town on a motorcycle, drink and whatever else, earn a reputation for being difficult to work with, and acquire your death-Porsche—all by the age of twenty-three—if you're not bent on departing young.

That's why we love James Dean—he died before we even knew we were in love with him, before he could be found wanting, before the studios could cramp his style and turn him into an eight-by-ten glossy. The studio actually forbade anyone but its own photographers to shoot him, but fortunately lots of pictures were taken, leaving a legacy of incredibly elegant posing in New York–ish and western ways. We knew, both from stills and from the way he moved in his movies, that he was *bad*. Rock and roll. If he were still alive, James Dean would be cinema's version of Bob Dylan, if not Neil Young.

Martin Scorsese is an Italian James Dean, and early Clint Eastwood was as James Dean as a Republican can get. Even Woody Allen might be James Dean if James Dean were a scrawny, Jewish New Yorker. Like Dean, Allen's got the whine and the hunched shoulders. Daniel Day-Lewis in *My Left Foot* was James Dean, and Sid Vicious was James Dean as a dead fool. Anything in the mainstream that is beautiful and rebellious and tragic is James Dean—rodeo stars, Jennifer Jason Leigh, beatniks, Magic Johnson now. James Woods is James Dean with a stinger. James Dean is what's going on inside, underneath, while old men in suits lie from the podium.

In L.A. there are tons of unemployed teen idols, so actors with even a Hail Mary hope of being compared to James Dean are glad to play along.

James Dean was not a good role model, and yet all over America his posters still hang in girls' dorms. Nobody could wear jeans like James Dean—not all the Calvin ads on earth will ever touch James Dean in *Giant*. Nor will anyone come close to James Dean on a motorcycle, even though today *everyone* is up to their ears in jeans and motorcycles. What the sixties proved was that the decade's dreams didn't work, because if they did, things wouldn't be the way they now are. But we *do* still have Bob Dylan and Neil Young, and maybe the capitalist rampage here has been slowed and stalled by the James Dean element—maybe the reason America is nowhere near as bad, ecologically, as the Eastern Bloc countries have turned out to be is that James Dean was among us, promoting contempt for hypocrisy, encouraging the sentiment that led his contemporary, Allen Ginsberg, to write, "America, go fuck yourself with your atom bomb."

Luke Perry says, "Being connected to James Dean is the scariest thing. He's such a strong image, and it makes him look like the object of a game for me. And it's not what I'm shooting for. I'll try and be an artist, I don't always want to be the brooding guy in the T-shirt, I want to play pimps and doctors and lawyers, cowboys. If only people will let me be an artist and not the next James Dean."

Of all the young men being heralded as New James Deans, Luke Perry and Jason Priestley of *Beverly Hills 90210* are the major teenage heartthrobs, mainly because of the characters they play on the show—the way they're lit, and their sideburns. After seeing what happened with Johnny Depp, the Fox network has figured out that you can't have too many teen idols. These two are total crush material—though the story line is always some do-good plot, who can notice when you're in a love trance?

Perry says, "For whatever reason, we've all been hurled into the spotlight. I can't go to the market to get anything to eat. Luckily, McDonald's has drive-through."

On the show, Priestley plays a supersensitive, down-to-earth, unbelievably sweet guy, Brandon. He's the one you most want to be. The fact that in person he seems to be the same kind of man isn't to say that he's not a good actor. Like Michael J. Fox, he's short and Canadian, but unlike Fox he refers to "priapism" in public. He bragged in an interview in *Sassy*, the magazine for juicy teenage girls, that unlike his character, he's not the least bit innocent, that he smokes and drinks like any other twenty-two-year-old, and that he's been living in L.A. for five years—enough to put an end to anyone's innocence. He smokes and drinks like the old James Dean.

The youngest among the NJDs is Bojesse Christopher, who is only twenty-one and already a member of the Actor's Studio, not bad for a kid from a small town outside Santa Cruz. He's the only NJD who sounds grateful for the inspiration that comes with the James Dean comparisons. "He left a lasting impression on people because he took a lot of chances," Christopher said. "You need to spark new things— as long as when you fall it's on your face, you're going forward. If you don't find any lumps on the back of your head, you're OK." It's easy to see why he was cast to play Patrick Swayze's brother in *Point Break*—he looks a lot like Swayze, except cherubic. Next he's doing "a movie called *Dark Horse*, with Ed Begley and Mimi Rogers. I play a supersensitive, nice, down-to-earth, unbelievably sweet guy—believe it or not, it's a stretch to play a nice guy."

Dana Ashbrook is the NJD who is most dazzling in person. On *Twin Peaks* he was so dark and brooding as Bobby you couldn't tell that in the flesh he looks like that weird-streak English actor, Rupert Everett the Beautiful. Ashbrook arrived at the photo shoot shrouded in baggy black clothes with a black baseball cap over the Best Hair in the West, and dark glasses over the Eyes, which are so freakishly blue that all the makeup women, stylists, and photo assistants—grown women used to great looks—were left engorged, in creamed-out oblivion. If I weren't old enough to be...well, I'm glad I saw him before I was too old to appreciate it.

The *Twin Peaks* feature film will include Ashbrook as Bobby again, but in the meantime, being one of the new breed of Hollywood kids, the twenty-four-year-old has his own production company and is trying to produce movies no one else will do. "We're trying to make small, moralistic films," he said, "to further universal spirituality." He just finished a short film called *The Coriolis Effect*, which, he said, "is about love, infidelity, and bad weather."

Jamie Walters, who costarred with John Travolta in *Shout* (and therefore went virtually unseen, such is the Travolta-loathing in the air), is the NJD who looks most like the McCoy. He's also the least Hollywood showbiz of these guys, having moved from Boston to New York to attend NYU film school. "I got a job at the Canal Bar as a waiter and as a bartender. A customer came in and said he could get me a job doing commercials, so I went on a Levi's audition and I got it. Then I began getting acting jobs and decided to take lessons."

He's the only NJD without a publicist and the only one I could actually talk to without feeling his career agenda pulsing beneath the surface. He's not so much "on" as he is along for the ride.

"Since I've come to L.A.," he said, "I've experienced tons of rejection and learned how to cook. Part of the fun of being in L.A. is not liking it. Not liking it builds character." He plays Frank James on the *Young Riders* TV series and will assume a small part in a Cameron Crowe movie called *Singles*. He and Luke Perry knew each other in New York and on auditions were often mistaken for each other, though they are nothing alike. Perry has an almost Edwardian quality about him, an elegance that would work in a hero from any age, whereas Walters could only have happened après James Dean. Maybe we just always want more James Deans. Especially now, when there are so many suits lying from so many podiums.

The young actors with even a Hail Mary hope of being likened to James Dean are happy, of course, to play along with our fantasy. In L.A. right now there are cubic tons of unemployed teen-idol material, all of whom believe sincerely that if they got a chance to be on a show like *90210*, they'd damn well put up with any comparison and not do anything to endanger their careers. Once it actually happens, who you become moves beyond your control, which—let's face it—is a cold shower. James Dean himself probably had no idea he was the

New Frank Sinatra (or was it the New Rudolph Valentino?), but that's where things were leading.

We need these young, beautiful men to remind us that there's something besides the liars in suits. We need these wonderful boys to seem misunderstood. As the Rolling Stones sang, "the little girls understand." In a mall in Florida the little girls, ten thousand strong, mobbed Luke Perry, breaking plate glass and injuring twenty-one of their number in the stampede.

James Dean was rock and roll before anyone knew it wasn't a fad, and he was rock and roll before it was Disneyized and turned into role-model material. He was the role model for people who hated role models, and what we still want is *more* James Deans, and no one will ever be James Dean enough.

Even James Dean hardly was the artist long enough to live anything approaching a full life. But anytime someone slinky in a T-shirt and jeans with messy hair comes by, we'll think he's the latest one, and though others might think he's nothing but a soap star with a look, or the newest fad—well, maybe one of these new James Deans will last long enough to become someone else.

Esquire
May 1992

GREAT LEGS

THE FIRST man whose legs I'll never forget was a lifeguard in Santa Monica. It was an overcast day and no one was on the beach except him, age twenty-two, and me, a mere fourteen. He was one of those perfect, too-beautiful L.A. beachboys: blond hair, blue eyes, tan as a summer vacation and tall—over six feet, maybe six three. His legs came up to my waist, it seemed to me, and though I remember his smell—Sea & Ski—and his voice—a kind of moonglow tenor—and I remember him crushing me in his strong, tan arms in a kiss, it's his legs that I still think about. He stood there, as I fled after the kiss, with those long, elegant legs silhouetted against the gray-blue of the painted lifeguard shack. Sad, lost romance.

I was too young to be fooling around with lifeguards, but my preference for legs was solidly in place even then. Tan legs meant perfection, and nothing else would do. Of course, no one with California-beach, lifeguard legs—except maybe Tom Selleck—has even survived those days. So it was lucky that my life, and my tastes, changed suddenly in 1964 when the Beatles and their scrawny English legs scissored across Ed Sullivan's stage. Lifeguards were a thing of the past; Liverpool was *it*.

Before the Beatles, guys with legs that skinny (Henry Fonda, for instance) wore the baggiest pants they could find and hoped you wouldn't notice. But once the Liverpool look arrived, being the skinniest guy around was a badge of honor. When you look back at photographs of the sixties, what you see are little stick legs in black suits with Cuban-heeled boots. And you just know that under those toothpick-thin trousers, the legs were ghost white. But it didn't matter.

I was such a sucker for George Harrison that how he would have looked on the beach in Santa Monica was the last thing on my mind. Scrawny was beautiful. It was in this phase of my life that I fell in love for the last time, and the man of my dreams was as skinny as George Harrison with legs like some Gothic bas-relief. But I'm still an appreciative student of men's legs.

There are, it seems to me, three basic styles of great ones: cowboy, athletic, and my beloved scrawny rock and roll. The cowboy legs most women can't help feeling weak in the knees about are Clint Eastwood's in those Sergio Leone movies. They are so graceful and divine that even my grandmother, dozing before the TV, sits up the minute the flute solo comes on.

The second type—the athletic legs—have come into style more recently, since many basketball players, Olympic champions, and other scantily clad men we might never have noticed have begun to appear frequently on TV. The great tragedy of the decade is former L.A. Lakers forward Magic Johnson's retirement. I'll miss watching him move so effortlessly on the court, his feet slightly pigeon-toed, smiling as if to say: "What shall I do now to slaughter these guys?"

Finally, there's the ultimate in scrawny rock and roll legs—Mick Jagger's. Your heart goes out to him; mine does anyway. I look at the other guys, I remember my lifeguard, but I'm always willing to give a ninety-eight-pound weakling the benefit of a doubt. For the quintessential L.A. teenager I once was, that's a legacy of these strange times and a tribute to the power of love.

Self
May 1992

CHAIRMEN OF THE BOARD

THE STORY that serves as formative mythology and personal inspiration for all businessdude-surfers is almost certainly not true, but who cares? It's about when Otis Chandler was still running the *Los Angeles Times* and was said to have these sedate business or editorial meetings during which a butler would come in carrying a note on a silver tray. Chandler would read the note, leap to his feet, apologize all around for his departure, and then run out the door. Someone would retrieve the note from the floor and read the two words written on it—SURF'S UP.

"He always surfed Dana Point—Killer Dana," John Perenchio, a lawyer and developer, told me. "It really made him mad when they built a marina there." Even a developer thinks development has gone too far when it wrecks somebody's shore break.

"I try and surf a couple times a week, in the morning, six thirtyish. If you get there at five o'clock, there are already people in the water. There's a whole yuppie emergence of surfers—lawyers, doctors. I've heard there's a group called the Surfer's Medical Association, and every year they go to Fiji for their convention, which means they surf."

Since almost anyone connected with surfing is famous for not being connected with anyone else, it's kind of surprising to hear that Perenchio and other surfers like him are organized into something called Heal the Bay, which is trying to clean up the water off Santa Monica. Perenchio's also involved in the Surfrider Foundation, which is trying to clean up the water off Malibu (other places too). When normal surfers get mad about what's happening to their water, they bitch to one another. But when businessdude-surfers get mad, they lobby.

There's also a group called Save Our Coast and one called Environment Now, and a surfer who's involved in both of those plus the two aforementioned organizations is Jeff Harris, MD. "One of my patients, who works with petroleum engineers, says we have the capability to make natural-gas cars, but the oil companies have all this gas-station infrastructure they don't want to declare obsolete. Meanwhile, Mexico City is drowning in smog. It's frustrating to rational people who know things could be better. I'm a family doctor in Malibu, and people come in all the time with ear infections and sinus infections from the polluted water. But when the surf's good, I try and get out there several times a month."

Malibu is filled with guys like these two, successful men in their prime earning years who jump out of bed predawn and climb into smelly wet suits to get a few rides in before work. Gavin Grazer goes, sometimes with his brother, Brian, who is director Ron Howard's partner in Imagine Films Entertainment. Gavin is thirty-three, started surfing at eleven, did it semipro for a while, and then got into a more sensible line of work, filmmaking. He was heading to Portland, Oregon, to make a comedy documentary. "I considered bringing my board, but up there the water's too cold and the sharks are too much. When I'm through I'll go to Puerto Escondido, the Mexican pipeline in Oaxaca. It's the most treacherous, gnarly wave around. But the water's warm." Will Karges goes, too. He's twenty-nine and the president of the Johnnies Café Pizzeria chain here. Before the restaurants, "I was a surf bum," he says, but even now, "when conditions are perfect, I play hooky."

Some of these guys are even able to convince you that surfing helps their businesses. Matt Rapf sells real estate in Malibu—"I sell multimillion-dollar beachfront homes, and it's perfect because I believe in it and can appreciate the lifestyle. But sometimes I'm showing houses to studio executives who want to know about square footage and I'm distracted because I see a great set of waves coming."

Tom Hackett is also in real estate, lives in Pacific Palisades, went to school in Hawaii. He's so busy with work that he does his surfing in the dark, between 10 p.m. and midnight. Isn't night surfing kind of dangerous?

"Yeah," he admitted. "But the more stress I can release by surfing, the more successful I can be at work. It's productive for me to go surfing two hours a week. It gives me the ability to work harder."

Maybe that's how Otis Chandler justified ducking out of all those business meetings. Today he's retired from the paper and is known to have taken up mountain biking with a vengeance. He moved out of his big house in San Marino into what can only be described as a highly glorified trailer on the surfing beach at Paradise Cove. He still looks like the kind of businessdude who has a butler with a silver tray, but he still has a flat stomach too.

Esquire
July 1992

PARTY AT THE BEACH

WHAT HAD I done? Here I was, flying into Miami, city of grand-parents and right-wing Cuban émigrés. As I looked down at the coastline, the man next to me said, "See, there's Miami Beach, where you're going. It's an island. Like Manhattan, you see? It goes against the coast. And there's Miami Itself. They're two different things. Entirely different. Miami Itself is a flourishing, great town. I love it. Miami Beach, why would anyone want to go there? It's dead, it's over, my parents used to drag me there. You get sick of Miami Beach, you call me at my hotel—I'll take you for a drink."

"Oh," I said, "thanks."

He was pretty cute for a funeral director. And not uninteresting, at least on the subject of L.A. gang funerals—the Crips and the Bloods—and how he had to hire extra security or they'd shoot each other even in graveyards. But still . . .

I was going to Miami Beach because, contrary to what my seatmate said, it was the place. The *new* place—the Art Deco District known as South Beach. The place with pastel buildings (I'm a fool for them) and all the New Yorkers (even *New Yorker* editor Robert Gottlieb shared a house there now) and so many fashion photographers and models that even as they set up their shoots they muttered that it must be passé. It was also the place where Chris Blackwell, the record producer who had always been ahead of his time in so many elegant ways, was opening a hotel, the Marlin, that I just had to see. I had a friend there, Susan Brustman, a publicist doing the film festival, who told me, "You'll love it here. I can get you into all the parties. It's like L.A. in the fifties—before it got ruined."

She had never been in L.A. in the fifties, but the idea that anyone would try to seduce me with a promise so ephemeral mowed down my reservations. L.A. in the fifties, which I did experience, was even more a mirage than Miami is now, because nobody in L.A. at the time appreciated it except the odd artist, and I do mean odd.

"If you let me know in time," she said, "I can get you a room somewhere, even though there's a boat show and the whole place will be impossible."

"In the Art Deco part?" I asked. It seemed a dream.

"At the Raleigh," she said. "There's one room left. I'll call Zarrilli."

"Who?"

"He's one of these hotel guys, except I trust him," she said. "He bought this great hotel. They're fixing it up still, but you won't mind. It's right on the beach, you can sunbathe topless, and they've got *great* coffee."

"How far from the airport?"

"Nothing in Miami Beach is more than fifteen minutes from the airport," she said.

That made it sound like a good town to me. And if worst came to worst, I thought as the plane landed, I could always write a piece about Crips funerals instead.

Stepping outside to find a cab, I smelled this pearly, silky, feminine, luxurious, tango-salsa air and suddenly knew that what my friend Jeanette Aaron had told me the day before I left was true: "If you can't get in the mood in Miami, Eve, you can't get in the mood. Period."

It was as though I'd left America. And of course, in a sense I had. Miami is the only city in America that's tropical. It's the only city that in parts, at least, feels more like Cuba than the United States, with all those expatriates who make things lush and fill the city with their own dreams and keep the place hanging in a kind of limbo, while the Havana that actually exists hangs on the horizon like an unpaid debt. Even McDonald's in Miami has Cuban-style coffee. The thought occurs to you, as you feel such tropical air, that here is a city in which anything can happen: torrid romances and violent deaths, immigrant dreams realized and dashed; a city as warm as true love if they like who you are, and as cold as heartbreak hotel if who you are is not OK with them.

I got a Haitian cabbie—one of the lucky ones, the ones who got to stay. He had his radio tuned to French Haitian religious music, trying, no doubt, to douse the pure, unadulterated lust in the air with "Moulin La Toujou" by the Happy Singers. We had flash showers, three in the fifteen minutes it took to reach the Raleigh. As he paid to go over the bridge, I was reminded that we were going to an island, Miami Beach—unlike Miami Itself, which looked like an island too. Water everywhere was the theme; huge cruise ships in the harbor, water planes and boats galore.

The Raleigh turned out to be a seven-story confection in creamy white, mint green, and plum surrounded by photographers' vans, Jeeps, TV-commercial crews, and Winnebagos, with a huge stairway leading up to the double front doors. Inside was a large, terrazzo-floored, high-ceilinged lobby with a newly installed café to my right where I could smell coffee and see magazines for sale. It was homey already.

"Hi," said a widely smiling girl behind the desk. "Welcome to Miami Beach. I'm Suzy."

"Hi," I said, glad she wasn't dressed better than I was.

"And this is Kenny," she said, pulling away from the shadows—or what he wished were shadows—this dark-haired John Cassavetes–type guy with light eyes and an almost furtive, totally un–hotel-type manner. "Kenny Zarrilli," she explained. "You need anything, ask for me or him or anyone down here."

"Hi," he managed. He seemed too young to me to have a hotel, midthirties at most. He had on worn black jeans, a T-shirt of faded olive, and tennis shoes. If this was how the Raleigh was run, I knew it was the place for me. Kenny peered at me as he shook my hand, then turned and left, going off to direct some construction crews in the back.

"He used to be an investment banker in New York," Suzy told me on our way up in the elevator, "and he was really great, but he got bored. The last thing he did before he went out on his own was the Beverly Center in L.A. He got the financing when everyone said it couldn't be done."

"The Beverly Center," I said, remembering this funny, huge shopping mall with a caterpillar escalator outside, which at first everyone hated but now can't live without. "Really?"

I couldn't imagine this guy in a suit.

The elevator opened onto a rather long hallway with orange carpeting, which we walked down until we reached my room. Suzy opened the door, and suddenly there was this view that went all the way to Spain, or some infinite direction over the Atlantic. The furniture was simple—no rattan—and easy. The bed was covered with a brown paisley spread right out of the sixties and had big floral-printed pillows. Recessed in the walls were a CD player, cassette deck, and TV. On a neat little table in the corner was an orchid in a small vase.

"Wow," I said, "far-out." (I always say "far-out" when I'm dumbfounded.)

"Kenny did everything," she said. "He designed it or approved it."

The only trouble with the room, in my opinion, was that I hated leaving it.

When I finally did leave, I walked all over Miami Beach, up and down Ocean Drive, looking at all the old hotels that have come alive once more. The Raleigh was on Collins, which I would learn made it quieter at night. Washington, the third street over, was dotted with thrift shops, Latin juice stands, Hispanic and Jewish businesses, and places like Lulu's, with its Elvis motif, and Don't Say Sandwich to Me, a place where locals go at 4 a.m. to watch horror movies on a large TV screen and eat before going home.

Nowhere at all did anyone approach me for money or look dangerous. The streets themselves were so clean that when my shoes started killing me, I walked barefoot a few blocks home.

My second day in Miami Beach, I made the mistake of calling an old musician boyfriend from my rock and roll days who lived in Coconut

Grove and who, hearing my voice, said urgently, "Wait right there, I'm coming to get you. I'll take you to Miami Itself."

For the next eight hours, my old boyfriend passionately made the case for Miami Itself as opposed to Miami Beach. He drenched me in history, the rich, luxurious houses all over the city with yachts and boats and rowboats in their backyards, Brickell Avenue and its current architectural impressiveness, and the white I. M. Pei building, which at night glows red or blue or purple and green from color gels thrown over it for fun. He showed me the huge cruise liners and told me about "tonnage." He showed me three golf courses, one where Nixon played in Key Biscayne; a park with raccoons; the ancient mansions with banyan trees all around; the private schools and the black ghetto; the Little Havana section and the Mayfair Mall in Coconut Grove, the world's most beautiful mall but also, somehow, the least successful. By this time, my eyes were crossing from Miami Itself. "I want to go home," I said.

By way of apology, he said he'd take me to the Chris Blackwell party. Of course I'd already heard about the party. It was to celebrate the official opening of the Marlin, even though it had been open for a while. "It's going to be hard to get in—very VIP," he said. "But Chris is an old friend of mine. Both my ex-wives want me to take them."

As I came up the wide steps of the Raleigh, I saw Kenny Zarrilli behind the front desk. He looked as far from a hotelier as, say, Edward Villella.

Kenny made more sense the next morning, when I saw him having breakfast with a cluster of businessmen in suits, with briefcases and computer printouts. Kenny was in a suit too, looking bowed but untamed, like "I may be wearing this suit, but not for long." It was one of those Armani things that was supposed to be casual, though no outfit with a tie in Miami Beach could be anything but painful.

"What's the matter?" I asked Suzy behind the desk.

"It's these bankers," she said. "They want Kenny to manage another hotel."

"Besides the Raleigh?"

"*And* the Hotel 100 he's doing now," she said. "Down the street. A really big hotel."

If all this sprucing up was news to me, it was simply amazing to anyone who gave up on Miami Beach in the sixties. The whole concept of Miami Beach had been a sad joke, with its Arthur Godfrey Road and its Jackie Gleason Theater. The art deco buildings had had their apartments chopped into tiny rooms for pensioners. The city of Miami Beach kept hoping for some Big Developer to come and change the place into every other Florida beach town, a condo-filled, ahistorical blight on the landscape, where nothing of memory would survive.

Luckily, the Big Developer fell through. And as in L.A. during the fifties, a "scene" was quietly born, because the strip was so cheap and the buildings so cool, in a throwback kind of way, and the beach right there at your feet. While serious vacationers were all in Europe waiting in line at the Louvre (which had once been cheap and fun), the people who have always created action—gay men—created a new home. Along with local preservationists, they helped push through new limits on development south of Sixteenth Street. Now any building plan has to pass two stringent boards of review, with even more of the neighborhood likely to be restricted soon. After what happened in L.A., SoHo, and Europe, people have learned that when a scene's chief charm is its architecture, developers will come—and now even London looks wrong.

The result of this has been a pastel vigilance—art deco buildings in Necco wafer shades of pink and green and yellow. Somehow, the Marlin's facade of toast and lilac worked best of all. With its outside tables topped by lavender umbrellas and its foyer set off by mauvy sofas, it was a set piece in some new kind of elegance that doesn't yet have a name. In the bathrooms, the walls were checkered in primary colors that matched those in the little "Jamaican" café called Shabeen, where that morning, for the first time in my life, I tasted fresh pineapple juice squeezed with fresh ginger—sweet and exotic.

The furniture in the lobby, the magazine racks, the T-shirt stand—

all had been touched by the same hand and made new and beautiful. The bar was like some under-the-sea Botticelli set, and it was there, not long afterward, that I got to actually meet the woman who had created all this beauty.

I'd known about her for years. In London in the sixties, Barbara Hulanicki had designed the ultimately great Biba, a clothing store I had heard about but never seen. When the place closed in the mid-seventies, she'd moved to Brazil to design clothes for Cacharel and Fiorucci, then eventually came to the States to do hotels and restaurants and nightclubs such as Woody's on the Beach, Semper's, Bolero, and Match. The day I met her, she looked ready to go on a Kenyan safari, dressed in khaki shorts and a khaki vest—although the vest was loaded with tools, not guns or cameras. Or maybe she'd *been* on safari and just come back: she looked that tan. But her blond hair was straight and soft, a reminder that she was still fashion, no matter how rock and roll the money behind all this might be. She was now redoing the Netherland, condos on Ocean Drive that Chris Blackwell had bought.

We sat in Shabeen and had lunch, but she was too preoccupied and exhausted to be as brilliant as what she did. "It's so hard to get anything here," she said. "It always takes a week, where anywhere else you'd have it right away."

We both looked around and she dived into her pineapple-ginger drink, too beat to do more than drink in silence, which I was happy to let her do since her work was enough. The only other thing she could manage to say was, "I'm glad you like it. It did turn out, didn't it?"

On any given day in Miami Beach, you're bound to see at least one fashion shoot in progress. The whole place is a set. Models who aren't working walk the streets in the simplest clothes, like girls at summer camp, with no makeup, as if just getting dressed up reminds them of work. Still, you can spot them amid the great hordes of grazers making their way up Ocean Drive.

No one walks very fast. Nowhere's very far away, and what, after all, is the hurry? Even when people make "plans" in Miami Beach, I noticed after a while, they show up a little later than they're supposed to. By the time they do, you've run into other people who are urging you to go with them, and the evenings, especially on weekends, are mad with parallel possibilities.

"It's always very lazy here," said Tatiana, who owns this great shop called Satyricon, on Española Way. "It's always four o'clock, cocktail hour. It's the tropics, too, and that sort of slows things down. I just love it here. I was on my way back to New York, coming through Miami Beach after a vacation six years ago, and I just never went back. I left my apartment, all my stuff. I just let my friends there have it. I love it here—I could never leave."

It makes sense, I suppose, that the hippest street is the sleepiest-looking. Lincoln Road, unlike the other streets I'd seen, still shows vestiges of its retirement community, and there are still little bead shops where old Jewish ladies buy sequins to sew on sweaters. But ever since a very hip gym opened, and a place where they teach flamenco dancing and another where they do belly dancing, Lincoln has been filled with casual strollers. They don't seem to mind that this old-fashioned pedestrian-only street still looks abandoned, that its Saks and Bonwit Teller and Cartier pulled out twenty-five years ago, that there's not so much as a Gap or a Banana Republic anywhere. They *like* that.

In fact, there's not a single Gap or Banana Republic in all of South Beach, which is one of the great things about the place. You have to go up to Bal Harbour or over to Miami Itself for those stores, which is sort of ironic, considering that all these fashion photographers and models are on shoots here for every chain and fashion magazine in the world.

One day, in a used jeans store on Washington, I heard this guy ask, "How do I know what size these are?"

"Guess," the girl running the place replied.

Oh, there's a Woolworth, if you get desperate for shampoo or razor blades, and there is a department store called Burdine's hidden behind Lincoln Road. I only discovered it in the middle of my second week when I was desperate for Vitabath, but really Miami Beach discourages not only buying things but wearing them. Everyone is so casual.

Or they were, that is, until the Marlin party.

Chris Blackwell, I had heard, fell in love with Miami Beach because no one wore "clothes," and it reminded him of Jamaica, where he had grown up and where everyone just waddled around in any old thing, not caring. But as rumors of that party percolated around town, people began wondering what they were going to wear. Grace Jones was flying in; even Madonna might show, or so I'd heard. Bermuda shorts would simply *not* do.

I myself, luckily, had brought with me this extremely risqué navy blue dress that was so tight, short, and low cut that even in L.A. I wore it into bars at my peril. Also, my hair was short and unnaturally white-blond enough to fit right in with Madonna's Marilyn look and to show that my roots and heart were with her. "Do you have an invitation to the Marlin party?" Suzy wondered when I came into the Raleigh one evening. "Because you can have mine. I'm going to New York for a few days."

"You're not going?" I couldn't believe it.

"Kenny will take you," she said. "He wants to go."

By then I had become somewhat used to Kenny Zarrilli's style of hotel management—i.e., he was running everything, but you couldn't prove it if your life depended on it—and like a lot of people who knew him, I had begun to think of him as extremely funny. Like, to his construction crew he'd say, "Use your brain. It's free."

Zarrilli and I had the same oddball taste, so we wound up one night sitting at the bar in this club called Mac's Club Deuce, which he thought I'd like: "It's half gay, half straight, half rich, half poor, half drag queens, half real models. You'll love it."

First we'd tried to go to the DiLido Beach Hotel to see a drag show called *La Cage*, because, as Kenny said, "It's so funny, you'll laugh. Nothing else in Miami Beach is funny." Unfortunately, we arrived just as "Bette Midler" and "Madonna" were leaving (in full drag). "It's Sunday night—we only do one show," they said. "Come back next Friday."

Just out of curiosity I went inside. It was a perfectly preserved fifties nightclub, with padded booths, darkness, a bar, and a stage where the show would have been if we hadn't come too late. It had marble floors and that kind of fifties Miami Beach flavor that you see at the Fontainebleau, and it was a couple of blocks from the Raleigh, right at the foot of Lincoln Road.

"We could go to the Warsaw," Kenny said. "You've never seen that either, right?"

I was ashamed to admit that I'd never been, because in Miami Beach right now, the Warsaw Ballroom is the eventual destination of everyone out on the town all night, a major gay nightclub that people told me was "just like Studio 54."

We walked three blocks to the Warsaw. It was eleven thirty, and when Kenny called in from the front, we were invited upstairs to meet the owner.

The Warsaw was as much of an excuse for a Den of Iniquity as Miami Beach could muster. In L.A. today there are places where people with pierced genitals do weird things on stage with chains and thongs, but for Miami Beach the Warsaw was as modern as could be. It was entirely black inside, flat black, with strobes and the *loudest* music man has ever known, music that became the bodies of the big dancing men and the small dancing women. Although the place looked entirely too crowded to me, Kenny apologized for its being so empty and for my not being able to see it on a more typical night.

We made our way up narrow side stairs to a mezzanine, from which we had a closer view of an enormous dark-red broken heart about eight feet in diameter, hanging over the dance floor. To me, it seemed the real heart of South Beach, broken because AIDS has killed so many gay men and because those who were left had come here from New York or L.A. or San Francisco to spend their days in the soothing sun and their nights dancing here at the Warsaw to forget. It was they who had created this wonderful scene, in spite of the sadness, the tragedy, and the hearts broken by so many, many funerals.

We stood watching for a while, and then Kenny led me down a black hallway. He opened a door at the end, and we found ourselves in this office with Louis Canales, the man responsible for talking everyone in New York into coming to Miami Beach. Louis calls himself a promoter but is much too soft-spoken and casually dressed to be anyone's idea of that word. With him was George Nuñez, the Warsaw's owner. Both had liquid brown eyes and no tan and looked to be in their late thirties, languid and sweet.

"Hi," Louis said to me. We'd met once before, at a dinner on Lincoln Road. He took my hand, kissed it, and said, "I hear you're the fiercest person on the beach."

"You've been to the Alexander, haven't you?" George asked. He'd noticed that Kenny had a jacket on, which meant he was dressed up, which meant the Alexander, where in fact we had made a stop early that evening. In this scene, I'd learned, everyone knows where everyone is going or has been by what they're wearing.

"What I love about Miami," Kenny said, "is that if you want to get dressed up, you only have to put on a jacket."

"I know," George said. "When I lived in New York and was in the jewelry business, I had all these suits. But now I don't even have trousers. Just jeans."

By now, everybody knew Madonna was in Miami Beach to shoot that book of sexy pictures and that she was looking for a house. (She bought one, but in Coconut Grove.) Louis Canales had spent all day with her, but nobody said anything, and since Louis always looked tired and adorable, he didn't look any the worse for wear.

It was midnight by the time we got over to the Deuce. The place was packed with a mixed jam. Kenny and I sat at the bar, which was curved so you could look at people across from you. You didn't have to strain, in other words, to get a load of the drag queens. On the walls were mirrors, and above the mirrors on the back wall was this neon reclining woman that the TV producer Michael Mann had given to the bar after using it as a prop in a scene from *Miami Vice*. The Deuce smelled like all the gin mills in all the casbahs in every town from Fairbanks to Tierra del Fuego, but the people were more beautiful.

Usually, in real life if I have to stay up past eleven o'clock, I complain, but by one in the morning I was so caught up in wondering who would come in next and what they'd be wearing that I didn't want to leave. "Oh," Glenn Albin said when I told him the next day how I hadn't wanted to leave, "you were what we call here 'into the Deuce.'"

Thank goodness I was only drinking Diet Coke, because the next day I got the message that Chris Blackwell wanted to see me.

I'd been curious about Blackwell ever since my old rock and roll days, when I'd been an album-cover designer-slash-groupie—and I do mean "slash"—for Denny Cordell, who owned Shelter Records, and all the girls spoke of Chris Blackwell in the most hushed terms. They'd say, "Well, Denny is cute, but Chris is just so elegant and beautiful and . . . charming."

By then, Blackwell was already a legend, having started Island Records out of a small office in Kingston, Jamaica, in 1962 to bring local talents like Laurel Aitken ("Little Sheila") and Millie ("My Boy Lollipop") to American and British audiences. He had discovered and signed the Spencer Davis Group, with its fifteen-year-old singer Stevie Winwood, and when Winwood had gone on to form Traffic, Blackwell had produced that group as well. Jethro Tull, Cat Stevens, King Crimson—Blackwell had done them all, then almost single-handedly popularized reggae, making stars in the process of Bob Marley and the Wailers, Toots and the Maytals, Burning Spear, and more. Along the way, he grew as renowned for his loyalty as for his instincts. He nurtured bands until they clicked—most famously U2 in the early eighties, when no one else would touch them.

Although today Chris Blackwell doesn't have as much money as, say, God, he probably has more than you or I do (unless you're Ahmet

Ertegun or David Geffen). Grown men despair when they think about him, especially men in rock and roll, like my old boyfriend in Miami. "I heard he sold Island to PolyGram for four hundred million dollars, and he's still managing the record company," my poor friend moaned. "And even if he had to give back loads to banks and lawyers, he still must really be rolling in it."

What he's done with it is to expand: first into distributing movies (*Mona Lisa*, *The Trip to Bountiful*, *Kiss of the Spider Woman*) and now into real estate in a very big way right here in Miami Beach. His Island Trading Company has not only bought and refurbished the Marlin, it's done the Netherland and may soon do the Tides. Almost every day I heard rumors that he was buying up more. It was like a game of Monopoly where you've got nothing left but the utilities and a bunch of mortgaged railroads and your friend has all the money, has hotels on all the yellows and greens, and is about to build on Park Place and Boardwalk.

The odd thing for me about meeting Blackwell at last was that I hadn't asked to see him. He'd asked to see me. Someone must have told him that I was hanging around the Marlin, because the next thing I knew there was a message at the Raleigh from his assistant, saying that Blackwell would see me at one o'clock in the afternoon, at the Marlin, in the Shabeen café.

Considering this was the day of his party, that seemed to be cutting it pretty close. I entered the Marlin a few minutes early, and there was this manager, Wendy, who had fluffy brown hair, a New York pallor, and a worried attitude. "I know he really wants to meet you," she said, "because you're his *first* appointment."

By the time Blackwell arrived, at one thirty, both Wendy and I were nervous wrecks (he's famous for getting distracted, showing up eight hours or three days late for appointments). But soon enough, his famous charm—and a beautiful smile that made him look like Kirk Douglas in a pirate movie—mesmerized and calmed us. What I noticed right after the smile were these wonderful blue eyes and this not-too-long, but still rock and roll, Irishly blond-red hair. He had on a black T-shirt, black pants, and some kind of shoes so anonymous I don't remember them—maybe just sandals.

"What," I asked, "can I do for you?"

He looked—if he could have looked that way—to be momentarily at a loss for words. I mean, you don't often have people from the press throwing in the towel so early.

It felt good to throw him off guard, but I immediately felt guilty and asked a straight question. "So," I said, "I heard that you bought this because you came down to Miami Beach three years ago and didn't want to stay at the Fontainebleau."

"Yes," he said, "I was supposed to stay in one of those places, but I changed to some place nearer here. When all the developers fell through, I came back about a year later and all that was here was crack users and elderly couples. I thought it was so great that I looked around for something I could afford. And this I could afford. I couldn't afford anything on the ocean. Things on Ocean were three times as much, so I bought this."

His accent was upper-class British, toned down by this sense of not wanting to intimidate people. And there was a gleam behind him, a hidden agenda that promised that if things were different, he'd be perfectly happy to forget all this and just have fun.

"I think there are some people who capture the imagination of their generation," I gushed, "and you're one of them."

"Which generation is that?" he asked, and began laughing this mad Irish laugh that cut across decades and pompous remarks like mine.

"A blurry generation," I offered.

"The sixties to the nineties." He laughed, and so did I. "I must say I was thinking about that the other day, and I feel very lucky I was in England at that time. You know, someone was asking me if there was any other time that reminded me of this here in Miami now, and I said, 'Yes, London in the sixties.' It was great then, and it's great here now."

One thing that wasn't on his bio was the fact that he's a part owner of this extremely low-down (lascivious almost) fast-food chain in L.A. called Fatburger, which is so infamously great that you see rock stars' long limos parked outside the one on La Cienega in east Beverly Hills and chauffeurs sent inside to load up on this thing they invented, or perfected, called chili fries—i.e., the best and greasiest french fries, with chili (gummy, horrible, bad for you) ladled on top.

No human being is constitutionally able to lead a life of eating chili fries. They'll kill you. In fact, pretty soon L.A. is going to have a Chili Fries Anonymous.

"I've heard you own Fatburger," I said. "You should be ashamed."

"Why?"

"Because they're so bad for you," I said. "It's a lot like drugs, those chili fries there—*really* bad for you."

"But they're so great!" he exclaimed.

"The only thing good about them," I said, "is they make you happy."

"Well," he said, laughing, "that's a *start*, isn't it?"

Finally I could see he was getting that look that busy men get, and so I said I'd better let him go. He asked if I was coming to the party that night, and I said, "I was going to go with this rock and roll guy who lives in Miami, but both of his ex-wives are coming, and now he's chicken."

"Tell him he'll have fun," he said.

"That's not his idea of fun," I replied.

"Well, anyway, *you'll* come, won't you?"

He gave me one of these great blue-eyed looks, and I said to myself, Not only me but a dress to *die* for.

I had two choices. I could go along with the high-command dress code decreed by Louis Canales, who said "just casual." Or I could wear this Donna Karan clinging thing with a zipper down the front— red, which now that I was so tan nearly made me glow in the dark. I decided that since I *had* the red dress, it should be worn.

At eight thirty, as arranged, I came into the lobby to meet Kenny and saw that he had sensibly decided to wear what he already had on—white jeans and a T-shirt. When he saw me, though, he added a vest.

At Kenny's request, we went first to some book party on Washington, where I saw all the people I'd gotten to know in my two weeks in town. But when it was time to leave, I spotted Kenny, up to his ears in some conversation with Bruce Weber, the—ahem—photographer of cheekbones and cheeks.

"You go on," Kenny said. "I'll meet you there."

"OK," I said, and so off I went. A typical Miami Beach "we'll catch up with you later" parting.

Five of us wandered through the jasmine night. The moon was almost full, the potential unlimited.

Until, that is, we got within a block of the party. Chaos! There were cops, barricades, searchlights. Hundreds of people waving invitations were trying to catch Louis's eye, while he tried to accommodate what turned out to be three thousand people in a room that held six hundred (and *that* many only if you counted the vacant lot next to the Marlin, where one of Blackwell's bands was playing and people were supposed to dance).

If I'd been by myself, I'd have gone straight home, but I was with new friends whose idea of a challenging situation was just this. One of them managed to catch Louis's attention with a perfect East Coast money voice, and Louis managed to let us crawl through, and I wound up with this thing I still have, a large necklace that says MARLIN—BACKSTAGE PASS.

The lobby was a crush, the bar was a crush, and nobody wanted to be outside dancing. They all wanted to be right there in case Madonna came. Everyone knew Madonna had flown into town the day before; everyone knew that Isabella Rossellini had also flown in; and Grace Jones, too—and everyone wanted to be there to see if she danced topless on a table. I found myself on a balcony, where I could stand above the crowd and look down on great arms, great legs, gorgeous girls, beautiful boys—everyone trying just to get a drink, food having long disappeared. In their midst stood Chris Blackwell, looking gorgeous.

It was like the restaurant Evelyn Waugh described that everyone went to after a car race, "where only the overbearing and obnoxious could get tables, and only the vile and outrageous could get served."

Not that anyone could get served.

Much less *out*, as I discovered when I tried to leave after about fifteen minutes.

Later, I heard that the "real party," the one with Madonna and Isabella Rossellini and the VIPs, had been upstairs on the roof. The person who told me this then said that he was kidding, but I didn't believe that. If I were Chris Blackwell and my friends were all in town and I wanted to spare them, I would put them on the roof too.

Especially if I wanted them to be able to get a drink.

Or an hors d'oeuvre.

Now all parties in Miami Beach, my friend Glenn Albin told me, are judged by the Marlin standard. "Since that party," he said, "everyone has started dressing up. Before, they'd just go out in their usual clothes, but now, ever since the Marlin, we've noticed that if there's a party, people wear clothes."

So much for Chris Blackwell's coming to Miami Beach because it was easy and casual.

Still, all I needed were mornings like the one I woke up to the next day—the sky clear, the water blue, the *Pinta, Niña*, and *Santa María* out in the distance—because a calm day is all the casualness I need. I gingerly strolled past the Marlin to see if it had survived the previous night. Not a lavender umbrella was out of place. Had the party been just one more mirage?

What I loved about Miami Beach, I decided as I packed to leave, was that what it wanted to be was something to look forward to—a mirage unrealized, a half-finished vision. And I loved the water, water everywhere that was so blue and so tropical and so clean and so seductive, and the people with boats launched from their backyards, great boats and rowboats and even canoes. The whole of Miami is a city rising out of water, reflected in water, shimmering in water, mingled in water. Alongside it lies Miami Beach, like one of those cruise liners that suddenly shudders into view, huge and festive, the brass of dance-band music wafting over the water. Except that it is such an old and weather-beaten ship—a ghost ship, almost—its pastels worn by the sun and by sea-spray air, moored to the mainland by its bridges, its vow to return about to be remembered.

"What I love about this place," Chris Blackwell said, "is that it's so sexy. I mean, it *is*, isn't it?"

"What I really love," Kenny Zarrilli said, driving me to the airport the afternoon I, sadly, had to leave, "is that the airport's only twelve minutes from the hotel. I love getting into Miami at six thirty in the morning and suddenly feeling that air. The tropics! You get off the plane, and suddenly you're here."

He hugged me goodbye and said, "You'll be back. We'll have a party for the pool."

Two weeks before, the idea of flying across the country to celebrate the finishing of someone's swimming pool would have struck me as monumentally ridiculous. Now it seemed like a perfectly sensible excuse.

A tropical city in blue water with pearly air. It turned out I was right about my hair—it couldn't be too blond. And Jeanette was right about Miami—if you can't get in the mood in Miami, you can't get in the mood at all.

Condé Nast Traveler
August 1992

HIPPIE HEAVEN

THE SIXTIES were a dance that began because everyone was so sick of the uptight fifties, they just went hog wild, and then wilder and wilder. One English boyfriend of mine in those days told me about a party in Washington, DC, where a young girl dressed as a mime/princess went around blessing all the guests with a lily as she was about to leave. When she got to the last man in the room, a large executive filled with Scotch, and was about to touch him with her flower, his eyes began to bulge and his throat grew taut, and he snarled: "You don't scare me!"

But she did. That was the point.

He knew exactly what a girl like her meant.

Maybe the reason some of us so long for the sixties to come back is because the world has gone so seriously dismal, it makes the sixties look like they had character—flaky or not. After the eighties, if you begin wearing long fringe, suede hip-hugger bell-bottoms, and boots, you're no longer some "material girl," but someone intent on more important, higher, spiritual things—the rain forest, jobs with heart, recycling.

Of course, we know that the minute you throw away a long-treasured costume because it'll never come back, it comes back. Knowing this, I never did throw my sixties things away because for one thing I still wore them anyway, even when they were grossly out of style, and for another, to me they were art. Especially the red rayon forties dress, cut on the bias, that I'd worn the nights I waited in the Troubadour bar in West Hollywood, looking for trouble like Jim Morrison. Or my navy wide-leg sailor pants with the thirteen-button front (giving sailors thirteen chances to change their minds, was the idea—not that I ever did). These were the original bell-bottoms and not the Cher cut that came later, when the waistbands hit the hips and looking like a hula dancer became of the essence. I still have those pants, and I've worn them since 1967 when I bought them in an army surplus store. I look elegant in them and people have asked me if they're Chanel, they're so classic and well cut.

I showed a guy I know photos of the latest Perry Ellis, Betsey Johnson, and especially Anna Sui designs and asked him what he thought. He said, "It's 1968, right?"

In the actual sixties there were no designers; there were girls who made clothes for their friends or small shops selling one-of-a-kind things. In Los Angeles it started with a store on the Strip called Belinda's and with people like Trina Robbins who made Renaissancey clothes to wear. People wanted to look like storybook characters, to wear clothes that meant something. One of the things our clothes meant was "We don't believe a thing they say."

My sister began by making a maroon suede dress. Her boyfriend had learned about leather from a sandal maker in Chicago. He knew what tools you needed to work with leather, and together they made this dress, in 1967. "I wore this dress into this shop on the Strip, Belinda's, and the girl took one look and asked if I could make four more, and I said yes."

A month later, she'd followed her boyfriend to London and the next thing she knew, her boyfriend had designed a line of suede and leather hunting shirts they took to Blades on Savile Row, one of London's oldest tailors, who loved this line so much, my sister told me, that "they said, 'we'll take lots, but you don't know how to cut, we'll show you.'"

So, it being the sixties when anything went, my sister, a twenty-one-year-old American with a talent for sewing, was taken down to the basement of a Savile Row tailor and taught how to make real patterns, because, before then, all leather clothes had been boxy and depended on fringe or people not caring if things really fit or not, and these old men taught her, in three weeks, how to cut patterns that really fit—and from then on, she was in business in a very big way.

Eight months later, they returned to Los Angeles and opened a shop on the Sunset Strip named for my sister, Mirandi (she'd changed her name from Miriam, another thing you could do in the sixties without being thought too weird), and there, in 1968, with rock and roll coming into full bloom—next door to a place called the Psychedelic Conspiracy, everyone's favorite paraphernalia store—she had her own store.

"Our first customer was a guy in the Mafia who had rolls of hundred-dollar bills in his boots, and he put in a thousand-dollar order and we were off..." She made clothes for Steppenwolf, David Crosby, Stephen Stills, and Graham Nash, Cream, the Jefferson Airplane, Sharon Tate, "and this black suede tuxedo for this drug king to get married in."

She also made clothes for Jim Morrison: "Two suits, leather, with extra pants and a laced crotch, like sailor pants. And snakeskin lapels. With a stash pocket concealed in the lining." Mica Ertegun wanted a black glove-suede calf-length coat with snakeskin lapels, double-breasted with a fitted bodice and flared at the bottom—like a Russian princess, lined with green brocade silk. This was the year she was named to the ten best-dressed list. She sounds awfully well dressed to me now—"glove suede" sounds divine.

Eventually, my sister got divorced, quit making clothes, and began a career as a rock-concert promoter. But then she realized rock and roll was too hard. Today she's a therapist, seeing young girls in their early twenties with major crushes on very bad boys—which is recycled revenge, if you ask me.

I myself, in those days, was nothing if not in love with very bad boys, the worse the better, I realize now, although in the sixties the boys were very sweet and the only flaw you could find in them was that they were dealers or else rock stars, which made faithfulness impossible. Except that it didn't matter then because the worst things you got were social diseases that were only embarrassing—they didn't kill you.

In the sixties, nobody wore padded shoulders; they wore tiny fitted jackets and shirts. Men weren't supposed to look "buff," they looked scrawny and poetic. Guys on the streets, tan, dressed like pirates with long blond curly hair flowing past their shoulders, and eyes of periwinkle blue, and high cheekbones would look at me as I passed and say *I* was beautiful. I couldn't believe it. "You're the beautiful one," I would say, "look at you!"

"Hey, I live over there in that house with the blue door, if you want to come hang out," they'd say.

In those days I learned to tell people they were beautiful, and indeed, everyone seemed to be.

On Hollywood Boulevard yesterday I saw two young men, in their early twenties or late teens, both with long flowing hair—the high cheekbones, the tans, etcetera. I was in a shoe store, looking at these great purple shoes that reminded me of the old days, when these boys came in and one said, "Hi, we're both vegetarians and don't like animal products, do you have any boots not made of leather?"

They were both in jeans, T-shirts, and sneakers (no leather), and the girl managing the store said, "No, we don't."

Later, on the street, I came upon these boys again and said, "Are you from San Francisco?"

"Yes," they said, "how did you know?"

"Something about you," I said, "reminded me."

In San Francisco, of course, there are still hippies and in Berkeley, lots of them. And they have "raves" where two or three thousand people stay up all night, outdoors, and dance. If that isn't hippieness, I don't know what is.

In Miami Beach there's a renaissance of recycling old buildings, those gorgeous art deco two-story hotels and bungalow-court places that we still have in L.A., except not as well tended, and there I met a beautiful guy with a yin-yang tattoo on his shoulder and that laid-back intensity kids used to have in the sixties, and it seemed to me that Miami Beach right now, with all its thrift stores, very cheap rents, and nonstop nightlife, might be a perfect place for the sixties to be recycled too.

The weirdest thing in the world is seeing a style return that only a year ago was considered ugly by everyone who was anyone, i.e., bell-bottoms—in fact, a friend of my sister's just flew into L.A. from London and said, "I'm so happy to be here so I can buy some pants that aren't bell-bottoms."

A friend of mine, Caroline Thompson, who wrote the screenplay for *Edward Scissorhands*, told me that in London, where she went recently, "the kids are all in platform shoes with bell-bottoms, the guys have long hair and wear John Lennon glasses. And they were hanging out in Leicester Square singing 'Hey Jude.'"

According to a girl in her twenties I know in L.A., what really galled everyone enough to not mind the sixties coming back in a major way was the Gulf War. "That really made everyone mad," she said. "I was at UCLA and the kids were just furious. And Rio. And Clarence Thomas."

It's no wonder that kids have taken to wearing old clothes and hanging out in beatniky coffeehouses and talking about psychedelics.

Near my neighborhood in Hollywood, hippieness has sort of sprung up overnight. There's a block on Franklin Avenue where a coffee shop called the Bourgeois Pig is right next to an alternative-magazine store called the Daily Planet, which sells wild tracts from Berkeley and tattoo and piercing quarterlies. Not too far away is Big & Tall Books, which is also a café and is open until 2 a.m., jammed with aspiring hippies eager to talk all night and all day. On Vermont Avenue in East Hollywood, there are almost three blocks of hippie-ness, beginning with Chatterton's, which was always on the beatnik side; the Onyx coffee shop, which is cappuccino city; the Los Feliz theater, which runs great movies from far and wide; a men's store called X-Large, partly owned by Michael "Mike D" Diamond of the Beastie Boys, which has such great clothes that artists I know in San Francisco drive down just to shop there; and other little places, like the Amok bookstore, which has this great catalog entitled *Fourth Dispatch: Source Book of Extremes of Information in Print*. And the

Dresden Room, where old people living in Los Feliz Hills used to eat prime rib but which is now jammed with just plain weirdos from around the neighborhood in their twenties, thirties, and forties, eager for a dark place to hang out and drink beers. The Dresden Room is the kind of place hippies would never have enjoyed because they had no ironic detachment, but nowadays the innocence of the sixties has been cut by extremes of information, and ironic detachment is all the rage. It adds balance.

It occurred to me that when things on the outside get too disgusting and wretched or boring, kids will turn to things on the inside to see beauty. A friend of mine who manages rock groups said, "In London right now they're drinking Ecstasy punch as we speak. It's like mescaline, acid without the side effects. It makes everyone happy and stay up all night. Things are so bad there." Psychedelics are everywhere—mushrooms, DMT, Ecstasy. I hear that LSD is having a comeback—and I'll tell you, it can be a refreshing spiritual experience akin to selling your house and moving to Tibet. Even the rumor of LSD could make people rethink their idea of what to wear.

When I was a hippie, the main social rule was under no circumstances was anyone to be a bummer—you had to have a personality so full of sweetness and light that someone completely wrecked on LSD could run into you and think you were holy. We used to think that if only we hung on with enough of a vengeance, things would have to get better—kinder and gentler and certainly more colorful. Every time we saw the remotest evidence of this, we'd sigh, "It's happening, it's happening."

By which we meant "they" were getting it, that pretty soon the war would end, police would blend into the scenery, and Latin American dictators would divest themselves of their worldly goods and even Richard Nixon would show up wearing flowers. We thought beauty was power.

Of course, we were wrong.

In the sixties going to thrift shops and dressing up in the styles of another era became de rigueur: we began recycling the past and using it to bring romance, drama, and "it's happening" into the room with us. For very little money, girls could wear great clothes of days gone by and, because we were young and beautiful, get away with it. "Their" wives wore stuff from Paris, the couture creations that could make entrances at charity balls and opening nights at the opera, and things to wear shopping while buying other things to wear shopping.

The fact that the things in Paris now look like things you can get in the thrift stores, is, to me, amazing.

If today the women who lunch in New York are going to begin having dinner parties wearing long fringe, platform shoes, low-slung bell-bottoms, and headbands, or cut-velvet vests, brocaded-satin jacket lapels, tons of colors, tons of bracelets, and Cher-type short-skirted dresses with full sleeves and a renaissance flavor (Cher *avec* Bob Mackie), if thirties-style dresses by Marc Jacobs for Perry Ellis cut on the bias with tons of sequins and transparent blouses, if faux-fur vests and crushed velvet from Betsey Johnson and turquoise blue gloves, if Janis Joplin–type floppy hats with ridiculous feathers return, then it's happening, it's happening.

But what, really, is happening?

In the early sixties, before the big buildup in Vietnam had begun and the Beatles hadn't even left Liverpool, the polls showed that nearly 80 percent of the American public trusted the government in Washington ". . . to do the right thing." In the summer of 1992, only 20 percent feel that way. The numbers are completely reversed. It's hard to believe that everything we tried to free up in the sixties—the heavy-handed police dealing with "people of color," the small minds who championed backwater values and regarded women as a "splinter group," the ones who hated sex (or said they did, from pulpits, before they were photographed sneaking out of motels), the ones who didn't want anyone to have fun except them, the ones who savaged the coastline with oil rigs and polluted—is still with us; it's hard to believe that the sixties ever happened. It's enough to make you throw out your clothes from those days, but I never did. I suffered the eighties in silence, partly because it took me a whole decade to get sober and partly because I couldn't believe that such ugliness was so merrily multiplying. That people would forget about each other and settle for BMWs instead.

Perhaps people are just so tired of how awful everything is, they've given up and decided to just have fun in a cheap and simple way. We're afraid of the environment and extinction, we're afraid of the future, we're afraid of "urban unrest," and perhaps this is a way to stave off the stares of the homeless, because hippies had a great way of making being homeless seem a sensible idea. They had crash pads, and as my sister remembers, "In the sixties, panhandling meant you refused to be part of the system."

Since today you can't get in the system even if you're dying to compromise your politics, recycling seems our only hope. If we can recycle the spirit of "it's happening, it's happening" along with those expensive clothes from Paris, maybe having fun will come back into fashion. And fun isn't to be sneezed at. The sixties were fun. The trouble was, we thought fun was enough. But if we don't watch out, the only people having fun are going the be the three people who own everything.

Of course, this sixties surge of Anna Sui, Perry Ellis, and even Christian Lacroix could be a "trend." But if these platform shoes, hip-hugger bell-bottoms, and long fringe are just another "trend," I'll eat my Italian red straw hat.

Because one of the things one learned from the sixties is that the price of freedom is eternal vigilance and, though thinking about running things wrecks your peace of mind, even MTV is airing "Choose or Lose" ads to get kids to vote.

When an entire generation gets dazzled by a drug with the density, force, and newness of LSD, we can't really blame ourselves for hip-hugger bell-bottoms—we couldn't get our pants all the way up. And when through our marijuana-clouded living rooms we saw the non-war on TV or the napalm photographs on the pages of *Ramparts* in 1968, and when suddenly an entire generation became As One waiting for the next Beatles album to come out, and it does, and it's *Sgt. Pepper*, and when Jim Morrison calls himself an "erotic politician," and when an entire generation laces itself into high boots and long, flowing street clothes, giving each other flowers and beads, and sets out to prove we didn't "need" war, alcohol, or families because we were each other's family, and when the new star is Jack Nicholson, then not just a girl dressed like a psychedelic princess, blessing an old man from the old school, but an entire generation was met with the words, "You don't scare me!"

But she did. We did. That was the point.

Vogue
October 1992

BILLY BALDWIN

IN THE lobby of the hotel where I was supposed to meet him, I thought a man sitting in a chair might be him. He was sort of cute, but washed-out. Then I thought, suppose in real life he is washed-out. "Are you ... um, William?" I asked.

"No," the washed-out man said, "I'm not."

Suddenly I see him enter the almost-empty lobby in this Santa Monica hotel by the ocean, and of course this ordinary man I thought was him is nothing like him. He is tall, he is gorgeous, he is wrapped in a charismatic aura that, from afar, is unmistakable. He comes closer and I say, "You are ... ?"

And he says "Are you ... ?"

His voice is exact—the exactness of a New Yorker who doesn't want to be mistaken for an Angeleno. He's just passing through on business, otherwise he'd be where they are smarter and faster.

Even though William Baldwin (his friends call him Billy) was in *Flatliners* and *Backdraft,* two movies that weren't exactly the greatest shows on earth, most women know who he is, partly because of his more famous brother, Alec. "You mean, the cute one," they all say. But in the next few months everyone is going to know who William Baldwin is because he has two new movies coming out—*Sliver*, with Sharon Stone, opening in May, and *Three of Hearts*, with Kelly Lynch, due out this fall.

"What's *Sliver* about?" I ask, after translating his order, "A breakfast shake," into L.A.-ese—"A smoothie."

"Sharon Stone's character moves to a building where Tom Berenger and I live...."

"What's Sharon Stone really like?" I ask.

"Classic Hollywood sexpot," he says, facetiously. "Anyway, a love triangle emerges among the three of them, and that's where the fun starts. One of the characters is a voyeur, which is an interesting topic. I think everyone is a voyeur."

"I agree," I agree.

"You pick up the phone, you overhear a conversation because the lines are crossed, do you hang up?"

"Not me," I confess.

"Something similar happened to me recently. I was in my apartment in New York looking out the window when I saw this completely nude woman standing in front of her window. I was fascinated. All of a sudden she walked away. I waited fifteen or twenty seconds, but she didn't come back. I was hoping she would come back."

"Yeah, and take off some more clothes!"

"There were no more clothes to take off," he reminds me.

We both gaze out of the window, but there are no naked ladies outside, only the blue Pacific Ocean, so I decide to change the subject to something less naked.

"So," I say, "does Chynna live in New York?" He goes out with Chynna Phillips of Wilson Phillips, which is one reason men never say mean things about him. They see he's completely unavailable to other women.

"She lives here," he says.

"How did you meet?" I ask.

"We met in the MGM Grand Terminal at the Los Angeles airport." It seems that everyone in Hollywood thought they would be a good couple, and then, oddly enough, it worked out. They've been together for a year and a half.

"She seems like a shy person," I say, remembering when I saw her once at a birthday party, hovering around the edge, not joining in with total abandon as the other kids did.

"She's like me," he says, "she's shy around people she doesn't know."

"You seem like a nice person, and she's a nice person, that's probably why everyone suggested you get together," I remark.

"They never met me so they couldn't say whether I was a nice person or not, they just thought that we'd look good together or something."

"Well, you seemed like a nice person in *Backdraft*!"

"That could be good acting," he counters.

"Naw!" I insist. "It couldn't be good acting! It has to be that you're really sweet."

"I know a lot of guys who are tremendous assholes who come across as good guys, and I especially know a lot of really good guys who come across as tremendous schmucks on-screen. So it's got to have something to do with acting."

Since we're talking about acting, I decide to ask him what he thinks about his career so far.

"Well, it's pretty boring to chart a course for your career," he says. "When the good material comes, you just do it. I read a script last night that was pretty good. It was to play Sir Lancelot. It would be like *Robin Hood*."

"Don't do it," I reply. "Too sincere. You're already the cute Kevin Costner, and *Robin Hood* didn't do him a bit of good."

He begins to laugh, but once you start talking "career" it becomes too much for a normal person, so I change the subject. "I hear you used to work on political campaigns."

"In college I majored in political science, and then I went to Capitol Hill to work for Tom Downey, a congressman from Long Island."

"You didn't do anything there, right? Nobody does anything in Washington." (This was my Hollywood opinion leaking out.)

"No!" He was very nonplussed. "I *worked*. You're going to make me look like some kind of..."

"Doll," I offer, "some huge doll."

"Some sex symbol!" he cries, chagrined. "I hate those words! I hate the word 'star'! I hate 'celebrity'! I hate 'hot'!"

"How about charisma?"

"That I love," he looks mollified, "that's credibility, respect. Not one of those flash-in-the-pan words."

I write down "charisma," hoping to spell it right for his sake.

"So when I worked on the Hill, I actually did work."

You might think he had parents who were politicians, but he didn't. His father was a schoolteacher and his mother was a schoolteacher turned market researcher. He grew up in a Long Island town called Massapequa.

"We called it Matzo-pizza because it was half Jewish and half Italian. I was neither. I'm Irish. All my friends had Italian names filled with vowels."

"I love Italians," I say. "They're so beautiful. I'm half Cajun and half Jewish."

"That's interesting," he replies. (Really, if you were me, you'd have believed he thought so.)

Sadly, I eventually ran out of tape or I could have stayed there listening to him until the earthquake came and buried us up to our necks. As we said goodbye with his eyes matching the blue Pacific behind us on the horizon, I thought that if I were Chynna Phillips.... Well, but who is.

Mademoiselle
March 1993

THE AMERICAN SCENE

LOS ANGELES: ANGELS WITH ATTITUDE

Los Angeles has always been a city fueled by fame; its current underground scene, lorded over by a tight-knit group with hopes of stardom, is no different. What is different is that the club scene here thrives on two distinct—and invisible—planes. For those who wake up before sunset, a handful of hip coffeehouses, all located in West Hollywood, provide office space for L.A.'s "will-bes." In places like Small's, the Living Room, Big & Tall, and Bourgeois Pig, people in their twenties and thirties hang out for hours, planning their acting careers, playing Ping-Pong, and drinking cappuccino.

At night the second layer of L.A.'s under-undercurrent awakens. Neon is over. The haunts have plain doors, no signs, no grand entrances—every place looks like a garage that went out of business. There's the T Room, dead looking outside, vibrant red-vinyl walls within; Roxbury (on Thursdays only—deejay/party giver Brent Bolthouse's night); and King King, which you'd swear had been boarded up.

Occasionally you'll see hopefuls try to gain access: A '55 Chevy pickup glides up to Gaslight, and out hop three incredibly beautiful women. A young man tries to latch on to them. He makes it as far as the threshold and says to the door-woman:

"I'm a friend of Brent's."

"Oh?" she says. "How long?"

"A year."

"Well," she replies with a straight face, "I've been his friend for five years. Come back when you've known him as long as I have, and I'll let you in."

DALLAS: DOWN AND DIRTY IN DEEP ELLUM

The psychic metronome that rules Dallas ticks from the strictly conservative Right to the kind of stylized scene you find in Deep Ellum, the nickname used by black jazz musicians of the 1920s to describe the neighborhood that grew up downtown, on the east end of Elm Street, not far from Southern Methodist University. For decades Deep Ellum has attracted a mixed artistic population, but it was long considered to be on the wrong side of the tracks; by the late eighties the city government finally realized the area's potential and began gentrification, lining the streets with elm trees and streetlights.

Now nightclubs, health-food stores, and psychedelic shops are interspersed with older businesses—hardware stores, carpet installers, old elephant-walk bars—that persevere, like their counterparts in the Haight, the East Village, and Venice Beach. True Deep Ellumites might feel that their turf has become Dallas's Disneyland; for others—like the socialites arriving for the Cattle Baron's Ball or Lynn Wyatt's occasional hoedown—it's still on the edge. You're sure to find them, late at night and still in evening clothes, slipping deep into "Ellum Street."

The compact district is a Texas-style jumble of unpredictable attractions: low-down barbecue, upscale Mexican at Eduardo's Aca y Alla, vintage cowboy boots at Blues Suede Shoe, tattoo parlors, and piercing salons. There are also night spots like Club Dada, where rock singer Edie Brickell got her start, and Club One, where well-built guys in slave drag frolic with nearly naked dancing women, all aswirl in dry-ice fog and colored lights—a very *adult* sort of theme park.

Esquire
Spring 1993

SAN FRANCISCO: PSYCHEDELIC PUNKS AT HOME

We're in San Francisco to investigate the punk revival people have been talking about, but the moment we meet our guide to the scene— a kaleidoscopic woman named, simply, Tornado—we know we're onto something much more encompassing. Whereas punk was stripped-down and bare-bones, the situation here is more layered and eclectic. These kids—whose ages range from early twenties to midforties—are too colorful to be called punk and, in fact, vehemently resist the label (to them, punks are depressed people dressed all in black). Their look is actually a haphazard pastiche of several teen-anarchy fashion statements: grunge, rave, hippie, punk, seventies. It's a Dead Boys II Men scene. In-a-Gadda-Nirvana. Guns N' Roses singing punk classics on their current *The Spaghetti Incident?* album.

And such a scene must naturally have its contradictions. Since dropping out is not a viable activity these days, a pierced young man might hold a job at the Audubon Society. And stressing the culture in counterculture, a would-be Nob Hill socialite may have her butler serve magic mushrooms to her guests.

For Tornado and her friends, who earn livings as designers, hair-dressers, massagers, and caterers (shades of summer of '69?), both style and lifestyle are a happy convergence of whatever's in the air. "I knew when I moved here six years ago they had earthquakes," says Tornado (who grudgingly allows that she does have a last name, Terhune). "But then, I'm not against natural chaos. I like dealing with the unexpected." And so must anyone looking at her. Tornado herself is a natural chaos of conflicting styles: Her hair's a bright red-and-yellow rave tangle, her outfit a mix of hippie paisleys and polka dots, and her black work boots smack of Seattle grunge. This former Vidal Sassoon model has decorated her crib—a third-floor apartment in a Victorian house on Potrero Hill—in a painted swirl of lavender, gold, and pistachio. And furnished it with a multitude of art, including an altar to her friends and a towering throne.

Tornado's roommate, Rebecca Corbett (who calls herself Polywog), is another example of San Francisco's wild style. With her multicolored Day-Glo dreadlocks, giant tattoo etched on the shaved back of her head, and Brooks Brothers pajamas, she's as much a part of the decor as Tornado is. "I'd like to model for J. Crew," she tells us, out of nowhere.

Polywog trained to become a ballerina like her friends in the American Ballet Theatre, but she's ventured too far into that other world of body modification. She's too pierced for pliés, too tattooed to twirl in the classics. Unfortunately, the Golden Gate Bridge doesn't span *Swan Lake*. But now, as a club deejay, she still gets to spin.

Tornado takes us to the Phoenix Hotel, where bands like Nirvana stay when they're in town. Like us, they love the tapes of frog and cricket sounds that management plays at night. And the pool with Marcel Duchamp's name painted on the tiles. Tornado proclaims the hotel "totally the coolest." Also on her cool list: the Sound Factory, DV8, Red Dora's for lunch, and Club 181. And friend D'Arcy Drollinger, a composer of musicals who designs nightclub doors on the side.

In Lower Haight, we drop in on Blake Perlingieri, who is responsible for the many extra holes in Polywog's body. As we enter, Blake and roommate Eric Jones are up to their ears in piercing God knows what parts of their own—and their clients' (including third roommate Bret Williams)—anatomies. "To me, body adornment is a personal experience and manifestation of internal aesthetic expression," Blake says, "as well as a mode of spiritual discipline that escapes absolute definition." Could he be more specific? "Culturally speaking," he continues, "all primitive societies have done things like this since the dawn of time. It's a basic, intuitive practice. I'm practicing a ritual. It's a religious thing."

It's also a painful thing. It hurts just to look at Blake, whose earlobes have been stretched grotesquely by the huge silver weights hanging from them. Eric's done the same thing to his ears. Once upon a time in Haight-Ashbury, everyone was beautiful, man, groovy. Now it's not enough to be groovy, you have to actually be *grooved*. The trends currently in the vanguard involve more than a modicum of pain: shamanic piercing, branding, and tattooing, and even corseting women's waists into a Scarlett O'Hara-like eighteen inches. ("Oh, bondage! Up yours!" screeched Poly Styrene back in the punk days of loud fast rules.)

From Blake's it's off to a 4,500-square-foot loft where Denise Schwalbe, a hairdresser, rooms with Jeffrey DiGregorio, a self-described "artist-traveler." The loft is a magical, almost hallucinogenic space, broken up into small Alice in Wonderland rooms. Instead of the expected Jefferson Airplane anthem "White Rabbit," though, we're treated to a "techno acid" soundtrack as we look around. The music seems to course through our bloodstream, and we feel almost invulnerable enough to walk the tightrope they've got stretched across one of the rooms. Almost.

Nancy Eastep, another roommate, is a clothes designer whose creations are sedate enough to be sold in San Francisco's straighter boutiques. She's having her hair colored cinnamon by Denise. "It'll look nice in the sun," Denise tells Nancy when the job is finished. The sentiment is more love bead than safety pin. Just as we're thinking about transforming our tresses to turquoise, we spot a big tabby with white paws and ask Denise if she's ever thought of dyeing those feline feet. "No," she says. "I wouldn't do that to a cat." A punk would have, in a second.

Other days in the city bring other characters, most of them festooned in a tossed-together combination of retro clothes from thrift stores: fuzzy sweaters, plaid skirts, upgraded grunge with sequins, marabou feathers, high heels or Doc Martens, vintage jackets, coats, and shawls—a cacophony of visuals, like a big love-in on acid. And Tornado, who has The Look down pat better than almost anyone else here, is a true representative of what's happenin'.

So it turns out that on the long, strange trip called San Francisco, punk has only been along for the ride—a hitchhiker who left an indelible impression. But because Haight-Ashbury's vestigial hippie-dippy love trip will never completely go away, it's had a severe effect on its black-and-white passenger—punk got colorized.

Esquire
Spring 1994

A CITY LAID OUT LIKE LACE

"BRET ate potato chips and peanut butter for dinner last night," my friend Ajay said. "I ate Ben & Jerry's English Toffee Crunch ice cream, a whole pint, in bed until I achieved a state of mellow remove."

"The remote control to nothing," my sister said, recalling what another friend had remarked when she saw all the television and stereo equipment lying in wreckage and all that she could unearth was the remote.

I myself was knocked conscious by my great old Rudolph (Rudy) Valentino book, a collector's item given to me by my old boyfriend Dan, who, in 1971, was here for another earthquake and left L.A. because of many things, earthquakes being one of them. This book was on a shelf, unsafely, at the foot of my bed, and thus I was Rudy awakened.

My friend Ajay and I decided that if we had to live in a tent city, we hoped it would be in Roxbury Park (in Beverly Hills where they have the croquet games). "It would be catered by Wolfgang Puck, the blankets would be handed out by someone from Giorgio's and the water would be some Ramlösa or whatever."

"Yeah," I said, "and you could barbecue with mesquite."

Though it was all coming back to me—what they tell you at the Red Cross earthquake preparedness class, which my friend Caroline and I had signed up for after the Oakland earthquake jitters had captured our imaginations. What they tell you is that the kind of food everyone wants in a disaster is peanut butter and jelly sandwiches or peanut butter and anything. Peanut butter being one of the great safe foods you can store for years—it keeps so well because of the oil. And peanut butter being most people's idea of comfort.

It has become common to be a disaster victim (courtesy of CNN, which always has as many orange flames as possible, scaring my friends from coast to coast). It's even more common to freak out from the disasters of others (also courtesy of CNN). But in spite of everything, what happened during the riots—that feeling of complete anarchy— was a lot worse than this earthquake. Because this time, for one thing, our police chief and mayor are on speaking terms. It was during those riot days that we learned that you could phone out during disasters but nobody could phone in. So you had to call all your friends and say, "Reports of our death have been edited by CNN to make things look worse than they really are."

What people take from their houses or apartments, given fifteen minutes before they run for their lives, are family photographs, underwear, and their pets. Which makes you think, maybe we don't need all that much stuff after all.

And what we learn is that people shouldn't live in certain places. New York in the winter; L.A. during earthquakes, riots, floods, or fires; the Midwest when the Mississippi overflows; Florida and Kauai during hurricanes and various other places for various other reasons.

A very brilliant and gallant millionaire I know who made a fortune from computers, Jerry, moved a couple of years ago to a chalet in Sun Valley, which he believed would be a better place to raise his child and live with his wife than horrible L.A. with all its bad publicity in reality and fiction. However, recently I saw him at one of those Sunday brunches I often go to and asked, "Jerry, you're here on business?"

"I'm not here on business," he said. "We moved back."

"You're back?" I said. "You moved back?"

"Yes," he said. "My brain died. I need action."

But of course with L.A., the reason this place is so nice is the reason it's so temporary, like lace. Yesterday I drove out to the Valley, to Sherman Oaks, where places I used to like going to are now ground down, shattered, have huge strange cracks in them, and otherwise seemed shaken to their cores. ("Oh my God!" I said over and over and over.) The reason so many people love this place, the weather—hot desert by the ocean—is the reason for the fires, for the floods that come raining down, for the earthquakes that aren't done tearing up our coastline. The reason they came here long ago to make movies, the reason (among others) Rudolph Valentino could become the world's first sexy male star—the way he looked riding a white horse through the desert in a sheik outfit with his noble handsome face and liquid brown eyes was that the desert nearby could be the sandy terrain with the palm trees in the background that so set off this story of Arabian nights. A story that couldn't be shot really in any other state but just here, where everything was laid out like lace at the edge of an ocean.

If we live here, we should, like the sheik, live in tents, ready to pack up and go at any time. My friends and I decided last night at dinner, the thing to have is a rubber house—something that bounces during earthquakes—with rubber plates. And rubber freeways. Not that I ever drove on the freeways anyway, since, to me, they've always been much too scary just on an average day with average bad citizens, one to a car.

In a few months, when this all settles down, what people will realize is that this weird new subway they built to take people to downtown L.A. held up so well—we hardly heard it mentioned. Perhaps people in Los Angeles will finally become good citizens taking the Metro Rail.

My brains are still scrambled but perhaps this is what we needed here: earthquake preparedness. Diminished attachments, happiness to be alive and have your friends alive, and peanut butter.

Newsweek
January 31, 1994

HELLO COLUMBUS

I'VE NEVER understood the thrill of Lombard Street. To me it's like a dumb blond—all curves, no character. For romance and history and *fun*—all I love about San Francisco—I head for Columbus Avenue every time. "Columbus is a *passeggiata*," says my new friend Alessandro Baccari, who loves the neighborhood so much that he made a museum of it, the North Beach Museum, right on the mezzanine of EurekaBank. *Passeggiata*, Al explains, means a very slow walk. "It's the kind of street where you promenade and browse and philosophize about life."

Columbus even stands out on the map, a great diagonal slash across the city grid, splitting square blocks into triangles. From the Cannery near Fisherman's Wharf, it plows a border between bohemian North Beach and the marbled town houses of Russian Hill, nipping a corner off Washington Square, then plunging alongside Chinatown until it stops—stops dead—at the corner of Washington and Montgomery Streets.

To understand why it does that, you have to know how nature shaped the city, first by gold and then by fire. Before 1848, North Beach *was* a beach, San Francisco was sleepy Spanish Yerba Buena, and Columbus Avenue wasn't anything at all. In the frenzy of the gold rush, the cove was filled in, miners built shacks and saloons upon it, and Columbus became a demarcation line between the infamous Barbary Coast and the fast-growing town. Except that it wasn't Columbus at all. It was just Montgomery Avenue then.

Then came the Great Fire of 1906—only nonnatives call it the earthquake; the natives who survived it were much more worried about their houses burning down. The Italians, many of whom had saved their homes by spreading red-wine-soaked sheets across their roofs, were the immigrants who could rebuild the rest of the city. And they did, even though they'd endured much prejudice, and would continue to do so even after. For their brave, hard work, the city fathers renamed Montgomery Avenue after the Italian to whom they all felt indebted for being there in the first place.

Columbus, even before it was Columbus, was the Italians' market street, lined with simple Victorian-style two- or three-story wood-frame houses whose owners ran shops on the main floors and lived above. At the foot of it was the cannery, where fifteen hundred workers canned peaches. Now the Cannery is a shopping mall, where I started my most recent walk by buying socks patterned with watermelons. On the top floor is the Museum of the City of San Francisco, complete with newspaper headlines from 1906 declaring STARVING DOGS ARE DEVOURING SCORES OF BODIES and with remnants of Hearst's folly, a thirteenth-century Spanish palace ceiling brought from Europe.

From the Cannery I browsed past North Beach Leather, where at least two generations of aspiring cool people bought their first suede mini or black leather jacket. Then up the avenue's slight rise, past the extremely high hills on my right where the San Francisco Art Institute lies, past the Gap, which began in San Francisco, past the playground's high ivy walls that hide the fact that old men play boccie all day as always. The Italian presence in North Beach is still a major force, though the Chinese are gaining, there being more Chinese and fewer Italians in this world.

I passed Bimbo's, which you'd think was filled with bimbos but instead is a hip club where the latest fashion in avant-garde theater seems to be a group called the Broun Fellinis, so popular in an underground kind of way that society debs pick up art students waiting in line to get in at night and everyone in their twenties knows which Broun Fellini is which.

*

Urged on by visions of the Victorian pastry baseball cookies that I knew lay just beyond, I passed right by Washington Square, which isn't a square at all (it has five sides) and has a statue of Benjamin Franklin (not Washington) but *is* the happy center of life in North Beach. I always think of Joe DiMaggio and Marilyn Monroe, because they had their wedding pictures taken outside that great Saints Peter and Paul Catholic Church, even though they weren't allowed to get married inside because the Church objects to divorce. Out front is a small park with a green lawn where elderly Chinese do tai chi on weekend mornings, enchanting a city that feels jaded about most everything else.

On another corner is an adorable place called Mario's Bohemian Cigar Store that probably was a cigar store but has been a luncheon-ette (dinnerette, too) since any of my friends can remember. My film editor friend Nancy told me, "I love sitting there. It's just like the forties, looking out at that little park, eating great sandwiches—it's really my favorite place in the whole city."

"Every place in San Francisco is like the forties, practically," I pointed out. For to me, at least, most of San Francisco seems like a backdrop for some great World War II movie where sailors and nurses fell in love and life was pure and innocent and pretty girls wore hats, stockings, and cute little suits with trim waistlines.

Farther along, I came to my favorite part of Columbus, the massive Italian pastry section where I first found out about cannoli. This time I met a girlfriend at the Stinking Rose, a newish garlic restaurant that isn't bad for a tourist trap. You have to salute a place that celebrates the concept of putting garlic where its mouth is so devoutly that it even makes garlic ice cream.

After lunch, I strolled up to City Lights Books, which is almost exactly as I remember it from the fifties, when my parents took me to San Francisco to hear Allen Ginsberg read "Howl" and the truly shocking part, for me, was that a grown man wore sandals. Ginsberg and Jack Kerouac (who at one point lived right behind, on Grant Avenue) and Lawrence Ferlinghetti and Gregory Corso and the many beatniks who came along with them—mostly from Greenwich Village, so that the Italian pastry shops and espresso bars of North Beach seemed like home—brought nightlife to this part of Columbus. They also carved a place in history for City Lights, which opened in 1953 and still probably has more alternative publications and books than there are alternative people. For now, I passed it by and walked to the avenue's end, to the building that I think is the most adorable in the world.

A wedding cake of a place, the Sentinel Building was one of the city's first "sky-scrapers," complete with elevator, and one of the few buildings that withstood the quake of 1906—even though it was still under construction at the time—because no expense had been spared in its structural design. Unfortunately, those expenses were mostly graft money, and Abraham "Boss" Ruef, who hoped to locate his offices there, was temporarily unable to finish the job because of an eight-year stay in San Quentin. He did finish it, however, and today his legacy is proudly occupied by Francis Ford Coppola, whom I hoped to catch a glimpse of if I was lucky.

On the seventh of eight floors I found Tom Luddy, who's a staff producer for Coppola—he worked on *The Secret Garden* and *Wind*. It was getting on to midday, and talk turned, as it naturally would, to lunch. "I often think I'll go somewhere Italian," Tom mused, "but if I feel I'm getting a cold, I always go to the Chinese restaurant Brandy Ho's and order the smoked ham in garlic cloves, because it's so powerful it can cure anything."

I said goodbye to Tom, but as I was waiting for the elevator on the seventh floor, Francis Coppola himself emerged and offered to take me up to his office on the eighth-floor penthouse, where the view was the best. In fact, Francis's office is the most beautiful room in San Francisco and probably the world. "This is the one place in my entire life I've never let be photographed," he said, mysteriously. All around were extraordinary inlaid-wood murals designed by Dean Tavoularis, his favorite production designer, depicting scenes from film history.

I had last seen Coppola in the early seventies, when he was starting on *Apocalypse Now*. I remembered a sloppy guy in horrible khaki shirts and work pants. Now he wore a suit of brushed charcoal gray silk, with the most beautiful rose silk shirt, and he gave off this glow of good health and good cheer. Thank God for us all that *Bram Stoker's Dracula* was a hit and that Zoetrope can continue and Coppola doesn't have to move to L.A. and hustle. At least not yet, anyway.

I spent the afternoon back at the Phoenix Hotel, lying around the pool with all the cute and young but surprisingly quiet rock-and-rollers who stay there—it's my favorite hotel in San Francisco—but went that evening to Tosca, everyone's favorite Columbus Avenue bar, which is just a block from the Zoetrope office and right across the street from City Lights Books. It was once a café and still serves "corrected" cappuccino with brandy, a throwback to Prohibition days. It has walls the warm brown shade of a Leonardo da Vinci drawing and one of those great long bars you see from days gone by.

Jeannette Etheredge, the owner, agreed to talk to me even though all I did was introduce myself and say I was a friend of Tom Luddy's. The walls, she said, "got like this through years of smoke. They used to be white in 1919 when it opened, and so were the lampshades on the chandeliers. Now the walls are dark, and the shades have turned dark red. Nothing has been changed—it's all exactly like it was."

Thirteen years ago, when the original owners of Tosca decided to close the place, Etheredge bought it with the express intention of keeping it just as it was. She even kept the jukebox exactly the same. "Everyone on that jukebox is dead except Frank Sinatra," she pointed out. Then she took me into her private office off the bar and showed me the photographs of her with Lauren Hutton, Sam Shepard, Dennis Quaid, Matt Dillon, Ginger Rogers, and Nicolas Cage. Many stars come here still; the bar was even used for a scene in *Basic Instinct*.

Outside, the *passeggiata* was in full swing—people talking, kissing, ambling along, dropping in at the Italian pastry shops for after-dinner slides into creamy bliss. Here, it seemed to me, was the essential San Francisco: a city of lights, a city of radiant beings, a city of taxis and tourists and back alleys, a city of crazily shaped enterprises, of too-high hills and too much romance from long ago, where the past and the present blur into each other, so that whatever happened once might happen again if you could turn the right corner and find the right little entrance at just the right time.

Chances were you'd find it somewhere on Columbus.

Condé Nast Traveler
April 1994

NICOLAS CAGE

IT WAS one of those gray days, as gray as the blue-gray of his eyes, in fact, which made it too cold for us to sit out on his beach patio and talk. So when I arrived he was standing there, beside his '67 Corvette Sting Ray, the kind of automobile that could only belong to a guy who was once a kid raised, so romantically, in Southern California, projecting in its metallic sleekness an image of the boy no girl could say no to.

"We'll take my car," he said. "And go somewhere, OK?"

"Great," I said, having grown up in this town, too, and knowing what cars like this meant—the allure of flying along the coast, so seductive to those raised in a place where cars were everything fun in life. And fun was everything.

"I used to have a boyfriend with this car," I said. "He got up to 140 miles an hour on the Pacific Coast Highway, but we were passed. Totally dusted."

"By what?" he asked.

"A Cadillac," I said. "The guy driving was older and his wife had blue hair."

"Never underestimate those," he said.

"Old guys?"

"No," he said, "Cadillacs."

With that he slid in beside me, having opened the door and made sure the belt of my sweater was inside, and off we purred. "I have to drive this real slow at first," he said. "I haven't been home for three months."

His pace was sedate; he was almost polite to his car, just as he was

317

polite to me. There's something almost cautious about Nick Cage in person, which I didn't expect from a man who pounced that way on Cher in *Moonstruck*. There's something almost plodding, which comes out in his voice—one that has the insistent hesitancy of James Stewart—a lack of slickness, in fact, which is the opposite of the Corvette and everything I always thought it stood for.

In the list of his movies, from *Valley Girl*, where he began as the eccentric outsider who wins the girl by lack of slickness, to *Birdy*, where he was the sad friend, to his latest, *It Could Happen to You*, Nicolas Cage has managed to go from sweet to crazy, from sane to wild, from serious to madly funny, from eccentric to as clean-cut as apple pie. And he's done it in a way that is so totally real that he's never boring.

A couple of nights ago I was at a Beverly Hills dinner where someone said, "I think he's just the greatest actor, but is he a star enough for the malls?" He seems not to want that "star" kind of career, the kind where you can make one movie a year, always as the same person.

Recently I saw his two latest movies: *Red Rock West*, a film noir thriller that has already become a cult classic, in which he plays a loner trapped in a web of lies, violence, and danger, and a totally mainstream romance, *It Could Happen to You*, in which he plays what he called the nicest guy in the world. And, because that's who he's supposed to be, he *is*. He even looks years younger, and I remarked on it.

"Yeah, I was working out every day," he said, "and really taking good care of myself. Thanks."

We pulled into the Malibu Inn, this great old, traditional diner, and he said, "Is this OK?"

I had this sudden panicky feeling that he might prove to be one of the many L.A. actors I know who cannot go to even the most mundane of restaurants without ordering food that wasn't on the menu, or food fixed some exotic way that the people who worked in the kitchen would have to rethink life as they knew it in order to prepare. I also had a premonition that Nick Cage might prove to be one of those actors who cannot go anyplace where waitresses work without flirting with them, especially if they were cute and young.

But the real Nick Cage opened my car door for me, led us through the front door of the restaurant, and got to our booth without a single waitress incident. Once settled, he ordered oatmeal and strawberries, and he put the strawberries on top of the oatmeal like a normal person. Not only was he not the Cage you might have expected, he didn't even seem like an actor to me, though from a very young age he was determined to be one, from the moment in the seventh grade that he saw James Dean in *East of Eden*. Particularly that scene where Dean gives the money to his father, his father rejects it, and Dean cries—the moment that Cage realized that no other job was possible.

He was born Nicolas Coppola—the son of Francis's brother, August Coppola, a college professor—in Long Beach, California, and lived there during his childhood. His mother, Joy Vogelsang, was a dancer/choreographer. From the time he was six, "she was ill," he said. "She was very fragile. She suffered from severe depression. She had to go away for many years at a time; she would come in and out. But she was also a very highly tuned, sensitive person, mentally capable of extraordinary expressions and words that evoked a kind of poetry, in the way she would talk. That's the best way I can look at it, but she's fine now."

Nevertheless, he thought Long Beach was a great place to grow up. "I loved my childhood; things were so vibrant then.

"My first six years, my formative years of life, were from '64 to '70. The Beatles have always been earmarks to chapters in my life. I remember I was driving in a car with Francis [Coppola] and his family, and I must have been quite young. He was listening to 'Baby, You're a Rich Man,' and the words 'How does it feel to be one of the beautiful people' came on, and I was thinking, 'Yeah, he really deserves to listen to this, doesn't he?' He was right at the height of *Godfather II*, and I vowed to myself that one day I'd be able to listen to that song, too, as a reward to myself. And it wasn't until *Valley Girl* came out and people liked it that I felt I deserved it."

He remembered, "I used to make people laugh, just naturally—that was my means of expression. That's how I made friends, by being funny. Then I discovered Elia Kazan movies, and that scene with James Dean, and I decided that's what I wanted to do, and I didn't want to be funny. I refused to be funny, to make my friends laugh. I started to be serious, and used that many, many years in my work."

His father then moved the family to Beverly Hills and Nick went to Beverly High, where the highly regarded drama teacher, John Ingle, put on musicals. Nick was in one, *Oklahoma!*, but he hated the school and quit when he couldn't get into *West Side Story*.

"When you say Beverly Hills High School, no matter how you say it, it sounds obnoxious," he said. "You can't really complain about Beverly Hills High because everyone's going to read it and go, 'Oh, poor you,' *91240*, or whatever that show is. But I'm being completely sincere. I did not grow up with money; my father was a teacher—money didn't come easily for him. What I did experience was a kind of strange frustration when I found I could not get girls to go out with me on the bus. And I didn't have a car. No girl would go out with me."

I mentioned that his original problem of getting girls at Beverly High now seems to have been more than alleviated, and he backed way up and said, "Listen, I know I've said in the past that I became an actor to meet girls, and I did. But now I'm thirty years old and I'm interested in the work—I'm *really* interested in it. It gets me out of bed, it keeps me going. I need the work."

Nick went straight from Beverly High into the work world. While his name was still Nicolas Coppola, he landed a pilot for a sitcom with Crispin Glover called *The Best of Times*. "My dear friend Crispin would hate it if I mention that job, because it was not good. It didn't get picked up, thank heaven."

Then he read for the Judge Reinhold role in *Fast Times at Ridgemont High* but only got a small part, which was nearly cut out. At that point he decided to change his name to Nicolas Cage, and under this name he read for director Martha Coolidge (who later told him that if she'd known he was Francis's nephew it would have colored her perception of him). "It was my very first audition under that name, and I got the job just like that." The job was *Valley Girl*. He was only seventeen.

There are two other directors he's eager to work with: David Cronenberg and Martin Scorsese. "I met David Cronenberg and he's a very nice man, really passionate about insects. I share his fascination. I told him about eating that cockroach in *Vampire's Kiss* and it bothered him, not because it was disgusting but because I killed a cockroach."

About Scorsese he said, "I met him, too. He was very gracious. I was nervous because I'm such an admirer, and he struck me as being just passionate about film. I found it invigorating. I could listen to him talk forever; he's just so pure."

There was a time not long ago when he had become "so selective about movie roles that I found that I hadn't done anything in two years. And basically an actor is only an actor when he's acting." And an actor who isn't working is also forced to amuse himself by breaking girls' hearts, getting nailed in tabloids, or being seen at midnight in a red convertible with the top down, rock and roll blaring, or at the Westwood Hamburger Hamlet with Charlie Sheen, a white limo outside, the two of them in the bar together the way men will do. "God, he was so obnoxious," a friend of mine who saw him said. "Can you believe it? Looking for girls right on Fairfax at midnight!"

"Well, did he get girls?" I asked. (It sounded like a sensible idea to me. Fun, even.)

"Yes, but," she huffily sneered, "I mean, *really*, how obvious can you get!"

Today he has a model girlfriend, who lives in L.A., and a three-year-old-son, Weston Coppola Cage, by ex-girlfriend Christina Fulton, with whom he shares custody. "Until I had a child, I was consumed with myself, consumed with the work; it was all about me. Now a day doesn't go by that I'm not thinking about my son and worrying. I do think I worry too much."

He arrived yesterday from Canada, where he spent three months shooting *Trapped in Paradise*, directed by George Gallo for Fox and costarring Dana Carvey and Jon Lovitz. He was in town for only a day and a half, to visit his son before flying to New York. "I'm going to be in this movie *Kiss of Death* with David Caruso. I play the old Richard Widmark part, the killer. I'm supposed to be King Kong big, with a goatee, in two weeks. It's directed by Barbet Schroeder, whom I've wanted to work with ever since I saw *Barfly*."

He was still lithe and boyish from the movie he'd just done, but I'm sure, being the real Nick Cage, he'll really be a killer in two weeks.

I checked my tape recorder to make sure I'd gotten everything. Nick mentioned once in the midst of all this that mechanical things all break around him—answering machines, cars—"It's a curse, a genuine affliction; I'm not kidding."

And so we left, going once more outside where he stood beside me to open my door, this very cautious, polite, serious, intelligent man with a bad-boy car and a beautiful voice; the gray-blue day behind him seemed now to come from the color of his eyes—so sad, blue, and quiet.

"Well," he said, "this has really been fun." I was relieved. Fun was always the criteria where we grew up, the object of desire.

We got into the car and he drove us back up the coast, where I said goodbye and that it had been fun meeting him, too.

Harper's Bazaar
July 1994

GIRL'S TOWN

I LOVE other cities—I do. Whenever I go to San Francisco or New York, I wonder what I'm doing in the land of smoggy freeways, earthquakes, fires, and floods. Still, when I get back to L.A. I'm always glad. Nowhere else is it possible to pass for cute long after the point where you're obliged to conduct yourself like the matronly age you are. If you don't, people will accuse you of not having good taste—of being too L.A. for words.

I mean, only in L.A. can you be Cher, all in black leather riding a Harley down the Pacific Coast Highway. Let's face it, if she were in New York, she'd have to be attending those loathsome Upper East Side dinner parties or charity balls to meet cute guys, and except for John Kennedy Jr., there isn't that much of a selection. Because in New York—or worse yet, the rest of the country—women who aren't girls are supposed to look, well, no fun at all, that's for sure. They're supposed to dress in classical attire befitting their social station. Even when casual, they've all got the same hair—almost shoulder length and held back by a barrette—the same loafers, the same white jeans, the same pastel cashmere sweaters. Cher, in other words, they're not. They eschew tattoos with a vengeance. Nor do they have Cher's appetite for guys her own age: twenty-four.

In L.A., it's so much easier to look healthy, because here nobody looks askance at you for running around in gym clothes. In fact, for some of us, gym clothes are all we'll wear. In fact, there's something fabulous about these great new running bras—you can look very sexy *and* like you don't care. I used to feel I had to apologize for everyone here using their skin and Lycra as outerwear. Eventually, I realized it's what I love about L.A.—it keeps juices coursing and interest high. If you don't want to think about such things, you should stay home or move to Seattle.

Ever since L.A. was invented, there has been a great battle between those who thought women should behave like they do in other places and women who didn't think about it because they were too busy working, being in love, and not caring how they looked but rather how they felt.

From the very beginning, women coming here found that even the lowest-paid waitress was breathing the same balmy air as the richest socialite. The weather was democracy itself, and though the first women running things were the same as everywhere else, they were forgotten when the second generation began running things— women like Mary Pickford, who by the age of twenty-six, in 1919, formed her *own* movie company with Douglas Fairbanks, D.W. Griffith, and Charlie Chaplin. They called it United Artists so the *artists* could get the money.

Pickford also sold herself as "America's sweetheart"—a nice girl content to stay home and be cute, when in reality, she was a rabid worker who had been supporting her family since she was five and known as Baby Gladys in a vaudeville act.

Unlike the rest of the world, Los Angeles was a place where girls could be inspired by the feeling that even if they didn't wind up in a castle like Pickfair—visited by kings and queens—they were part of this same air. Even when the air turned to smog, it was still untainted by a socially stifling mind-set that insisted talented girls belonged in the demimonde—never the *monde* itself.

Historically, "townie," or working-class, women could never get anywhere by doing anything, with the sole exception of Joan of Arc, and we all know what happened to *that* girl. Until Los Angeles, where women not only captured people's imaginations as stars but also wrote movies, were editors, and otherwise jumped into full-time, highly paid, marvelous occupations that required brains and fast minds but no social connections.

Anita Loos went to work for D.W. Griffith; June Mathis, an influential figure at Metro and a writer, too, discovered Valentino. By the 1930s, smart women who weren't even that cute could get as great a job as a star like Judy Garland.

Hollywood, which was a geographical location in L.A., became a mythological state. Here, for the first time in the world, was a gold rush that wasn't just for men, a land grab available to the lowest of the low, a place where nonvoting dish mops could become golden icons like Greta Garbo, Mae West, or even Penny Marshall.

If you hated L.A., like Garbo, you could take your money and hide in New York, and nobody out here minded or accused you of bad taste or disloyalty. If you loved L.A. but were lazy, you could rest on your laurels, like Mae West, and cultivate musclemen. Nowadays, you can live overlooking the city, like Marshall, wearing only a sarong, on the phone to the hottest stars extant, all trying to get her to direct them in whatever she's doing next.

Los Angeles has always been a great place for women in sarongs, in harem pants, in shorts, in dance togs—barefoot and breathing the same soft, free air.

For other women, the place is impenetrable. I once heard an Upper East Side matron trying to explain why she'll never come to California now that Swifty Lazar isn't here anymore to have parties. "I don't know anyone there," she said. "Why would I go?"

"Los Angeles," the man next to me said, "is a cold shower to women like her."

To women like her maybe it is, but to women like me, like Pickford, Garbo, West, and Marshall, it's the rest of the world that's cold. Los Angeles for us is that warm night when the scent of jasmine, orange blossoms, and love inspires us to become who and what we want to be. Because here it has been done, it's part of the history of our century.

And in spite of quakes, floods, fires, and traffic, the cold showers here are never as bad as winters in other towns, where you sell your soul to survive, where wearing the right clothes, marrying the right man, and having good taste are everything. Where the worst thing you can be is "too L.A."

Los Angeles
July 4, 1994

THE MANSON MURDERS

I WAS IN the bath when the phone rang in the Spanish duplex where I lived alone in the heart of West Hollywood, surrounded by hippies, rock stars, dealers, and others who clung to dreams of making it—or at least of never having to return home to Arizona or Seattle or wherever. They lived there and thought that perhaps they might someday be invited to Cielo Drive, to be under the night skies with the peacocks.

I was standing naked and dripping in the hallway, listening to my old boyfriend Peter say, with a note of "get ready" in his voice, "Did you hear the news?"

"News? What news?"

We were all enchanted, under a spell of peace and love and LSD that we thought had changed the world. In those days, people might drop by for one joint, get hung up on some transformational conversation, and wind up staying for the whole day or three weeks and then leaving for different skies, other adventures. And it was going to last forever.

We were all under the same spell, but still I had always been paranoid in the worst and most obnoxious way, afraid not only of the West Hollywood Sheriff's Department but also of "joy"—of "scenes," of the hints of orgies, of too much happening on drugs, of girls who lost their heads. I knew people like that, their minds wiped clean by some acid/speed combination that left them standing rigid with tears streaming down their faces, and I was afraid of being one of them, dropped off at the UCLA psychiatric clinic.

I couldn't smoke a joint without hearing the West Hollywood

Sheriff's Department kicking down the door. I couldn't be high without knowing that cops five miles away could tell and were coming to bust me. Everyone said, "Well, try LSD, you can't be paranoid on that!" But I was.

Still on the phone, I ran to my front door and locked it. "Why would anyone do that to Sharon Tate?" I asked.

I had seen Sharon Tate only once, in Rome in 1961 at the Café de Paris, a vision of such loveliness, and yet somehow this incredible gift hadn't protected her—nothing had protected any of them. My friend M., a tailor who made suede clothes for Sharon and Roman Polanski, had been up to their house on Cielo Drive with her husband, and she said, "Some weird kind of evil flirtation stuff was going on between them and us. My husband was necking with Sharon, so I never wanted to go back up there again."

We all heard the rumors, of European movie types picking up hitchhikers, tying them up, filming them—whips, sodomy, and strange young girls who'd go along with anything just to be there. Into this vacuum of freedom, an ex-convict named Charlie had wandered and worked out a system where he would be God, a star, and if that didn't work, then . . . there was always plan B.

After the killings, Roman Polanski, who knew a thing or two about wickedness, said, "If I'm looking for a motive, I'd look for something that doesn't fit your habitual standard—something much more far-out."

It took a short time for the police to figure out what had happened (murderous guru's hippie disciples take their killing spree to throats and bellies of the beautiful people of Cielo Drive), and during that period a woman named Catherine, with whom I'd gone to grammar school, joined the Manson group. When he was on trial, she and some other followers etched crosses in their foreheads and then *crawled* down Sunset Boulevard toward downtown, where Charlie's trial was taking place. I was walking to the store for my morning cookies and coffee when I looked down and saw Cathy, but I figured giving her a cookie wasn't the point.

As we were learning about Manson, going out at night in your car became, for women, a scary adventure. Once those pictures of him and his family started appearing on the front pages, hitchhikers could no longer depend on people as they had in the luxurious days of free everything.

My friend Sandra Sharpe told me, "One night, I was up in the hills on this winding and deserted road, rounding a bend, when this guy jumped out from behind a bush, waving a flag. And I just *freaked*. And then two more guys with headbands waving rags jumped out and yelled at me, and I put my foot on the gas really hard, went around the curve, and drove straight into a movie being filmed. I practically crashed into the buffet!"

The enchantment had fled in the night. The charm had broken; we had heard the screams, and they were ours.

Esquire
August 1994

JACKIE'S KIDS

TABLE 7, that's Jackie Collins' station at Le Dôme, the Sunset Strip restaurant that was once a powerful lunch spot but seemed, the day I entered, to be slacking off—although maybe it was because O. J. Simpson had just been declared a "fugitive" and anyone powerful who would normally be going out for lunch didn't. Except us, that is. Not only was I there, I was incorrigibly early as usual. So early that I sat in my car for fifteen minutes, trying at least to be merely on time, only to find when I entered the restaurant that Jackie Collins was not only already there but she had bought a copy of one of my books and was waiting for *me*. "I'm such a fan of your work," she said in one of those English voices that wraps around you with cozy welcome and simultaneously promises more spine-tingling lowdown than even her books deliver. "I can see you're like me—we both like to observe, but we like to be involved at the same time." "Great table," I said, noticing its strategic location. I had never met Collins before. On book jackets, she looks assembled by teams of stylists and lighting artists; in real life, she looked like she sounded: friendly with an edge of worldliness. With her warm brown eyes, tousled brown hair, black Armani jacket, black boots, and black leggings, she could have been an elegant beatnik—a sexy but dolled-down, more human version of her sister, Joan. Her hands fiddled with a clutch of clunky silver objects hanging almost to her waist. "It's a designer called Robert Lee Morris, who has a shop in SoHo I love," she said. "I don't smoke, so I have to hold onto something. These are lucky, they're fun and they're phallic." I found myself feeling not so much that I was with some invented superstar like the ones on her book covers but rather with a sort of glamorous bohemian with a very low-down streak that causes incredibly dirty thoughts to come bubbling up uncontrollably and which, on paper, sells millions and millions of copies.

More than 120 million copies worldwide, in fact, and published in thirty-two languages, starting in 1969, when her first, fabulously scandalous *The World Is Full of Married Men* debuted in England; moving on to her first gigantic American hit, *Hollywood Wives*, which came out just in time for the eighties; through her Lucky Santangelo trilogy (*Chances*, *Lucky*, and *Lady Boss*); past her books *Rock Star* and *Hollywood Husbands*. "I get this table because I like to see what's going on," she said. "But when I'm working, I don't go out too much . . ."

This statement was immediately belied by the arrival of Barbara Davis (that's Mrs. Marvin Davis to you), who stopped by our table and invited Collins to a private screening of *Beverly Hills Cop III* at her house the next night, which Collins gladly accepted.

The truth is, you cannot be around Jackie Collins for five minutes without feeling plugged-in. She's a cottage industry of droll asides and hot tips on everything adventurous, fun, and in. She loves going to the Pleasure Chest on Santa Monica—"I can prowl around watching people"—and was probably the first on her block to go to the Gospel Brunch at the House of Blues and the Atlas, at the corner of Wilshire and Western, where, on Tuesdays and Thursdays, the dance floor is filled with amazing tango types in sultry clothes—even a man who, in the darkish light, seems like Valentino himself. ("I would love to take tango lessons," she said.)

"I'm not good at doing ladies-who-lunch," she admitted. "The kind who talk about the help or the new makeup or which plastic surgeon they're going to. I'm one of the boys, actually. When I'm at a party, I like to sit with the men, play a little pool, and hear what's going on. Guys will come and talk to me about their relationships, how they feel about women. I love those conversations."

Many of those conversations, in one form or another, make it into Collins' books. It's the *clef*—the sense that her characters and even their most outrageous erotic adventures come from an insider's knowledge of real life in the jet set—that makes her novels so seductive.

She's been in the john when everyone is doing coke; she's been at the beach house when the drunken director is seducing the underage starlet. Reading Collins, you know you're chewing on slices of the real—albeit decadent—thing. And her newest, *Hollywood Kids*, due out this month, is no exception.

Having just finished reading the unbound manuscript, I was still full of the story of Cheryl Landers, daughter of studio head Ethan Landers, who, for something to do, goes into the madam business, finding and supplying gorgeous actress-model-hookers to the rich and famous of Hollywood.

"I started this book before Heidi Fleiss," Collins said. "So it's a lovely coincidence, having one of the kids in my book being a madam, but still, there's a lot of that going on here, isn't there?"

"Yes," I said, "Los Angeles has never been shy."

One of Collins's main sources for the inside scoop on Hollywood kids was L.A.'s limo drivers. "People do things in limos they don't do in real life," she said. "Young Hollywood uses them a lot, and they think the drivers don't exist!" Other sources were "the waiters at Bar One, car attendants, and hairdressers."

"I could have told so much more," said Collins, "but nobody would believe what Hollywood kids are really like."

Apparently, in addition to being crybabies, they've all slept with one another. "There's one particular person I wanted to write about, but it's just too unbelievable," Collins confided, and then proceeded to tell me a story so sordid her editors banned it from the book—and so would the editors of this magazine. Suffice it to say, it dealt with a producer, some call girls, and a glass table—and that Salvador Dalí wouldn't have been surprised. "I tried a toned-down version of it, and my editor kept saying, 'Your heroine is so raunchy. Do people really talk like this?' And I said, 'Fuck, yes!'"

"Well, I guess they haven't been to the Viper Room," I said.

"I love sensuality—erotic sensuality," Collins said, expressing a sentiment that made me think more of the Italian Riviera than *Melrose Place*, where both men and women tend to be quite calculating about whom they sleep with. "That is one thing that's actually a little lacking in Los Angeles, because people here are so into perfection."

The main character in *Hollywood Kids* is Jordanna Levitt, a "cross between her breathtakingly beautiful mother and her craggy macho father...more European than American," who drives around in a white Porsche. Kind of a cross between Sofia Coppola and Bridget Fonda...maybe. Her emotional history is that her mother committed suicide when she was still a child, her brother jumped out a window and killed himself when she was sixteen, and her best friend, Fran, killed herself the following year. In other words, a typical Hollywood childhood. Jordanna can't forgive her veteran producer father for keeping her at a distance or for marrying four too-young types.

She hangs out at a place that sounds almost exactly like the now-gone Helena's, called Homebase Central, where she meets four other sons and daughters of Hollywood royalty: Cheryl Landers; Grant Lennon Jr., an agent and "the dissolute son of Grant Lennon, a movie icon"; Marjory Sanderson, anorexic daughter of a "billionaire television magnate" (Tori Spelling?); and Shep Worth, son of aging sex symbol Taurean Worth (Liz? Cher?), who has a long line of ex-husbands. These kids have all had "too much, too soon. A Porsche at sixteen. Handfuls of credit cards. European vacations. The best tables at the hottest restaurants. And endless lavish parties." And they're all looking for something that will fill up the void inside them.

Also tossed into this stylish ragout are a *Vanity Fair*–style journalist widow from Connecticut named Kennedy Chase; an up-and-coming actor-producer named Bobby Rush, whose father, Jerry (a star of Kirk Douglas's magnitude), has made drunken passes at all of his girlfriends; director Mac Brooks, whom, in typical Collins fashion, we first meet with his wife, movie star Sharleen Wynn, about to have sex in their yellow Rolls-Royce; a retired but cute New York cop who comes to L.A. looking for his ex-wife and daughter; and, last but not least, a *serial murderer* who speaks in *italics*.

But my favorite character is Charlie Dollar, "hardly your average matinee idol. He was overweight with a comfortable gut, fifty-three years old, and slightly balding. But when Charlie Dollar smiled, the world lit up . . . for Charlie possessed a particularly wild stoned charm that was irresistible to both men and women." Now if *he* isn't a dead ringer for Jack Nicholson, I don't know who is.

The book braids three strands: AIDS in the background like the plague; the impulse to be sexy and fabulous; and the practical plodding of life, where days have to be filled somehow, if not by work then trouble, since we all know what idle hands lead to, especially in Hollywood. Let's just say it ends not with a bang but with a gigantic shoot-out up in Laurel Canyon.

Despite the high drama, Collins prefers to keep her eye on ordinary happiness in *Hollywood Kids*. After all, at the end, Jordanna finds what everyone really needs in life: a job, true love, and the ability to stop blaming her bad childhood for her rotten temper. "They all seem to have some beef with their childhoods," I said.

"I know," she replied. "That's so wrong. I'm a great believer that you seize your own life. You know, when you're twelve, you should say, 'OK, I'm not going to blame anything on my mother and father—this is what I'm going to do with my life, and I'm going to make the most of it.'"

The truth is, Collins feels sorry for Hollywood kids. A great sadness seems to hang over their decadent little monster heads—the result of never really getting to see their parents or feeling they can never match their parents' success, all while being raised in the lap of luxury. What fascinates her is the knowledge that, though the world envies these kids, they themselves realize what a sour prize celebrity is.

Collins's own childhood wasn't exactly stiff-upper-lip British. Her father was a theatrical agent in London, and she had a relatively sophisticated home life. Both parents were well along in years, and sister Joan was eighteen when Jackie was born. "Growing up, I read the whole time and lived in a fantasy world," she said. "I was English but pretended I was American and couldn't reveal my own identity, and I wouldn't hang out with other kids. I would go home and write and then sneak out the window and go to the movies."

This picaresque youth screeched to a halt with Collins's expulsion from school at fifteen. "I was thrown out for smoking, being truant, and waving at the resident flasher," she said wickedly. "We used to walk past him in our little tennis uniforms every Tuesday afternoon, and he would be flashing away, and I would point and laugh and say, 'Oooh, it must be very cold today.' I only came to school on Tuesdays to see the flasher. The rest of the time, I'd get these great notes from my mother to get out of school."

In 1956, she packed up and came to Hollywood to stay a few years with her ultraglam movie star sister. "Joan was living at the Chateau Marmont and having an affair with Warren Beatty, and I thought we were going to share this rather affluent suite. But what happened was, I was sent up to his little attic room, and Joan left town to go on location. So I bummed around town on my own for two years. All the 'research' I did then has proved extremely useful!"

Collins then moved back to England, where, at eighteen, she indulged in her first, rather volatile, marriage to Wallace Austin, a "very cute, very manic Jewish-prince drug addict." They lived in London, where Austin's principal occupation was gambling. "He was in his thirties, and we would do wild things like go for dinner in London and end up on a plane to the South of France, where we would gamble for twenty-four hours." Collins had her first child, Tracy, in her first year of marriage, and then hit rough seas.

"I had a little child, a maniac husband who hid his drugs from me, and a dying mother—it was a very traumatic time. I feel when I write about people who have drug problems I really know what I'm talking about, because, well, he killed himself."

Austin died from a drug overdose, but by then Collins had divorced him and begun a brief but action-packed acting career that included roles on *The Saint* and *The Avengers*. Then she wrote her first book, *The World Is Full of Married Men*. "I was fed up with the way married men came on to me. I'd say, 'Well, what about your wife?' and they'd all say, 'Oh, my wife's different—she's happy staying at home.' I thought, What two-faced, double-standard sons of bitches. I've got to write about this!"

She also thought it would be nice to make some money. And, unlike so many books written for that reason, *Married Men* actually became a best seller, was published in thirty-two languages, and caused a homegrown scandal as well. Members of Parliament were not pleased to find single women behaving that way—that is, fucking around and not caring about marriage. Collins laughed at the memory. "The English are so stodgy—and decadent at the same time."

When she was well established in Britain, she met her second husband, Oscar Lerman, an American twenty-five years her senior. "He saw my picture in a magazine and came to London to search me out. A friend fixed us up on a blind date, and we *hated* each other. Then, a year later, I would see him at the Ad Lib, this discotheque he owned where the Beatles and the Rolling Stones would hang out. He invited me to a Diana Ross concert, and I wanted to see her, so I went. On our second date, he asked me to marry him!"

Lerman encouraged her to shoot for an American best seller and decided they should move to L.A., so she could gather material for *Hollywood Wives*. One of the London clubs Lerman owned was the ultrasuccessful Tramp, and when they arrived here in 1980 he opened a West Coast version, and the couple socialized with the same jet-setters they'd met in London. Today, she spends time with the Davises, Billy and Audrey Wilder, and Sidney and Joanna Poitier. "And I have lots of younger friends through Tracy, like Tony Danza," she said.

"Are you friends with Joan?"

"Yes," she said, "we're good friends. But she lives in Europe, and I live here. When I go there, we have dinner and vice versa. We're sisters—we're not joined at the hip!"

Lerman died two years ago of prostate cancer. "We had a wonderful life," she said. And two daughters, Tiffany and Rory. Now a very unsedate widow, Collins has no desire to return to England. "L.A. is the most beautiful place," she said. "Flying in at night is just an orgasmic thrill. And I love the people; they've all got a story. I love the *excitement*. Even the earthquakes give the place a kind of edge. Everything's open twenty-four hours. You can get mugged day or night."

Over our scallop salads, I wondered if any of her children had been caught up in the flagrant actions of Hollywood kid-dom. But strict Catholic schools in London and Los Angeles, plus her own vigilant mothering skills, apparently kept Collins's three daughters on the straight and narrow. Unlike her fictional families of divorced parents and mothers who kill themselves or are alcoholics or otherwise impossible, Collins stayed happily married, never left town except to publicize books and was way too sensible to give her daughters Porsches at sixteen. Now, they're grown and flown: two in London, one still in Los Angeles.

Rearing them, Collins said, there wasn't much downtime. "I would basically be two people. One was Jackie Collins the writer who went on talk shows or to her husband's club. The other was a mother, taking them to and from school, and writing in the car at stoplights. Then I would go home and cook them dinner and deal with their homework and get them to bed. And then, about ten every night, I would put on makeup and get dressed up and go to my husband's club, where I would sit entertaining people until two or three in the morning."

The truth is that during the eighties, she and her husband "hated" to have to socialize at Tramp. "However exclusive a Hollywood club is, you can't keep out the drug dealers and hookers," she said. "The stars want the drug dealers around, and the single guys want the hookers around. So they all bring them in, and before you know where you are, you're knee-deep in drug dealers and hookers. But for me, it was all grist for the mill."

"I'm sure they entertained you with lots of stories," I said.

"Oh yeah—exactly."

Nowadays, Collins lives in Beverly Hills. So fertile is her mind, she's working on not just one book but several. She's looking forward to producing the *Hollywood Kids* miniseries, and while it's obvious she enjoys living life to the hilt, she is equally happy writing about the even more orgasmic adventures of her titillating characters.

"I feel like I'm turning into one of my heroines," she said. "They're all based on girls who claw their way to recognition. They feel strong, and I want to show that women in general are strong, that they don't have to be pushed around and be victims."

"Do people pour out their hearts to you because they know you're a writer and they want you to tell their side of the story?" I asked as we finished our lunch.

"I think I'm just an extremely good listener, which is rare in Hollywood," she said. "You know, everyone's looking over your shoulder at the door to see if someone more famous is going to come in, somebody they should be with rather than you. I hate that. If somebody gets my attention, they get my undivided attention. I guess men like that."

"Plus, you probably give them funny replies."

"Exactly! Show me a decrepit old billionaire, and I'll show you a fan," she said with a wicked laugh.

We had finished our cappuccinos and were out in the hideous blast of noonday sun, and yet the traffic on Sunset wasn't bad, it being a sort of slow day—O. J. still not having been found and his Bronco's slow-motion stampede along the freeways yet to come.

As I drove home, I thought how Collins's books are not really about shopping (only her villains shop) or even sex. She writes about emotions—and dreams coming true. And, OK, so there *is* sex. "All we're looking for," she had said, "is to wake up in the morning with someone who makes you happy, who makes you laugh, and with whom you have great sex."

Had she found it?

"Well," she said modestly, "I sort of have—at the moment."

Los Angeles
September 1994

KEEPING TIME IN OJAI

IN THE 1994 Ojai Music Festival Playbill, Michael Tilson Thomas, the musical director, wrote: "I can clearly remember the clear, dusty California days, shadowed by live oak and sycamore with the music and presence of Ingolf Dahl, Igor Stravinsky, Aaron Copland, Lukas Foss, Alice Ehlers, Sol Babitz, Mel Powell, and Pierre Boulez to name but a few..." My father, Sol Babitz, was the first violinist in the orchestras then, plus one of the originators of the Ojai festival, which he loved because they played interesting and early modern music.

Tilson Thomas was dedicating this music festival to his memory of those earlier times, times I too remember, though I cannot remember when I first went to the Ojai music festivals because I was too young, but I remember every year, in around April or May, my father would get out these various sheets showing an orchestra's seating arrangements for different pieces of music, and he'd be on the phone, day and night, acquiring musicians to fill those seats—and the great ladies of Ojai would allow these musicians and their children to come stay during the festival weekend, so what I remember first, being one of the children, was the lane scented with orange blossoms and honeysuckle as we drove to Mrs. Grant's house. She was a classical kindly old American lady with spectacles, with a beautiful old bungalow house with a stone porch, filled with remnants of travel in China, like a ruby-handled letter opener. She had an orange grove behind her house and something of a farm with chickens and cows too; it was paradise, a house inside full of books and culture, and outside the Country in the way old California was "country." And in the backyard, she always had kittens that my sister and I considered just further evidence that the best place on earth was Ojai.

In the mornings Mrs. Grant would make my sister and me fresh orange juice and cinnamon toast and then we'd go play with the kittens and we definitely hated being dragged to concerts and considered one of the fabulous things about being an adult that we'd never have to go to a concert again.

In later life, what I loved about concerts were the intermissions where you could find great funny people who talked a mile a minute and were deeply civilized, but still to this day, the idea of being stuck, having to sit through a concert, drives me somewhat over the edge, though once I'm there, I usually find something funny enough or transcendent enough or amazing enough to capture my imagination, at least for a few moments.

Last year, my friend Paul Ruscha and drove up to Ojai and stayed for two nights, not with Mrs. Grant, who is now, alas, dead and her home but a sigh in my memory, but at the fabulous Ojai Valley Inn, which has lately undergone a $35 million makeover and is now a place transcendent among golf fanciers, though even for the ordinary person, the lanes lined with honeysuckle and the balconies of jasmine are a thrill, as are the great birdcages outdoors filled with spectacular parrots and various other things and the indoor birdcages filled with gorgeous chirpers too. For breakfast, their open buffet is so decadent that Paul could hardly walk after actually *eating* eggs Benedict, which I guess is OK because I am his sole beneficiary though if I weren't, I'd rather he stick to the oatmeal and all the great fruit they had as well as the divine muffins and incredible waffles with maple syrup. (On Sundays they actually had blintzes, which for a Republican-type golf place is amazingly Jewish.)

Ojai today is almost exactly like it used to be, the corner with the pharmacy where I used to buy books when I was little is still the corner with the pharmacy and nothing in the town has been allowed to go the least bit slick—there are no malls, no gigantic discount drugstores, no "improvements" that wreck life and make you think California isn't that great after all.

If nearby Santa Barbara is the bastion of hidebound city planners absolutely refusing to allow anything but exactly what's already there to be built again and so determined that the city never even take so much as water from Los Angeles so it won't have to pander to ignorant nouveau "improvements," then Ojai is equally bent on quaintness, though being inland and farther away from the hoi polloi, it's got a gentler, quainter, sweeter grace that, still today, is exactly as marvelous as it must have been in the twenties when it became somewhat of a town and definitely as it was in the early fifties when I remember my first concert rehearsal, for Stravinsky's *L'histoire du soldat* conducted by Edward Rebner, which included a kind of theatrical event, the devil, the solider with his violin (my father played that part), and the princess—and the devil jumped out from under the bed, giving me nightmares for years and years afterward.

When Paul and I went to the concerts, we sat in the front where I never sat before, since in the olden days when we were children, it was better sitting out on the lawns with picnics and others equally uninterested in music and more interested in the birds or the stars at night. They played a Lukas Foss piece, described as "ungirdled silliness" or something in the Playbill, which did make everyone laugh because it was like Bach only with sampling, things stuck in like Spike Jones did. It was so wild and funny. Sitting way up front, it was practically like being in the orchestra yourself, and it's great that only about eight hundred people can fit into this bowl because it's possible not only to park but also to get the feeling that you're in something personal and special, rather than the way most concerts are today, where it's so computerized and vast, you can't wait for the intermission to go stare at people in their clothes.

The Clothes at this concert were mainly khakis, walking shoes, sweaters, and pants, nobody was dressed amazingly, but then it was all outdoors and cozy and inspired and brilliant anyway, the way the originators like my father and John Bauer hoped it would be, and the way Mrs. Grant and the other wonderful ladies of Ojai long ago imagined—civilization in the country, a perfect combination, a divine melding of the outdoors and the very, very sweetly cultivated—one of the great things about living in Southern California as it started out to be, and somehow still manages to be.

The tug-of-war that goes on within me about sitting through concerts at all, and the feeling that concerts are really the most sublime thing on earth and probably ought to be gone to as much as possible, still causes me trouble, but if you have to go to a concert, it's probably most wonderful to go to these in Ojai, held in June, under the stars or gentle shade, hearing a young orchestra filled with technique and spirit and enthusiasm, and with the least expensive seats, the ones on the lawn behind the small bowl, where you can eat your picnic dinner and be there but not *too* there, the perfect way to hear music on a soft, California lawn, the air perfect, the people gentle, civilized, and kind as the avante-garde used to be and still, today, is.

Between concerts, we went to Suzanne's, this elegant place, except it was too early for us to have dinner, so we just had gazpacho and I had iced tea, Paul had a beer. Later, in Santa Barbara, we went to a cute French restaurant called Mousse Odile, where for the first time in the years since I went to Paris, I found celery root just like it's supposed to be, perfect, and the best bread on earth too. Even the coffee was so great, Paul bought some to take home with him, but then Santa Barbara has always had secret great places and one of its secrets is that twenty-five miles inland is Ojai with its orange groves, music festivals, and the beauty of country life lived in the grand manner of people who want to be out where they can see stars at night, but not *that* out.

Wherever Mrs. Grant is, I hope she's in a place as divine as her farm in Ojai, but I doubt anything could be more divine than the place I remember, the kittens, the ruby-handled letter opener from China, and the cinnamon toast.

Westways
June 1995

SANTA FE
Angels We Have Heard on High

WELL, if you think Santa Fe in summer is beautiful but just a little bit corny because it's so perfect, in the winter Santa Fe is beautiful but *not* corny.

Of course, there are many wonderful things to do in New Mexico any time of year but basically they all boil down to looking at the sky. You can go shopping in Santa Fe or skiing in the mountains above and look at the sky, come out of any place at sunset and look at the sky, go to the nearby pueblos, where even the Indians look at the sky and have been for eight hundred years. Or you can completely stuff yourself at lunch and go outside, look at the sky, and suddenly all the fat grams you've consumed just become one with the Great Zen of Realized Dreams that permeates Santa Fe and suddenly you know all you have to do is walk the entire gradual hill of Canyon Road—a place lousy with art galleries and fraught with cute-stranger eye contact—and suddenly, voilà, your dessert burns off and you're ready for tapas that night at El Farol.

If you suddenly decide you have to go to Santa Fe in December and you take the Shuttlejack (it's called) from the Albuquerque airport, you'll be amazed because it's a foot and a half higher up for passengers than regular buses and you can see all those hills shaped like Hershey kisses and the land that goes from beaten tan to rose to iron rust as you get closer and closer to seven thousand feet above sea level where Santa Fe mysteriously endures, in beauty, a realized dream. By the time I arrived the snow had all melted from the sunshine all day and I had no idea, when I got to my room at the Inn on the Alameda, just how wonderful it was to be in a place that had fireplaces and piñon wood to burn when outside there was snow.

In the morning, when I left the inn, if I turned right I'd soon hit the Old House, and if I turned left, I was just a short block from Canyon Road, the boulevard of realized dreams most days. In Santa Fe proper, they made a law in the 1950s that any building newly erected could be any shade of brown it liked, with trim either brown, white, or blue like the sky. I learned this on the elegant and fascinating walking tour that meets in front of the Eldorado Hotel at 9:30 in the morning, led by this ex-Angeleno named Alan who explains that everyone and everything in Santa Fe is from somewhere else; it's the land of the romantic exile, a land, he said, "based on three things—the geology, the three different cultures [Spanish, Indian, and Anglo], and the altitude."

It is a city, to me, that depends on the influence of my two favorite elusive artist geniuses—Georgia O'Keeffe, whom we all today know for her skies, bones, and obedience to the spectacle she beheld out her doorstep, and Evan S. Connell, writer of the greatest book of American history ever attempted, *Son of the Morning Star*, a book about Custer's last stand from not only the Anglos' but the Indians' point of view, and it was so lucidly and brilliantly written and about such shocking and amazing cruelty and weirdness that though I picked the book up just to browse through it because I had to wait for something, I soon was gripped in amazement and couldn't put it down for three days till I was finished. Plus he wrote *Mrs. Bridge*, about how horrible being a good American woman can be.

My goal on my first night was to see a school's Christmas pageant, but I got lost on my way there because as I was out wandering on foot looking for the place, I suddenly heard angels singing from inside the Loretto Chapel. Actual angels, their voices cascading in breathless crescendos like from heaven, coming from inside the church. I tried the front door but it was locked, so I dashed around to the side entrance, and when a woman standing by the door asked if I was late I said yes, brazenly crashing a rehearsal of the Santa Fe Women's Ensemble where they were putting the finishing touches on a new piece of Christmas music, modern music mixed somehow with Bach-type harmonies, made totally angelic by the sopranos, contraltos, and altos, totally angelic women's voices so pure, so divine, such a realized dream for all with ears to hear—and they were going to perform in this incredible church on Friday and Saturday evenings, though I unfortunately wouldn't be there.

So if I were going to Santa Fe in December, I would call the choir and find out when they will be performing and then be there with bells on since to go to such an altitude, seven thousand feet, to hear such voices is surely one of those things that cannot ever be duplicated anywhere else.

The next thing I knew, I was back under the cold night skies, and luckily, the great new restaurants, like Cafe Pasqual's, were just a couple of blocks down the street, so it was easy to walk there, still under the spell of the angelic voices, and if you love fresh salmon and a totally romantic place to eat, this is one of the most elegant places on earth—and if you like, for lunch or breakfast, they have a large round table for people who come there alone, to sit and meet others, which is very cozy yet elegant—a typical Santa Fe style of life. For breakfast, there's Celebrations, on Canyon Road, where I had pancakes fit for General Custer, Mrs. Bridge, or Georgia herself—or for lunch, the Shed, where the blue corn enchiladas and the chocolate dessert . . . And there are a great many stores and in December they smell of sage incense and sell lots of dresses and skirts, vests and jackets, in dark jewellike shades which, if you buy them there, will remind you of Santa Fe forever.

I prefer Santa Fe in the winter—no one's there but the angels and the sky, the clouds, the sunsets. Spirits hang in the air, exiled in this romantic place made from the geology, the three cultures, and the altitude.

It's not even in America, this place.

Westways
December 1995

LOVE AND KISSES

WHEN I was growing up, we girls spent every waking moment trying to be more kissable. Every one of our assets we exploited: our curly
hair, our long eyelashes, our scent, our toothpaste, the way we talked—
all to become adorable enough for boys to want to kiss us when we
played spin the bottle and its more sophisticated cousin, seven minutes in heaven.

You can get pretty disorganized kissing for seven minutes in a
closet, but when I was twelve years old, we combined the two games
so that when the bottle landed on a boy, you not only got to kiss him
but also got to spend seven minutes with him in a closet—in "heaven."
I can't remember if anyone ever really lasted the full seven minutes—
parents and chaperones being the clever killjoys they were—but this
was the fantasy we girls had: The bottle would land on the cutest boy
(in those days, his name was Doug), and we'd get to kiss forever.

When I was in junior high school, my favorite thing to read was
love comics—pre–Harlequin romance stories about women wishing
they could kiss someone but being unable to do so until the last frame.
Boys read adventure comics, crime stories, Western trash. And when
boys went to see a pirate movie with Errol Flynn and he kissed Olivia
de Havilland at the end, they would squirm with nauseated revulsion
and hide their eyes in the same way girls did when people were grue-
somely killed. Fortunately, this boy stage didn't last forever.

It is almost as though kissing were invented by Hollywood as the
only sensible ending to love stories—the golden moment when "happily ever after" was supposed to begin. I don't think boys would have,
of their own volition, kissed girls were it not for the lessons they

eventually learned from the movies. At best, in pre-Hollywood times, if people kissed it was in illustrations of a gallant knight kissing her ladyship's gloved hand, or in hearsay from the Bible like "So she caught him, and kissed him, and with an impudent face said unto him ..."

In junior high there was a boy all the girls were crazy about, Shaggy. He had the blackest hair, long enough to fall over his eyes, and in the hot sun he smelled of Brylcreem, a scent that ever since has hit me as an aphrodisiac. For almost a week of afternoons we would sit out on the concrete steps that surrounded the cafeteria, reading *Mad* magazine. We would laugh at the same things, and then he'd walk me to class and kiss me—both of us aflame with burning desire.

One Friday night Shaggy dropped by my house in a car with a bashed-in windshield—not a good sign, since anyway he was only fourteen and way too young to drive. "We can't go in that car," I said. "We'll get busted." But he was fast and he wanted more than mere kissing. Suddenly one day he dumped me for this hot tomato named Julie with very impudent red lips. I didn't see him much after that, but the truth was that if I could have done more than kiss him to keep him kissing only me, I would have. It was only later I discovered that some guys will leave you for hotter tomatoes no matter how far you go—love being the unfair thing it is.

In high school, I knew another boy who had the lips all the girls wanted to kiss. We used to dream about kissing him, just as all the boys in school used to wonder what it would be like to kiss this girl named Cami, a cream puff in a tight skirt and powder-blue sweater to match her eyes. One rainy day during lunch, those two kissed each other in front of the whole student body and we all went limp. Time stood still for all of us—the moment more hot and steamy (and more innocent) than sex could ever be.

Kissing involves all of your senses: sight, because you wouldn't want to kiss anyone not striking you as adorable enough to touch your lips; sound, because once a kiss starts, moaning ensues and you hope it's inspirational; smell, though who knows what to make of the current testings on men that reveal what turns them on most is the smell of pumpkin pie; touch, because touching is why we kiss someone at all; and taste, of course. In more ways than one, taste is everything in kissing.

But there is one sense you don't need to worry about in kissing, the stuff mothers used to call "sense enough to come in out of the rain." This is the kind of good, "sound" sense that you need to have in your friends, but it's not what you need in a lover. People who kiss you can get away with a lot, especially if you want to kiss them again. A lover who's been mean to you can, with a kiss, stop you from leaving, if feeling you might never kiss him again makes you miserable.

Kissing, if it's done on both cheeks, is camaraderie; if on one cheek, is coy; but on the mouth, it can go anywhere—uphill to heaven or downhill to hellish squalor. The great thing about a kiss is its potential, its possibilities, its main line to commitment.

Looking at photographs of people kissing, we are like voyeurs. We always hope that in the wonderful act of kissing, passion will take over, which is how we wish it to be for Rhett and Scarlett and all the stars who kiss in movies. We hope that even though it's their job and they're only actors and they're surrounded by film crews, we *hope* that when they kiss, the kiss will get out of hand and take over and turn into passionate romance.

Long ago, I came across a great book of Jacques-Henri Lartigue photographs with an elegant gold cover. In this book were pictures of his beautiful girlfriend in her incredible svelte stylishness. And I realized that the photographs we take of people we love—or that they take of us—symbolize to us what love is, like remembering the thrill of a kiss in the rain long, long ago.

There are many kinds of kisses. Teen-lust kisses, kisses that bring comfort and joy and make life worth living, kisses of life and death and close calls, kisses of spontaneous victory, tribute, and relief. But the kisses I want to remember, the ones in which the world turned to mush, could never show up in a photograph—even if one could have been taken in a pitch-dark closet.

The last man who kissed me seriously was way too young for me and beautiful enough to be a lot of trouble. His shoulders were like angels' wings and his eyes like turquoise pools. He took me for a ride on his BMW motorcycle, and when he said goodbye, he kissed my cheek. Unlike other men's kisses, this one landed straight in my dreams....

But I can't be dreaming about him; it would end in complete disorganization of my senses, like memories of spin the bottle—a game that could start here on earth and end up in heaven.

Vogue
February 1996

SCENT OF A WOMAN

WHEN I was twenty-one, one of the great mortifications of my life was that the only damned thing that didn't smell horrible on me was a perfume by Avon called Here's My Heart. This was way before Avon got hip, and the scented cream came in a fake plastic Dresden-blue container with a white top. The first time I wore Here's My Heart, I was fifteen and went out to a beatnik coffeehouse where this particular guy, a guy who was all-city football quarterback, a guy who was so wild that all the women were afraid of him, a guy who owned a red convertible, a guy who had golden hair and green eyes, took my hand as I entered this coffeehouse and went ape over my perfume. He was kneeling at my feet, begging for my phone number (he was eighteen)!

So it wasn't as if Here's My Heart didn't work. It's just that it didn't sound or look like anything that belonged on a beautiful woman's dressing table. (In fact, I would put empty atomizers on mine, just to have the look of perfume.) I could not find a single sexy perfume in the department stores that smelled on me the way perfume always seemed to when it was wrapped around beautiful women—and since I lived in Hollywood, there were a lot of beautiful, great-smelling women around. (I smelled good, too; it was just I hated to admit it was Here's My Heart by Avon because, jeez, it just wasn't dignified!)

I would search Saks and Magnin's and all the other big department stores. Every time I met a woman who smelled wonderful, I'd find out what she was wearing, then run out and try it. Except on me, it never smelled the same. The first perfume I decided was malarkey was Joy, which my cousin and aunt could both wear without it smelling like gasoline. But on me, like most perfumes, it did. My mother, on the other hand, had such a great genetic gift, she could wear Chanel No. 5 and actually have it smell exactly the way it does in the bottle. (Whereas if I put it on, I smelled like old stationery.) In theory, I loved the smell of Fidji and Je Reviens and Fracas and various other French perfumes, but they either were too sweet on me or would give me a headache. Even Shalimar, which so many women smelled delicious in, made me smell like the Whore of Babylon. In fact, the only thing that I actually didn't mind the smell of was Vitabath, which in those days you could get only if you knew stewardesses who flew it in from Switzerland. It was called Babedes or something.

Finally, my friend Jack, who used to know a stewardess who'd bring back Vitabath, invited me to the house of a friend who had a pool. "It's great," he said. "He's away and we can go swimming. He's in Paris with his wife. He wrote *Charade*, so he's in Paris a lot. His name is Peter Stone."

I had just seen *Charade* (it came out in 1963) and was still quivering with how great Audrey Hepburn was, how marvelous she looked—her eyes, her voice, her Givenchy clothes. The clothes practically stole the movie. I couldn't believe we were going to the house of someone who had had anything to do with this movie, even if he was out of town.

With his wife, in Paris.

Jack and I arrived on a hot, clear summer day, and he told me to change in the bedroom, where Peter Stone and his no-doubt beautiful wife would be if they weren't in Paris. I looked at the dressing table and saw that, unlike a lot of women in Hollywood, she had only one kind of perfume, a single bottle called Le De Givenchy—the same guy who designed the great clothes for Audrey.

I opened the bottle, and my God, the stuff was the best perfume I had ever smelled.

Horrible as it was to steal perfume, I put some on, fearing that in five or ten minutes or an hour, it would smell terrible.

But it didn't. It smelled divine.

It was not a knock-'em-out, drag-'em-down-the-stairs kind of scent. It was just the most elegant, ladylike, pretty perfume ever invented by God or man. It was exactly what you'd think Audrey Hepburn would wear, to go with her pearls, her eyes, and her voice. It was the scent of unbelievably good taste, with just an edge of blissful sex.

It was happiness.

It was not a statement about the dark side, it was not vampire history, it was not black. It was sunshine and beauty, something you could wear with a bathing suit or jeans.

Maybe it was an L.A. perfume, because most people I knew in L.A. just loved Le De, whereas in France and in New York, people couldn't smell it at all.

I've heard it referred to as a "green" scent, which I suppose is the same category Vitabath falls into, but it has a subtle violet-and-rose smell and yet it lasts and lasts. It doesn't reach out and strangle anyone. You have to lean close—no, closer . . . no, really close; here!—to smell it at all. But once you do, you want to drown in it, like in a lake of heaven.

My father, who smoked cigars, so he should talk, claimed that anyone who wore perfume gave him a headache (except for my mother in Chanel No. 5), but even he didn't mind Le De, because he couldn't smell it, and when he did, it didn't overpower his cigar.

And then the unthinkable happened. They took Le De Givenchy off the market—or at least cut back its distribution to the point where it became impossible to find. This is something Andy Warhol would have picketed Givenchy with me for (Andy Warhol has an extremely funny section in his autobiography *The Philosophy of Andy Warhol: From A to B & Back Again*, in which he says that whenever a product is "improved," the manufacturer should leave the original, unimproved product on sale, too, because a lot of people don't want what they already like pulled from the shelves). I used to buy $140 bottles of this stuff so as to be sure to have enough for any eventuality (it would take me about two years to run out). Then one day I woke up, and I couldn't find Le De anymore—not even in France, as I discovered when I sent my adorable friend Paul Ruscha to Paris to a sort of "perfume museum," where they kept a stock of perfumes that had been rudely removed from your life without so much as a fare-thee-well.

I went on a quest for my Holy Grail, Le De Givenchy. Without it, I never felt I was on full power—I met a man who was unbelievably funny, smart, and tall, and we did have a relationship, but the thing that was missing was Le De. It was as if I were trying to have a passionate affair without my inner scenery, without my ability to flirt, without my elegance and femininity. It was really sad and embarrassing, lying in bed with someone, totally naked, without my Le De.

I longed for Le De Givenchy, the way my sister and I wore it for everyday, just for all over everything (Le De had staying power, especially if you tried to funnel some into an atomizer—it would stay on wood forever). It made us feel like the Persons of Elegance we aspired to be and thought we were in Le De, whereas real Persons of Elegance—those rich people—wore the worst perfumes, things you'd have to really love them a lot to tolerate the smell of. In my opinion, that's what some of those perfumes were invented for. "If you can stand me in this perfume, I know you really love me" is the secret code of some of these terrible heavy perfumes and the ones that smell like old ladies' candy. (In *Carousel*, there is that great song sung by the girl who falls in love with a fisherman: "The first time he kissed me, a whiff of his clothes knocked me flat on the floor of the room. / But now that I love him, my heart's in my nose / And fish is my favorite perfume!" So you never know, do you?)

Anyway, miracle of miracles, they have rereleased Le De Givenchy, suddenly, and it's now available at Saks. My cousin has already gone out and bought three bottles, my sister's rushed there and gotten one, and I have broken out a small quarter-ounce of perfume that I had saved but feel I can now wear again anywhere, even to fall in love, because we're going to get enough this time to last the rest of our lives. It isn't fair that they take these things off the market. They should at least warn you when your persona is about to be pulled.

Vogue
March 1997

I USED TO BE CHARMING

HERE'S what you would have witnessed if you happened to be standing outside the Raymond restaurant in Pasadena on April 13, 1997: A '68 VW Bug comes to a stop, a woman flies out, skirt aflame. She drops to the ground by the side of the road, rolls on the grass, setting the grass along the side of the road on fire, and then against the green bushes, setting those on fire too. "Oh no, oh no!" is all she can manage. That woman was me.

In fact, about thirty feet away, a poor Sunday-brunch couple getting out of their car did see the whole thing. They stopped in their tracks and watched as my skirt burned off, as my skin turned to char. "Can we do anything to help—?"

"Oh no."

The thing is, this wasn't the first time I had been nakedly embarrassed in Pasadena. Years ago I was immortalized in the old Pasadena Art Museum playing chess against Marcel Duchamp totally naked. But now it seemed more likely that the result of the embarrassing episode would be the very opposite of immortality: it might possibly be death itself. Back then I'd said "oh no" too—but to myself.

I got back in my car, grabbed my pink wool sweater, and put out the rest of the fire the best I could with it. The brunch couple watched in horror as I drove off.

I had just finished brunch with my mother; my aunt Tiby; my sister, Mirandi; and my cousin Laurie. Mirandi would be driving my mother back to her place, where I was also living at the time, and I looked forward to smoking the Tiparillo I'd been saving for the ride in peace and quiet. The cigar was one of those fashionable but hideous cherry-flavored ones I loved because smoking them made me feel like Clint Eastwood; everyone else hated them. I grabbed one of those wooden matches, struck it against the sandpaper side of the box, when all of a sudden the match fell from my hand. The gauzy skirt I'd put on to go out dancing later went up in flames; my pantyhose melted to my legs. Thank God for sheepskin Uggs, which protected my lower legs from burns. I tried swatting at the fire with my hands, but it was hopeless. At that moment I remembered the words of a fireman I'd met long ago, who told me that the real danger from fires isn't external burns but the damage that smoke inhalation does to the lungs, so I jumped out of the car. The skirt's wraparound ties made it impossible to remove. If only I'd had a nice swimming pool nearby to jump into, I would have been fine.

Here I was, I thought, over fifty years old, still so stupid that I was risking my life for a smoke. Was this the brick wall that Mrs. Hurly, my fifth-grade teacher, so confidently warned me that one day I'd end up crashing into "if I didn't pay attention"? Had I managed to avoid all the damage I had done up to this point, breaking hearts, being unreliable, only to hit that brick wall because of a match? I imagined how pissed off my friends would be if they heard I actually *died* from trying to light a cigar.

I got back into the car. My hands felt like fire, but I managed to shift gears, steer, brake, and otherwise accomplish what any driver whose lower half didn't resemble a blackened mermaid could do. I was filled with adrenaline, unstoppable. News came over the radio of a fire in Pasadena. Was it the one I'd started? Thank God, no. I was still craving that cigar, but it was too late, the matches were somewhere melted into the car. And obviously I couldn't be trusted with such a luxury.

First-degree burns really hurt, like getting boiling water splashed on you or a serious sunburn; second-degree burns are those horrible things you don't want to have either; but third-degree burns, which is what I had, meant that my nerve endings were burned off. So I wasn't in much pain at all.

I drove slowly through Eagle Rock and then Glendale, because it was Sunday and the cops would be out, ready to give tickets. Now I was getting close to home. All I had to do was turn onto Franklin, make it the final few blocks to where my mother and Mirandi would be waiting. Unlike them, I was too chicken to take the freeway, so I knew they'd beat me home.

I pulled into the driveway and got out of the car, minus my skirt. I saw Mirandi standing with our next-door neighbor Nancy Beyde. Nancy's face had a look of pain; I knew her Sunday was completely wrecked and my sister looked just as horrified.

"What did you do?" she asked, following me back into the house.

"My skirt caught on fire, can you believe it? I'm going to put aloe on it." I still planned to go dancing with my old boyfriend Paul Ruscha later.

"Aloe?" she said, looking serious.

"Would you get a scissors and cut the waistband? I want to sue the skirt company."

Mirandi got scissors and cut the waistband, and there on the label was the name of the clothing company. She borrowed a codeine pill from my friend Holly, who happened to have some left over from a surgery, and called 911. A woman paramedic arrived, looking like I'd wrecked her Sunday too, even if she was a paramedic. I said, "It's OK. I was trying to light a cigar in my car and my skirt caught on fire."

She looked like she was sure I would die, but she didn't know me. My friends would kill me if I died.

I was admitted into the burn intensive care unit at Los Angeles County–USC Medical Center. I once read in *The Village Voice* that an artist was anyone over twenty-five without health insurance—well, that was me all right: over fifty without health insurance. Did that make me a real artist? My sister had explained the situation to admissions, and I'd been enrolled in the hospital's special program for people like me. My condition was listed as "grave"; burns, mostly third-degree, covered nearly half of my body, which is to say that the skin was gone. And I used to have such great skin.

The last thing I remember before falling into a heavily sedated sleep was meeting my night nurse, David. He was exactly the type to prevent me from dying.

"Oh, you're going to save my life," I said.

"You won't remember me," he explained, calmly.

But he came every night for the first six weeks I was there, so I did remember him. And later, he did save my life.

The doctor showed up the next morning, bright and cheery, with the news that I had a fifty-fifty chance for survival. The doctors confirmed that my jumping out of the car had in fact protected my lungs, so the prognosis wasn't as dire as it could have been. Mirandi burst into tears, but I took it the opposite way. To me, fifty-fifty meant I had a *good chance*. I'd have guessed something closer to seventy-thirty. But on the way to the hospital it occurred to me: All my life I had been very lucky, and why should my luck run out now? Having been through getting sober in a twelve-step program, I knew that even when things seemed horrible, there was always a chance that they could turn around. It was only later I'd learned that in addition to my main doctor, Dr. Nguyen, the famous and heroic Dr. Zawacki, the best burn doctor on earth, would be overseeing my case. He looked just like Jim Caan from *The Godfather* and his specialty was severely burned patients, the kind who, years ago, *couldn't* be saved.

I was being drugged into oblivion, yet not so much that I didn't wake up now and then and beg David to give me a cigarette. Finally, he called Mirandi on the phone. "She's begging for a cigarette, what should I do?"

"Put a patch on her," she said.

"There's no skin," he replied.

Kicking nicotine, as everyone knows, is the worst thing in the world, worse than kicking heroin, according to friends who should know. You can imagine what I was going through: not only was I in the burn unit but I was being forced to kick tobacco cold turkey. Well, I'd been miserable from kicking stuff before. Funny thing was, in recent years I'd been in the best physical shape of my life. I was working on a book about the ballroom-dance scene in L.A. and going out dancing every single night. I still smoked, though. If you're a writer, tobacco is all that works. I wanted to finish my book, so I had to smoke, is how I looked at it.

"So, Eva, a cigar, eh?" Someone had written my name wrong on the band around my wrist.

Every morning a different person would come in and ask the cigar question.

It was the only thing in the burn ICU that gave them a laugh, because the other guy in there, a Mexican man who'd burned 30 percent of his upper body trying to help someone on the freeway undo a radiator cap, was really not good for a laugh at all. But me? They just had to laugh.

"Have you *always* smoked cigars?" they wondered.

"No, it was just a fad," I tried to explain. "A Demi Moore type of thing."

The previous fall Demi Moore had been on the cover of *Cigar Aficionado*, a fat cigar in her mouth. I thought that would ring a bell, at least if they bothered looking at magazine covers.

But I couldn't tell them the whole thing, because once they began laughing, they didn't really want to hear about Demi Moore, much less about the fashionableness of smoking cigars.

It was decided that I would undergo two twelve-hour surgeries. In the first one, the doctors would remove skin from my scalp, shoulders, back, and arms. Two weeks later, they would staple it back on, reupholstering me with my own skin. And afterward I would be on a respirator and a feeding tube for weeks.

The first surgery took place on April 18. All through it, it seemed to me that I was floating above my body, I was watching the bloody operating room. The hospital had warned my family that it wasn't worth waiting around during the surgery, but my cousin Laurie insisted. When she first saw me after the surgery, I was bundled up like a burrito, my face and body swollen to three hundred pounds. We looked at each other and the word came to us at the same time: *abattoir*, the French word for slaughterhouse. All my life I had wanted to have a reason to use the word *abattoir*, but it usually escaped me, no matter how determined I was to remember it. Laurie didn't sit through the second surgery—one butchery in a lifetime is quite enough.

After some weeks on the respirator, I was well enough to have the intubation tube removed, though the feeding tube remained. Still, breathing was hard. It was from all the morphine, I suppose. I just couldn't breathe with enough conviction. David, my lifesaver, tried to warn me: "Eve, if you don't breathe, we're going to have to ask your friends to leave!" But my lung collapsed anyway.

It was practically a third operation, getting me on the respirator. God, it all comes back to me, what I put them through.

Now began the routine. Every day I was taken to a horrible weighing machine. I had been unable to get true REM sleep for weeks, and in my paranoid dreams, it seemed I'd been kidnapped by terrorist orderlies and taken to a secret place where they tortured the patients.

I was so weak, strong arms were my ideal. I began to regard the men able to move me to the weighing machine with the least fuss as my saviors. I'd never gone in for muscles, but now they were all I looked for in a man.

My other torment was physical therapy. Christine, the therapist, put me through an ordeal where I had to sit up and crawl across the hideously impossible bed (which I was too weak and mad to do). Once I was seated, the bed would be lowered with a loud *wham*, so I dropped about a foot, right into what felt like a pile of broken glass.

Pain was the whole point of the exercise. Only later did I realize that that crushed-glass feeling was probably exactly what jump-started my nerve endings, which had been completely burned away. One of the reasons nobody but saints wants to work with burn patients is that they only get better when there's more pain. Screaming from pain is the signal that you're getting better.

Burn patients are also susceptible to infection, so the number of friends allowed to visit during my recovery was limited to five: Mirandi, Laurie, Paul, my writing partner Michael Elias, and Carolyn Thompson, whom I'd known since the 1970s. Nancy Beyde, the neighbor who witnessed me pull up in my VW, naked from the waist down and burned to a crisp, wasn't on the official list, but she snuck in anyway.

It was Nancy who, when the doctors feared that I wasn't healing and there was talk of another surgery, consulted her homeopathic doctor friends. She smuggled in cantharis pills, something usually reserved for bladder ailments and blisters. She told me to relax (*relax?*) and slipped this smallest of tablets under my tongue. The doctors were amazed at my progress. I wasn't about to clue them in to Nancy's secret pills, because I was sure they'd regard them as ridiculous or else take them away. They were my secret.

My only consolation was the wonderful warm therapeutic Jacuzzi. Even though it was the world's hottest summer, and Carolyn was fainting from the temperature in my overheated room, the bath was the only place I ever felt warm enough.

The Jacuzzi was the first place I'd seen the staples, so many staples. And my legs: from my waist to my ankles, black, black, black. It seemed impossible that I'd ever stand on them again.

"How did they get black?"

"This is just the first stage," someone explained. "Eventually, they'll turn pink—and then red."

At least I hadn't burned my face, or run into a traffic pole headfirst. I was trying to remember my good luck. I held on to the happy thought of being well enough to go back to the Glendale Galleria, not far from my house. I dreamed of shopping at the Gap and Nordstrom, as shallow as that sounds.

To a lot of people, the idea of an extended bed rest sounds like heaven. But the truth is, lying in bed you get no respect and being a burn patient is a visit to torture land. Even though everybody knows that since time immemorial sleep is about the only thing that lets people get better, I was never allowed to doze more than two hours at a time without someone coming to take my vitals, putting one of those blood pressure things on, turning me over on my side, sticking needles into my wrists, and doing it so ineptly that I was bruised all over. Immobile in bed, on opiates, the constipation is terrible and enemas the only, horrible, solution. Everyone keeps telling you to "relax," which you have absolutely no way of doing anyway.

It was the modern era, so they put me on the latest thing, an antidepressant called Paxil. It didn't do anything for the insomnia but it did enable me to speak with enthusiasm about everything that was wrong with me. I would list my complaints, starting with my head (too cold, sticky rubber pillow), my arms (bleeding), my gut (constipated from the opioids), my heels (developing bedsores). Laurie would come and read Colette to me, but my body was so traumatized that every story just sounded like pain. I was paranoid and had incredible twisted ideas of what they were doing to me in the hospital. It wasn't till two years later, when I finally kicked the Paxil, that it dawned on me that the thing that was supposed to make me sane was in fact doing the opposite. I shouldn't have been surprised; one of the things I learned at AA was that the drugs that usually work for "normies" sometimes work wrongly for people like me.

Eventually my lovely therapist Christine was able to get me on my feet, and I was able to use my near-atrophied legs again to practice walking up and down the hallways. Suddenly I got nicer, and the staff was nicer to me. Unfortunately, despite everything, including flowers, being forbidden in case they gave me a virus, I did get a virus: VRE (vancomycin-resistant enterococcus). My room was quarantined for the remaining weeks I was at County. Only doctors and nurses were allowed in. Eventually they let up a little and the few people allowed to visit had to scrub up, put on sterile mint-green paper masks, paper coats, rubber gloves, and even booties, and deposit them in a basket labeled TOXIC WASTE in the corner of the room, which by the end of the day was piled almost to the ceiling and carted off with humiliating regularity. Even my beloved life-size poster of Magic Johnson, which I could glance over at when I needed to see his incredible smile, was incinerated in the end. Michael had brought the poster in memory of the Lakers games he used to take me to. We would sit in his third-row seats, and everyone who passed by, like Jack Nicholson, would wave hello. What a scene. Now Magic Johnson had HIV and like me was a shell of his former self (though a shell with mystique and beauty). Likewise the radio, which my friend Anne Rice had sent me, and whose oldies station provided some distraction, had to be destroyed too. God, that virus, that quarantine!

My appetite was nonexistent. The feeding tube that had been pumping thousands of calories into me until recently had naturally caused me to gain weight. After that I was faced with the notoriously horrible 1950s food at County General. Soon I weighed what I had when I arrived—another miracle of modern medicine. I begged my friends for something edible, and Michael brought me pasta with pesto, but my mouth was still sore from the respirator, and it hurt to eat even that. Diane sent me a gold box of Godiva truffles, but the thought of them made me mad instead of ravenous. Nancy brought me smoothies from Jamba Juice, our favorite.

One day I woke up craving a tuna fish sandwich like my mother used to make. It consisted of tuna mixed with chopped celery and lemon juice on whole wheat bread, nothing else. I mentioned this to Carolyn who brought me a tuna sandwich she made herself, only on white bread, with green pepper. My friend Sarah Kernochan brought me one on white bread with cucumbers, for Pete's sake. It was then that I realized that everyone in the whole world has their own idea as to what a tuna sandwich is. Now my sister and I have had the same dynamic practically since she was born, her being obliging and kind and me being horrible and ungrateful. But I knew I could call her, and that she and I being the only two people who understood what a tuna fish sandwich was, she could bring me what I was hoping for. I was glad because I knew that if I longed for this, life was possible again; the craving made me feel human. I would eat a few bites, feel full, and then stash it away in a little fridge on the floor. But then this imperious killjoy nurse, this caricature of Loretta Swit's character on *M*A*S*H*, declared that since I was contagious, there could be nothing of mine in the cooler: "Impossible. Unsafe."

"But it's all I like!" I cried.

"The hospital has egg salad," she said, primly.

The funny thing was, this nurse actually loved me and was a fan of my writing. But here she was, taking away my sublimely perfect tuna, and pawning off County General egg salad.

Finally the doctors took a look at my ass, pronounced it "healing," and made preparations for me to go to White Memorial, a rehab hospital not far from County. As miserable as I'd been at County, with its funereal teal blue everywhere, I was afraid to go to a new place. What would the staff be like? Would they be as great as David? What about the night nurse William, the only one who could stand me in my rotten insomniac moods, who would chat with me from 3 to 5 a.m.?

My sister assured me that compared to where I was, White was the Beverly Hills Hotel—all the beds had purple spreads and really the people were lovely.

And so, six weeks after my admission, I was wheeled out of the hospital on a gurney, screaming the whole way at the fresh, cold air. I hadn't felt an actual breeze in months; it was exhilarating.

*

I was greeted at White by all the nurses, as though assembled just to meet me. These nurses were beautiful; I was amazed. One, Maria Rosa, was especially kind, an angel, in fact. No more struggles with catheters, tubes, or needles. She was brilliant with them all, and she never told anyone to relax, a sure sign she was adept.

Here were the famous purple bedspreads. I had a room to myself and a window with a view. I even had my own telephone—not that I could stand its loud ring, given the state of my nerves. Of course I was still in quarantine, but this was a fabulous version of it.

Maria Rosa handed me a sheet. "Here's your program for tomorrow," she explained.

How delightful! I thought. Maybe they put me down for a massage—who knows?

At eleven the next morning, I was wheeled down to the Jacuzzi, where I was met by an extremely cute male assistant with whom I immediately fell in love, muscle-bound as he was. You know me and muscles. As far as I was concerned, Johnny Depp came in a distant second to this assistant. This brilliant flirt thought I was cute too, and he was the only reason I didn't fall into despair when I knew I had to go to therapy. "I used to be charming before I got here," I told him. It was the first time I'd been able even to imagine making any kind of joke since the accident.

"OK," he said. "You stand while we—"

"Stand?" I snapped. "I can't *stand*. You'll have to hold me." I hobbled to my feet, leaned back into the muscles, and "stood," which is to say leaned, for about forty-five minutes, while a girl picked at my skin with sharp tweezers, pulling at me while I screamed. This was the therapy.

Here, instead of being lowered into a therapeutic bath of warm water on my beloved gurney, as had been the practice at County General, I was seated in an electric wheelchair that plunged into frigidness. This water was so cold that pain was its essence. I screamed at every move—but then I was always screaming. I was used to it by now. At County the Jacuzzi was the only time I wasn't in pain, whereas here, it was the only time I *was*.

Finally, wrapped in a sterile white sheet, covered with a sterile towel, bandages taped to my body, I was wheeled upstairs. Lunch awaited me, and I actually felt a pang of hunger. Had the morning's exercise worked up an appetite? It occurred to me that maybe what looked like beef might not be bad.

It turned out to be barbecued beef and it was so good I actually gobbled it up. The vegetables too. I hadn't so much as seen a single vegetable my whole time at County. The nurse who came for my plate explained that White was a Seventh-Day Adventist hospital, and supplied its kitchens from its own vegetable garden. It was the most fun I'd had at a meal since that tuna sandwich my sister brought me. Oh well, I thought, at least I have something to look forward to.

The routine at White wasn't all that different from County General and I wasn't feeling much better, at least to start. Between the Paxil and being woken up for a vitals check, I never was allowed a minute to sleep. My digestion still wasn't "regular," so I wound up having to have several more enemas. And I was bored: at County there were videos (I must have watched *Tin Cup* eight million times), but here there was just the TV—with nothing worth watching. My friend and editor Vicky Wilson had sent me a history of the Byzantine Empire, which was fascinating, but I was still in too much pain to read. I longed to be left alone for one whole day, but I was subjected to standing and tweezing therapy even on Sundays. None of it really mattered, though; I loved this place. If you rang for the nurse, one would come and chat, and except for the weekends when the place was staffed by temps, we always had the same nurses—the same everyone. Because White Memorial's chief physician was a woman, there were no male doctors barging into my room laughing about cigars and calling me Eva.

The young Mexican man who had been in County General was here too. His burns, unlike mine, were visible: on his hands, his shoulders, his face, even. His family didn't speak any English, but I loved them; you could tell they were kind.

OPIUM DREAMS

Inside, it was the usual Sunset Strip restaurant. I managed to huddle myself upstairs to the Skin Bar. At the sushi bar sat a man who looked like a mixture of Tim Ford and Mick Haggarty, while at a table in the back, Bianca Jagger sat in a black-and-white outfit out of von Sternberg's Shanghai Express, drinking an orange drink.

On a white marble edifice at the sushi bar was a five-foot-high glass goblet, and inside it was a gorgeous girl dressed in a kind of gingham bikini, singing with all her heart "I Will Always Love You," the Dolly Parton song that Whitney Houston made such a big hit.

She was singing this to the Tim Ford/Mick Haggarty guy at the bar, who was waiting for me in order to aid and abet my escape. I was going someplace away, like the desert, so I could escape my fate and get with real *doctors, who'd feed me great food and let me sleep so I could get better in a more civilized fashion.*

I remembered then that downstairs in the restaurant was my old friend Carolyn Zecca-Ferris, whose father used to manage the Fairmont Hotel in San Francisco. Obviously, she was a woman used to dealing with all manner of surprise guests, and she had shown me her own private vegetable farm that raised special vegetables so perfectly organic that anyone (me) who ate them could grow new skin instantly and be all better in a few days of peace and harmony, instead of the hideous baths, gurneys, and staples that I had been forced to submit to at County General.

At the bar, the beautiful girl singing "I Will Always Love You" was singing this straight at the guy at the counter, and she was so beautiful, with such a beautiful voice, that if ever there was a siren designed to fog the mind of man, she was it. Yet my savior was ignoring her, gladder to see me than to be seduced by her, even with my sticky bandages, blood, lymph, blown-up with black legs.

"But first I want you to promise to introduce me to Fred Roos," he said, this being Hollywood, where there's a business reason for everything, including escapes from Alcatraz-hospital adventures. I was grateful

because I had Fred Roos's number in my phone book, which I somehow had with me.

"Let's call him now," I said, to prove I was game.

"Let's call him when you're well," he said. "It's four in the morning."

"Oh," I said. Was it four in the morning? "Jeez, Fred would have been mad."

Off we went in some kind of vehicle, arriving at a place with strange children, as dripping with ooze as I was, where the special vegetables were being sliced up in beautiful ways, so we could all get well. A San Francisco–style healing, where acupuncture and healers abounded, just in case you couldn't stand the AMA.

But then, damn it, I woke up, right back at White Memorial ...

I began to make progress.

I'd been sent from County General with bedsores on my heels. One day a surgeon of great valor came in. He gave me a tiny little opiate and with a small knife dug the bedsore first out of one heel, then the other. The scream of pain in my throat was so shocked that no noise actually came out. The pain was surprising. Nothing else, outside of a bikini wax, even came close. But then after my first bikini wax, I'd vowed I'd never subject myself to another.

Amazing tortures arrived for me in the form of occupational therapy. The surgeries had affected my hands and upper arms. In removing the skin from my arms, the doctors had cut too deeply. It was a long time before the incisions stopped bleeding. For two weeks I worked on desensitizing the nerves by clutching first a handful of sand, then beans, and finally dry pasta. It took about two weeks before I realized a magazine could touch me and I wouldn't scream. But it really took a year for the pain to fully subside. Until then, even the brush of a pillowcase was excruciating.

When it came to relearning to walk, years of dance lessons made me fearless. The social workers and therapists watched, frightened, as on the very first day my near atrophied legs miraculously climbed, first up a flight of stairs then down. But I had done much more daredevil things in tango. In fact, all the common things most people struggled to relearn, I learned with relative ease. The real problem was that the new tissue was not really adhering the way it was meant to. I was leaking so much that if I didn't keep my pants legs rolled up, they'd become all gummy.

There were tense meetings at White, when the social worker got together with the head doctor and the two bickered over how soon I could go home. The head doctor was determined to keep me there until I was as healed as much as possible. But after almost two months in rehab my time was up. They booted me, even though I was far from fully recovered.

Just before it was time to leave the rehab center, I was finally allowed flowers in my room. My agent at the time, David Vigliano, sent a miraculous bunch, one of those newfangled bouquets that look just like dripping petals. Anne Rice sent a four-foot-high arrangement that turned my room into the Four Seasons and was so alluring that people came from all over the hospital to get a look at what the Vampire lady had sent. Don Henley (that witchy man) sent white roses stuffed so tightly in this wicker basket that it took weeks for them to fade. And last but not least, Ed Ruscha, Paul's artist brother, and his wife, Danna, sent a breathtaking combo of huge sunflowers and gigantic irises, half van Gogh, half English garden.

Home in my condo, I was visited daily by a home-health aid. The agency sent a different one every day by some twisted logic, which meant that I had to explain on a daily basis exactly how to wrap around me the endless rolls of bandages I still required. After about two months, my sister found Heather, a physical therapist whose specialty was burn patients and who was universally adored—even if she did have a set of those sharp tweezers and knew how to use them.

The expenses added up. If my cousin hadn't figured out how to get discounted bandages from Kaiser Permanente, those things alone might have bankrupted me. I was fortunate to have friends who knew about finances. Michael Elias brought around Debby Blum, a whiz at setting up foundations. She made it so that people could donate money tax-free. Everyone from Steve Martin and Harrison Ford to Ahmet Ertegun gave generously. Laddie Dill held a silent art auction in my honor at the Chateau Marmont, which was pretty amazing. I was determined to sue the skirt company and make them pay, though.

Six months later, when I was finally on my own two feet, I visited the burn unit at County General. The doctors had told me that "nobody comes back." I took that statement as a dare, but I also wanted to see the people who had saved me, and to let them know that I remembered everything they had done. But the thing is that I hadn't really remembered at all. Dr. Zawacki, who I thought of as a kind of insane older Mickey Rourke, was just a benign smiler, happy to see me dressed and upright for the first time. And the whole place wasn't that obnoxious pale turquoise I'd thought it was, there was only a single curtain in that horrible shade. The Jacuzzi, which I experienced as kind of a baroque object of torture and relief, was just an ordinary long aluminum tub. My dark room was bright—I mean really bright. It was small too: the distance between the bed and the bathroom, which I thought must be a city block of pain, was no more than ten feet.

1997, 2019

FIORUCCI
The Book

THE FIORUCCI SCENE

Fiorucci is the name of a man, the name of a look, and the name of a business. A phenomenon. Walking into a Fiorucci store is an event. Milan. New York. London. Boston. Beverly Hills. Tokyo. Rio. Zurich. Hong Kong. Sydney.

Fiorucci is fashion. Fiorucci is flash. Fiorucci stores are the best free show in town. The music pulses; the espresso is free; the neon glows. Even the salespeople are one step beyond—they often wear fiery red crew cuts. But it is, after all is said and done, a store—a store designed to sell clothes. But the difference is all that sex and irony. Anyone who knows anything can see that finally the entire operation is motivated by the very same energy that lights the fire under rock and roll.

A couple of years ago I made my first trip to Fiorucci, in Beverly Hills, just off Rodeo Drive. I took along my friend Ann, to lend an air of veracity to the expedition since I knew that Fiorucci only sells clothes up to size 10, and I'm a 12. Within two minutes, I found a wonderful little violet petal straw hat that only cost $20 and which made me look like the past recaptured.

"Oh, you look beautiful," Ann promised. "It's just your color. It's perfect. You have to buy that hat."

I knew it was just my color; I bought it; I just had to. In two minutes, I was already looking beautiful. But not only beautiful—I was looking effortlessly amusing. Ann bought a tiny turquoise tube top. She put it on and she also looked beautiful—and effortlessly amusing.

Coming back down to earth, as we stepped out onto one of the richest streets in the world, I looked up at the sky, a nice proud loud blue, and I wished that Elio Fiorucci could have seen us: the sky and me and Ann. We were happy, and I know he, if only for a moment in his busy, conservative businessman's life, would have been happy. Luckily, there was someone else there to appreciate us. A guy driving by in a truck called out as he passed, "Hey, beautiful, where'd you get the hat?"

My heart gladdened to a loud violet. The light changed to green, and Ann and I slinked across the street. Her new tube top was so turquoise and my new hat was so violet. We really showed up.

"I think we should go there again tomorrow," Ann said. We had found a way to look beautiful every day.

Fiorucci is selling glamour. He is selling Hollywood to the world. He is selling disposable, flamboyant razzle-dazzle. Jungle-siren leopard-skin Sheena outfits, costumes of what you've always wanted to be when you were too little. And now you're big enough. He is selling pearls and rubies and sequins and satins. Dress-up Raymond Chandler silver screen ladies of romance, broken hearts, dramatic entrances, and tragic farewells. He is selling them to Brazil and Italy and France and New York and England and even to Beverly Hills itself.

Fiorucci is selling the future. Everything seems at home with the premise that this is the future we are living in and we're on the next galaxy. Before we left earth, we scooped up as many remnants of our civilization as we could. We managed to bring along the 1950s and rattlebrained fabrics designed with fields of boomerangs and flying rectangles on them in colors like pink, charcoal gray, and kelly green. We managed to capture some of the 1940s with shoulder pads, peplums, and skirts below the knees. The 1960s are there, represented by a rack of actual antique clothes from the previous three decades, as well as clothes designed to make everyone look like romantic costumed extras: cowboys and Indians and whores of Babylon. And from the 1970s there are jeans. The only square fashion item in the store. But then Fiorucci redesigned jeans and made them chic. Before Diane Von, and Gloria, and Calvin, and Yves. Long, long before.

Fiorucci is the whole twentieth century in one place. The atmosphere is electric. The music is selected by a specialist who keeps on top of such things as which group and which wave of music is now. And the tapes are played so loud they seem part of the interior design. In fact, once when I was taken through the Milan shop when it is closed to the public from 12 noon to 3 p.m., the store with no music felt decidedly bereft, like a lover stranded all alone without someone to dance with.

Neon blinking on and off, too-loud music, the momentum kicks you into outer space when you enter a Fiorucci store and the atmosphere is kept rolling right along by the fashions, the salespeople, and the fellow shoppers. The salespeople are striking representations of the Fiorucci "line." They will streak feathery varicolored patches into their hair which must first be bleached a dead empty white and only then tinged with moody blue, electric green, or Matisse cerise. Even a modest Fiorucci employee in ordinary, less pronounced styles—perhaps in simple too-tight jeans and a bulky sweater hanging down almost to the knees—when seen from behind with ebony hair laced with patches of one of these bright and cheerful crime-against-nature hair tints, can make an unsuspecting first-timer at Fiorucci feel like the world has passed her by forever and she'll never catch up. And for the first-time person to come up alongside another Fiorucci shopper wearing fuchsia construction overalls, an acid yellow and black striped T-shirt, and a purse made of crinkly transparent plastic with Marilyn Monroe's face stamped on it, it's clear that what is happening here is not just the obtrusive rock and roll culture or the dizzying upheaval of the blinking lights—it's the Fiorucci people themselves. They aren't like normal people. They aren't living on the same planet. Not even in the same galaxy. And certainly not in the same time slot going on outside in the rest of the world.

There are some Fiorucci employees you just can't help but stare at. Like the young guy in the New York store who goes around in the tightest black leather pants and the blackest turtleneck sweater and who at first appears to be built like a flamingo, with legs that are simply too long for a young man of his proportions. It turns out he's walking on the highest pair of high heels, the kind one is used to seeing in comic-book illustrations of the wicked dragon lady.

Or perhaps one will be caught up musing over one of the fresh, young, gorgeous girl employees of Fiorucci like the two leaning against the counter across the floor. One is wearing fake snakeskin cowboy boots dyed pale yellow, pale-yellow cotton shorts with little strawberries embroidered on them here and there, and then a demure little Swiss-girl smocked cotton blouse in palest aqua. Her colleague is wearing an outfit of scarlet zebra-skin fabric that looks like it's made out of reconstituted plastic wrappers and designed for street wear in Rio at *carnaval* time. Both girls wear the exact same shade of lipstick: Fresh Blood.

The one in the flying-down-to-Rio outfit is blond enough to pose for a Breck shampoo ad, if she would only wash her face. The one in the sweet pale yellow is a very black, black girl who looks like an Ethiopian princess. Both of them talk as if they're from the Bronx.

The floors in Fiorucci shops are wood, light hard oak. Light fixtures are naked. Being inside Fiorucci is like being someplace before it's ready. Fiorucci practically invented high tech, or at least they were the first to go commercial with it. Early in the 1970s, the first stores, designed by the Fiorucci in-house architects and the graphic-arts department, pioneered the clean, spare, industrial look that is now so vogue in shops everywhere. Though at first the idea of using laboratory beakers as drinking glasses and industrial metal shelves in your bedroom for your marabou negligees may seem like this-time-they've-gone-too-far, sooner or later one must admit that at least high tech works: it doesn't fall apart the way most things do. Not even—and in Fiorucci this is a real plus—from stage fright. For everything in Fiorucci is on stage. The lights are often turned up very bright; one is invited to peer as closely as one wants at every detail, one is almost forced to. Unlike other high-priced shops where a kind of supernatural calm is imposed by soft wall-to-wall carpeting, soft music, and restrained flattering lighting and even the racks must appear discreet, Fiorucci is selling energetic, adrenaline-driven jokes.

What America sells is itself: American know-how and Coca-Cola.

What Milan does is sell you what you already have, only better. In Italy, everything is designed, even bathroom fixtures; everything is a work of art. So it really should not be a surprise that it was Fiorucci of Milan who finally came up with a way to sell America back to America, to sell American jeans that cost three times as much as Levi's but are so well designed—or redesigned—that once anyone tries them on, that is that.

In 1977, Fiorucci was featuring four main items in its line: jeans, sweatshirts, T-shirts, and windbreakers. L.L. Bean in high gear. Gianfranco Rossi, who is Fiorucci's executive vice-president in charge of business and who now spends most of his time in New York commented, with a smile, on the line: "It was American. Only now it is designed right. Now it is Fiorucci of Milan."

The Fiorucci phenomenon. Take an old idea, redesign it, sell it back. Or better yet, take an old idea and recycle it into a new one. In the color spectrum of human endeavor, there are those at the indigo end who wish that everything would be ultimately stationary and last forever. And then there are those opposite at the bright-red end who believe that a day without ninety-seven fresh ideas is a day without sunshine. At Fiorucci, old ideas and new ideas are woven into fresh patterns and turned into flying carpets that sometimes shoot by so quickly that they are forgotten almost before they have happened.

Elio Fiorucci, president and guiding genius, and everyone who works for him, is constantly vigilant day and night, keeping a close eye on teenagers and anyone else they see who is the least bit interesting. They are looking for any new idea, any imagination in style that might possibly be incorporated into the Fiorucci look. The fastenings on a child's snowsuit. The spirit of a seventy-five-cent paper birthday tablecloth. Everything is constantly changing at Fiorucci. That's the appeal. The success of Fiorucci is that if you ever become hooked, you'll need to come back all the time, if only just to look.

Employees are given their head to travel around the world; they are shopping for ideas new enough for Fiorucci. When Elio Fiorucci hears that Milanese friends are about to embark on a business trip or vacation to Tahiti or South America, he takes them aside for a hushed impromptu conference and instructs them to keep their eyes open and send back anything, any little thing they see that might be of interest, to them, to him, to their children, anybody.

People who work for Fiorucci two years in Milan are encouraged to move to a Fiorucci somewhere else and stay two years to gain a new language and more friends; that way they'll have more access to new ideas. Even people who quit and go to work elsewhere seem to gravitate back after a year or so, using the knowledge they gained working in "the outside world" to enforce and strengthen Fiorucci with the very latest in business advances, research, and design.

Unlike some companies, Fiorucci does not harbor wrathful resentment toward people who leave; instead Fiorucci seems to regard anyone who ever worked for the firm as family, welcome always to return home, but please bring new ideas of course, for new ideas are what Fiorucci is all about. Everything needs to change—and often.

It's all part of the Fiorucci phenomenon, whatever that is. The Fiorucci phenomenon—the concept, the image—is almost impossible to pin down. If you don't understand and have to ask, you'll never know. It's like asking someone to explain a peach.

But people do know. If they care about fashion, if they're between the ages of fifteen and twenty-five and they aren't complete sticks-in-the-mud, if they read fashion magazines, if they live in New York or Beverly Hills or Boston or Tokyo or London or Rio, they know. Even if they don't live in those places or read those magazines, they know. Whenever something totally outrageous comes along in fashion these days, people always think it is something from Fiorucci, even when it's not. There is a new adjective in the fashion world: things are described as being "very Fiorucci."

And then there are always the stores. If you still need a definition, go into one of them; they're like photo emulsions. If you've got the ability to pick up from the negative, you pick up. Some people just don't. But even people who don't like the stores, or can't understand them, can always pick up something, a vibe, the music. And then, through that one thing you kind of get plugged into a network. Even the straightest, squarest person can find one little piece of merchandise or one little design detail to like. And then the whole thing just opens up for them. Suddenly it is all very familiar, and very Fiorucci.

Incredibly sexy young women who sing rock and roll onstage or get photographed for magazines wear Fiorucci, just as incredibly sexy older women at chic discos wear Halston and incredibly sexy Las Vegas bombshells wear Bob Mackie.

Celebrities arrive in limos to buy Fiorucci. Halston patrols the aisles to check out how the other half dresses. Andy Warhol is a friend of the store, a regular. Diane von Furstenberg and Jackie O buy their T-shirts at Fiorucci. And fourteen-year-olds hang out there. Wherever there is Fiorucci, there are kids.

To define a fashion outlook that appeals to rock stars, socialites, teenagers in from the suburbs, punks, and upper-middle-class fashion watchers is perilous. Elio Fiorucci himself refuses to enter the fray. As far as he is concerned, he says, "Fiorucci is either accepted or rejected." It doesn't matter which. They keep coming, and everybody has a good time. Controversy sells plastic evening dresses, and jeans. People are curious about what is going on out there in the future.

Picasso once said, "I make things first, others follow me and make them pretty." The creator or originator of ideas doesn't have to be the one to smooth off the corners and soften the edges; he is too busy doing more important things. Something of this philosophy also belongs to Fiorucci; many new ideas are presented first in Fiorucci stores, where they cause an outrage. Months, or years, later the same ideas appear in other stores, made pretty and even bearable by the passage of time.

To some who loathe Fiorucci and reject the entire place as a sordid example of fashion hype at its least appealing, the notion that they'll be wearing (perhaps in vastly toned-down shades and vastly toned-up fabrics) the very designs that Fiorucci is splattering all over his windows in multiples seems a terrible truth almost too depressing to think about.

"I go into that store," one fashionable New York woman says, "just to get myself ready for the outrages I'm going to have to endure in two years. Because I know once it's in Fiorucci, it's coming, and there's no getting around it."

Interestingly, the Fiorucci phenomenon is criticized and rejected for reasons that are hard to explain.

"Fiorucci is very Carnaby Street and out-of-date," one young man told me, "and it's very directional." Which means, I found out with some difficulty, "everybody else will be showing it next year." Fiorucci is directional, and you either like that or you don't. So we arrive back at the original Fiorucci paradox. It is out-of-date and also the coming thing.

Two other frequently heard criticisms of Fiorucci may help confound the issue. More than two people have said to me: "Fiorucci is terrible now. Nobody goes there anymore; it's too popular." A complicated idea. And the other common, convoluted criticism: "Everything in Fiorucci is just cheap junk. It's like a dime store—everything costs two dollars. And everything is so expensive there. They've got a hell of a lot of nerve charging those kinds of prices."

Obviously, ever so obviously, Fiorucci is the newest wave.

FIORUCCI HISTORY

The history of Fiorucci begins in Milan, Italy's large northern industrial city. If it were in America, it would be called Detroit. Since it is in Italy, the citizens, wrapped up in lives of industry, factories, and business, apologize for not being artists. They regret that necessity forces them to be practical. However, like people in all northern industrial cities, they are happy—happy as clams—to be producing and selling products and spending from dawn until dusk immersed in phone calls, meetings, and strategies. Milan may be only the second-largest city in Italy, but the Milanese think it is the most important city, the *real* Italy.

Originally, Fiorucci was a small shoe shop on the Corso Buenos Aires; it was owned and run by Vincenzo Fiorucci, the father of Elio.

In the early 1960s, people with money and snappy Italian taste had their suits tailored and their shoes made especially for them in Milan. The cobblers in Milan, men like Fiorucci the father, made hand-carved wooden models of your feet and kept them forever, so that they could always make shoes for you that fit perfectly and looked exactly right. Even today the Milanese still can't help referring to Fiorucci as "you mean that shoe store?"

In 1962, Elio Fiorucci, then twenty-seven, armed with three pairs of brightly colored plastic galoshes tied to a string, took a cab to the editorial offices of *Amica*, a weekly Milan fashion magazine, and inspired the editors to publish a photograph of these galoshes, telling where they could be bought. Like a hit single, the galoshes became an overnight sensation all over Italy.

And perhaps Elio Fiorucci's entire success was based on that simple transaction, for in a nutshell it included all the things Fiorucci ever does. First, he risked taxi money. Second, he knew that the particular galoshes he picked would strike magazine editors as news rather than as items in need of advertising. The magazine gladly parted with free space and a photograph. The galoshes became editorial material for the magazine. And last but not least, the galoshes themselves (which Fiorucci had imported and cornered the market on beforehand) were so cute, nobody could resist.

To this day, it is strict Fiorucci policy never to advertise. Fiorucci is news, not commerce. The simple idea remains a constant of the whole Fiorucci operation.

In 1967, Elio Fiorucci opened the first Fiorucci clothing store in Milan. In those days, it was just a one-room shop. Today, it is three floors of pulsating shopping space, located in one of Milan's many gallerias, the Galleria Passarella.

Gallerias are an early invention of Milanese merchandisers; they are the first true shopping malls. The largest and most beautiful galleria is the Galleria Vittorio Emanuele, built in the tradition of the Victorian Crystal Palace. The ceiling is wrought-iron curlicues and glass and is five stories high; the sunlight from above makes the loggias faintly radiant, a look that is distinctly religious. Which is all together appropriate, because merchandising is religion in Milan. Whenever one reads guidebooks to Milan, the four most important things one must see are: (1) Leonardo's *Last Supper*, which keeps fading and which they keep touching up; (2) La Scala, Milan's opera house and major claim to the arts; (3) Il Duomo, Milan's elaborate white marble cathedral, a religious fantasy dripping with loops of icing like a Viennese wedding cake; and (4) the Galleria Vittorio Emanuele.

The shortest route from La Scala (Art) to Il Duomo (God) is through the Galleria. Once you're in the Galleria, it is easy to forget where you were originally headed. You may lose yourself to shopping. The marble hallways, the baroque sidewalk cafés and the fabulous shops prove that Milan is well and prospering and has its priorities straight.

The Galleria Passarella is a secondary galleria across the street and down the block. The Passarella is not nearly so grand as the Emanuele, but it is more modern, caters to younger, hipper customers; after all, it is the same Milanese "in the blood" merchandising tradition that built it.

In 1967, when America was madly alive with the Byrds, Dylan, and LSD, and the object of dress was outrage, Milan was still as conservative and untouched as a prim private school. While America was throbbing with the Doors and Big Brother, there were no radio stations in Italy, let alone in Milan, playing the Beatles. Nothing. An utter wasteland. But you could go to Fiorucci. And hear anything. And dance to it in the aisles of the store.

It was almost as though rock and roll and Fiorucci were plugged into the same amp. The raw, tough teenage romance, the slant on things, was identical. But the perspective was different. Fiorucci was rock and roll and merchandising combined as equals; neither ever took over completely. And the store's involvement with rock maintains to this day a firm grip on both adolescent passion and minding the store.

Even in the beginning, even in that first fledgling Fiorucci store, it was always all about fun. And, since from the very start Elio Fiorucci was amused by life itself and determined not to remain in the slipper-store business; he could hardly fail to be amused by London's Carnaby Street, the quintessential 1960s look, one of the biggest popular fashion concepts of our day. Here the mods, young kids who listened to the Who and the Beatles and worked very hard so they could buy all their clothes on Carnaby Street—even if it meant sharing a one-bedroom apartment with five people—could look as chic as Jane Asher.

Carnaby Street was Mary Quant's hemlines refusing to believe in modesty, a store named Biba presenting its merchandise in mirrored swankiness while rock and roll played into the very cracks of the dressing rooms; raspberry-velvet-Indian everything, white lipstick. Carnaby Street was the utter dernier cri in fashion presented with an air of amused intimacy.

The clothes would fall apart after you wore them only three times, but you only wanted to wear them three times anyway, and besides, they didn't really cost that much so who cared. They were fun. They amused Elio Fiorucci. So he went to Carnaby Street, every weekend, and bought everything in sight. Especially miniskirts. And he sold them by the hundreds at the first Fiorucci store on the sedate Galleria Passarella.

Soon actual miniskirts direct from Carnaby Street weren't enough. Neither were bright plastic galoshes. The essential genius of Fiorucci begins with the genius for choosing the right people, offbeat people with the ability to look at an obviously popular idea or thing, send it through outer space and bring it back light-years ahead of where it started. That supersonic swerve in interpretation that makes something the rage, not merely popular. These people (including designer Cristina Rossi, now Elio Fiorucci's wife) swiftly began to design Fiorucci miniskirts. And because they were from Fiorucci, by Fiorucci, they were utterly different from anything that had crossed the Channel before.

By the early 1970s Fiorucci was not simply the rage in Italy. Although being the rage in Italy might well have been enough, especially since even then Fiorucci was still the only place you could go and hear the latest music. For in all of Italy there still wasn't a single radio station playing Van Morrison or the Stones. Fiorucci had taken flight and was fascinating ladies and gentlemen of fashion all over Europe. America would know soon enough. Carnaby Street had not survived the unamused light of morning but Fiorucci had begun to sweep the globe.

In 1974, Montedison, Italy's largest multinational corporation and owner of Standa, Italy's largest utility, bought 50 percent of Fiorucci. And while it is generally true that when such a giant buys 50 percent of anything the real flair tends to be the first thing to bite the dust, Fiorucci once again went against the grain of tradition. Fiorucci was not swallowed up by peculiar notions of corporate normalcy. The purchase by Montedison quite simply made Fiorucci even more Fiorucci. If such a thing is within understanding. The original small group of designers magically transformed themselves into a thing calling itself a design department. One shop in Milan became many stores and franchises until over three thousand shops all over the world displayed vivid little window stickers announcing that they were Authorized Fiorucci Outlets: PUNTO VENDITA AUTORIZZATO-FIORUCCI.

For a line of clothing, for so many stores, for such a point of view to maintain a reputation for over a decade as *the* place to go if you come up with a weird thought or something new and wonderful, cannot be an accident. There must be something underneath, some structure that is forceful and yet subtle enough to support such ephemeral spirit and scatter it over the globe.

What Fiorucci has done is to capture a kind of international ideal of teenage promise and bottle it. Fiorucci's aim, the illusion it creates, is that all your conventional reservations and stubborn navy blues are nothing more than prissy hangovers from a past life that is no longer useful. We're going to have to live on what's left, to recycle the remnants of things past, to survive. And in this future time, which is now, we'll be glad for a little color, a little black joke in sticky orange plastic that has been wittily designed into a belt shaped like a cat with ruby rhinestones for eyes. And we'll be glad that instead of stores that have become browbeaten into beige, elegant subtlety, there is a store with the wisdom to produce sunglasses in purple and chartreuse with glitter rainbowing into rims the size of Cadillac fins.

THE FIORUCCI LOOK

In the world of high fashion, clothing designers all believe that the women who wear their clothes won't wreck the line by being larger than a size 10. All the women who wear the clothes will have bodies that are so perfect that even if they take their clothes off their bodies are sensuously held taut by muscle tone.

The invention of the notion of going braless on the top and wearing pantyhose on the bottom has changed the world of fashion. After all, a woman who doesn't need a bra and who is sheathed below in gauze does have complete freedom of movement. For all intents and purposes, she is naked, and that's what designers want.

It is perfectly clear in the fashion magazines that designers are only interested in customers who are lithe, who have nothing to hide, who are "comfortable" with their liberated bodies. Little black classic dinner suits worn by models who are eighteen years old, little tailored jackets with only one button and that will reveal absolutely everything if the model inclines her body a mere forty-five degrees forward, see-through fabrics, and slit skirts—all these standard elements of good design have one kind of woman in mind. She is a size 6, she is without a false sense of modesty; she buys clothes not to keep warm or conform to social custom but rather to add a touch of color to her look, or to set off her green eyes, or to complement a new and outrageous shade of nail polish.

Fiorucci designers are no different. They also believe that clothes are really created only to liven up a dull-but-perfect naked size-6 body. Fiorucci clothes are designed to be worn only by beautiful young girls with long slim legs. (The pants Fiorucci makes are cut extra long so they'll fit these perfect girls.) Elio Fiorucci admits his preference for slim girls: "To manufacture only small sizes is doing a favor for humanity. I prevent ugly girls from showing off their bad figures."

When a woman who is a size 12, like me, goes into Fiorucci, it's a very cold shower to find out that there aren't even any size 10's left; the one they had last week is already sold. A size 12 can only conclude one thing looking at all those size-6 clothes: Fiorucci clothes are really silly, and they're not for real people anyway. For people who are a 6 or 8 or 10, the clothes in Fiorucci are designer clothes sold at cheap prices. For people larger than a size 10, it is perfectly obvious that Fiorucci clothes are nothing but a collection of sleazy, flimsy, tacky things that would fall apart if you wore them more than once and besides, who can wear them anyway?

But it's nice, I suppose, that somebody can wear the stuff. After all, the Fiorucci experience is not confined to wearing it. Watching other people who can dress that way and then do is something to be grateful for too.

After the issue of size is settled, Fiorucci's approach to fashion diverges sharply from the mainstream. Fiorucci is antifashion; it is, first and foremost, a creator of new trends. The Fiorucci look is a delirious shambles of fragments from everywhere, every time, everything. It is easy to get confused in a Fiorucci store and conclude that they've gotten America and history all mixed up. They've piled up images from the 1950s atop the 1940s and mixed it in with the 1970s and some futuristic punk. And it is the preoccupation with glamour, with every Vargas pinup, with every B-movie starlet, with every overdone chorine, which sets the tone. In Fiorucci you are far from the elegant understatement of fine cashmere and slippery silk.

The obsession with Frederick's of Hollywood garishness is not a failure of education on the part of the Fiorucci design department in Milan. They know what's cooking in the couturier world; they just don't care. And the Fiorucci customers love them for their nerve.

The Milan store began in 1967 as a revolutionary new idea. Elio Fiorucci wanted to provide an alternative for shoppers. He brought the youth culture from London and presented it to young people in

Milan who went gaga. They had barely seen jeans and T-shirts and glitter; now they could buy it in the chic ambiance of the Galleria Passarella. The Milan customers today, thirteen years later, are almost the same people. They are young, slightly intellectual and/or artistic, a little bit "fringe" in a nice sort of way. They are the people who don't want to become bankers. They disco, they work in the day in shops or offices, and they pride themselves on their awareness of the world outside Milan.

In America, Fiorucci customers pride themselves on the same virtues: they are young, or young at heart; they are chic, and they like to think of themselves as being very avant-garde. In New York, wearing Fiorucci used to mean that you ran with Andy Warhol and the *Interview* magazine crowd, that you spent all night flouncing around discos, and that you were booked every late afternoon for art gallery openings. But Fiorucci merchandising is more sophisticated than that, and now the typical Fiorucci New York customer is practically anybody. A secretary on her lunch hour can't resist buying a pair of $50 jeans. A wild and crazy advertising guy runs in after work to pick up a T-shirt for his weekend at the beach. A college professor buys, on sale yet, a crew-neck sweatshirt with little flowers on it. The wife of an accounting mogul breezes in and finds herself unable to resist a satin cowboy shirt with glitterized fringe. Anyone can afford something at Fiorucci and everyone wants to wear the Fiorucci look, or at least part of it. Only the fashion purists, the serious disco people, ever dress entirely in Fiorucci. Eclecticism is much more workable.

Fashion eclecticism of course is a very Fiorucci idea. Nothing in Fiorucci is really original, except that it all is. Everything comes from something or somewhere else, and that's the way it is supposed to be. The Fiorucci people are information junkies. They gather information the way squirrels gather nuts, against a future use. Everything—the clothes, the graphics, the store fixtures—is all derivative.

Fiorucci people like to collect what they call "mass-culture facts." A mass-culture fact is a piece of the culture observed. For example, the emergence of rock music as a major force in the youth culture is a mass-culture fact. The ecology movement as a seductive political cause is a mass-culture fact. The new interest in utilitarian and highly functional design is a mass-culture fact. On their own, mass-culture facts are interesting. Connected to fashion, they become inspiration. Fiorucci designers observed the new interest in utilitarian simplicity, and they turned jeans into a fashion item. They observed, firsthand in Milan, the advent of terrorism as a political tool, and they invented brightly colored parachute-cloth jumpsuits. They turned workmen's lunch boxes into purses, in both plastic and in metal. Industrial goggles became sunglasses. Overalls now came in turquoise and it-hurts-my-eyes acid yellow.

Nothing is sacred. The Fiorucci designers are masters at taking an ordinary object or material and turning it into something else, and that something else is usually fashion. (Although Fiorucci has experimented with manufacturing nonfashion items. They have made dinnerwear, ashtrays, clocks, and other household items. Nothing fazes them. At one point they even designed, but never produced, a line of cigarettes.) At Fiorucci, design is whim, and whim is fashion.

One of the favorite words in the Fiorucci design lexicon is "recycle." It means reuse, change, reassemble, reinvent. It means thinking in modular units. Recycling is the central principle of design at Fiorucci, and like most other things at Fiorucci, it is best explained by example. While I was in Milan the designers were experimenting with using the pebbled rubber material found on Ping-Pong paddles. They were only at the prototype stage, but I'm sure in six months they will have perpetrated Ping-Pong fabric vests or address books. They took a severe and strictly functional-looking military belt buckle and made it into a funny fashion item by manufacturing it in pastel-colored see-through plastic. The display box for Fiorucci sunglasses is an oversize version of an old-fashioned box of American kitchen matches. They make a $30 clutch purse out of Pirelli rubber floor material. And the ultimate Fiorucci recycle job: see-through plastic jeans. Fiorucci does more recycling than Alcoa.

If you find the concept difficult, you are on the wrong frequency. Take a deep breath, look carefully at any Fiorucci product, and think. Notice its design elements; you're sure to have the vague feeling that you've seen this somewhere before. You haven't really, but you have seen pieces of it. You've seen lightweight luggage made out of heavy-duty plastic cloth before, but you've never seen it in fluorescent colors. You've seen red polka dots before, but never on a $400 white leather jacket. And surely you've seen soap before, but never soap shaped like little macaronis. That's recycling. And the recycling is funny. It's what accounts for the chuckles you hear all over the store; the little shocks of recognition from pleased browsers and amused customers. They can shake their heads no all they like, as long as they walk out carrying one of those famous Fiorucci shopping bags, one of which is recycled from an old American mesh onion bag.

In a way, the shopping bags are the key to the whole thing. They carry the goods, they carry the ever-changing logo, and they catalog the years of Fiorucci success marching along. The shopping bags, like everything else at Fiorucci, are designed with care; they must "represent," with exactitude, the ideas that Fiorucci is recycling at any given time. The shopping bags are themselves a form of recycling. They carry the stuff and the image simultaneously. Their imagery is the best of Fiorucci graphics, carefully supervised by Fiorucci's graphics department head, Franco Marabelli.

Judging time in chunks of graphics is perfectly natural to Franco. He talks easily about various graphic phases in Fiorucci's history. Sometimes the dates overlap, sometimes the graphics. But he always seems to be remembering some very specific notion or concept that the Fiorucci people were interested in that year. Thus, Franco talks about the Year of the Angel, because in 1979 Fiorucci produced shopping bags with an image of two Victorian cherubs looking very foxy in Lolita-style heart-shaped sunglasses.

In 1975, Fiorucci people got interested in the ecology movement, and the graphics reflected their concern; thus, a Period of Nature. The Year of the Fruits (1978) presented lush tropical Hawaiian prints, white pants, and panama hats. (The graphic phases reflect what's going on in Fiorucci fashion as well as being connections to mass-culture facts.)

And then there was the Year of the Pinup, which seems to have

been almost every Fiorucci year. Also the phases of time called Fiorucci
Fly and Fiorucci Space, both in 1976, both having to do with mass-
culture facts about spaceflight and other kinds of air travel. Recently,
there has been another Airplane Period. And for the 1980s Franco
predicts a Geometric Period, to be followed shortly by a Fluorescent
Period.

Take a look around you. Franco is never wrong, and he is never
just talking about his own graphics presentations. Franco is a good
index of the fashion future always, because he has a lot to do with
making fashion at Fiorucci, which, as we all know, means it will get
to the rest of us in very short order. As one Fiorucci poster puts it
(this one with the angels in sunglasses). "Fiorucci, Since 1492." These
people know what they're doing.

The Fiorucci phenomenon is more impressive than you might
think. I asked Franco Marabelli and Mark Sawyer, who does the New
York windows, to list some Fiorucci firsts, things they can remember
they pioneered—notice how common these ideas have become. In
the realm of merchandising and store display, which is increasingly
important in this consuming-crazed society, Fiorucci was first with:
flat two-dimensional wooden mannequins for in-store display; mass
displays of a single item; clothes displayed pressed between two sheets
of Plexiglas; "theme" windows that tell a little story or set a dramatic
scene, and metal poles instead of mannequins. They didn't invent
hardwood floors, but they certainly understand what many layers of
polyurethane can do.

As pioneers in the fashion world, the Fiorucci designers are relent-
less front-runners. If they didn't invent it, they rediscovered it first.
Which amounts to the same thing in the fashion design business,
since fashion historians are quick to point out that fashion runs in
thirty-year cycles always: if it's not the bosom being emphasized, it's
the legs, and then the bosom returns.

The Fiorucci fashion firsts are difficult to catalog, because things
happen so fast in the fashion world that it is sometimes difficult to
track an idea, and because the Fiorucci people don't care about chro-
nology.

They are delighted when one of their ideas becomes everybody's idea. That's the point. A partial list of Fiorucci firsts should suffice.

In 1976 Fiorucci popularized gold lamé. They made it into everything: shoes, bags, boots, jeans, belts, and luggage. Ditto colored metallics. They made lamé in different colors.

In 1977 they reintroduced fishnet stockings to a world which had sorely missed them since their last reappearance in the early 1960s. And just for the shock of it, they tried miniskirts again in 1977, but bombed with them. They've had to wait for everyone to catch up with them, and sure enough, miniskirts are back on the streets of New York and the runways in Paris. In 1977 they also got interested in animal skins, and suddenly everyone was wearing leopard, zebra, tiger, or snakeskin anything.

In 1978 they stretched out and redesigned their clothes in Lycra and spandex, and for fun, used a lot of military fabric for "silly" clothes, to contrast with the Hawaiian prints and fruits and flowers they had scattered everywhere. In 1979 they started using little star prints, and little stripes in bright candy colors—you know, the 1950s updated.

In process now at Fiorucci are the geometrics—futuristic fabrics derived from the futuristic 1930s and featuring flying boomerangs and starbursts of yellow, green, and blue. Similar to the ones the Big Designers are using, but the BDs do them in silk, with matched colors. At Fiorucci, the fabric is cotton sometimes, rayon a lot of the time. If you were there in time, you saw it at Fiorucci first.

The best, biggest, most amazing Fiorucci first of all is jeans. American jeans. The ultimate American product, conceived by pragmatism, turned hot and fashionable by some upstart young designers from Milan in 1970. Jeans were invented in the nineteenth century for cowboys to wear—they were designed to be serviceable, long lasting, tough, practical, and washable by any cowboy. Easy to care for, easy to wear. Fiorucci connected with the mass-culture fact of American ingenuity and practical know-how and rocked the fashion world. The first Fiorucci jeans were almost exact copies of Levi's, the quintessential American jeans, the originals. Fiorucci copied every detail, including the orange thread used for the welt seams and the little tiny change pocket in the front. But they went one step too far, and Levi-Strauss got miffed. Not at the whole thing mind you, Levi-Strauss is too big not to be flattered by imitation. What they really didn't like was the little red Fiorucci label sewn into the side of the back pocket. That was the Italians going too far. And so everybody went to court and Fiorucci promised never again to put their little red Fiorucci label in the side of the back pocket. They moved it to the center back belt loop. Fiorucci fans are delighted, in 1980, to see Levi's for sale with little red Levi's labels on the center back belt loop. Justice is done. Fiorucci was first with the new, chic place to put labels.

Jeans are the centerpiece, the mainstay, of the Fiorucci empire. They sell over three million pairs a year, because that's all they can produce. The demand exceeds the supply. The jeans come in fuchsia and peach and periwinkle and jade. Some of the Fiorucci jeans turned baggy in 1978; it took a couple of years for everyone else to think baggy, but finally it happened. In 1979, some of the Fiorucci jeans turned transparent; they were produced in see-through plastic, but the idea didn't catch on. "The plastic made you too hot," Franco explains, as if that were the only necessary explanation. They made jeans in gold lamé, but no one at Fiorucci can remember what year. It was too long ago.

The jeans are called Safety jeans, because their label design was derived from a box of Safety brand matches. They changed the fashion world. Simply. The Fiorucci jeans are the beginning of a whole new way of thinking about fashion. Gloria Vanderbilt owes Fiorucci a lot. As do we all. As does John Travolta, who orders his jeans custom-made by Fiorucci, dozens of pairs in every color.

The Fiorucci people are glad to oblige. They grin and twinkle with glee at reports of their influence and success. And when something doesn't work, when it doesn't sell out immediately, they shrug their shoulders and go on to the next idea. Practically nothing in Fiorucci, except the jeans, is ever manufactured more than once, regardless of how well it sells or how many requests are received for it. Perhaps it is simply too boring to spend your life making only one blouse, just to get rich. The Fiorucci designers would rather try out something new; it's more fun. And fun is what they're after. They'd much rather try something crazy, float it, and take their chances.

One of the funnier ideas they tried didn't work at all, but they had a good time. In 1978, Fiorucci tried selling Paolo Buggiani's "artist's jumpsuits," each individually signed by the artist, each one numbered as if they were prints or lithographs. Fiorucci threw a big party at Xenon, a New York disco, to kick the idea off. It didn't work; the jumpsuits didn't sell. But no one minded. Fiorucci sold over one million dollars worth of Fiorucci merchandise last year in Arab countries; the Arab Fiorucci girls wear their jeans under their chadors. So it equalizes.

Some of the ideas work really well. For years Fiorucci has been manufacturing transparent plastic rain slickers in bright colors that sell for $2. The pink one caused a sensation when it was worn by a bare-breasted model on the cover of the German magazine *Stern* in 1978. The slickers represent, in a $2 bargain, the essence of Fiorucci design. The most important thing is to be witty. The second most important thing is to make clothes that lots of people will be able to think of lots of uses for. And the third most important thing, which is always the thing you notice first, is that everything is all backward and upside down and recycled and redefined.

Fiorucci thrives on its perversion of form, its refusal to do things the way everybody else does them. They don't use silk; everyone else does. They used fake leopard skin when no one else would. They used plastic; everybody else was embarrassed to. They combined lush magenta and limpid yellow when no one else could imagine it. They love tacky rayon blends; everyone else who uses them tries to disguise them into looking like natural fabrics. They defy. They dare. Fiorucci is out to break all the rules, to destroy the integrity of the original form or material.

It is quite common, for example, at Fiorucci, to see ordinary Vassar-girl type skirts, the kind that *Women's Wear Daily* is calling "preppy," as if that's not what they've always been called, cut exactly as they've always been cut. With little pockets in the side seams and buckles at the waistband, everything just right and in place. Except that at Fiorucci they are made in shocking, fluorescent, visible-from-three-blocks-away bright yellow. So you won't miss that this is something new and something now. Fiorucci makes ballet-dancer tutus out of stiff plastic. They make briefcases out of aluminum toolboxes. After all, if you can turn jeans into fashion, the shameless variations and possibilities for the future are endless. The only thing they seem to worry about at Fiorucci is that maybe someone isn't getting the joke. They remind me, over and over again, as we look around the design studio, that their things are very funny. They want me to like things because *they* like them. They are happy in their work. Fiorucci people resent not being taken seriously. They are serious about being funny. They want us to laugh with them, not at them. And the distinction is extremely important to them. They are skilled designers, graphic artists, fashion mavens, and merchandisers. They work hard at creating an atmosphere of freedom, of devil-may-care abandon. They want it all to look casual. It does. But that doesn't come without a lot of work and care. The Fiorucci spirit is light and bright. Like all fashion people, they work ahead. They are looking at the future, and they are amused.

ATTENTION TO DETAIL

It is the details that have made Fiorucci. It is buttons of red and blue and rust and green running down the front of a man's shirt. It is lightning bolts of metallic thread darting off the surface of an otherwise undistinguished plaid cotton. It is a sliver of shoulder pad where others, less wise, would simply have avoided the issue. It is attention to detail. The exact thing that made those first Fiorucci galoshes Crayola-colored, unlike the rest of the galoshes in the world that had always been dreary black. What else but the detail of color made these galoshes into "news" for a fashion magazine? Not the fact that galoshes are rubber boots capable of keeping rain off your feet, the colds from your head, the accidental traffic splatters from your stockings. It was the idea of cheerful, playful galoshes in fanciful colors so happy that your mood would improve the instant you looked down at your feet slogging through a mess of puddles.

Colors are often the detail Fiorucci uses most. An overgrown Shetland sweater doesn't appear at Fiorucci in calm, Brooks Brothers colors, it comes in candy-apple red or a soaring lemon yellow. Jeans must have all that stitching on the outside, but it will be done in fluorescent orange.

Along with all the pulsating colors and brazen necklines go endearing details of construction. A girlish cotton skirt with scalloped trim has an elastic waistband that also has belt loops and a cotton belt to match, just in case. A T-shirt with the most flattering neckline imaginable is made perfect for all time by the detail on the back of the neck: it is reinforced like a sweatshirt, so this T-shirt that you obviously are going to love will never unravel at the neck like T-shirts you love always do.

Because this is Fiorucci, all this picky attention to detail is not reserved only for clothes. Inside a Fiorucci store sticks of neon radiate just so, haloing a practical but unamusing pillar smack in the middle of everything. There is no such thing as whipping in and out of Fiorucci; there are only slow strolls and after an hour or so you are bound to get thirsty. Then you'll be offered free espresso in a midget Fiorucci cup, a chance to relax or listen to the music or talk with a Fiorucci salesperson.

What if Milan is the fashion capital of the world and flooded with buyers and journalists and media types of all sorts? Don't those people need help finding a place to eat, shouldn't they at least be reminded of La Scala? Thoughtful Fiorucci issues a casual-looking brochure including a map of Milan, a listing of restaurants and their prices and directions for how to get places with the least aggravation.

Nobody in the fashion industry expects to pay full price for anything to wear; they are walking advertisements. To receive a discount in a Fiorucci store you must have a card to present to the orange-haired person with the long lime-green fingertips tapping the till at the cash register. And the card should be a nice plastic one like a credit card. It will have a cluster of brilliant red cherries drooping somewhere on it: the discount percent will appear in a floodlight beam.

Attention to detail is spotting military medals in an antique shop, being captivated by their stern glitter and crisp ribbons and understanding everyone should have a Fiorucci medal. Soon there is a poster that is more than a poster. Twenty medals march smartly across a Hong Kong red background, each medal a gum-backed sticker ready to be peeled off the poster and smacked onto a chest in need of a bit of dash.

Nothing sits still at Fiorucci. Everyone is constantly in midflight, on-the-wing, going in circles, jumping up and down. Ceaseless motion. No one can stay still long enough to be concerned about the overall impression, the flamboyant splash, the outright commotion Fiorucci creates in the outside world. They are hummingbirds.

The details are what count, the details are interesting. Real life pales when you are preoccupied with designing skirts with gathers in the back that flare out over a woman's behind and make her look like a Fabergé penguin.

While it is true that occasionally even in the fashion business one must sit still long enough to write something down, there is no rule that says you must do this on plain white paper. Fiorucci stationery changes as often as the Fiorucci logo does, and then some. There is special stationery for the New York store, for various departments in the New York store, for Zurich, for London, for Boston, for Beverly Hills. The public-relations office in Milan has its own stationery design while three offices away the press-liaison people have yet a different design on theirs. When the Via Torino Fiorucci opened in Milan in 1975, it had its own private stock, even though it was less than a mile away from the original Fiorucci. A "flight" theme was invented and matching stationery duly issued during the brief period Fiorucci organized charters and made travel arrangements for fashion buyers. Even interoffice stationery, which the public never sees, never remains the same for very long. If a graphic somehow manages to hang on for more than three weeks or a month, somebody is going to notice that detail and immediately move right along with a new one to replace it.

Then there are the labels. Quite aside from the fact that almost everyone else used to put them on the inside and Fiorucci found it more amusing to always put them on the outside, these never remain the same for long. One day a pair of jeans may sport a small fabric label with a row of caballeros, but when the next shipment arrives they'll sport a tiny three-frame cartoon or a stately buffalo.

Whether or not the price of things at Fiorucci is a painful shock or a delightful surprise, one thing is certain. The design of the actual price tags themselves doesn't change any less frequently than the stationery or the labels. One is a pinup girl in shorts whose legs are scissored up in the air, looking as though she's just landed on her fanny, very surprised. Another is a voluptuous smiling brunette wrapped in a towel, leaning forward so her cleavage shows. The pain of the price you pay can be made amusing if the price ticket looks like a joke drinking glass from the 1950s. Another label, with bright red in the background, shows a cutie pulling a T-shirt up over her head, exposing a fraction of her gorgeous self, just a fraction.

The price of things at Fiorucci is very uneven. Cheap plastic slickers that come neatly tucked into plastic envelopes cost $2. Dresses that are lined, have delicate and elegant designs and complicated sleeves cost $170. Funny-looking rough leather belts stamped to look like leopard skin with a leopard's head at one end and the tail used as the tip that slides through the buckle cost about $12.

A velveteen suit in pale yellow costs $75 and looks just like an usher's uniform from the 1930s with an epaulet on one shoulder and a string of jet black beads looped under and over the shoulder's arm. You could search the rest of your life for such an outfit—$75 is just fine.

A heavy cotton T-shirt with a flattering collarbone-level neckline, that is impossible to find anywhere, with sleeves ribbed at the wrist, a loose T-shirt that makes a body look sexy without trying—the sexiest way to be—costs $21. A small price to pay for a casual deception.

A summer dress of 100 percent cotton is $64. The cotton print looks like it jumped off the French Riviera from a Lartigue photograph in the elegant 1920s. It's an old-fashioned sundress for wearing on the yacht. Large sloppy 100-percent-wool sweaters that cost $60, as they would in any store, come in red so bright, green so vivid, and blue of such mad desire that you'd pay $60 just for the color alone.

I suppose one of the reasons it is so often thought that Fiorucci things cost the earth and fall apart the second time you wear them, is because of the overlayer of glitz and razzmatazz, the sequins and glitter and acrylics in tiger skin seem all that's in the store at all when you first walk in. But the price tags on the well-made things, which a newcomer naturally gravitates toward as a haven of subdued sanity, indicate the place ain't cheap. This confusion is easily overcome by anyone who refuses to let the glitz and music mow them down and who makes a determined, stoic effort to discriminate from the $15 T-shirts with neon glitter spelling DISCO BABY and the hundred-dollar ladies' dresses that are lined and faced and designed and which, when worn, look like a true creation of wit and style and detail that you can wear, as my mother says, "Anywhere."

What is made cheaply and fly-by-night and only for fun is not expensive. What is made carefully, lined, and studded with details used on "better" dresses is expensive, not enormously expensive, but what you'd expect to pay.

The price of things ought to bear a relationship to the quality, and the Fiorucci people are the first to admit that not everything sold in every Fiorucci store was intended to last a lifetime. It is also true that there is a certain charm in having something that costs $50 last longer than a quart of milk in your refrigerator. Fiorucci is a company that specializes in design, not in manufacturing.

Fiorucci clothes, which are sometimes complained about for having poor workmanship, are produced in such small quantities that it would cost too much to sell them if they were manufactured with the same quality controls used when millions of units are manufactured. And since virtually nothing Fiorucci makes is ever produced more than once the problem becomes clear. Especially when one remembers a lot of Fiorucci manufacturing is done in Korea (rubber things like shoes) or Romania (knitted items).

Does it really matter, this question of quality? If what you are buying is outrage, or the knowledge that you are just ahead of what is about to happen, quality is not your prime concern. You have to keep your sense of humor and come back next week. Maybe there'll be a party.

Fiorucci is always throwing parties; for Valentine's Day, to celebrate the publication of Andy Warhol's new book, or because *Wet* magazine of the West Coast should be properly introduced to the East Coast. Part of throwing parties, parties that are more fun to be at than anywhere else that night or afternoon, is paying attention to the details. Champagne is one of the most enduring allures of party giving. "Fiorucci must have the best," protested Angelo Careddu, a former Fiorucci person and now a public-relations consultant to the Fiorucci New York store, in a recent somewhat heated conversation with a liquor store proprietor. It was party time once again. Angelo had noticed that the champagne sent for the last party had simply not been of the same high quality as that sent for the party before last. "You must understand," he said, "Fiorucci must have the best."

A Fiorucci party doesn't necessarily get planned down to a gnat's eyebrow. Organizing a party in conjunction with *Interview* magazine or with Studio 54 (during its respectable heyday) is likely to require some restraint to keep the guest list under control. But for other more informal, though equally festive occasions, the more-the-merrier rule applies. During Christmas 1979 the New York store either stayed open awfully late one night or had a Christmas party. You decide. There was no advertisement in *The New York Times,* no mention in *New York Magazine*'s Best Bets section, no babbling radio commercials. But somehow, someway the word circulated. The store would be open for twenty-four straight hours the Saturday before Christmas Day. Hundreds of people milled around outside waiting to be allowed inside by friendly but efficient guards. For inside Christmas shopping had become one big party. Betsey Johnson was there in a pink net tutu and a clown's face autographing her T-shirts, Fiorucci's version of a stocking stuffer. A spirited punk rock band set the pace while Fiorucci employees on roller skates whizzed around offering panettone (Italian Christmas bread), and the very best greetings of the season.

Publicity is Fiorucci's expertise and it comes their way readily just because they are Fiorucci and do sensible things like stay open for twenty-four hours so you can get your Christmas shopping done. It's a question of style. When one remembers a few years back that one of the TV networks paid some advertising agency a million dollars to design a new logo only to discover at the unveiling that the logo was almost exactly the same as the one used by a small station in the Midwest (they'd designed it for practically no money), it pays to remember just how far an abundance of style can get you. It is one of the mysteries of this age that Fiorucci, which can't remain the same for one minute, is always being recognized for its "image" by the media, whereas companies that lavish trillions of dollars on marketing research and psychological folderol all look alike. If you pay the right kind of attention to the right details, things like publicity seem to take care of themselves.

Nobody at Fiorucci pays more attention to detail than Franco Marabelli, one of the original employees from Fiorucci's early days. Besides supervising all the graphics and inventing how the stores look, Franco does lots of the actual designing himself. Clothing, posters, purses, gift items—at one point or another Franco gets involved.

For the past several years, Franco has lived in New York City and had to speak English from morning till night, practically. He is sent out to circulate everywhere—Los Angeles, Chicago, Hong Kong, Zurich, Paris, Tokyo, Rio. Franco spins around the world like a top and poor Franco is a homebody who really would be quite glad to live in Milan and walk his dog. Only now he lives in New York and his apartment is so small the only kind of dog he can fit inside it is a teeny-weeny Lhasa-looking thing.

"When I am back in Italy," he told me, "I again will have a big dog. A dog I can put my arms around like this..." (his arms encircling an imaginary future dream dog the size of two Santa Clauses).

"What kind of dog is that?" I asked.

"A Great Danish," he said. "My favorite dog. You know this breed, Great Danish?"

When Franco zeroes in on an interesting detail, one that completely strikes his fancy and that you'll see in two months as, say, a belt buckle, the evidence of a sighting is announced by Franco's involuntary *chè bella*. Following Franco around during one of his rare earthbound periods is to be misled into thinking that the entire spectrum of the Italian language begins and ends with *chè bella*. *Chè bella*s ebb and flow, constant signs that Franco is picking up on details.

Fiorucci doesn't forget any of the little things, including children. Fioruccino (little Fiorucci) is a Fiorucci sentimental nicety. In the natural order of things, there is the time between birth and perhaps twelve years of age called childhood. It is the time before a person is big enough to fit into a size-6 pair of jeans and certainly before feet have made it to the satin-mule stage. It was for this time that Fioruccino, the children's version of Fiorucci, was born.

Fioruccino is winsome right down to the poster of a small child dressed in Chinese peasant blue, knee-deep in a vegetable patch, head buried deep inside an unfurling head of cabbage, peering fruitlessly for the exact place babies come from. In Milan, where they love babies—even babies born from cabbages—the Fiorucci store has an enormous Fioruccino department. Elegant Italian matrons outfit their bambinos here for any occasion. "*Ecco*. I really think Fiorucci is practically the only one who should be allowed to design children's clothes," one pleased mother told me. "Everything else is so boring."

All the other Fiorucci stores also have special small areas for Fioruccino. Fioruccino has its own shopping bags, clear plastic ones with a giant red robot or a goose looking at itself in a mirror. A Fioruccino poster will feature robots marching around on it performing homey, unindustrial tasks like sweeping floors and watering plants.

A robot dog in the far corner of the poster is observing their spacey domesticity. Fioruccino clothing is somewhat miniaturized grown-up Fiorucci, the milder sort. It's vivid little T-shirts and sweatshirts, practical little overalls in sassy colors, socks with silly trim. With Fioruccino clothes, again the detail is the thing.

THE STORES

You can tell you've arrived at Fiorucci before you walk in. The windows are spectacular. You absolutely have to stop and stare. Something is different here; something is going on. They're peculiar, not like other windows. In the 1960s what went on in Fiorucci was called a happening; that word isn't au courant anymore, and we don't seem to have come up with another. But it is still going on at Fiorucci, only more so. And weirder.

On Valentine's Day in 1979, the New York store put a live pinup girl by the name of Niki in the window. She was lounging around in a Hollywood-bonbon boudoir, powdering her nose, and waiting for her Valentine.

In the Beverly Hills Fiorucci on Valentine's Day in 1980, the window featured a new album by the Specials, that month's hot new-wave ska band. The album was propped up casually amid what looked like a burned-out Valentine store, a place where the paper hearts had survived a grenade attack, but just barely. Fiorucci had connected with another mass-culture fact, and was tuned in to the latest craze. Ska music was here to stay, for a month at least, and Fiorucci center-staged it. And of course Fiorucci loves Valentine's Day; it is one of their favorite holidays.

But any day can be a holiday if you're in the right mood. A summer day, for instance. A couple of years ago the New York store created a 1950s window. It was an all-American-looking sort of patio setting—complete with Astroturf, plastic webbed chaise longues, a lawn mower, a bicycle leaning against a brick wall, a barbecue grill, and beach balls. The Fiorucci people think all that American backyard stuff is funny.

And it is funny, especially in the window of a store selling sequins and glitz and crazy plastics. The connection is made; the culture is observed.

Fiorucci also celebrates bigger holidays, like Christmas. Several years ago the Milan store did a very elegant Christmas Eve window. Two mannequins sat in the window surrounded by the clutter of a very classy party: an open champagne bottle, beautifully wrapped gifts, a huge real Christmas tree. Both the man and the woman were in evening dress, except he was wearing a plastic rain slicker over his dinner jacket, and she was wearing pointy rhinestone-trimmed sunglasses. And there was a reindeer standing in the room with them. You can't pass that kind of window by without doing at least a double take. It arrests; it cries out "pay attention to me"; and who knows what it means? Probably somebody at Fiorucci thought it would be funny.

Sometimes everyday objects are funny. Franco Marabelli found a Japanese artist in London who was creating fancy displays made out of tin cans. So Fiorucci did a whole production number in the London store with them—they constructed display units for the clothes out of cans and used them to spell out FIORUCCI on the wall. It was an amusing culture fact—cans are utilitarian and beautiful too. Just like taillights from bicycles, out of which they designed a very shiny window display.

Perhaps the most outrageous Fiorucci window in anyone's memory was the 1979 beefcake window in the New York store. Fiorucci decided to have a laugh, and cause some stir, so they invited three contestants from the man of the year contest being run by *Blue Boy* magazine to lounge around the window. Without exception, every passerby stopped dead in his or her tracks to stare at live male pinups doing their stuff.

Sometimes the Fiorucci windows are more orthodox, but they're still not like anybody else's. Clothes are displayed pressed between giant sheets of Plexiglas; somehow that makes the clothes look like art, or at least like cultural artifacts. Other clothes are displayed hanging on metal poles or plumbing pipes; they look like crazy, happy scarecrows with their heads mysteriously gone. Shoes are displayed down front so you can see them well. And shoes don't just sit there in Fiorucci windows; they walk along, or they dance.

And the windows are always color coded. Not in the monochromatic, subdued, "matched" way of other store windows, but in the nutty Fiorucci way. One week everything in the window will be lime-green—bright lime-green—and that may include ten pairs of the same lime-green running shorts shown with a matching lime-green briefcase, all of it lighted with lime-green neon. Or it might include a mannequin dressed in a silver lamé evening dress tying the laces on her silver lamé skates. Anything goes; the funnier the better.

The Fiorucci windows in New York are designed by one of the true Fiorucci people, Mark Sawyer. Mark is half-Syrian and half-Italian, twenty-three years old, and has the biggest nose in New York. It is a really big nose, and it looks just great on him. He explains his history before Fiorucci: "I came to New York from Syracuse. Well, I didn't really come to New York, I left Syracuse."

Mark started at Fiorucci after serving an apprenticeship doing PR work at Studio 54. One day he walked into Fiorucci, and they looked at him and offered him a job. He *is* Fiorucci. On the day we met, he was wearing toreador pants from the 1950s, ladies' high-heel shoes, and a gigantic shocking pink–and-yellow pullover sweater with the numerals 1980 emblazoned on it in bright colors. The sweater was designed by Betsey Johnson, who runs a concession boutique in the New York store. Betsey had asked Mark to wear the sweater to test people's reaction to it. I reacted. Mark noticed me react, and reassured me: "I don't usually wear stuff like this. Usually I wear very off-the-shoulder stuff, as if I'd just been dragged into an alley. You know, very Sheena stuff."

For all his outrageousness, he is sweet and kind and wants to please. And he does the windows. Mark recognizes the importance of the windows to the Fiorucci image, and so he tries very hard to come up with window concepts that will shock. One of his more outlandish ideas was to dress a window to look like the inside of a luxurious private jet—which had just crashed. The guys upstairs nixed that idea—too morbid they thought; the amended version was still effective. The posh jet cabin was littered with an empty glass, a full ashtray, an open magazine—but there were no mannequins. The cabin was mysteriously, unaccountably empty. It made you think. Maybe just because you never see a plane cabin empty. Maybe just because you wonder where those folks went. Maybe because Mark managed to communicate his original idea without actual evidence of it.

He is a master. His windows create a situation, a little vignette that never has a beginning or an ending, but is clearly very dramatic. Something is always about to happen, or has just happened. The Fiorucci windows are very much of the new school of window display. Stores in New York and Los Angeles and Boston are veritable surrealist still lifes—strange dramas being enacted by mannequins with blank stares. It is the latest gimmick in display merchandising. And of course you saw it first at Fiorucci.

Once you get inside a Fiorucci store, you feel just wonderful. A whole new world opens up to you. Before I saw Fiorucci, I thought there were only two kinds of department stores (well, two and a half counting Bloomingdale's). Department stores were either stately Saks Fifth Avenue style, with beige wall-to-wall carpets and the hushed-but-cultured voices of Forest Lawn or they were type two, the Sears/Penney's type where you just go in knowing what you want and find it and that's that—the sensible type. But suddenly, two minutes after stepping into a Fiorucci, it dawned on me that Saks—with its atmosphere of leisured, muffled plush—was invented to make you feel old, or at least experienced. In Saks you're supposed to feel as if you've been around the block a couple of times and you know the good stuff from the bad, and of course you haven't got time for the bad. And at Sears you are supposed to feel typical, reliable, efficient; the tire department is always only steps away from the sweaters.

But in Fiorucci, oh, in Fiorucci you feel the world is your oyster. You're young again, and full of energy and life and that driving rock beat. Anything and everything is possible. Just sashay down those wide and gleaming hardwood aisles, boogie a little to the beat, stop and chat with a salesperson, or another customer (true, they're often hard to tell apart), and finger the goods. No one will bother you; no clerk in Fiorucci ever hovers. Rather, they smile and wink. We're all in this crazy world together, and isn't life fun?

Even the light in Fiorucci stores is perfect. They don't use fluorescent lighting, because they think it is ugly and they think it is unhealthful, and they are sure it makes the clothes look bad. So everyone in Fiorucci looks natural, as natural as you can look with magenta hair and poison-green jumpsuits and lots and lots of makeup. Everything is geared up to look like a circus, a happy zany three-ring show that you can wander around in to your heart's content. No one expects you to buy anything, unless you really feel you want to.

The customers browse, the clerks browse (to look casual), and even the furniture moves around because someone might change his mind about the best way to display zebra-printed portfolios. So all the fixtures in the stores, including display and light fixtures, shelves, racks and tables, are movable. Even the dressing rooms. Anything can be recycled into another use.

Franco Marabelli says that everything has to move and be changeable: "It helps the dresses sell." Bigger stores have learned this lesson well; department stores are all currently redesigning themselves into movable boutiques, small departments with a theme that make the customers feel less inhibited, more intimately connected to the merchandise.

All the Fiorucci units are custom designed by Fiorucci's team of in-house (Milan) architects: Anita Bianchetti, Evelyne Zurel, and Stefania Sartori. The architects work full-time drawing renovation plans for recycling old buildings and redesigning display units and store interiors. Blueprints of everything ever created for Fiorucci are always beautifully rendered; they are more Fiorucci art, although they adorn only the offices of the architecture staff and are never seen by the public. But then everyone in Milan with the least bit of poetry in their souls has a degree in architecture—it's the city's favorite art form.

This detail, this custom design work, costs plenty, but it is what makes each Fiorucci store look so distinctive and function so well. It is in the end this obsession with detail, with having every little thing done to exact specifications, that makes Fiorucci what it is.

The first Fiorucci store opened in Milan in 1967; it is still in its original quarters. It began as one room, but as business boomed it spread first upward into a mezzanine and then down to the basement floor. Because the shop grew in a sort of catch-as-catch-can manner, it seems lopsided. You never quite feel that you're on the main floor. Instead, it is a series of levels—a look that is now being imitated in American shops that deliberately build platforms and mezzanines to create smaller spaces for more personalized shopping. The street floor of the store is high-ceilinged and narrow—you never feel comfortable there, exactly—it seems to be mostly a checkout desk and a concourse leading you up or down. The basement is where the action is. It is wide and low and sprawling, and has a few little levels of its own. One tiny room is attached to it by a couple of steps down, and suddenly you're in a space under a stairwell. There I found two young guys, about twenty years old, practicing the ancient Italian art of mural painting. Just like Leonardo doing the *Last Supper* just down the street nearly five hundred years before, these two were painting a wall decoration. This one updated. They were painting a South Seas island tableau, with a girl diving straight into the blue ocean, her hair flying behind her, and bikini tan lines the only evidence of Western civilization on her sleek body. A beach ball bobs on the surface of their blue water. It's a lovely scene.

"This is where we sell bikinis," one of the salesmen told me. He was wearing an I LOVE MARCEL DUCHAMP T-shirt, and was grinning from ear to ear. He tried to tell me what was so wonderful about Fiorucci: "We are getting this wall ready so that just before everyone goes on their winter vacation to the sun, they can come here and buy bikinis. You see, no place else in Italy can you buy bathing suits in December. Only in summer. But in Italy everybody goes away around the first of January, so we sell them. Lots of them." More Fiorucci iconoclasm, more defying of the rules. More sales.

The music tapes played in this Fiorucci are the same as those played in all Fiorucci stores. If you happen to walk into the Milan store in the middle of a winter blizzard, you'll hear the same raging punk rock and roll you'd hear back home in the Beverly Hills Fiorucci where it is hot and smoggy. And the merchandise is the same, or almost the same. In Milan the things are more conservative, more sedate, more subdued—if these words can ever be applied to Fiorucci. In New York, anything goes, the flashier the better; in Milan a little restraint is still required. But there is recompense: the prices are lower in Milan. Import duties and the cost of shipping merchandise account for this difference, but it is difficult to stop myself from buying one of everything. It's like the old days—everything so cheap. Right here on the Galleria Passarella. The salespeople in the Milan store usually stick to plaid—loud plaid—pants, turtlenecks, and cowboy boots. One young woman had a poodle haircut like Elizabeth Taylor in the 1950s and she wore one of those little silk neckerchiefs knotted around her neck. She looked like a lot of the girls in my high school. A young man in the jeans department has a *Blackboard Jungle* ducktail, slicked back with greasy kid stuff. The two girls working in the basement were flamboyantly glamorous with blond wavy hair. One wore a kelly green sweater, plaid jeans, pink plastic galoshes, and chunky pink plastic jewelry—matching bracelet and earrings. The other had a slinky zebra-print black-and-white jersey outfit, a jumpsuit that zipped up to her chin. She wore it with high black boots, and, happily, no whip. After all, even if she does work at Fiorucci, this is Fiorucci Milan.

And alas, the Galleria Passarella store is now the only Fiorucci Milan. There used to be another one. In 1975, when Fiorucci and Montedison went into partnership, Franco Marabelli was allowed to design a second Fiorucci store in Milan. And it was his masterpiece. The Via Torino store was a reflection of the luxury of freedom given an architect to design without necessity, with the freedom to make a space do what he wants it to do.

Photographs of it show a glass roof like the roofs of the gallerias all over Milan; the ceilings were three stories high, and plants were hung in the open space to create a sort of Crystal Palace feeling. The store had a wonderful espresso bar, and once housed the Fiorucci restaurant, which of course had its own special tableware and served hamburgers Milanese. The restaurant and coffee bar became a meeting spot, a place for listening to music and talking, and if you got tired of the talk, you could browse around the occasional art exhibitions held there—in among the clothes. For this was, after all, a store. A store that had a full stereo setup, complete with a disc jockey, because the store did a lot of record selling; it even wholesaled records to other outlets in Italy.

At Fiorucci, one thing nobody seems to mind admitting is that something didn't work, didn't make money, and was abandoned. Apparently that's what happened to the Via Torino store. Various explanations, none of them full or complete, were offered. The store was a little off the beaten track, too far for an easy walk from the center of town where all the best stores are. The Via Torino neighborhood had declined slightly, and it had become more Sears, less Fiorucci. They had shoplifter trouble. And maybe two Fioruccis in one town, even if that town was Milan, were too much. It was a wonderful store, and served them well for a time, and they all miss it. But the future beckons. And Beverly Hills is just a plane ride away.

The building in which Fiorucci of Beverly Hills is installed is an old redecorated movie theater, a luxurious first-run place that was plenty ornate before Fiorucci moved in. In came Franco and his team, and now it's *really* gaudy. They repainted the original murals; they felt they needed brightening up. So now the oasis scenes, the elephants, camels, and palm trees have been painted in every possible rainbow combination—finally, Fiorucci has really outdone and overdone itself. It is as if these ornaments weren't spectacular enough—so Fiorucci added a rainbow of colors. Neon lights blink to add a little more color, and the music pounds. And then there is the counter where makeup items are sold for Fiorucci faces: demonic shades of lipstick too dark for anyone except a person up to no good. Alabaster-white powder for a mime's face. Glittering pink powder for a daring shoulder or a beckoning cleavage. Rouges and eye shadows that promise too much.

It is almost as if it is all too much. To decorate an old movie theater with a mock-Turkish dome, to try to turn Hollywood into Hollywood. To put zebra-skin prints and sequins and rhinestones into an already overdecorated fantasy world. And right in Beverly Hills! Just off

Rodeo Drive, which everybody but everybody now knows about, and comes to gawk at even if they can't afford its silly, ridiculous high prices. It was here, in my own territory, that I found myself asking the same question about Fiorucci—and still not having an answer.

How do they make it work? In Milan, which is so full of dreary seriousness. In Rio, where they've understood bright colors mismatched and *carnaval* craziness for hundreds of years. In Tokyo, where they have so much money they don't know where to spend it first and anything from the West is immediately chic, even Louis Vuitton plastic. In London, where the New Youth world began, and where Carnaby Street has been defunct for a decade. And in New York, with its roller-coaster-paced cynicism and its provincial seriousness.

The opening of the store in Beverly Hills was a madhouse. The fire department marched in and closed the opening before it opened; some little regulations hadn't been observed properly, and the crowd of thousands outside trying to get in spelled trouble. So the opening was put off a night, by which time the press had cranked itself up about this new outrage being perpetrated on unsuspecting consumers, and so the crowds were even bigger for the second night of the opening. And the store is still open, two years later. Maybe they really could sell the Brooklyn Bridge—in puce.

Nothing could ever be as Hollywood as Hollywood already is. And it is in the Beverly Hills shop, rather than in New York or Milan, that you realize just how heavy Fiorucci's dependence is on Hollywood. How indistinguishable a pair of Fiorucci rhinestone-studded sunglasses or a pair of tight toreador pants is from their Hollywood originals. Hollywood shoppers, especially the ones willing to wear clothes before everyone else is wearing them, have a difficult time at Fiorucci. They've seen it all before, at supermarkets in the Valley, at joints on the Strip, and yet this is Fiorucci, and they've heard what a hit it is in New York, so something must be going on.

I talked to Carolyn Zecca, a Fiorucci girl from way back in 1970 when she lived in Milan. Carolyn now does public-relations work freelance for Fiorucci in Beverly Hills, and I asked her about this problem of bringing coals to Newcastle. I asked her to tell me what Fiorucci really is, what its image means. Carolyn, who speaks with a clean, direct, childlike sanity, suddenly turned Fiorucci fuchsia: "What is the 'image' of Fiorucci? Why is everybody always asking that? I hate that word 'image.' It's got to go. Next time I talk to Elio Fiorucci I'm going to tell him we can't use that word about Fiorucci anymore. It doesn't mean anything. Fiorucci is Fiorucci. That's it. There is the store. There are the people. There are the clothes. That is Fiorucci."

Probably everybody's favorite Fiorucci is the one in New York on Fifty-Ninth Street between Lexington and Park. Just half a block away from Bloomingdale's. Everyone in the neighborhood calls this God's Country. The store, which opened in 1975, is the showplace Fiorucci. It and the Milan store are the only stores actually owned and run by Fiorucci people; the others all over the world are franchises.

The store is beautiful. It is everything a Fiorucci store should be. It's a circus, a show, a bazaar, a meeting place for strangers, a rendez-vous spot for friends. It's a chance to look around and see what's going on with the nutty Italians, and have a cup of coffee, and listen to the cheerful music, and get the feeling, if only for a little while, that this is the way you lead your life.

There is even a downstairs—a wide, spacious place with low ceilings and louder music. They put the staple stuff down here, the jeans, the men's shirts and sweaters, the shoes, the Fioruccino for tiny tots. One day while I was visiting, Diana Ross sailed in—with two kids in tow. They bought T-shirts and she was halfway through buying a pair of silver lamé boots before anyone recognized her. But someone did, and the word passed among the salespeople. One of them sped upstairs to the tape deck and put on "Stop! In the Name of Love." Suddenly Diana Ross was there buying a pair of shoes and she was also there acoustically—so loud that she became a part of the atmosphere. We all looked up, the sound was palpable; her presence was felt. The whole place lit up in one broad smile of recognition. And then Diana smiled, and the whole *world* lit up. For Diana Ross is exactly the kind of person to inspire Fiorucci people—employees and customers alike. With her boas, her sequins, her glamour, and her eyelashes, she has always been a star; she never lets her audience down by appearing ordinary, not even her audience while she does an afternoon's casual shopping.

She was approached and greeted and thanked for stopping in by one of the salesmen, Joey Arias, who also answers to the name of Joey Fiorucci. He is called that so often that he has given up making the distinction. Joey is true Fiorucci. He is twenty-five, an L.A. boy, father a Mexican and mother a German. He was raised in downtown L.A. where he went to Cathedral High, a Catholic school. And where he was not a big hit in hennaed hair, tweezed eyebrows, and Springolators. He went to college at L.A. City, "in the arts," but dropped out after three years because he was wasting his time, he says. He came to New York in 1976, "to celebrate the bicentennial." And New York has never been the same.

Joey is a real original. He wears his hair punk style, slicked back and it is pink, or purple, or teal blue, depending on his mood or on the mood of the chic salon that does his hair free, for the publicity. (Everybody asks him where he has it done, and he is glad to give out the name and address.) His looks are outrageous. He appeared on *Saturday Night Live* as a backup singer for David Bowie. They all wore dresses. When I asked Joey if his mother had seen him on television and what did she think, he laughed out loud: "She loved me. She asked me to send her the dress I wore on the show."

When Joey isn't working at Fiorucci, where he sells, and supervises the other salespeople, and meets the celebrities, and gives interviews, he designs clothes and performs in avant-garde rock gigs with his friend Klaus Nomi, another way-out number. In its book concession in the New York store, Fiorucci sells black-and-white "art postcard" photos of Klaus and Joey, for $5 each. They are stars.

Practically every Fiorucci employee I talked to told me they were deliriously happy to be working in Fiorucci now, but what they really want someday is to be stars. Singers, actors, celebrity stars. Andy Warhol (who once said that everybody will be famous for fifteen minutes) is such a regular in the store that he is considered "a special friend." Anyone who comes in more than once is already a "regular friend."

I felt I was onto something, this star thing, and so I went upstairs to the administrative offices to rest my feet and talk to some of the behind-the-scenes types. Did they all want to be stars too?

Celeste Reyes is a twenty-year-old Puerto Rican girl with a face so open and so trusting that you worry for her. She works as an assistant in the public-relations department upstairs, and loves her job. But what she really wants is to be a singing star. She came to Fiorucci in a fairly typical way. As a teenager, she was hanging out at Reno Sweeney, a rock place that features new groups. One of her friends there told her that anyone who dressed the way that she dresses ought to work at Fiorucci. She had never heard of the place, but went to have a look. She was hired immediately. I asked her what it was like to work at Fiorucci and she answered, with a grin, "Oh, my life has changed completely. For instance, I would never have been allowed to get into the best discos if I hadn't worked here. I love it here. The best part of my job is the excitement of the Fiorucci phenomenon."

Which is really some phenomenon. The clothes are crazy, the employees are from outer space, and the customers are no different. Or wish they were no different. Everyone is there to get a little piece of the action. Lots of the customers look like ordinary people, looking for a thrill, taking a spin through the store. Or ladies and gentlemen wanting to learn, to figure out what, if anything, they can buy to make their lives just a little bit glitzier, lots snappier, funnier. Always funnier. Or they come to look at the employees who are watching the customers look at the employees. Circling, smiling, sharing an unspoken communication about isn't-this-all-too-silly. And it is. What Fiorucci is selling is junky chic. And the whole world is buying it.

BEHIND THE SCENES

Across from the Milan Fiorucci store is a perfectly ordinary-looking office building. Inside this building, on the second floor in a space not much larger than four motel rooms, is a jumble of Fiorucci offices.

Squeezed into this unpalatial territory are four departments: promotion, architectural design, graphics, and DXing.

Nestled in a sunlit corner is the graphics department. The space is small and so is the department, only five people. They are in their early twenties and, of course, have rippling Italian names: Augusto Vignali, Guglielmo Pellizzoni, Adriano Chieregato, Sauro Mainardi, Carlo Pignagnoli. Buried in mountains of Prestype and useful ephemera these five churn out the unending stream of graphics that have become Fiorucci hallmarks. Shopping bags, posters, stickers, clothing labels, price tags, decals for windows, stationery, and fabric designs all spin into existence as "The Harder They Come" blares full blast in the background. The whole place is a good-natured visual assault. Suspended overhead on a thin wire, a brilliant lipstick-red high-heeled shoe spins, its lining bright white and scalloped like a pastry doily. Shelves are littered with French children's books, fishing magazines, seed catalogs, and soup labels. A photograph of a sumo wrestler is tacked to a bulletin board along with a postcard of the flamboyant drag performer Divine and advertisements for armpit-hair remover and marital aids.

It is almost a relief to spot next the office of Leonardo Pastore. He is the public-relations man who receives buyers from around the world and it is probably because of this that his office is the only one on the floor that is not absolutely awash with graphic flotsam and jetsam. His department spills over, however, with the madness known as DXing.

In CB radio jargon DXing (pronounced *dixing*) means communicating across long distances and in Fiorucci, which really is a place with its own language and way of thinking, this seemed a witty thing to call the office in charge of handling research. Of course, it would be easy to complain that no matter what you call it, it's still public relations but once inside the actual office it seems beside the point.

Fiorucci information is gathered together, organized, and DXed to the media by Giannino Malossi, Margherita Rosenberg Colorini, and Karla Otto. Operating in an atmosphere of genial chaos, they present the Fiorucci image to the press and the public.

Phones are ringing wildly, conversations are exploding in a flurry of languages, hands are flapping madly like fish fins. Even when Italians talk on the phone, even when they know the person they are talking to can't possibly see them, they are still explaining what they mean with their hands. The DXing staff does not sit still, not for one minute.

Their slapdash quarters are piled with periodicals. The latest copies of what seems like every magazine published on earth are carefully scrutinized. *Slash, Interview, Elle, Lui, Marie Claire,* Japanese art magazines, *Playboy, Rolling Stone, Stern, Wet, Music Echo,* rock newspapers from everywhere. They pore over these magazines and papers, for this is the stuff that tells someone in Milan just what is really going on around the world. And this is of the utmost importance in a country in which you must actually make an appointment to make a long-distance phone call. Anything in print that could pertain the least little bit to Fiorucci, could offer even the smallest hint of something new or different, seems to end up somehow in the DXing office.

The Fiorucci version of a reference library extends along the wall. Here are books on pinup art and old postcards, car repair manuals, brochures about trucking, an elegant volume on erotic art, art books on Vargas, Picasso, O'Keeffe.

The three people who spend the most time in the DXing office contrast neatly with one another: Margherita Colorni radiates ultra-ladylike charm and pleasant directness. You would tell, you would want to tell, this woman your most intimate problems. She has the look of someone who would understand anything. She wears the most subdued sort of Fiorucci with elegance and panache. It was Margherita who came up with the idea of setting up a flea market of antique clothes in the Via Torino store around 1975. It was very Portobello Road and so successful an idea that it lasted for what passes for eternity at Fiorucci. One year.

Karla Otto is a twenty-five-year-old Dresden shepherdess in bright Fiorucci clothing. She is beautiful, all tomato-red lips, azure eyes, and whippet-colored hair. She is also smart, able to slip effortlessly in and out of German, French, English, Italian, and Japanese. At eighteen she headed for Japan because, she says, she was overcome with fascination at the whole idea of Japan and the language—the little tables, the flowers, the kimonos, everything. Once she left Germany and arrived in Japan, someone suggested that rather than teach German to earn money, she ought to become a model. Anyone with eyes could have seen that with Karla's body, all lank and slouching, and a face of such sweetness and style, Karla was never for an instant meant to spend so much as a minute doing something as boring as teaching someone how to speak German.

Giannino Malossi is the mastermind behind the DXing office. A serious, intense bearded young man who wears his lighthearted black Fiorucci sweater trimmed with wistful strips of flamingo pink fiercely. Giannino is a radical intellectual who studied the humanities in college and who is mad for the Slits. He firmly believes that fashion and politics meet at every turn. He is an obsessive fan of American music, English rock and roll, and What's Happening Right This Minute. It is Giannino who decides what tapes will be played in all the Fiorucci stores.

One of Giannino's pet projects is the Fiorucci *Fanzine*. Fanzines are those weird little publications that might be issued by some fanatical science-fiction zealot, mimeographed, stapled by hand, and mailed to other science-fiction zealots. Sometimes fanzines aren't about science fiction, they are about rock in San Bernadino, or about Kristy McNichol.

For Fiorucci, the Fiorucci *Fanzine* is "a moment of communication and information." To people outside Fiorucci, the *Fanzine* is a cross between a broadside, a poster, and a road map. It is a periodical of flexible content, published pretty much according to whim. There is no ironclad publication schedule. *Fanzine* appears when the spirit moves the DXing office to conjure one up, though in general you can count on one to appear whenever a new Fiorucci store opens. When the Beverly Hills Fiorucci opened in 1978, *Fanzine No. 1 Speciale Los Angeles* was given away free in Fiorucci stores worldwide. On the cover, overdeveloped young men were shown clutching surfboards as they trotted across the sands of sunny California. Inside, a newspaper-style guide to "Electroluminescent Los Angeles" dipped lightly into the pleasures of Venice, Disneyland, Watts Towers, freeways, Hollywood, the Valley, and flashy street art.

From his tiny overcrowded desk in the DXing office in Milan, Giannino Malossi, a twenty-eight-year-old information junkie and music fanatic, manages to know practically everything.

"New wave is passé," he told me in passing, one afternoon as he was plotting Fiorucci's musical path through the next season.

"Well, if new wave is passé," I asked, "what hope do we have?"

"Outer space and ska," he said, without a moment's hesitation.

When Giannino and the DXing staff are not predicting the future, they catalog the past. For twenty days and twenty nights they slaved to put together an exhibit for the 1979 Triennale.

It has long been a tradition in Milan once every three years to put on an enormous art and design show called the Triennale. In 1968 a protest closed it and Milan stopped hosting the show; the whole thing ceased to exist for eleven years. Eventually the authorities declared that if Milan didn't hold the exhibition before 1980, the honor would be given to some other Italian city. Milan rose to the challenge in the nick of time.

The people who run the Triennale decided to allow fashion design to be represented, and Fiorucci was allowed to be included in the show. Until this born-again Triennale, fashion design had not been thought serious enough to be on display with things like furniture, bathroom fixtures, espresso machines, bicycles, and dentist tools. To be invited to show fashions there was considered by Elio Fiorucci to be a terrific breakthrough.

The Fiorucci exhibit took place in a kind of miniature Hollywood Bowl. Standing in front, the audience viewed the exhibit on three screens, side by side like a triptych. Three slide projectors simultaneously clicked three different sets of images on three screens, tracing the history of fashion since 1945. Rita Hayworth, Queen Elizabeth, Dior, and photos from *Vogue* collided with stills of Frank Sinatra surrounded by screaming girls as the tape in the background played Sinatra singing "Monterrey." For twenty minutes the slides clicked brazenly through the years. James Dean, Frankie Avalon, Elvis, Jackson Pollock, Twiggy, Avedon, space suits, Miró, Jean Shrimpton, Calder, Liz Taylor, Kennedy, pedal pushers, Timothy Leary, Veruschka. The music hopped from Bill Haley to Marilyn Monroe singing "My Heart Belongs to Daddy" to "Da Doo Ron Ron" to the Beatles until the entire thing collided in one big *splat*, exploding in mangled color with tangled noise. Suddenly someone is singing "My Way," Frank Sinatra's most sacred hymn, only it wasn't Frankie, it was Sid Vicious of the Sex Pistols and *his* way of singing "My Way" made it sound maniacal. And the clothing was equally blasphemous, a sweatshirt showing two different colored wristbands, girls with peculiar sunglasses wearing twisted mockeries of all that has ever been glamorous or beautiful, girls who were obviously going Fiorucci's way.

That night, after the Triennale exhibition wound up, an entourage of various colorful people came along from the main event for dinner at La Torre di Pisa, Elio Fiorucci's favorite restaurant.

Like many busy Milan businessmen, Fiorucci takes almost all of his meals in a restaurant. And, because like all of us he likes what he is used to, Elio Fiorucci seems to only think of La Torre di Pisa when he says, "Let's go eat."

La Torre di Pisa is a kind of bohemian-looking trattoria tucked into an alley. A place you must know about in order to find it. The sort of place that always has a little white sign on the front door indicating they are full. But La Torre di Pisa is always ready, no matter how crowded, to seat Elio Fiorucci and however many people he shows up with.

It was here I sat at a longish table, in a room decorated with framed strips of antique wallpapers, talking to an Italian woman journalist who writes for *Vogue* and her friend, a designer of Olivetti typewriters. The conversation we were having was slightly, well, slightly more serious than those I had previously had with Fiorucci designers who tend to be very young and therefore so enchanted merely being in the kind of dazzling fashion world of Fiorucci that nothing on earth but Fiorucci seems to matter. So the conversation drifted toward the protests that had forced the closing of the Triennale in 1968. I couldn't believe terrorists stopped a thing like a design show.

So far I had been unable to bring up the idea of terrorists. It seemed to take just too much political nerve to mention them amidst the perfections of La Torre di Pisa's fresh tomato-and-basil appetizers. But terrorism had been on my mind. That week five professors and five students from a Fiat management school had been lined up and neatly shot in the kneecaps. This terrible event had been bleeding all over the headlines. The people of Milan were dumb with sadness and pain, making it almost impossible for them to smile when they shook my hand, though, for an Italian not to smile somehow when they meet you would, of course, indicate the end of the world.

Most of the people I had met in Milan were connected with Fiorucci and several things prevented me from talking with them about the terrorists. For one thing, the young people who are lucky enough to work at Fiorucci consider the capitalist system not so bad, especially since it is the capitalist system that has gotten them this job where they are involved with such a glittery public and designs that have received worldwide acclaim. And when the job at Fiorucci means you have connections with the rest of the world—London, New York, Tokyo—and all the glamour of those places is somehow yours.

It was much easier for me to learn about the Autonomy and the Red Brigades from the people sitting next to me at dinner because they were not actually working for Fiorucci, not so bound up in glamorous Fiorucci ambitions.

"It isn't so much that I'm against the terrorists," the designer said, "but rather the violence. It is the institutions that they object to. But the institutions have treated the workers violently themselves. It is a terrible paradox. A complex situation. One must be very careful not to make judgment. I think it all started with the Autonomy...but then...."

The Autonomy, it seems, was a time in Italian politics a few years ago when it was suddenly decided by terrorists and students that it would be a much better idea if there were really no government, no police, and no laws. Instead, the people themselves would decide how much they could afford to pay for a movie, and then just pay it. This Autonomy, which was particularly strong in Milan, was supposedly kept in check by a group called the Red Brigades, who would see to it that nobody went overboard and simply "liberated" TVs from stores.

During this period Fiorucci graphics and various Fiorucci projects reflected some of the more peaceful aspects of the Autonomy's solutions to problems. It was a time when people talked about growing their own food, using solar energy, and living in communes. Even though Fiorucci is obviously a capitalist organization, it had somehow managed to reflect some of the philosophies of the Autonomy.

Though I am not really a deep student of the political situation in Milan, I can nevertheless draw some conclusions about all this. It seems to me that Fiorucci managed to be on the side of the Autonomy while maintaining a perfectly respectable capitalist business, merchandising the profitable output of workers—and yet being on the side of the young and their dreams. Of course, Fiorucci is full of paradoxes, but this particular one is a gaily waving flag.

The journalist and the designer sipped their wine in silence, and by this time, since they'd explained as best they could what the Autonomy was, I too felt that the problems of Italy would never be solved.

"But," I said, remembering when I lived in Rome over ten years before and everything, or so it seemed to me, was perfect. "It seems so un-Italian for these terrorists not to want to have fun."

"What do you mean?" the designer asked.

"I mean, revolution and kneecaps are so serious."

"I think the terrorists do want to have fun," the designer said. "Terrorism is an act of pure form. Terrorists just don't know exactly what they are doing. Just as we don't know what we are doing."

Of course, it's occurred to many people in all countries, capitalist and otherwise, that no one quite knows what they're doing, but it now dawned on me that to say that terrorists don't know what they're doing too isn't altogether true.

Everyone went back to sipping their wine again.

The sounds of La Torre di Pisa picked up. A three-piece band made up of a bassoon, a sax, and a clarinet, suddenly swooshed into the restaurant playing a ridiculous *oom-pah-pah* version of *La Traviata*.

A blond model who'd been eating dinner across the room and had now finished was coming toward our table to talk to Elio and some of the designers. She leaned forward to smile, in spite of kneecaps and sadness, and to be kissed hello. The girl had removed her jacket and lifted her shirt, showing her incredible new rust-colored satin Fiorucci jeans which, when she turned around in a movement of splendor and elegance, revealed a derriere of such primal glory and shininess that she nearly brought La Torre di Pisa's roof down, and the music *oom-pah-pahed* euphorically into heaven.

She held the pose, continuing to stand there, an incredible display. "Enough of terrorism," the designer said, "now for satin asses."

From movies like *Red Desert* one remembers the wildly sprawling suburbs of Milan covered with refineries, wheezing machinery, and smokestacks. And Corsico, where Fiorucci's main office is located, fifteen minutes from downtown Milan, is just such a suburb.

Standing in front of a large, white, medical-complex type building, all conservative and serious, for the first time Fiorucci looks like Business. You can understand how a corporation like Montedison would come to buy half of what would seem to be a frivolous fluke. For here, if nowhere else in one's encounters with the world of Fiorucci, they aren't kidding.

Getting off the elevator on the top floor, thoughts of Montedison quickly disappear. The moment you step out of the elevator, things get silly again. The walls are nicely trimmed with bright yellow stripes, and little flying rectangular neon sticks swirl across the reception-area wall. The charm is back. It settles over your shoulders like a pink angora cardigan. Franco Marabelli stares at the wall for a second, tilts his head and reaches over to adjust one of the neon sticks just so.

The people who work here in Corsico are much less fast-lane than the ones in downtown Milan or in the stores in general. Here they are relaxed, the music isn't the Sex Pistols, and you can think.

Without exception, everyone in the building is dressed with élan.

Even the most conservatively dressed accountant has a touch of Fiorucci about him somewhere. Perhaps this is simply an example of what it's like to have a job in Italy, but even if one has to work in Corsico out there in a blanket of industrial haze, it doesn't seem so bad.

Corsico is a mass of accountants, quality-control supervisors, designers, stylists, models, inventory-control people, seamstresses, textile experts, and secretaries. More than three hundred people work for Fiorucci in Milan, most of them in Corsico. In Corsico, as in every other part of the enterprise, people who work here try to explain that Elio Fiorucci's genius is his ability to hire the right people. Like innocent children, they seem somehow to expect that being hired by Fiorucci, whether it is to add up long, dull columns of figures or to design sunglasses, is a sign of his expertise.

Nevertheless, innocent children don't succeed in business. Whenever people think that Milan is a deadhead city and that Fiorucci is just a bunch of happy children from sunny Italy, I can't help thinking that if only Fiorucci would put out a postcard showing this office building in Corsico, amid the landscape of factories, people wouldn't insist that Fiorucci isn't really an actual business.

This deadly earnest expanse of suburb has nothing to do with the Fiorucci posters of a blond Venus wrapped in blue plastic, those vinyl behinds on topless girls with spiked high heels, that girl in a metallic purple bathing suit gazing at a swordfish.

Yet as businesslike as Corsico is, a feeling of coziness pervades. There is a sense of intimacy like that in a boutique, a cottage industry stranded in cement. Karla Otto steers me from one department to another. "Here are the eyeglass people, this is the department that keeps track of gift items, things like stationery and unusual soap and clocks. Do you like this bracelet? Meet Elyette. She collects Barbie dolls."

In the accessories department I am shown a plastic orange, about five inches in diameter, with green leaves, that has been sawed in half and turned into a purse. I meet a person named Sara Nannicini who "coordinates styles." And what it seems she does is make sure that the jeans don't become *too* impractical a color, so that they still will be worn by people who were only in the mood for jeans just the tiniest bit too far-out, not whole-hog.

I am surprised when I realize that most of the people I am meeting here are in their late thirties and early forties. They aren't the teenagers with scissors you think they might be.

Rows of enormous tables are covered with patterns, just like Seventh Avenue. Scissors, pins, and rolls of brown paper for making patterns are scattered here and there. And dress dummies. Even the dress dummies in Corsico are jazzed up, not content to be merely dumb gray or tan, but instead determined to be periwinkle or turquoise, side by side, clashing. Eight sewing machines, where a new idea can be quickly run up, put on a model, thought about, adjusted— or changed or abandoned or tried again. Yards of plastic lace lie unfolded across a billiard-size cutting table, waiting to become God knows what. A glass cookie jar sits overflowing with scraps of fabric.

I meet Tito Pastore, head stylist of Fiorucci and brother of Leonardo of the public-relations office in the Galleria Passarella. Tito has been with Fiorucci practically since the beginning. He has slicked-back hair, narrow wraparound sunglasses, a shiny black leather jacket with screaming pink velour lining, the sort of fabric usually reserved for bathrobes, and a face so classic that you've seen him in every painting by every Italian master. Tito understands the world of haute couture perfectly, and he could care less. For at Fiorucci he has "*libertà.*"

Corsico has everything. Even a buttons and trimmings section, where everything is arranged obsessively in rows on white cardboard cards and neatly labeled. Buttons you would enjoy just owning, let alone having on a dress or shirt. Duck buttons, pig buttons, clear plastic ones shaped like little bows, mother-of-pearl ones in the shape of little crescents, heart ones, four-leaf clover ones. Plus collars of every shape and intensity of color lie waiting, spangled and sequined and shining.

Corsico began to seem less an office building than a toy-land for adults. And when the chief accountant wearing the stodgiest clothes leans over and suddenly there is a glimpse of a Fiorucci vest sweater with silly flowers all over it, the impression intensifies. None of the offices has that scared-office-worker feeling. Typists lean against desks and chat easily for a few moments and no one comes out and turns red.

While we toured the design studio, I suddenly noticed one of those plastic mesh bags with two small handles at the top that women all over Europe use when going to the market. Except this one was bright orange. I sighed, broke my promise to myself not to ask for any gifts, and said, meekly, "Oh, could I please have one of those?"

"Do you really like it?" Franco asked incredulously. "We think it is so dull, so boring, not a Fiorucci color, not loud enough. We have almost decided not to manufacture them."

I shrugged and said that I was no marketing expert, and because I'm a size 12 I'm certainly not the perfect Fiorucci girl, but I liked it. Franco thought a moment, wrinkled his brow, and thought another moment. Then he walked over to the phone, called some distant factory, and ordered two thousand of the bags made up for shipment to New York.

I was horrified. Me, making merchandising decisions at Fiorucci! But what if they don't sell? Franco shrugged and said, "They'll sell. If you like them they'll sell." I felt positively woozy. And then amazed at the way these people do business. So casually and with such calm. Well, not calm, but ease—with abandon.

Strolling along the corridors of Corsico, dotted here and there with potted green plastic trees gaily decorated with pink-and-green bows, we arrived at the "inspiration room." To truly appreciate the inspiration room it is important to remember that Fiorucci actually pays people to knock around the world looking at things, returning with new Ecuadorean embroidery, Canadian boots, or whatever the kids in Kyoto are wearing. Thirty-one-year-old Maurizio Brunazzi, who used to shuffle paper in a big company, now spends his days and nights as a fashion buyer and scout for Fiorucci. He was introduced to Elio Fiorucci at dinner one night in Milan by Franco Marabelli. Fiorucci liked him, liked the way he dressed, and offered him a job. At first Maurizio turned him down, because: "I was very tired—I didn't want to start a new job. But finally Franco and Elio convinced me, and I started to work. I cannot imagine leaving Fiorucci. It is home, it is family for me, and I love my work."

He ought to love his work—Maurizio has what looks to me like the best job in the world. He shops for a living.

Everyone who works for Fiorucci shops for Fiorucci even if that is not all they do. Almost everyone at Fiorucci can tell of being kept on the payroll while they just went somewhere, possibly on vacation, and kept their eyes open.

The inspiration room is where what they buy is kept. Here in this room with no windows are straw tourist purses plastered with sombreroed Mexicans asleep against felt cactuses, fatigue jackets, Hawaiian shirts, plastic earrings, dinner jackets from the 1940s. Plastic laundry hampers and wooden baskets overflow with bikinis, ties, scarves, mittens.

Running down the middle of the room is a wooden platform about fifteen feet long devoted exclusively to shoes. Shoes of every conceivable sort—Bass Weejuns, running shoes, little kids' sandals, spectator pumps, buffalo-hide sandals from the 1960s (the kind with the little loop that goes over the big toe). And these are not just new shoes, the Bass Weejuns have a penny tucked into the little slot over the arch and have certainly been to high school, if not college, and the running shoes have been around the gym a few times. When space runs out on the shoe platform, the shoes are hung here and there from meat hooks.

The inspiration room is a dry-cleaned swap meet. All this stuff is just sitting there waiting to be considered by the stylists and designers at Fiorucci now, or maybe in two years, or when someone goes through the room and just gets caught up by a detail they never noticed before. A blouse might catch someone's eye—the neckline is OK but the sleeves should be different and the fabric is hopeless, but when it has been run through the time machine here in Corsico and ends up in some off-the-wall window display in London or New York or Buenos Aires some months later, it has become Fiorucci. It is designed better, and it comes in nineteen colors.

This is the ultimate in recycling. For it results in a product entirely different from the original in the way that a nifty little bottle-green V-neck letterman's sweater from the 1950s turns up at Fiorucci in a color no high school would ever have chosen. And this new color dazzles the whole point of the 1950s and high school and late-fall afternoon football games and turns a relic of teenage rite of passage into something God never intended.

After the homey jumble of the inspiration room we visit the only place in all of Corsico that actually looks almost like the office of the head of a $65-million-a-year business. It is the place where Elio Fiorucci himself comes to work. Here it's all stark and plain. Enormous windows are covered by white cotton shades to cut the industrial glare. His desk is teak and big. He has no papers anywhere, but then he has no files nor in-and-out boxes. There isn't a hint of business in sight, unless you count a telephone with a few extra buttons. An enormous bowl filled with bourbon- and Scotch-flavored hard candies and a giant rock crystal ashtray are the room's only nod to the human condition. Everything is the palest sand color, subdued and simple. *Classico.* Except for the green plastic tree with pink-and-green bows.

The placidity of Fiorucci's office is in part due to his secretary Telma Malacrida. She is the kind of secretary, all poise and charm and savvy, that businessmen pray for and too rarely find. She appears to be in full control of the empire, all the answers at her fingertips.

People usually expect Fiorucci-the-store the first time they meet Fiorucci-the-man. But like so much here, meeting Fiorucci-the-man is a complete shock, a nice shock, but nonetheless a shock. He is dressed so conservatively that he all but fades into the muted tints of his office. His clothes, in the most reserved colors, are well made and cut from good fabrics; they are never conspicuous. "I have never dressed myself in anything coming from Fiorucci," he has said. The look of Fiorucci-the-man is the antithesis of the look of Fiorucci-the-store. But the charm of Fiorucci-the-man is indisputable.

Elio Fiorucci, upon meeting people for the first time, is so terribly confused, sorry, and depressed that he's not Fiorucci-the-store, that anyone expecting to meet Fiorucci-the-store is simply stunned into silence. "Oh," Karla Otto sighed, "he is such a dear, dear man. So wanting to be friends, but so sorry that people meeting him expect things, I don't know, you know what I mean?"

"Jazziness," I suggest.

"Yes," she says with relief. "Hipness. You know—worldliness. That sort of thing. He's embarrassed to be Fiorucci in front of new people always."

"I do not find myself a phenomenon," Elio Fiorucci has said over and over.

He sits quietly at his giant teak desk. He is waiting for me to speak, to haul out a tape cassette or a pencil and riddle him with questions about what he thinks about important subjects. He is listening. He is perfectly available to hear anything I say.

In fact, he seems to be waiting this very moment for me to speak so he can participate by listening. And I will find that the way Fiorucci listens is more intense and concentrated and full of burning energy than most people put into telling someone they love them. His way of listening, his peculiar simplicity, naturally in the beginning confuses people into nearly being struck dumb.

The Italian I had once nearly been able to speak disappeared the moment I arrived in Milan. So usually one of the young stylists would translate for us.

"I am sometimes shy," he says (the word in Italian is disarming: *timido*). "But the thing I like most is to speak with people, to communicate. I always feel embarrassed in the beginning because I never know what people expect, but I like people so much."

Fiorucci-the-man excludes nothing, he is open to all possibilities. He listens, he watches, he travels, he asks questions. Fiorucci calls the people who work for him, that unending array of graphic artists, designers, and stylists, "technicians of taste." And he describes what they are doing as "recomposing with taste." They are going against the tide, creating the things they believe people yearn for in clothing. Things that "function," things in "nonelegant colors." Fiorucci believes that "the only vulgarity is not to be chic."

Talking fashion philosophy with Fiorucci, however, can be as jumpy a proposition as the music in his stores, for five minutes later he is telling me that "color can be elegant." Fiorucci believes what he is doing is providing people with a choice, that people like to be able to pick and choose, mix and match with abandon. This was what he had in mind in 1967 when he shuttled back and forth between Carnaby Street and Milan with suitcases filled with miniskirts. For at that time in Milan people who cared anything at all about fashion had two choices: high fashion or *classico*. High fashion was a discreetly perfect navy blue Chanel suit, the hemline held absolutely plumb with tiny brass chains sewn by hand into the silk lining of the skirt. And *classico*, well *classico* was what Fiorucci-the-man looks like today. It was, and is, down-soft cashmere, pale beiges and grays and browns, simple oxblood-colored hand-sewn loafers, snappy gabardine, and true wools.

In Milan in 1967 there was nothing in the middle. Fiorucci widened the choices, made it possible for people to go to his store and choose not just complete outfits, but bits and pieces, putting their own look together, creating their own fantasy. And about high Italian fashion Fiorucci insists, "Gucci is a no-freedom concept. By 1990 there will be no class distinctions in terms of dress or fashion. People will just wear what they want."

"I am not a creator, I am a businessman," he says. It is the disarming modesty that does not allow him to speak directly about the extraordinary group of people he has brought together. His collaborators, his "technicians of taste," all attribute sheer genius to Fiorucci when it comes to picking the people to work with him.

"He gives people the possibilities to experiment with all expressions. Design clothes, everything. He is very wonderful choosing people. It is his big talent," notes Cristina Fiorucci. Cristina who is beautiful in a kind of noble, tall, and blamelessly uncomplicated way, Cristina who was picked by Fiorucci very early to be a stylist. And she has simply said again what every other person at Fiorucci said whenever I asked what they believed the real secret of Fiorucci-the-store to be. And, most touchingly, these people Fiorucci has chosen so wisely, these people choose to date their personal histories, their very lives, from the time they began to work for him. They simply do not admit, or very rarely admit, to having had a life before Fiorucci. They believe this as absolutely as they believe in Fiorucci's genius in picking them. They are probably right.

Fiorucci is always ready to settle down to a good long talk about how different Europe is from the United States. "In Europe we are forced every day from when we are children to worry whether we are doing the right thing. In America, you seem not to bother about such things."

"Well," I reply, "in America we seem only to discover God when we are about thirty-five—like Bob Dylan—and crash right into Him."

"In Italy, we know younger," he says, sadly.

"In America," says Fiorucci, "everybody seems to know who they are. They are so much *more* what they are, than we are here in Europe."

"That's because in America people aren't all dragged down by centuries and centuries of facts and traditions and—I mean, look at Milan," I said. "Here you think it's important to preserve history. In America we know that what's really important is a place to park."

"One of the main problems," Fiorucci says, "is to know whether it is right to manipulate the environment."

"You mean, like your shop?" I ask.

"Both with my shop, the clothes," he says, "and . . . with women."

To speak of America with Elio Fiorucci is to speak always of New York. "I like New York very much," he says. "It is the capital of America. You can breathe the grandiose air. People say that if I have a negative quality, it's that I never get enough. But in New York, I get enough. The sense of power in New York—everything is going to happen better in New York."

Although Elio Fiorucci spends a great deal of time in Milan, and even more time being all over the world, he has officially moved his wife and family to New York. It may be that his whole reason for moving to New York is his love of the city and his feeling that here at last is a place that has "enough." So now Elio Fiorucci resides in an apartment on the Upper East Side in New York City where all the taxi drivers speak English. Everyone he meets at parties speaks English, the entire place more or less speaks English twenty-four hours a day.

And of the rest of the world, what did he think of the rest of the world?

"How do you like L.A.?" I ask lightly.

"Los Angeles makes you frightened," he says. "Because it is crazy. The horizon is very long, like Africa."

"And Tokyo?" I ask.

"In Tokyo the town is not very beautiful but the people are terrific, very vital."

A beat passes while I desperately try and think up another town. Oh, Rio. A new Fiorucci has just opened there.

"Fiorucci clothes go very well there. It is always summer, always time to go to the beach. The women are very tall and very beautiful."

Fiorucci loves women more, so it would seem sometimes, than life itself. It's a good old-fashioned Frederick's of Hollywood type of appreciation. This fascination is a theme that can be traced throughout the history of Fiorucci graphics from those first romantic, wispy posters in the 1960s of windblown, leggy blonds in cotton-candy colors to the stiletto heels and gleaming thighs on Fiorucci stationery to the most stunning rear end ever to appear on a shopping bag, an airbrushed bottom rimmed with thin, white lace.

And it was in response to a question about the Fiorucci view of women that I heard just one thing that Fiorucci had said that made me suspect that he was not just a simple, shy, peasant genius, totally innocent of everything but hard work and neon stretch thighs. Someone I know told me, "You know, finally one day I just couldn't help it, I had to say it, and I asked him 'Don't you think your clothes are degrading to women?'"

"You said that?" I asked. "You said that to this man who's taking you and all these other people out and you're his guests and you said that?"

"Yeah," she said.

"Well, what'd he say?"

"He wanted to know if it was really true that Americans sleep together on the first date."

"Oh," I said.

It has been said of Elio Fiorucci that "He is always six months ahead of himself and one year ahead of his time." This is, of course, true. It is true in part because over his basic Saint Francis of Assisi humility, he is a changeling. At any moment he can be a misunderstood millionaire with a poetic soul describing the pleasures of eating a ripe fig, a lecher, a graphics junkie, a shy schoolboy, a concerned citizen worried about politics and the destruction of the ozone layer. He can be so on-the-money, so insightful about those too-young girls with their swan-like bodies, their flirtatious rosebud lips, their jailbait-green eye shadow, that it makes your head swim. He knows what red these young girls want when they ask for "one in red" and Fiorucci knows red better than any man alive. But he also knows purple brilliantly and has a natural-born genius for loud blues.

That he is unconventional and right, well mostly right, or at least so damned close it doesn't matter, is possible because he is not in the least afraid to fail. He doesn't mind if he makes a mistake. Because the basic assumptions will have been correct. Fiorucci just keeps doing things that everybody else says won't work and mostly they do work. And when they don't, there is no gnashing of teeth, no fruitless hysteria; there is some shoulder shrugging, but no break in the pace. It's nerve.

"Are you glad that the store has your name?" I finally ask. "I mean, you're so shy."

"Yes, I am glad to have my name on the store. Because even though I am afraid people will be disillusioned because they are waiting for someone colorful, at least they come to meet me and then I am glad."

And the way he listens to you, sometimes you think perhaps that he is only pretending to be shy. He doesn't really sound all that *timido* when he says things like, "I want to dress the world."

1980

OTHER NEW YORK REVIEW CLASSICS

For a complete list of titles, visit www.nyrb.com or write to:
Catalog Requests, NYRB, 435 Hudson Street, New York, NY 10014